SECRET MAP
of the BODY
Visions of the Human
Energy Structure

SECRET MAP of the BODY

Visions of the Human Energy Structure

consisting of

The Great Mirror
Praise-Biography of the Precious One from Lhadong
by Chen Ngawa Rinchen Den

and

The Hidden Description of the Vajra Body
by Gyalwa Yangönpa

Translated from Tibetan and Annotated
by Elio Guarisco

Edited by Judith Chasnoff

Shang Shung Publications

Cover drawing: Painting of Tönpa Garab Dorje by Drugu Choegyal Rinpoche
Cover and interior design: Kasia Skura

Shang Shung Publications gratefully acknowledges the generous support of the Ka-Ter
Translation Project funded by the Shang Shung Institute Austria toward the publication
of this book.

Published by Shang Shung Publications,
an imprint of the Shang Shung Foundation
Merigar
58031 Arcidosso (GR)
http://shop.shangshungfoundation.com

ISBN: 978-88-7834-139-5

Contents

FOREWORD

I AM VERY GLAD that here, the biography and an important work of Gyalwa Yangönpa have been translated into English. Yangönpa was an exceptional yogin of the Drugpa lineage, known for his high realization, who left an indelible imprint on the teaching of generations of Tibetan masters of different traditions. On the table beside my pillow, I keep old handwritten books by Yangönpa and by his teacher Götsangpa that were brought from Tibet to save them from destruction.

Reading these teachings is a great inspiration and support for practice. Every word is a living Dharma that shines with their realization: reading them is like exploring the beautiful vast space.

Drugu Choegyal Thutop Yontan Gyamtso

PREFACE

I CAME ACROSS Gyalwa Yangönpa's *Hidden Description of the Vajra Body* (*rdo rje lus kyi sbas bshad*) in 1998, while translating for a Tibetan doctor who was giving a three-month course in Tibetan medicine at Shang Shung Institute in Conway, Massachusetts. Having inserted a few sections of Yangönpa's text into a book he had prepared for his classes, the doctor pointed out to me its particular relevance to Tibetan medicine. This sparked my curiosity, and I eventually decided to translate it in order to study its content and make it available in English. I have since come to realize that the *Hidden Description of the Vajra Body* is a unique work whose importance far exceeds its scanty notions of traditional Tibetan medicine.

Reading through the *Hidden Description of the Vajra Body,* I became curious about the person behind the book, and convinced that the eventual publication of the translation would be more meaningful if it included the author's biography. So I ventured to translate *The Great Mirror* (*me long chen mo*), the most extensive and complete biography of Yangönpa, written by his main disciple, Chen Ngawa Rinchen Den (1202-?).

The translation of the text on the vajra body was undertaken at different moments over the last ten years, as my understanding of its content developed. The text is straightforward. Its language is not particularly difficult to grasp, but the principles and reasons behind many of Yangönpa's explanations are not easy to understand.

Their clarification would be the task of a complete commentary that does not yet exist.

Nowadays, it is becoming increasingly difficult to find Tibetans who are able to fully comprehend these ancient texts. Lacking such support, in translating this text I relied principally on the knowledge I acquired during the many years I worked in Darjeeling on the translation of Jamgön Kongtrul Lodrö Thaye's *Encyclopedia of Indo-Tibetan Knowledge*. However, to avoid falling into erroneous personal interpretations, I have always tried to discuss difficult points and concepts with my colleagues.

I have provided an introduction that will hopefully assist the reader to approach Yangönpa's personage and text. Any inconsistencies or errors will, I am sure, be corrected by future writers.

Reading through Willa Blythe Miller's 2013 dissertation, *Secrets of the Vajra Body: Dngos pa'i gnas lugs and the Apotheosis of the Body in the Work of Rgyal ba Yang dgon pa*, has been very interesting and useful.

I wish to express my gratitude to those who helped me with this project. In particular, Oliver Leick, the director of the Shang Shung Institute of Austria, tirelessly worked to secure financial donations so that I did not have to worry about livelihood issues. I wish to thank Adriano Clemente, with whom I often consulted on the translation, and whose advice certainly improved its accuracy. The editorial work of Judith Chasnoff has surely enhanced the overall quality of this book. I thank the staff of Shang Shung Publications for their constant and inspired work, and the Padmakara Translation Group for allowing me to use some passages from the *Treasury of Precious Qualities*.

Drugu Choegyal Rinpoche graciously allowed his beautiful watercolor of Garab Dorje to be used on the front page of this book, and its owner, Giorgio Dall'Orto, an expert in Tibetan art and literature, gave permission for its photographic reproduction. Choegyal Rinpoche also provided the foreword.

I wish to thank Chögyal Namkhai Norbu, renowned incarnation of Drugpa Ngagwang Namgyal, for being a constant inspiration for my life and work. Chögyal Namkhai Norbu personifies the knowledge and behavior of the exemplary human being and amazing spiritual practitioner that was Yangönpa.

After several years of intermittent work on this project, I am happy to now be able to bring to light something of the amazing life and thought of an extraordinary yogin, whose legacy has penetrated the teachings of the masters of all the lineages that succeeded him.

Elio Guarisco
Lake Como 2015

PART ONE
Translator's Introduction

THIS BOOK

This book contains two translated works: Gyalwa Yangönpa's *Hidden Description of the Vajra Body* (*rdo rje lus kyi sbas bshad*), preceded by this master's biography, *The Great Mirror: A Praise-Biography of the Precious One from Lhadong* (*rgyal ba yang dgon pa'i rnam thar bstod pa ma 'am me long chen mo*), written by his main disciple, Chen Ngawa Rinchen Den.

For the translation of the biography, I used an edition of the original that was published in 2002 by the Gampo-pa Library, Shree Gautam Buddha Vihara, Swayambhu Kathmandu, Nepal, under the chief editorship of Khenpo Shedup Tenzin. Khenpo Shedup Tenzin, a Bhutanese lama living in Nepal, deserves special credit, not only for publishing this biography and undertaking the preparation of a new version of Yangönpa's *Collected Works*, but for his untiring dedication in collecting and reprinting many Tibetan works, including some that have become quite rare.

The translation of the biography proved particularly challenging. Written in the eleventh-century colloquial language of Western Tibet, it contains many expressions that are neither used nor known today. Frequently, the subject of a sentence is not clearly identified, and different personages are called by the same appellative.

After I had prepared a draft of the translation, while staying in the Kathmandu valley for about a month in the spring of 2013 to clarify some of the biography's difficult passages, I sought the assistance of a native speaker. Lama Guru—the former attendant of the late Chögye Trichen Rinpoche, and who is also collecting the works of Yangönpa—kindly and patiently offered me his interpretation of those passages. When I reexamined the translation on returning to Italy, I found that many questions still remained. I consulted the Bönpo lama Geshe Namgyal Nyima, who presently resides in Germany. Reviewing the doubtful and uncertain passages with him, I resolved more of my doubts. But since a few unresolved points still remained, I decided to ask Chögyal Namkhai Norbu for further clarification. Rinpoche kindly agreed to sit with me for several hours, patiently checking these points and expressing his understanding of them. Alak Zenkhar Rinpoche also offered me his interpretations of some sections of the biography when I visited him in London in November 2014. Although I cannot claim to have made a perfect translation of Yangönpa's biography, I did my best within the time frame permitted by the circumstances.

Other sources of information on Yangönpa's life include *The Blue Annals* by Gö Lotsawa Shönu Pal (1393–1481);[1] *A Feast for the Learned Ones: A Religious History* by Pawo Tsulag Trengwa (1504–1564);[2] *The Sun That Blooms the Lotus of the Doctrine: A Religious History* by Padma Karpo (1527–1592);[3] and Ngagwang Kalden Gyamtso's *History of the White Crystal*.[4] Three short texts recording events of Yangönpa's life are his *Inner Autobiographical Accounts;*[5] the *Secret Accounts of the Life of Gyalwa Yangönpa,*[6] written by one of his main female students, the Old Lady Yulo, together with Rinchen Dan; and the *Secret Autobiographical Accounts.*[7] Moreover, a biography of Yangönpa composed by Sengdrag Rinpoche (1946–2005) was published in Nepal in 2011.[8] But this appears to be essentially the same as *The Great Mirror,* purged of the more enigmatic passages and including some additional information on Yangönpa's lineage, the history of Lhadong monastery, and the hermitage of Lhading.

For the translation of the *Hidden Description of the Vajra Body*, I mainly used a computer-transcribed version contained in the collection *gsang chen thabs lam nyer mkho rnal 'byor snying nor*, typeset and published in Beijing by the People's Publishing House (*mi rigs dpe skrung khang*) in 1991. In this publication, the author is named as Sakya Gyaltsen Palzang.

I also consulted this text as found in the three currently available versions of Yangönpa's *Collected Works*, one published at Phajoding monastery in 1976,[9] and one at Tago monastery in 1982.[10] In addition, I had at my disposal a copy of the text, in cursive Tibetan, drawn from an incomplete manuscript of Yangönpa's Collected Works published by Kargyud Sungrab Nyamso Khang in Darjeeling in 1973, which exists at Hemis Monastery in Ladakh.[11]

During the process of translation, I charted the differences between the various versions, intending to include them in the notes to this book. However, as I was revising my translation, I realized that the version published in China in book form, which had obviously undergone a thorough revision, with a few exceptions, was by far the most correct. I decided to rely mainly on that version, and omitted references to the others.

Yangönpa's *Hidden Description of the Vajra Body* contains interlinear notes. These must certainly have been added later, and are not the words of Yangönpa. In the Beijing version, the interlinear notes have been revised, corrected, and frequently relocated within the text. They are therefore somewhat different from those found in the other versions, which are at times quite messy and contain obvious errors in grammar and meaning. In only a few cases are the interlinear notes helpful in clarifying the meaning of the text. Many are redundant, and seem to have been written by someone who lacked a high standard of learning.

Interlinear notes are also present as comments on quotations drawn from the tantras, and occasionally serve to clarify the general meaning of these passages.

The quotations from the tantras presented in this book are often problematic. The wording of many passages differs slightly from that contained in the Derge Kangyur. Several explanations may account for these discrepancies. Yangönpa may have had access to alternate versions of these tantras, possibly translated by different translators. Changes in wording may also have been introduced in error by editors, publishers, and so forth. When the discrepancies are particularly striking, I have noted them and reproduced, for comparison, the same passages as they appear in the Derge Kangyur and Tengyur.

This translation was also informed by four brief commentaries to the *Hidden Description of the Vajra Body*. Although they are preserved in the Collected Works of Yangönpa, all were written by Chen Ngawa Rinchen Den, his chief disciple and biographer. They are:

1. Summary of the *Hidden Description of the Vajra Body* (*rdo rje lus kyi bsdus don*), a three-folio text that lays out the structure of the *Hidden Description*.

2. Explanation of the *Difficult Points of the Hidden Description* (*sbas bshad kyi dka' 'grel*), a seven-folio, and apparently unfinished, word-commentary on the opening section of the *Hidden Description*.

3. *Extraordinary Essential Points of the Hidden Description* (*sbas bshad kyi gnad thun mong ma yin pa*). This eight-folio text is Chen Ngawa's record of Yangönpa's oral elaboration on selected points from the *Hidden Description*.

4. *Treasury of the Essential Points of the Hidden Oral Instructions of the Hidden Description* (*rdo rje lus kyi sbas bshad kyi zhal gdams sbas pa gnad kyi gter mdzo*). This five-folio text contains oral explanations of some reputedly secret points in the *Hidden Description*.

YANGÖNPA'S TIME

Gyalwa Yangönpa Gyaltsen Palzang (1213–1258)—commonly known simply as Yangönpa—lived in an era following a long period of political fragmentation when the centralized Tibetan empire had collapsed, a situation that persisted from roughly the ninth to the eleventh centuries. During the next two centuries, Tibet was dominated by the Sakya Lama, who enjoyed the support of the Mongols. In 1240, when Yangönpa was twenty-seven years old, Tibet was invaded by an army of thirty thousand Mongol troops led by Doorda Darkhan. But a year later, when all the Mongol princes were summoned back to Karakorum for the appointment of a successor to Ögedei Khan, they withdrew. In 1244, Köten Khan, the second son of Ögedei, ordered another invasion of Tibet and summoned Sakya Pandita to serve as his chaplain. When Sakya Pandita arrived at Köten's court and cured the ruler of an illness, the Khan converted to Buddhism and became his student. Thus began the special relationship that made the Sakya rulers of Tibet. In 1253, Chögyal Phagpa (1235–1280) succeeded Sakya Pandita at the Mongol court and became the spiritual teacher of Kublai Khan. With the Khan's support, Chögyal Phagpa and his Sakya school became the preeminent political force in Tibet.

The Sakya hegemony over Tibet continued until the mid-fourteenth century, although it was challenged by a rebellion by the Drigung Kagyüd. This revolt was suppressed in 1290 when the Sakya and the eastern Mongols burned Drigung monastery, killing ten thousand people. Sakya rule came to a definitive end in 1358, when central Tibet came under the control of the Kagyüd school. By that time, the lines between the Nyingma, Kagyüd, Sakya, and Kamdampa schools of Tibetan Buddhism were clear.

Yangönpa's Early Life

Yangönpa was born in the region of Latöd of Tsang, one of the two main provinces of Central Tibet, in the year of the Female Water Bird, 1213. His native village was Chucha, close to the monastery of Lhadong, in Kungthang, the central plain of Ngari, not far from the Tibet-Nepal border. This monastery was the source of Yangönpa's other name: Lhadongpa, "the one from Lhadong." The name Yangönpa is taken from that of a hermitage in which he remained in solitary retreat for some time.

Yangönpa was born of the Tön clan to a Nyingma family that had been the source of many *siddhas*. He was the family's youngest son, having two older brothers and an elder sister. His younger brother, who possessed a great knowledge of Tantric literature, passed day and night in meditation practice. His mother, Chöthong, considered to be a wisdom *ḍākinī*,[12] was probably Yangönpa's first teacher. As a boy, he was tutored by his father's elder brother, Trubthob Darma, a great practitioner who was known to have meditated uninterrupted for sixty years.

His father, Chung Lhadongpa (whose actual name was Chosam), a lay master connected to Lhadong monastery, passed away at the age of seventy-five when Yangönpa was still in his mother's womb. Prior to his death, he left a testament prophesying that the coming child was an emanation of enlightened beings, and naming him Regent of Blazing Splendor. Thus, at a very tender age, the boy would say: "I am the Blazing One, the little man of illusion."

It is said that soon after his birth, he pronounced the words "I take refuge!" A child prodigy, he was able to read and write without being taught. At the age of five, he was already reciting scriptures for the benefit of the people, and thus it became known in the area that an emanation of the enlightened beings had appeared.

Yangönpa began his religious education as a young child through informal meetings with various masters. When he was five years old, he met a lama known as Mikyöd Dorje who had come to his place disguised as a beggar, and was recognized by no one but Yangönpa. This lama was in fact the renowned Nyingma master Latöd Mikyöd Dorje, who was a student of the famous tertön Nyangral Nyima Wözer (1124–1192) and was known for his transmission of the Avalokiteśvara teachings from the *Mani Kabum*.[13] Sometime after their first encounter, when Yangönpa was eleven years old, this lama once more came to meet him and asked the boy to sing a song. In reply, Yangönpa sang:

Salutations to the lord, the master.
I, the Blazing One, the little man of illusion,
Have awakened the predispositions of my former actions.
[Because] the master's blessing has entered me,
My view is not framed into a concept.
My meditation is devoid of any object.
My conduct is beyond acceptance and rejection.
My goal is freedom from hope and fear.

Mikyöd Dorje, greatly impressed, folded his hands before the boy and, shedding tears, declared, "This boy of ten has fastened the belt of the Dzogchen teaching. He is an amazing son of Samantabhadra! Take refuge in this manifestation of enlightened beings."

Thereafter, he bestowed on the young Yangönpa the transmission of the Hidden Treasures of Nyangral Nyima Wözer, and the teaching on the Pacification of Suffering.

At age six, he began his formal studies with the lamas known as the Pulmar brothers.[14] The biographical sources provide no details regarding these early masters of Yangönpa. A lama Pulmar is mentioned in *The Great Mirror* as the teacher of Yangönpa's father. In any case, under the tutorship of the lamas Pulmar, Yangönpa received the initiation for the *Guhyagarbha Tantra;* studied the Dzogchen tantras and their accompanying instructions; the teachings of the Kadampa; the Pacification of Suffering and the Cutting of the Demons; and the *Path and Its Fruit* with its commentaries and instructions.

At age eight, feeling unready to become head of Lhadong monastery, he requested and received instructions on the practice of the Mind cycle of the Dzogchen system, which introduces one to the true nature of the mind. It is said that at that time, a nonconceptual realization of the mind's nature arose in him. Maintaining this knowledge, he came to perceive things as manifesting from the creative energy of the mind's nature, and experienced the mind as space-like emptiness, primordially beyond concepts.

At age nine, Yangönpa moved back to his home place and was installed as abbot of Lhadong monastery. On that occasion, he gave religious discourses that greatly impressed large crowds of people. It was then that he came to be known as Lhadongpa, and his renown as an amazing child, an emanation of enlightened beings, began to spread far and wide. Having possessed prescience since infancy, he openly exhibited it to everyone until the ḍākinīs told him to desist.

Although Yangönpa lived as a layman until age twenty-one, during that time his conduct very much resembled that of a pure monk, for he neither ate meat nor touched any alcohol. Every aspect of his external behavior, his speech, and his attitude inspired people to have faith in him. From his biography it appears that he did not have to exert any effort in learning, and was, from the beginning, a self-arisen saint. But four masters devoutly referred to in his writings as the Four Precious Ones certainly contributed to Yangönpa's full spiritual maturation.

THE HERMIT OF KO CLIFF

The first of Yangönpa's four precious masters was Kotragpa Sönam Gyaltsen (1170–1249), known as the Hermit of Ko Cliff. It is said that from ages eleven to twenty-two, Yangönpa served as his apprentice.[15] Born in the Tingri region near the Tibet-Nepalese border, Kotragpa was a mountain yogin who traveled the land requesting teaching from various masters of different lineages. One of the most significant instructions he received was that of the *Path and Its Fruit,* descending from the eleventh-century female teacher Machig Shama. Assiduous practice of these instructions for twenty-four years in secluded mountain hermitages and caves yielded Kotragpa visions of deities and masters of the past, clairvoyance, boundless knowledge, and magical abilities. Thereafter, he came to be known as the Dharma Lord Kotragpa.

Kotragpa invited the Indian master Vibhūticandra, who was then staying in Nepal, to Tibet to give a special transmission of the Six-Branched Yoga of the *Kālacakra Tantra,*[16] which Vibhūticandra had received in a vision from the siddha Śāvaripa.[17] This became another of Kotragpa's main spiritual practices.

Although Kotragpa was primarily associated with these two lineages of teaching, later historians in Tibet have been uncertain as to where to place him among the various Tibetan schools. He lived in an era favoring a liberal approach to the learning and implementation of spiritual practices, one in which the Tibetan schools' sectarian identities had not yet become fully fixed. Because of this, he is considered a kind of precursor to the nonsectarian approach that greatly influenced such nineteenth-century eastern Tibetan luminaires as Jamyang Khyentse Wangpo (1820–1892), Jamgön Kongtrul Lodrö Thaye (1813–1899), and Chogyur Dechen Lingpa (1829–1879).

From his personal attendant, Yangönpa became Kotragpa's foremost disciple, receiving all his teachings, initiations, and esoteric instructions. In particular, it is said that Kotragpa empowered him in the practice of Vajravārāhī, the favored meditational deity of Yangön-pa, and in the teaching on the Intermediate State[18] originating with Machig Shama. Kotragpa also officiated at the twenty-two-year-old Yangönpa's full monastic ordination. On that occasion, Kotragpa gave him the name Gyaltsen Palzang. Kotragpa held Yangönpa in such high esteem that, prior to his death, he entrusted his monastic seat to Yangönpa alone.

In his eightieth year, Kotragpa sent a letter to Yangönpa saying that he would not live much longer, and asked him to come quickly. Unfortunately, the road was blocked by Mongol troops, and by the time Yangönpa arrived, the master had already passed away. But, as per Kotragpa's wishes, it was Yangönpa who presided over the funerary rituals.

THE VULTURE'S NEST YOGIN

While still a layman, on a begging tour near Shri Mountain,[19] Yangönpa met another teacher with whom he established a deep relationship and who would greatly influence his spiritual career. This was Götsangpa Gönpo Dorje (1189–1258), the Vulture's Nest Hermit, an early and exceptional master of the Drugpa school.

With Lorepa Wangchug Tsöndru (1187–1250), Götsangpa Gönpo Dorje was one of the two main students of Tsangpa Gyare Yeshe Dorje (1161–1211), the founder of the Drugpa lineage. From these two students originated two major offshoots of the lineage, the "lower" and the "upper." The upper lineage gave rise to numerous subsects, including the Yangön Kagyüd, stemming from Yangönpa himself.[20] The lower Drugpa spread mainly in Bhutan, having been brought there by Ngagwang Namgyal (1594–1651). The Yangön Kagyüd later became known as the Bara Kagyüd, after Barawa Gyaltsen Palzang (1310–1391).

Götsangpa was born in Lhodrag. It is said that as a child he was very handsome, and skilled in singing. One day, four singers from Tsang came to him and sang:

With Gyare, the Master of the Teaching of Ralung
    monastery,
There is the happiness of this and future lives.
If you practice the precious divine Teaching,
    go there!
If you sincerely practice our Teaching, go there!

On hearing these words, Götsangpa experienced an intense longing, and went to Ralung. There he met Tsangpa Gyare, who ordained him as a monk and gave him the name Gönpo Dorje. At that time he was nineteen years old and Tsangpa Gyare was forty-seven. A mere eighteen days after Götsangpa received Tsangpa Gyare's instructions on the practice of Mahāmudrā, he clearly perceived the true nature of reality. Upon Tsangpa Gyare's passing, at age twenty-three, Götsangpa returned to Lhodrag, where he remained for three years in strict retreat. At age thirty-two, he began another three-year retreat in Tsari. At thirty-six he arrived in Shri, where he stayed for another three years in the Khyungkar and Yangkar caves. At age thirty-eight, he went to the Vulture's Nest cave, where he remained in retreat for seven years. Thus, he came to be known as Götsangpa, or the Vulture's Nest Hermit. At forty-five, he went to Tengdro, where he remained for thirteen years. Then he spent nine years in Dechen Teng and Ganden in Nyanang; two years at Senge Ling and Hongthang; and two at Dorje Ling. He passed away at the age of seventy.

Among his main students were Yangönpa, the disciple with equal realization; Ugyenpa, the one with equal conduct; and Chirkarwa, the one with equal devotion.

Upon seeing the face of Götsangpa for the first time, Yangönpa fell into a swoon of divine grace. This marked the beginning of a deep master-student relationship that lasted until the year in which they both passed away.

At the feet of Götsangpa, Yangönpa learned the yogic practices related to the channels, energy-winds, and vital essences that are the focus of the "path of method," as well as Nāropā's *Five Points That Dispel Obstacles*,[21] which provide instructions on the famous six yogas of Nāropā: inner heat, illusory body, clear light, dream, intermediate state, and transference of consciousness.[22]

Assuming that Yangönpa's earliest and most complete biography, *The Great Mirror,* is in chronological order, after meeting Kotragpa and receiving the Vajravārāhī initiation from him in his early twenties, he entered a period of intense retreat at Yangön hermitage, during which he recited that deity's mantra four million times.[23] After meeting Götsangpa, Yangönpa chose as his retreat place the hermitage of Namding—a rock formation on Shri Mountain that various masters had prophesied as a favorable place for his spiritual exercises—and plastered its entrance shut.

There Yangönpa remained in strict seclusion and almost total isolation. It is said that for eleven months he sat uninterruptedly in the lotus posture, a feat that, according to *The Great Mirror,* had previously been achieved only by Ga Lotsawa, a translator who had studied directly with the renowned Indian master Abhayakaragupta.

Withstanding the pain and illness caused by this practice, he came to a definite understanding of the energy structure of body and mind, and gained control of this structure. It appears that the experience and realization he had at this time led Yangönpa to write the *Hidden Description of the Vajra Body.*

Visionary Encounters with Lama Shang

In his dreams, Yangönpa met Lama Shang Yudrag Tsöndru Tragpa (1123–1193). Also known as Kungthang Lama Shang, or simply as Lama Shang, he was born in Tsawaru, in the Kyichu river valley of the southern region of the present-day Tsal Kungthang district. His father, Shang Dorje Sempa, was a lay Tantric practitioner of the Nanam clan. During his childhood, his mother, a former nun, encouraged him to pursue a religious education, and took him to listen to the discourses of the female teacher Majo Darma. Later on, he engaged in formal studies with Sambu Lotsawa. While still in his teens, he went through a period of despair due to the death of his parents, and also due to his disquiet at his past performance of animal sacrifices in the course of training in black magic. While in this state, wandering around eastern Tibet, he met and studied with Ga Lotsawa, one of his key teachers. But the event that most impacted his spiritual career was his 1154 meeting with Gompo Tsultrim Nyingpo, known as Gomtsul, a nephew of Gampopa Sönam Rinchen. Since the Kagyüd subsects were still not well organized at this time, Gomtsul was the most important and influential Kagyüd figure. Through Gomtsul, Lama Shang had important mystical experiences and received all the transmissions and authorizations of that tradition. In the early 1160s, Gomtsul was called upon to mediate between monastic factions in property disputes that had turned violent. In these battles, even the two main temples of Lhasa, the Jokhang and the Ramoche, had suffered severe damage. Successful in his mediation, Gomtsul appointed Lama Shang to protect Lhasa from further damage.

In 1175, Lama Shang established his monastery of Tsal Kungthang just north of Lhasa. He gained control over most of central Tibet, and thus became one of that period's most powerful rulers. As a ruler, he was apparently not averse to the use of force and violence, and so he remains a controversial figure. At age sixty-one, Lama Shang suffered a life-threatening illness, and thus remained secluded in virtually unbroken retreat, affording no one the opportunity to meet him until the end of his life. From him stems the Tsalpa Kagyüd tradition.

Although Lama Shang died twenty years before Yangönpa's birth, while in his twenties, for reasons unknown, Yangönpa had a series of dreams about him in which he received blessings, teachings, and prophecies. On one occasion, Yangönpa had an extraordinary dream in which Lama Shang conferred the Secret Dream Practice. Inspired by these events, he made a pilgrimage to Tsal Kungthang temple to offer prayers and to practice before a statue of Lama Shang. For this reason, even though Lama Shang died before he was born, Yangönpa is sometimes counted as one of Lama Shang's "minor disciples."

Later, Yangönpa had an encounter with another master who would greatly influence him. This was Sakya Pandita Kunga Gyaltsen (1182–1251).

The Crown Jewel of Tibetan Scholars

Sakya Pandita was the fourth of the Sakya school's five patriarchs and the sixth holder of the Sakya throne. He was a major player in a movement to renew Tibetan Buddhism by strengthening its connection with its Indian origins. As a monk, Sakya Pandita was instrumental in promoting close adherence to a pure monastic discipline; as a scholar, he promoted knowledge of the so-called "five sciences."[24]

He was a prolific author as well as a translator of Sanskrit texts. His exceptional reputation as a scholar attracted the attention of the Mongol rulers who established the Sakya dynasty that ruled central Tibet. The beloved nineteenth-century Dzogchen master Paltrul

Rinpoche considered Sakya Pandita, Longchen Rabjampa, and Tsongkhapa as the three Mañjughoṣas, or wisdom deities of Tibet. For the Sakya school he was, of course, a link in the transmission of the *Path and Its Fruit*, which he also passed on to Yangönpa.

Yangönpa met Sakya Pandita for the first time when, on his way to Sakya, he passed through the region where Yangönpa was staying in retreat. In their informal meeting on the outskirts of town, Yangönpa established his first contact with that extremely learned master by revering him greatly, and thereby received numerous reading transmissions.

Their relationship was consolidated when, in the following year, Yangönpa traveled to Sakya to meet Sakya Pandita once more. On that occasion, Yangönpa became the fortunate recipient of initiations and teachings, notably the *Hidden Description of the Path*[25] that had been directly conferred on the Great Sakyapa Kunga Nyingpo (1092–1158) by the Indian mahasiddha Virūpa[26] in a vision. Sakya Pandita entrusted him with these teachings and encouraged him to freely transmit them to others.

Sakya Pandita's explanations and views certainly influenced those expressed by Yangönpa in the *Hidden Description of the Vajra Body*. In fact, Yangönpa uses several quotations from Sakya Pandita and acknowledges his contribution to this work. In the context of the explanation of the fundamental nature of the body, Yangönpa states:

> These [places and channels] have been described by presenting, without contradiction, the viewpoints of the *Hevajra* and the *Cakrasaṃvara* tantras. "Such an explanation," said Sakya Pandita, "... is an oral instruction on the *Hidden Description of the Path*."

After describing the channels of the chakra of the secret place, Yangönpa remarks:

Such explanations accord with the teachings of the *Path and Its Fruit*. Thus, they represent the viewpoint of the great, glorious Virūpa that has been transmitted through Sakya Pandita.

And in his concluding verses, he states:

> [In particular], this great treasure of profound and vast
> essential points,
> Comes through the blessing of the glorious master
> Heruka [the matchless Sakya Pandita].

His Most Cherished Teacher

The last of the main Four Precious Teachers of Yangönpa was Drigung Chenga Tragpa Jungne (1175–1255). Drigung Chenga was born in Nangchen, eastern Tibet. He became a novice at age eleven, and for three years received guidance from Yelpa Yeshe Tseg, a disciple of Phagmo Trupa. At fifteen, he felt the urge to leave for central Tibet. Having arrived in Drigung, he met Jigten Sumgön, founder of the Drigung Kagyüd tradition, who, placing his hand on Drigung Chenga's head, said: "This child is bright, and his past accumulations are great. Seeing the way you wear your hat, you will make a great meditator." It is said that at the moment the teacher touched his head, Drigung Chenga experienced a state of contemplation in which everything was of the same flavor and free of any mental representation.

Drigung Chenga was provided with a hut in which he meditated for several years, and then for two decades he served as the attendant of Jigten Sumgön. Then, Jigten Sumgön appointed him abbot of Densathil monastery,[27] where a dispute had arisen as to where Gampopa Sönam Rinchen's writings should be preserved. There he passed most of his time in monastic activities, and did not teach, but dedicated himself to meditation. When, in 1234 or 1235, the abbot of Drigung Thil monastery near Lhasa passed away, Drigung Chenga agreed to become his successor. He passed away at the age of eighty-one, and marvelous signs were observed at his cremation.[28]

Even before personally knowing Drigung Chenga, Yangönpa had developed an enormous admiration for him. One year before he actually met him, Yangönpa had a dream about Drigung Chenga that prompted him to go to Drigung Thil. There, Drigung Chenga accorded him a warm and reverential welcome. It was to Yangönpa alone that he offered all the essential instructions he possessed, placing particular emphasis on the Yantra Yoga and other practices related to the vajra body.

While at Drigung Thil monastery, Yangönpa also received the complete transmission of Phagmo Trupa's teachings from Drigung Chung Dorje Tragpa, who succeeded Drigung Chenga as abbot of Drigung Thil. Thus, Yangönpa became the holder the Drigung lineage's entire body of teachings.

OTHER TRANSMISSIONS RECEIVED

Besides the Four Precious Teachers—Kotragpa, Götsangpa, Sakya Pandita, and Drigung Chenga Tragpa Jungne—Yangönpa received particular transmissions from a number of other masters.

From Lama Dzingbu he learned the Mahayana Mind Training, Atiśa's *Lamp of the Path,* and other teachings of the Kadampa; the *Guide to the Bodhisattva Conduct;* Machig Labdrön's *Cutting of Demons;* and the Dzogchen teachings.

From Lama Tröchungpa Khyungtön Zhigpo he received the *Guhyasamāja Tantra,* the *Six Yogas of the Kālacakra,* the *Mountain Teaching* [called] *Large and Small Vases of Nectar,* the *Seven Teachings of Nyö,* the *Dream Teaching on the Pacification of Suffering,* and the *Cycle of Teachings of the Oral Transmission of the Ḍākinī.*

While still young and not yet a monk, from Sangye Repa he received the *Four Hidden Teachings*, the *Five Points*, the *Seven-Day Inner Heat*, the *Cycle on the Innate of the Glorious Galo*, the *Secret Practice of the Guru*, and *Compassion Striking the Mind*.

While visiting Drigung Chenga at Drigung Thil monastery, from his successor the abbot Drigung Chung Phagmo Trupai Wönthog Dug, he received the *Cycle of Profound Teachings of Phagmo Trupa*. From Jalung Bumkangpa Lungtön Shigpo he received the transmission of Mahākāla, the Four-Armed Guardian of the Teaching, and the Teaching of Shang.

From Repa Dorje Yeshe and the Drangtön brothers he received the *Cycle of Teachings on the Path of Method*.

From his paternal uncle Drubtob Darma he received the teaching on the rituals of the Nyingmapas.

From his mother, Chöthong, he received the Amoghapāśa with Five Deities.

From Pardrog Manlungpa he received the cycle of teachings of the Drugpa lineage. From Lama Nepa he received some profound teachings of the Drigung.

In addition, he attended and studied with nine excellent contemporary teachers, such as Chowo Lhatsun Sokhawa, Lama Pulmar, Trangtso Trawopa, Kyese, Khenchen Tsultrim Nyingpo, and others.

Yangönpa also received many teachings in a state of clear light, in particular from Shang Yutragpa, and Drogön Tsangpa Gyare. From the secret ḍākinī Tashi Tseringma he received the *Liberation from the Narrow Passage of the Intermediate State*.

In all, Yangönpa had about forty teachers who looked after him, either through their actual physical presence or through their wisdom body. In some reckonings, Götsangpa, Kotragpa, Sakya Pandita, and Drigung Chenga—the Four Precious Ones of Incomparable Kindness—plus Mikyöd Dorje, Dzingbupa, and Tröchungpa are known as the Seven Teachers of Great Kindness. These, plus Sangye Rechen,

Yangönpa's uncle Trubthob Darma, Chowo Lhatsun, and Pardrog Manlungpa are his Eleven Special Teachers.

Nevertheless, it appears that of all his teachers, Drigung Chenga Tragpa Jungne was the one with whom Gyalwa Yangönpa had the closest relationship. In *The Great Mirror*, we read:

> Generally speaking, there were some twenty-four teachers with whom [Yangönpa] had a spiritual connection; among them, there were four undisputed and incomparable Precious Lords. The one who was the essence of the Lord of the Family[29] was the Precious Lord of Drigung.
>
> It was by invoking this master, father and son—essence of the sixth buddha Vajradhāra, essence of the five dimensions of awakening—that all the qualities of Body, Voice, and Mind came all at once [to Yangönpa], like a vase filled to the brim. Through the blessing of their minds [becoming] indivisible, [Yangönpa] joined the end of the row [as the most recent holder] of the Kagyüd [tradition] that transfers the wisdom of realization, the ultimate transmission.

This close relationship—and the fact that Drigung Chenga Tragpa Jungne and his successor entrusted Yangönpa with all the Drigung Kagyüd teachings—would place Yangönpa chiefly in the Drigung rather than the Drugpa lineage in which he is usually included. It seems safe to assume, however, that Yangönpa himself did not have such a limiting sense of belonging, and would have been unconcerned in which lineage he would be included by others.

Yangönpa was the repository of diverse lineages transmitted through masters of the Nyingma, Kagyüd, Sakya, and Kadampa schools, and he mastered all the teachings he received. This contributed to the rich blend of learning and realization that informs his written works, such as the *Hidden Description of the Vajra Body*. In its colophon and elsewhere in the text, we are told that Yangönpa's writing on the vajra body reflects his own experiential knowledge, but is based on a synthesis of the instructions and methods passed on to him by his four precious masters.

Accomplishments

Yangönpa spent most of his time in meditation at Namding monastery on Shri mountain, which he himself had founded, but he also stayed at Lhadong; Lhading; Khyungkar; Tricham, Pardrog, Chag Ngur, and Kang Pule, where he continuously gave spiritual teachings.

Following his periods of intense retreat in these places, and in particular, after meeting Kotragpa and Götsangpa, Yangönpa was gifted with a number of miraculous powers and extraordinary abilities that he used throughout his life to inspire faith in students, cure illness in himself and others, and protect the local population. Most important of all, he achieved the realization of Mahāmudrā, the true nature of the mind and of everything, for which all the ancient Kagyüd masters are renowned.

It appears that, for an extended period, Yangönpa combined and alternated yogic practices related to the energy structure of the body and mind with the visualization and recitation of the mantra of Vajravārāhī, his favored meditational deity. This grounding in the understanding of Mahāmudrā and Dzogchen yielded extraordinary meditative experiences, wonderful visions of deities, special teachings received in dreams from the ḍākinīs, boundless clairvoyance, the ability to prophesy the future, the ability to influence the course of events, and the power to conjure nonhuman guardians and protectors of the teaching to assist him in his manifold activities for the welfare of people.

As a result of his spiritual accomplishments, Yangönpa attracted large numbers of followers who gathered in the hermitages and caves clustered in his area. It is said that once his fame had spread, he had more than ten thousand students from every corner of Tibet. He took care of them by giving the appropriate instructions for meditation, as well as providing them with food and other necessities. His field of activity was not restricted to the confines of the monastery walls or the peaceful atmosphere of mountain hermitages. He actively demonstrated his qualities of compassion and knowledge in the secular milieu. In fact, much of his time and many of the resources he received from devotees were selflessly spent in settling disputes among families, communities, villages, and regions of the country. He used his powers and knowledge to protect the local populace from attacks and devastation caused by the Mongol troops who, in that period, repeatedly invaded Tibet. And he even demonstrated technical skill in building bridges wherever needed, personally participating in the work.

Yangönpa lived his life demonstrating perfect altruistic conduct. Despite being an exceptional individual gifted with powers, knowledge, and wisdom, throughout his life he remained natural and humble, caring for the lowly and never refusing requests.

One is struck by the accounts of Yangönpa dedicating his life to help, protect, and instruct others with boundless love and compassion, without making the slightest distinction as to social class or position. And he did so not as a self-aggrandizing display, but as the spontaneous manifestation of his natural way of being.

YANGÖNPA'S PASSING

In the summer of the Tiger year (1254), he remained for a week in strict seclusion without eating, drinking, or speaking to anyone. The wondrous signs that manifested during that time were witnessed by all the people of the region. Perhaps these were omens indicating that he would not live long.

Yangönpa passed away in 1258, the year of the Male Earth Horse, at age forty-six. Though relatively brief, his life was remarkable. He quickly traversed the landscapes of the spiritual path by spending half his time in secluded meditation and half working for the welfare of others through teaching and other altruistic activities.

He himself said:

> My life is unobstructed. From age nine, when I became a spiritual teacher, up to now at age forty-six, for thirty-seven years I have worked for the benefit of others. Thus, I have established a connection with many beings. On some occasions, I also brought disciples to spiritual maturity and liberation. May the great moon of the Kagyüd transmission long endure.

It appears that, about a year before his death, Yangönpa no longer wished to stay at his home monastery of Lhadong. Knowing that he would not live much longer, he encouraged his students to request any instructions they might need. He gave away all his material possessions and indicated to his students that he would not be returning. At that time, he also wrote his testament and left it among his books. He then went to Pardrog to meet Götsangpa.

The spiritual father and son expressed to one another their intentions to pass away soon. Yet, as is the custom, each of them offered prayers requesting that the other remain.

Yangönpa left for Chag Ngur, where he said he would stay for eight months, but after six months he showed signs of illness. He then moved to the hermitage of Namding. Although he indicated that he was seriously ill, he neither accepted medical treatment nor ordered the performance of rituals to overcome the illness and extend his life. Saying that illness and death constituted no problem for him, for everything he experienced was sheer bliss, he declared:

> From the beginning, I made few promises as to the length of my life; I will not live long. The disciples are more numerous in other [worlds]. Even if [I have] a short life, it does not matter, [as] all my direct disciples—those who have a connection with me—will be liberated presently. It is just as [is mentioned] in the sutras: "Many buddhas, such as the Buddha Purna, became enlightened in the morning; turned the wheel of the Dharma at midday; and passed away in the evening. All who became their disciples were brought to spiritual maturity on the same day."

On the auspicious eighth day of the lunar month, he met with all his students and gave them words of encouragement, so that they could face the sorrow and grief of his approaching departure and continue their spiritual quest as before. He gave away all his possessions without keeping even a single needle.

One day, he gathered his important students to tell them that he had written his last wishes as to how his body should be dealt with after death and what was to be done thereafter. To their request that he identify his reincarnation, Yangönpa replied that his emanations were already present in India and elsewhere but that, in the future, he would come in four emanations, and as countless emanations. He gave strict orders that his disciples not treat him as a cult object after his passing, but keep things simple with regard to the erection of statues, temples, and so on, in his memory.

Then, on the morning of the nineteenth day of the fourth month of 1258, just as it was getting warm, he passed away.

The clothes in which Yangönpa died were given to Götsangpa, who then declared, "This is a being who is accomplishing the benefit of others." During that same year, Götsangpa also passed away.

Yangönpa's Writings

At the insistent requests of his students, Yangönpa composed the so-called *Four Profound Dharmas and Four Ornaments,* including:
1. *Three Mountain Teaching Cycles, with the Ornament of Advice*
2. *The Path of Direct Instructions, with the Dispelling of Hindrances*
3. *Miscellaneous Topics, with the Ornament of Fragments of Teaching*
4. *The Collection of Songs, with the Ornament of a Table of Contents*

Among these, the most renowned are the Three Mountain Teaching Cycles [including their commentaries] with the Ornament of Advice. The Three Mountain Teaching Cycles are:
1. *Mountain Teaching, Source of All Qualities*
2. The *Hidden Description of the Vajra Body*
3. *Liberation from the Narrow Passage of the Intermediate State*

The *Ornament of Advice* consists of six works, collectively titled the *Six Mothers:*
1. *Five Key Points of Fierce Breathing*
2. *Secret Conduct of Dreams*
3. *Six Lines on Emptiness*
4. *Transference of the Red Hūṃ*
5. *Healing Sickness and Provocations with Hūṃ*
6. *Sealed Teachings on Retaining Vital Essence*

Yangönpa's works were widely read, quoted, commented on, and integrated into the writings of important later masters of all Tibetan schools.

We find references to his teachings and writings in the works of Tsongkhapa (1357–1419), founder of the Gelug school; the third Karmapa Rangjung Dorje (1284–1339); the eighth Karmapa Mikyöd Dorje (1507–1554); the master of the Dzogchen Mind series Sogdogpa Lodrö Gyaltsen (1552–1624); Jamgön Kongtrul Lodrö Thaye (1813–1899), proponent of the nineteenth-century nonsectarian movement; Tseleg Natsog Rangdrol (1608–?), an important master of both the Kagyüd and Nyingma schools; Raga Asya (1613–1678), learned tutor and student of the great Nyingma tertön Namchö Mingyur Dorje (1645–1667); Jigmed Lingpa (1730–1798), the visionary promulgator of the Innermost Essence Teaching of the Vast Expanse; Tagpo Tashi Namgyal (1513–1587), the author of two famous works on Mahāmudrā; and probably in the works of many others.

This indicates the extent to which later masters of all schools appreciated Yangönpa for the understanding demonstrated in his writing, and the extent to which the nectar of his teaching pervades all Tibetan schools, without sectarian distinction.

YANGÖNPA'S SPIRITUAL LEGACY

Yangönpa trained many realized disciples and practitioners who were beyond worldly attachment and who continued his legacy. Chief among them was Chen Ngawa Rinchen Den. Chen Ngawa was born in the region of Tingri in 1202. As a small boy, he made pilgrimages to various sacred sites, and following this, developed the aspiration to follow the spiritual path. Once, when he was five, some mountain people told him of an extraordinary emanation of enlightened beings who was living in Lhadong. On hearing this, out of faith, he felt that he should meet this emanation. When he met Yangönpa, who was residing in Tingri, he felt great reverence, and an effortless meditative state was born within him. To facilitate the formation of a spiritual connection between them, Yangönpa taught him the practice of the Union with the Master and the Four-Line Mahāmudrā teaching.

When he was eleven years old, Chen Ngawa went to Lhadong, where he remained as the master's attendant for thirty-five consecutive years, without missing a day, until the master passed away. Because of this, he was called Chen Ngawa, meaning, "in the presence," or in this case, "attendant." Historically, it is not uncommon for such a close relationship based on devotion and service to result in the devotee's inheritance of the master's transmission.

Since he was always with Yangönpa, we can presume that Chen Ngawa received most of the transmission that Yangönpa had received from Kotragpa, Götsangpa, Sakya Pandita, Drigung Chenga, and others.

Chen Ngawa authored *The Great Mirror,* the earliest and most reliable biography of Yangönpa, and compiled the master's *Collected Works* for future generations. His commentaries on Yangönpa's works include one on the *Hidden Description of the Vajra Body,* which is included in Yangönpa's *Collected Works,* and one on the *History of Transmission of the Mountain Teaching,* which describes the circumstances leading up to Yangönpa's composition of that famous work. In his life, Chen Ngawa Rinchen Den raised the banner of practice and came to the realization of the natural state.

There was also the master's nephew Lore Chökyong Pal, known to have attained mastery of the practices involving channels and energy-winds, and to have attained the realization of the "unique flavor" stage of Mahāmudrā practice. When Yangönpa passed away, Chen Ngawa and Lore Chökyong—the master's best students—took up residence in Namding hermitage.

The five students who were prophesied to become holders of the teaching were Sherab Dorje; Rigdzin Zangpo; Tönpa Yönten Pal; Könchog Pal; and Dütsi Nyingpo.

The main recipient of the *Mountain Teaching* was Senge Gyalt-sen. The main recipient of the *Hidden Description* was Shang Pen Dewa. The main recipient of the *Instructions on the Intermediate State* was Tönpa Yönten Pal. The main recipient of the *Seven Days Inner Heat* was Amtso Ritropa. The main recipient of the teachings on the *Enhancement through Illnesses* was Yöngom Kunden Pal. The one who received the *Teachings on Meditative Experiences* was Chose Degyal.

Those who received the teachings on the Base, Path, and Fruit were Tarseng, Dzongkhawa, Trulku Tsanglung, Gyaltsen Bum, and Gompa Shagdor.

The students who served the master were Yönten Zangpo, Yeshe Zangpo, Kunga Zangpo, Yeshe Gönpo, and Rinchen Pal.

Gompa Tepapal and Gompa Yeshe Dorje were the students who received the lineage of profound histories.

Old Lady Yulo received the *Secret Biography*. Other important disciples were Thungchung Shakya Senge, Dharmakoṣa, Chöje Tragpa, Tsibri Yönten Gyamtso, Choden Changchub Zangpo (also known as Kunkhyen Kangtröd), Lobpön Sangye Pal, Chose Yeshe Pal, Lengom Tepawa, Khenchen Chödingwa, Chöje Dziwo Repa, and Gyaltsen Zangpo.

There were also 108 cotton-clad yoginis, such as Majo Tsultrim Gyen; Majo Chönyi Dze, who showed the signs of proficiency in the practice; and many other excellent practitioners.

Chen Ngawa Rinchen Den himself had several realized accomplished disciples, including Surphugpa Rinchen Palzang, the siddha Nyima Gön, and others. But his chief disciple was Surphugpa.

Surphugpa had approximately thirty disciples skilled in accomplishing the benefit of others, including Kunkhyen Surphugpa Rinchen Pal, Chöje Barawa, and Ripa Shönnu Gyaltsen. However, his main student was Barawa Gyaltsen Palzang (1310–1391).

Barawa was a prolific writer who produced many treatises, including the *Three Cycles of Teaching [Titled] the Boat to Liberation*. On the rocks of Bari he established a hermitage called Töndrub Ding. He was the source of the so-called Bara Kagyüd lineage that spread Yangönpa's teaching throughout southern, central, western, and eastern Tibet, and even as far as Bhutan.[30]

Unfortunately, although Yangönpa's teachings have influenced all the schools of Tibetan Buddhism and his *Collected Works* have been published several times, it seems that they barely survive today as an independent system of practice in the Himalayan religious institutions, even in the Drugpa lineage.

Yangönpa's Vision of the Vajra Body

As mentioned above, sometime after his encounters with Kotragpa and Götsangpa, Yangönpa dedicated himself to solitary meditation in mountain hermitages. During this time, he consolidated the meditative experiences that would eventually lead him to compose the text known as the *Hidden Description of the Vajra Body*. It seems that a clear picture of his future work arose in Yangönpa's mind when, still in his twenties, he remained seated in the vajra posture for eleven months, and had a direct vision of the vajra body. *The Great Mirror* records:

> The Precious One himself said, "First, I meditated a great deal on the empty enclosure.[31] [Then,] by the power of [my] training in the pure illusory body, I actually saw the condition of the vajra body—[with its] stable channels, moving energy-winds, and positioned vital essences—just as it is. This is why I composed the *Hidden Description of the Vajra Body*.

His direct vision of the structure of subtle channels; of the colors, spans, and manners of flow of the energy-winds; and of the working of the body's vital essences enabled Yangönpa to present his own version of the vajra body, consistent—according to him—with the descriptions found in the various tantras that he quotes in his work, while resolving their discrepancies.

Given Yangönpa's references to Sakya Pandita and the Drigung transmission in the *Hidden Description,* it is likely that he composed the text during the last decade of his life, after his meetings with Sakya Pandita and Drigung Chen Ngawa. It was in their instructions that Yangönpa found his vision validated. Relying on scriptural authority as well, he ornamented his composition with numerous quotations from the tantras.

In his colophon, Yangönpa states that he composed the *Hidden Description of the Vajra Body* in the Bird year at Lhading. That would have been 1249, when he was thirty-six years old, since in the preceding Bird year of 1237, he probably had not yet met Sakya Pandita and Drigung Chen Ngawa.

However, instead of the title, the front page of the Phajo Ding and Tago editions provide the following puzzling introductory remarks that would seem to contradict the dates of composition just presumed, giving the impression that the conception of the text and its composition occurred almost at the same time:[32]

This *Hidden Description* came to his mind at Lhading, and he was set to write it down. But his pen broke, and he was unable to write, so he fervently invoked the teachers of the lineage, and was then able to write it down. So when he taught it, he always first invoked [the lineage teachers]. In the future, too, his followers should by all means make [such an] invocation.

Whatever the case may be, the *Hidden Description of the Vajra Body* is a medium-length treatise consisting of some thirty-four folios. It was written in a rough and unpolished style, almost as a sudden revelation, just as it arose in his mind. The second and third parts are particularly succinct and terse, and the book ends abruptly. It seems that Yangönpa deemed it sufficiently clear to meet the needs of the meditators to whom it was addressed, without providing lengthy elaborations. Although the *Hidden Description of the Vajra Body* does not set forth any yogic technique or meditative practice, it is intended to complement his many works on retreat practice and to support the practice of the yogin.

THE *HIDDEN DESCRIPTION*: OPENING VERSES

In his opening verses, Yangönpa salutes his favored meditational deity, Vajrayoginī; states the title of the book; and expresses his reverence for the vajra knowledge, the ḍākinīs, and the master. Then he pays homage not to a deity or to the Buddha but to the very vajra body that is the basis for treading the spiritual path, a divine mandala whose subtle aspects are the male and female deities.

In explaining his intention to write the book, he states that the nature of the body is difficult to appraise by those who follow paths other than that of Tantra and who, thus lacking access to this knowledge, are deprived of its liberating effect.

Yangönpa then reveals his qualifications for writing down such teachings. He specifies that he has relied on the masters, on the Tantric methods explained by them, and on his own direct experience; thus, his description is no arbitrary personal invention:

Having relied on [the way of Mantra] … I have gained
certainty through experience regarding the fundamental
nature of the hidden vajra body, the tantra of exegesis that

is the method that clarifies all teachings, that swiftly protects one with bliss, revealed to me by the master's kindness.

Throughout the book, the term *vajra* mainly connotes inseparability. This is clearly stated by Yangönpa when he explains that one's ordinary body, voice, and mind are at all times the enlightened Body, Voice, and Mind. It is for this reason that one speaks of the inseparable nature of vajra.

This nature is said to be hidden. Chen Ngawa, in his *Commentary on the Difficult Points of the Vajra Body*, tells us why this is so:[33]

As to the hidden fundamental nature of the body: it is "hidden" because people of lesser intellect—that is, those of the lower spiritual pursuits—have difficulty understanding the extraordinary points of the inseparability of body and mind. From one perspective, it is hidden from those who, without relying on a teacher, wish to practice [these points] that are locked by means of the six parameters and four modes [of explanation], by hidden instructions, by twisted quotations, and by tantras in disarray. From another perspective, it is secret because it is hidden, in the sense that the great innate wisdom is difficult to realize.

Thus, it is not the body itself but its fundamental nature that is hidden. There are layers or dimensions of the body that are not apparent but must be discovered and penetrated through yogic practice. The outer, coarse layer of the body serves as a kind of veil for the subtle layer. And the subtle layer serves as a veil for the reality source of all. Yet this reality may be discovered by working with the channels, energy-winds, and vital essence. Thus, the yogin's task is to employ appropriate methods to fathom the depths of the subtle layers of the body, according to the maps laid out in the tantras and the instructions of experienced teachers.

THE FUNDAMENTAL NATURE OF THINGS

In the *Hidden Description,* Yangönpa addresses the question of the fundamental nature of things.[34] He starts by citing Tilopa's instructions, which he had received directly from the ḍākinīs:[35]

The fundamental nature of things, the path,
And the steps of the fruit, come to light.

He then points out that it is this fundamental nature of things that is to be realized on the spiritual path. The process by which such realization is awakened in one's being is the spiritual path itself. The positive qualities emerging from such realization are the final fruit.

A few introductory words on the nature of Tantra in general, and the Highest Tantra in particular—which is the standpoint of Yangönpa's description—may provide the reader with clues to the content of Yangönpa's *Hidden Description.* Although the purport of the Highest Tantra can be communicated in a variety of ways, a very clear one stemming from the *Guhyasamāja Tantra* consists of the scheme of the "three continuities."

Here we translate the word *tantra* as "continuity" or "continuum," as it denotes the continuity of the true nature of the individual, a state that is always perfect, characterized as a timeless natural clarity. It is continuous because it has always been present, without interruption, regardless of the condition in which one finds oneself. This continuum has three facets: causal continuum, method continuum, and resultant continuum. In the Dzogchen teaching, these are known as the "base," "path," and "fruit."

Causal continuum denotes the mind essence that is never modified, regardless of the level of spiritual development or lack thereof: it is changeless, self-cognizant, great bliss. Method continuum refers to all the possible ways in which the mind essence may be recognized. In particular, in this Tantric context, it refers to the so-called phases of creation and completion.[36] Because all aspects involved in such recognition are interconnected, method is a continuum. Method is thus a contributory condition for the recognition of the mind essence that is itself the enlightenment or full realization that has always been with one.

Resultant continuum refers to the point at which, through such recognition, the individual becomes a base for the fulfillment of the welfare of others. This occurs when the adventitious stains that are preventing the mind essence from being recognized vanish with the dawning of the understanding that they have never really existed.

Stated differently, although all that is perceived externally and all that is experienced internally seem to be separate from oneself, this is not the case. It is like a hallucination caused by long habituation to nonrecognition of one's true nature. Even when such deceptive perceptions and experiences arise vividly and seem overwhelming, their origin—one's mind's natural clarity—is utterly untouched by the habits that create them. This is the causal continuum, or base.

Relying on the instructions of an experienced master, a yogin comes to understand that whatever is perceived and experienced is the mind's natural clarity; thus, he does not struggle to reject or confirm anything. This is the approach emphasized in the Dzogchen and Mahāmudrā systems. Those who are yet unable to come to this understanding are instructed to imagine a divine dimension in which the environment is a mandala, all beings are deities, and all experience is these deities' enjoyment. In this imaginative way of transforming the ordinary, they approach the mind of luminous clarity. In either of these two ways, one's knowledge is stabilized. This is the method continuum, or path.

Continuing in this way, although the mind of the yogin will still manifest as the entire field of the knowable, the dualistic impressions are absent and the mind is recognized as a great wisdom. Awakened activity spontaneously manifests to impartially fulfill the temporal and spiritual aspirations of countless beings. This awakened activity is the resultant continuum, or final fruit.

The causal continuum (or tantra) described as the mind essence is, in reality, the nature that pervades not only the mind, but everything. Thus, Tilopa's instructions, received directly from the ḍākinīs, tell us:[37]

The fundamental nature is twofold:
That of the body, and that of the mind.

These words are explained by Kongtrul Lodrö Thaye in his *Encompassment of All Knowledge*:[38]

The [fundamental nature] ... denotes the nature, or way of being, of all phenomena, inclusive of everything from form to omniscience. The [fundamental nature] ... is also called the "total seal at the ground stage," "primordial reality," "original lord," "affinity for enlightenment," and "essence of enlightenment." On that basis of division, there are two [fundamental natures] ... that of the body and that of the mind, when distinguished in terms of the way the [fundamental nature] ... manifests.

Yangönpa's particular understanding of the fundamental nature of things (*dngos po'i gnas lugs*) is revealed in his *Mountain Teaching*:

Source of All Qualities, where he defines the expression by breaking it into two parts: things (*dngos po*) and fundamental nature (*gnas lugs*):[39]

> In the context of the extraordinary path, the essential meaning of cause, path, and result of the Secret Mantra are taught as follows: All stationary and mobile things (*dngos po*) such as one's body with its aggregates, elements, and sense fields, have naturally existed as the mandala of the deity from the beginning. This is not created through the profound instructions of the master. Nor does it arise from the great knowledge of the student. The real state that so exists is the fundamental nature (*lugs*). Not recognizing things in this way is ignorance. Taking one's ordinary body and the external world—with its environment and beings—to be independently existent, is deception. In this state, manifold illnesses, provocations, emotions, nonvirtue, and suffering arise.

Here "things" in general, and the body-mind complex in particular, do not exist only as they ordinarily appear. Their real state is the deity mandala. With respect to the body-mind complex, it is the mandala consisting of the channels, energy-winds, and vital essences, whose nature is the deity, or enlightenment itself.

This mandala is not produced by spiritual exercises learned from the master, or through the student's creative imagination. It is inherently and innately present. Thus, not only the mind—which, by virtue of its essence, is aligned with the ultimate truth—but also the body and all phenomena represent that truth. Yangönpa's vision of the fundamental nature as twofold, expressed in the above passage, is essentially the same as that presented by Tilopa: "The fundamental nature is twofold: That of the body, and that of the mind."

But what is the fundamental nature of the mind? It is the *tathāgatagarbha,* or essence of enlightenment present in all beings from the beginning. In the Tibetan milieu, there two main strains of thought that describe the essence of enlightenment. One considers the essence of enlightenment as a potential that can blossom into enlightenment. The other holds that the essence of enlightenment already possesses all the qualities of enlightenment. The difference in these views is largely speculative, since in any case, for the enlightened qualities to fully manifest, that essence must still be recognized.

But basically, the essence of enlightenment is one's ordinary awareness itself, which cannot be defined in any way. It is awareness that cognizes itself; it is awareness and clarity; it possesses the nature of great bliss.

Although the essence of enlightenment is above conditioned existence and its transcendence, it nonetheless serves as the ground for the manifestation of all appearances. This is because, coemergent with it, is the unawareness that is nonrecognition of itself. This activates the subjective mind, and when the occurrence and motion of the subjective mind is not recognized for what it is, the sense of self manifests. Thus, when one's true nature is not recognized, the unimpeded creativity of this nature falsely manifests as subject and object.

At the beginning of the *Hidden Description,* Yangönpa emphasizes the need to know the fundamental nature of things as a precondition for grasping the nature of the spiritual path and the final fruit. The understanding of the mind's nature is thus indispensable. But, in keeping with the Tantric approach, he asserts that knowledge of the mind's nature or essence of enlightenment as expressed in the Madhyamika and the Cittamātra philosophical systems of Mahayana Buddhism is not sufficient. Mind is not an abstract entity separate from the body, but is completely embodied and inseparable from the body. Thus, one must first come to know the fundamental nature of the body. This is Yangönpa's main concern in the *Hidden Description of the Vajra Body:* to pinpoint the body's fundamental nature.

Yangönpa's *Hidden Description* unfolds as the three classic principal categories: base, path, and fruit. He places great emphasis on the base, which takes up most of the text. This is because his main focus is neither a presentation of instructions for treading the path, nor a detailed description of the qualities of the final fruit. His main focus is the description of the fundamental nature of the body.

In the section on the base, Yangönpa divides the fundamental nature of things (*dngos po'i gnas lugs*), which Tilopa presented as the dyad of body and mind, into four: the fundamental nature of the body, of the voice, of the mind, and of the three as inseparable.

Yangönpa's description of the fundamental nature of the body includes the formation of the body in the mother's womb; the channels and chakras; and a brief introduction to the topics of the vital essences, unclean substances, and thought. His description of the fundamental nature of the voice comprises the coarse and subtle energy-winds, syllables, and the voice as sound. As to the fundamental nature of the mind, he describes in some detail the vital essences, their formation, and so on; the cycles of the white and red vital essences; great bliss; the five wisdoms; nonconceptuality; and contemplation. He dedicates just one page to the fundamental nature of body, voice, and mind as inseparable.

The remaining two sections of Yangönpa's text describe how birth, living, and dying are the naturally occurring path and final fruit.

Yangönpa discusses body, voice, and mind, each under five headings. He provides these headings by citing passages that he ascribes to the *Vajramāla.* This title usually indicates the text that is an explanatory tantra of the *Guhyasamāja,* but the passages cited by Yangönpa are not found in the *Vajramāla* preserved in the Tibetan canon as it exists today. These passages are instead found in the *Non-*

dual Victory Tantra, a scripture translated by Marpa Chökyi Lodrö
and one of Marpa's Indian teachers, Shri Jñanagarbha, and which
is contained in the *Treasury of Teachings of the Drigung Kagyüd.*[40]
It may be that, in Yangönpa's time, the *Nondual Victory Tantra* was
also known as the *Vajramāla.* But this question remains unanswered
and will require further research.

It is to be noted, however, that some other passages quoted by
Yangönpa in the *Hidden Description* and ascribed to the *Vajramāla*
are indeed found in the *Vajramāla,* the explanatory tantra of the *Guhyasamāja.* Some questions also remain regarding Yangönpa's naming the *Saṃpuṭa Tantra* as the source of several passages he quotes
in the *Hidden Description* that are not, in fact, found in that tantra.

When Yangönpa introduces the idea of the fundamental nature
of the body, he does not simply refer to the ultimate nature of the
body as emptiness, as it would be understood, for example, in the
Madhyamika system. His explanation of the fundamental nature
of the body focuses primarily on the condition of the human body
itself. This comprises the body's various layers: coarse, subtle, and
very subtle. In his *Perfect Words,* Tilopa states:[41]

Concerning the presentation of the nature of the body,
There are the coarse, subtle, and very subtle [bodies].
These are inseparable from the ordinary [body].

The coarse body mentioned in this passage is the one possessed of
sense organs and so on: the body of flesh, blood, and bones that is
the basis for our experience of pleasure, pain, and so on. The subtle
body is the internal structure of channels, energy-winds, and vital
essences. The refined aspect of channels, energy-winds, and vital
essences, which transcends particles of matter and is of the very essence of wisdom, is the very subtle innate body: intangible emptiness and yet tangible bliss.

Each of these three layers is interconnected, overlapping, and inseparable. The three are collectively known as the vajra body.

The very subtle or innate body, being of the very essence of reality that is inexpressible and inconceivable, is not discussed by Yangönpa in the *Hidden Description*. Nor does he explore the coarse layer of the body in detail. Although he does not neglect the topic, his description of the coarse body is minimal, and mostly derived from traditional Tibetan medicine. Yangönpa's chief concern is the second of these layers, the subtle body, for this is the primary focus of yogic practice.

In Tantric physiology, the subtle layer of the body consists of channels, energy-winds, and vital essences. This triad also represents the subtle or inner layer of body, voice, and mind, which is not normally observable through the senses. The subtle layer of the body consists of the network of channels pervading the entire body. The subtle layer of the voice consists of the energy-winds that pervade both the body and the universe. The subtle level, or support, of the mind consists of the vital essences that, as the various essences of the body, give it its strength, vitality, and luster.

As mentioned above, the word *vajra* in the expression *vajra body* denotes "inseparability." Inseparability here refers to the fact that body, voice, and mind in their ordinary condition are already the enlightened Body, Voice, and Mind.

In the Mahayana, the enlightened being's Body, Voice, and Mind are the opposite of those of an ordinary being. It is only through a process of purification and acquisition of knowledge that the ordinary body, voice, and mind can become the enlightened Body, Voice, and Mind. But from the Tantric standpoint, Yangönpa points out that the nature of an ordinary being and that of an enlightened one are inseparable. This applies to body, voice, and mind. What binds the enlightened and the ordinary being together is the subtle layer of the body just described: the channels (subtle aspect of the body); the energy-winds (subtle aspect of the voice); and the vital essences (subtle aspect or basis of the mind).

Channels, energy-winds, and vital essences are the expression of the enlightened nature present in all beings. They are also the main focus of the Tantric praxis aimed at the recognition of this nature: the essential identity of ordinary body, voice, and mind and enlightened Body, Voice, and Mind. Thus, for Yangönpa, the "subtle body" as the dimension of channels, energy-winds, and vital essences is not only the basis for the application of the methods of awakening, but is itself of the nature of awakening. This is why, in the *Hidden Description of the Vajra Body*, Yangönpa places greater emphasis on the body than on the mind.

Yangönpa accompanies his brief description of the principal qualities of the channels, energy-winds, and vital essences with analogies: the channels are "stationary," and resemble a house; the energy-winds are "mobile," and resemble the owner of the house who also possesses the wealth contained within it. The vital essences, "positioned" in the different channels, represent the wealth. But he provides no rationale for his analogies.

The channels are the main pathways in which the energy-winds and various bodily fluids move. Their condition—pure or impure, blocked or unblocked—determines the quality not only of the person's health but also of his spiritual development. They may also be called stationary because they do not generally change course within the body.

The characterization of the energy-winds as the owner of the wealth stored in the house signifies that they control the channels themselves, as well as the vital essences present within them. The energy-winds exercise their ownership of the vital essences by distributing them throughout the body, and by controlling them in the course of Tantric practices through breath retention and other means.

The vital essences are "positioned" in the sense that they are made to flow by the energy-winds in various bodily channels. In the analogy, the vital essences representing the wealth itself are the most valuable and important aspect of the triad. In fact, the vital essences represent the potentiality that, in the ordinary condition, as sperm and ovum, are the origin of life; and in the spiritual condition, are the element that, as the basis of bliss, has the nature of the enlightened state. But the vital essences are also directly linked to concrete external wealth, for the condition of the vital essences grants good health and serves as a causal nexus for the possession and enjoyment of wealth.

Several centuries later, Jigmed Lingpa, in his *Treasury of Precious Qualities,* echoes Yangönpa's words and gives his own interpretation of the terms *stationary, mobile,* and *positioned,* as explained in the commentary by Longchen Yeshe Dorje:

To begin with, in the perfection stage that uses visual forms, primordial wisdom must be generated by mastering the channels, winds, and essence-drops. In order to practice in this way, it is very important to understand what exactly these components are. The channels are referred to as "stationary" because, in being the nature of the deity, they do not move. The wind contained within the channels is called "mobile" because it is [the vehicle of consciousness, and thus] the compounder of the three worlds. Supported, as it were, by both the channels and the winds, the essence-drop or *bodhicitta* is said to be "positioned," in the sense that it is conveyed back and forth and is set in various positions by the winds. This bodhicitta is by nature free from stain and is endowed with every perfect quality. A body that is endowed with the three coarse aspects of the channels, winds, and essence-drops is an extraordinary support and is referred to as the city of the vajra aggregate.[42]

Thus, the channels, energy-winds, and vital essences representing the subtle aspect of body, voice, and mind, respectively, form the main topic of Yangönpa's *Hidden Description of the Vajra Body,* which provides a map of Tantric physiology that is essential to the application of yogic exercises.

THE FUNDAMENTAL NATURE OF THE BODY

To introduce the fundamental nature of the body, Yangönpa cites the following passage from the *Nondual Victory Tantra:*

> As to the body, by virtue of the five awakenings,
> Channels, vital essences,
> Unclean substances, and thoughts,
> The phenomenon of the body exists.

He then proceeds to describe the factors of the body, beginning with conception and development of the fetus in the mother's womb. In this description, he associates conception and gestation with two sets of five manifest awakenings, the "outer" set, typical of the Yoga tantra, and the "inner," of the Anuttara tantra.

The five awakenings, in origin, were five moments in the Buddha's enlightenment as described in Yoga tantra literature. For the sake of future spiritual seekers, in this and in other Tantric literature, these moments are laid out as steps in the visualization of oneself as the deity. Although, in the Highest Tantras, they are considered a method of purifying ordinary birth, Yangönpa's association of these steps with conception and gestation aims to prove that there is no such thing as ordinary birth, but only birth as an awakened being.

The body is thus a spontaneous buddha, not one that has become so through spiritual practice.

There is no fundamental difference between the five outer and the five inner awakenings. The association of the five inner awakenings with the five wisdoms in the Anuttara tantra is also implied in the outer model of the Yoga tantra.

In Yangönpa's text, in the last nine of the ten lunar months of gestation, from the second to the tenth, the fetus is associated with the ten incarnations of Viṣṇu, beginning with the second month when it becomes elongated and resembles Viṣṇu's incarnation as a fish. In the genesis of the human body, we can say that the very subtle layer of the body generates the subtle layer, and that this in turn generates the coarse human body. In his *Encompassment of All Knowledge,* Kongtrul states:

> Accordingly, the aggregates, elements, and sense fields are all formed from the channels, winds, and vital essences; and these three, from mind nature, the essence of enlightenment attended by stains.[43]

Conception occurs when the mind and the accompanying pervasive energy-wind of a being seeking rebirth blends with the semen and ovum. Then, around the third week following conception, as the embryo grows, the first chakra or energy-center, that of the navel, emerges. From this, upward and downward, the central channel and all the chakras along its course originate. Then, the network of channels producing the various components of the physical body— including the senses—branch off from the chakras.

On the basis of the preexisting mind of the being seeking rebirth that has entered the mother's womb at conception, channels and chakras give rise to the various levels of conceptual and sensory consciousness. By the time the child is born, all components of the subtle body are complete, and thereafter, unlike the coarse body, the subtle body develops no further. The *Kālacakra Tantra* even states that after birth, two channels disappear daily.

The Channels

In the Tibetan language, channels are called *rtsa*, meaning "root." According to Tibetan medicine, because they ensure life, they are like the root of life of the individual.

The term *rtsa* in Tibetan medicine has a broad connotation. It refers to the network of blood vessels (veins and arteries); to the pathways of the energy-winds; to the lymphatic vessels, bile ducts, and other ducts; and to the nerves, tendons, and ligaments. So, when reading classical Tibetan medical texts, if the context is unclear, the term is often ambiguous. We find the same ambiguity in the context of Tantra.

There is a widespread impression that the channels mentioned in Tantra are immaterial pathways of energy-wind and mind. But Yangönpa's text and the Tantric texts themselves make it clear that the nature of the channels varies according to the content they carry: some carry energy-wind; some carry blood; and some carry vital essences. Yangönpa writes:

> As to the number of channels, distinguished in detail, they amount to ninety-five million. The channels containing blood equal seventy-two thousand. The channels in which the winds flow are 21,600.... The channels in which the vital essences descend are thirty-two.

From this description, it is clear that some of the channels described in the tantras are veins and arteries. According to Tibetan medicine, in addition to blood, arteries also carry energy-wind, and for this reason they are called "pulsating channels," as opposed to veins, which are called, "unmoving channels." The precise nature of the other, more subtle, channels remains an open question. Are they immaterial pathways through which energy-wind and mind move, or tubelike structures with some form of physical existence?

The Three Main Channels

In Tantric physiology, there are three main channels whose functions are of primary importance and whose position in the body reflects the principles of method, knowledge, and nonduality: the *rasanā, lalanā,* and the central channel. These are generally described as extending from the lower body to the head. The two lateral channels insert into the nostrils, while the central channel inserts at the crown of the head, or between the eyebrows. The position of the channels' upper and lower extremities are explained differently in different tantras.

The first channel to form in the womb is the central channel that provides the support for the life-sustaining energy-wind.[44] From this, myriads of smaller channels branch off, through which energy-wind and mind—which in Tantra are considered to be indissolubly united—are carried to all the parts of the body.

It is through the channels that mind is totally embodied; thus, mind can be affected by yogic practices that focus on the body. It is not necessary for mind to be affected through thoughts or other mental means. Mind's movement must be stilled within the innermost recesses of the body itself. With the stilling of the energy-wind within the central channel that represents nondual reality, mind loses itself, and reality shines forth.

The Tantric postulation of channels in which energy-wind and mind and vital essences flow raises the question of the relationship between the physiology of the observable human body and the

Tantric physiology of the invisible subtle body. This issue, which must surely have been raised even prior to Yangönpa's time, appears prominently in the *Hidden Description,* in its discussion of the central channel (Tib. *dbu ma,* Skt. *avadhūti*). This is understandable, for the central channel is the main focus of the yogic practices involving channels, energy-winds, and vital essences.

Without attributing them to anyone in particular, Yangönpa lists and debunks some erroneous attempts to identify the nature of the central channel. He refutes the notions that the central channel is imaginary, that it is the life channel,[45] and that it is the spinal cord.

The first notion seems to come from the side of Tantric practitioners. He dismisses this with the argument that, if the central channel were imaginary, all experience and realization gained from practices involving the central channel would also be imaginary.

The second notion, that the central channel is the life channel, certainly originates from the medical field. It should be noted that by Yangönpa's time, the *Four Medical Tantras,* the most authoritative text of Tibetan medicine, had emerged in its present form. Some learned physicians, who were also Tantric practitioners, had tried to bridge the gap between the Tantric and the more observable medical physiology.

Although, according to Tibetan medicine, the life channel is the basis for life, Tibetan doctors disagree as to its precise definition. What is agreed on is that when the energy-wind and mind enter the life channel, serious mental disorders ensue. Yangönpa refutes the identification of the central channel as the life channel by stating that, when the energy-wind and mind enter the central channel, there arise many positive qualities but no negative ones, as when these winds enter the life channel.

Yangönpa also dismisses the notion that the central channel is the spinal cord. This idea may have been inspired by the fact that the central channel is often said to be located in the center of the back. Yangönpa contends that the spinal cord lacks the characteristics of the central channel, and cannot be similarly used as the focus of yogic practice.

But what then is the nature of the central channel? Yangönpa states that it possesses four characteristics:

it is straight like the trunk of a plantain tree; slender like a lotus stem; luminous like a sesame oil lamp; and red like the lacquer tree's flower.

He then quotes several passages from the tantras that describe the central channel as a life-pillar extending from the crown of the head to the abdominal crease, entwined at the six chakras by the right and left channels; a place where, through yogic practices, the energy-winds enter and the workings of the ordinary mind come to an end.

Kongtrul Lodrö Thaye, in his *Phrase-by-Phrase Commentary to the Hevajra Tantra*, explains that:

The central channel (*kun 'dar ma*), which is of the nature of the inseparability of method and knowledge, stands straight in the body, its tip inserting into the Brahmā aperture. In males, its lower extremity inserts in the door of the gem of the vajra; in females, it inserts in the clitoris. Since it is totally beyond apprehended and apprehender, it is called, the "all-abandoner" (*kun spang ma*). Moreover, from the navel, having reached the Brahmā aperture, the central channel turns toward the point between the eyebrows.[46]

And in his *Encompassment of All Knowledge*, Kongtrul states:

The central channel ... originates from the power of energy-wind. It is known as "central" or "all abandoning" ...
because it has rejected the "extremes" of both the lunar
and solar winds, and because when the winds that flow in
the right and left channels enter and dissolve in the central
channel, the concepts of subject and object are overcome....
Its lower extremity, known as "conch-shell" ... controls the
emission and retention of semen.[47]

In Kongtrul's *Commentary to the Hevajra Tantra,* he adds:

The lower extremity of the central channel, from the meeting point of the three channels [downward], causes the
white part of the lunar bodhicitta, which has the nature
of Nairātmyā, wisdom, to descend; thus it is said to be
filled with Vajradhāra [holder of the vajra. The bliss] pervades all channels, and since bliss makes [the central chan-
nel] shake, [this channel] is called "all-shaking" (*kun 'dar
ma*).[48]

Yangönpa does not address the questions: If the central channel
is neither imaginary nor a physical entity, what is it? Does it exist
on a material or on an immaterial level? For him—the most adept
of yogins—the central channel was certainly something real, but
real in what sense? One possibility—as communicated by Rigdzin
Changchub Dorje to Chögyal Namkhai Norbu—would be a reality
pertaining to the realm of wisdom. Considering that the color and
size of the central channel visualized in tantric methods differs from
that observed in the body, how could it possibly reflect a concrete
physical structure?

However, in his *Advice on the Hidden Description,* Yangönpa's
successor Chen Ngawa struggles to supplement the master's expla-

nation with some words of commentary that seem to go in quite a different direction:

> Some, in consideration of the ultimate [sense], say that the [central channel] is merely imputed and therefore does not exist in reality. This is a misunderstanding. All the interdependent factors of the Secret Mantra tradition are set in place in the body. Therefore, if a relative, substantial central channel does not exist in the body, all the qualities pertaining to the central channel that have been explained would be meaningless. Therefore, on what would the two [vital essences, white and red], support-holders of life at the upper and lower extremities, rely? This is a complete misunderstanding of the Secret Mantra.[49]

Chen Ngawa continues with a rather murky explanation that locates the central channel in front of the life channel, and asserts that it has a subtle substantial existence.[50] However, he neglects to define his term, *substantial existence*, which could not refer to ordinary matter. Here, Chen Ngawa is probably attempting to discredit the idea that the central channel is just a work of imagination with no real basis in the human body, an idea that would render all yogic endeavor relating to the central channel imaginary, and thus incapable of having any real impact on the body and on the individual.

To sum up, the central channel does not pertain to the gross materiality of the body, and yet it is something that, as the focus of yogic practice, has concrete effects on body and mind; thus, it is real. The central channel symbolizes the nondual reality, a reality beyond concrete or not concrete; internal or external; and all other ways in which the mind may conceive things to exist.

This level of the central channel exists only while the coarse material body is alive. When the body perishes, states Chen Ngawa, the central channel loses its substantial existence. Likewise, once the body dies, all the other relative aspects of the subtle body present within the living organism disappear, and only its very subtle or ultimate aspects remain.

While the vajra body subsists during the life of the yogin who is familiar with it—particularly with the central channel—this reality is at the center of his body, subtle like a lotus stem. When this yogin inserts energy-wind and mind into the central channel, he discovers this reality, the true nature of things, an emptiness inseparable from bliss: this is the very subtle, or ultimate central channel. Thus, the central channel becomes the source of all good qualities for the yogin.

To reconcile the different notions of the central channel into a noncontradictory view that echoes Yangönpa's, we cite the words of Yönten Gyamtso, found in his commentary on Jigmed Lingpa's *Treasury of Precious Qualities*:

> The *uma* or central channel (*dbu ma*) is a sort of axis or life-tree along which all the chakras are located. It is not wholly inexistent as a causally efficient entity, for otherwise the qualities that arise when it is brought under control would be impossible to explain. It is neither the life channel (*srog rtsa*) nor the spinal cord (*rgyungs pa*), for these are coarse channels, and it is said that if the wind enters the life channel, madness and unconsciousness ensue, and this is contrary to the way the [real] uma is defined. Nevertheless, there is no such thing as an uma that is independent from, or unsupported by, these two channels. As Saraha says, "Wind and mind are supported by the life channel. Therefore, when it (the *srog rtsa*) is brought under control, the ordinary mind is naturally halted." And as the *Heart-Essence of the Ḍākinī* also says, "The *uma of skillful means*, the so-called *avadhūti,* is what ordinary people call the spinal

cord; and the *uma of wisdom,* the *ever-trembling* (*kun 'dar ma*), is commonly identified with the life channel. The *uma in which skillful means and wisdom are united* lies in front of the backbone and behind the life channel, and it is without blood and lymph."

There are three umas: the *localized uma* (*gnas pa'i dbu ma*), the *actual uma* (*chos nyid kyi dbu ma*), and the *ultimate uma* (*don dam pa'i dbu ma*). The first of these is, from the point of view of its actual condition, the channel that supports life. The second [which is the channel employed in the perfection stage practices] is the genuine central channel (*mtshan nyid kyi rtsa*) and is marked by four features. It has a luminous nature, it is unobstructed and intangible, and as long as the body, mind, and breath remain together, it is present. To that extent, it is not nonexistent. When, however, the body, mind, and breath go their separate ways, it disappears, and to that extent it is not existent. It is like a rainbow, which appears when the proper conditions are present, and disappears when they disperse. When one is meditating, one should consider that this uma is in the middle of the life channel. This is because both the universal ground (*kun gzhi*) and the life-wind (*srog rlung*) are supported by it, and thus they are in fact all of the same taste. Finally, the *ultimate uma* refers to the actual condition of the fruit: the absence of intrinsic being (*ngo bo med pa*).[51]

In the triad of the most important channels, we find the two channels that flank the central channel, the rasanā (*ro ma*) and lalanā (*rkyang ma*). These two channels represent the duality, the split that occurs when reality is not recognized and is thus perceived as the separate entities of subject and object, or observer and observed.

Thus, as the pathways for the karmic energy-wind, they are the initiators and perpetrators of dualism. In his *Encompassment of All Knowledge,* Kongtrul writes:

> The left channel, in Sanskrit lalanā (*rkyang ma*), originates from the power of the white aspect of the glow of pristine awareness. It creates the illusion of an apprehender. The lalanā is also called "knowledge" ... because it causes the lunar wind to flow from the left nostril. Its lower extremity controls emission and retention of urine. Fourteen channels branch off from the lalanā, spreading throughout the left side of the body.
>
> The right channel, in Sanskrit rasanā (*ro ma*), originates from the power of the red aspect of the glow of pristine awareness. It creates the illusion of an objective world, the apprehended. Rasanā is also called "method" ... because it causes the solar wind ... to flow from the right nostrils. Its lower extremity controls emission and retention of feces. Ten channels branch off from the rasanā, spreading throughout the right side of the body.[52]

According to this explanation, the rasanā is associated with method and the lalanā, with wisdom or knowledge. In Tantra, broadly speaking, "method" refers to all that is manifest and perceivable by the senses. "Knowledge" refers instead to the energy that is inherently present in the empty nature that is the manifestation's underlying reality.

In the upper part of the body, rasanā and lalanā insert in the right and left nostrils, respectively, and the energy-winds of the various elements flow within them. In the lower part of the body, rasanā discharges blood, and lalanā, urine.

In Yangönpa's explanation—drawn from the perspective of the New (Sarma) schools of Tibetan Buddhism, Sakya, Gelug, and Kagyüd—the rasanā is the right channel. It is red, and associated with the solar vital essence. The lalanā is the left channel and is white, and associated with the lunar vital essence. In these schools—perhaps reflecting the fact that Tantra was taught mainly to men—the two channels are visualized in this way irrespective of the meditator's gender.

It should be noted that in the Nyingma, in the Dzogchen Ati Yoga tradition of Total Perfection,[53] and in the Shang Shung Nyengyü transmission of Bön, the rasanā is white, and associated with the lunar energy. In men, this channel is on the right side of the body, and in women, on the left. The lalanā is red, and associated with the solar energy. This channel is on the left side in men, and on the right in women. This is clearly stated by Longchenpa, the great systematizer of Dzogchen in Tibet, in his commentary to the *Guhyagarbha Tantra* called *Dispelling All Darkness throughout the Ten Directions*:

> With regard to the nature to be known, in the vajra body there are two main channels: rasanā, the right one, white; lalanā, the left one, red; and avadhūti, the central, blue. These three life pillars serve as the support for the three doors [body, voice, and mind], and of the three poisons [attachment, anger, and ignorance]. When they are purified through the union of method and knowledge, they serve as the support for the three dimensions of enlightenment.[54]

This is stated even more clearly in Longchen Yeshe Dorje's commentary on Jigmed Lingpa's *Treasury of Precious Qualities*:

The consciousness of a being in the bardo, which is in the process of gaining the support of a human body in one of the three cosmic continents, enters in the midst of the semen and ovum in the womb of its future mother. It is within this support (the mingled essences) that the channels first take shape. This begins at the navel, where the knot of channels contains two "eyes" and is shaped like the knot used to hobble the three legs of a horse together. From this the body gradually takes shape. When the outer universe is formed, the quintessence of the elements becomes the central Mount Meru, and then by gradual degrees the golden mountains are formed, while the residue of the elements becomes the cosmic continents, the surrounding boundary, and so on. In parallel fashion, the quintessence of the male and female elements becomes the central channel or *uma* (Skt. *avadhūti*), together with the two lateral channels, *roma* (Skt. *rasanā*) and *kyangma* (Skt. *lalanā*), which are like pillars in the center of the body.

Within these channels are three seed-syllables. They are like the main figure and retinue (in a mandala), and act as the basis: outwardly, for the body, speech, and mind; inwardly, for the three poisons or defilements; and secretly, for the enlightened body, speech, and mind, as well as for "light," "increase of light," and "culmination of light." The various tantras and pith instructions describe the location of the syllables differently, but if the matter is discussed according to the function of the three channels, it seems sufficient to say that OM is in the roma, ĀH is in the kyangma, while HŪM is in the central uma.

The central channel is so called because, in terms of its position, it is situated between the two lateral channels and because, in terms of its ontological status, it is beyond the extremes of existence and nonexistence. At the upper end of the central channel is located (in the form of the syllable HAM) the white essence-drop obtained from one's father. It has the nature of skillful means. At the lower end is the red essence-drop obtained from one's mother. This is in the form of the shortened A and has the nature of wisdom. The upper end of the central channel penetrates the Brahmā aperture at the crown of the head, while the lower end enters the secret center below the navel. And between these two extremities, the central channel, which is of nondual nature, is the basis of the universal ground, which subsists in the form of the life-wind—the central channel being like space. On the right of the central channel is the roma, the so-called corpse or taste channel. This is so named to reflect its nature. Being unable to perform any function, it is like a corpse; but once brought under control, it is the channel that elicits the taste of bliss. On the left of the central channel is the kyangma, the so-called solitary channel. Its name reflects its character, for it is like an isolated rod that is not connected to anything else. When it is mastered by means of the pith instructions, the thought-free experience of ultimate reality occurs. It is thus the channel that elicits freedom from discursiveness.

The colors of the roma and kyangma are respectively white and red. In women, the position of the roma and kyangma is reversed, owing to their specific relationship with skillful means and wisdom. For them, therefore, the kyangma is on the right of the central channel. The three channels are the "mothers" of all the other channels—which is why their names all end in the syllable MA.

The central channel is light blue in color. The roma and kyangma branch out from the uma at the level of the navel, but they loop around it and constrict it at the level of the kidneys and so on, up to the crown of the head. By being thus entwined with the uma, they form a series of twenty-one knots.[55]

To sum up, for the New schools, rasanā, the right channel, is red and is associated with method. Lalanā, the left channel, is white and is associated with knowledge. For the Ancient (Nyingma) Dzogchen tradition, while retaining the same associations with method and knowledge, rasanā, the right channel in men and the left in women, is white. Lalanā, the left channel in men and the right in women, is red.

These differing views on the positions and colors of the two main channels flanking the central channel are reflected in the way they are visualized in the meditation practices of the various traditions. According to the Dzogchen tradition, Yönten Gyamtso writes:

The three channels may be evaluated according to their function. Blood, lymph, and the bodhicitta all circulate in the roma. Therefore, if one is skillful in working with the essence-drops, one's karma related to physical action will be exhausted. All craving for food will end, and one will be able to subsist on the food of *samādhi*. By contrast, the quintessence of the elements, as well as the wisdom wind, all circulate in the kyangma. Therefore, if one is skilled in working with this channel, the karma related to speech will be exhausted, and the need for clothing will be brought to an end. The ultimate uma has the nature of light. It is an empty, all-penetrating openness (*zang thal*). Therefore, if one is skillful at working with the wind [bringing it into the central channel], the karma of mental actions will be purified, together with all craving for drink. Dreams will

end, and finally one will realize ultimate reality beyond
the two extremes: the primordial wisdom of luminosity.[56]

Although Yangönpa defines the channels as stationary, this does not
imply that they always remain in the same condition. For example,
Yangönpa mentions a special channel of the heart chakra, the *maradarika*, or "liberator from the demon." Kongtrul Lodrö Thaye, in
his exceptional *Phrase-by-Phrase Commentary to the Hevajra Tantra*,
tells us that the ordinary function of this channel is to provide the
dominant condition for tactile perception, since the branches of this
channel reach from the heart to every pore of the skin. Another of
its functions is to draw the vital essence upward.[57]

Yangönpa explains that the maradarika is actually the posterior
of the central channel at the heart. The central channel is the source
of the nonconceptual state, for when energy-wind is inserted in it,
gross conceptuality ceases. It may be that Yangönpa's assertion that
the maradarika is the source of the nonconceptual state, totally devoid of mental fabrications, reflects the fact that the central channel expresses its most active potential in the heart region, where the
maradarika is located.

The mouth of this channel may be open, half closed, or closed,
depending on the person's level of spiritual development. For an ordinary person, the channel's mouth is closed and faces downward;
for a bodhisattva, it is half closed and horizontal; and for realized
beings, it is open and faces upward. In the ordinary condition, when
the channel is closed, it mostly generates unhappiness. Through yogic practice, when the mouth of the channel is turned upward, the
vital essence it contains is manifest, and body and mind are pervaded by bliss.

The maradarika is paralleled by another channel, the "mare's
face," located four finger-widths below the navel. The mare's face is

the seat of the fire-accompanying wind that governs the digestive functions. Although the mare's face extends up to the maradarika, in the ordinary condition, it remains separated from it. Being separated from its white balancing counterpart, the red vital essence of the mare's face that flares upward dominates the white vital essence of the heart, and this becomes the source of discursive thoughts and desires. It is only through yogic practices such as the inner heat that the two vital essences are reunited and thus become balanced and dwell in harmony, one reinforced by the other.

Having discussed the three main channels, Yangönpa then describes the channels that branch off from the four major junctures where the three main channels share a common interior. These junctures are the so-called chakras or "wheels," and the main ones are located at the head, throat, heart, and navel. Eight channels branch of from each of these, for a total of thirty-two channels that carry the vital essence to different parts of the body and perform different functions. In the external world, the places and organs to which these channels extend are associated with the sacred places of tantra.

Then, Yangönpa describes the channels of the genital chakra whose tips, according to his explanation, have the shapes of the six syllables—A, SU, NRI, TRI, PRE, and DU. These are the syllables of the six realms of existence, in that they serve as causes of birth in each of the six realms: that of the gods, demigods, humans, animals, tormented spirits, and hell beings.

At the right eyebrow, a channel that branches off from the genital chakra has the shape of the letter A of the gods' realm; a channel at the heart has the shape of the letter NRI of the human realm; a channel at the left eyebrow has the shape of the letter SU of the demigods' realm; a channel in the pubic region has the shape of the letter TRI of the animal realm; a channel at the navel has the shape of the letter PRE of the realm of tormented spirits; and a channel at the soles of the feet has the form of the letter DU of the hell realms.

These syllables, which are a fusion of channels, energy-winds, and vital essences mixed with various predispositions generated by actions, are the focus of the practices for purification of the six realms. Once purification has been achieved, the letters of the six realms are destroyed, and the visions of these realms, conditioned by habits, no longer arise.

All these channels, or the vital essence they contain, exist in the shapes of syllables, beginning with the syllable A, which forms upright at the navel, and the syllable HAM, which forms upside down at the head. Gradually, the five syllables of the heart: BHRUM, AM, DZIM, KHAM, and HŪM; the syllables of the sacred places in different areas of the body; and all the other inconceivable numbers of syllables arise. Within these syllables flow the energy-winds by which the sound of the voice is produced.

The Vital Essence of Bodhicitta

Commenting on the three final factors of the body mentioned in the *Nondual Victory Tantra*, "[vital essence of] bodhicitta, unclean substances, and thought," Yangönpa only briefly mentions the vital essence, since he will elaborate on it later in the section dedicated to the fundamental nature of the mind (*sems kyi dngos po'i gnas lugs*).

Bodhicitta is a term borrowed by tantra from Mahayana Buddhism, where it indicates the altruistic wish to attain enlightenment. Along with the understanding of emptiness, in the Mahayana, bodhicitta is one of the two essentials for treading the spiritual path to realization. Without the motivating force of altruistic intention, understanding emptiness is not considered sufficient for one to progress on the spiritual path. Thus, in the Mahayana, bodhicitta is the root of the path. But it is only an aspect of the mind.

In Tantra, however, as Yangönpa points out, bodhicitta is a factor of both body and mind. In terms of the body, as will be explained later, bodhicitta is the vital essence that nourishes both the coarse and the subtle organic components of the body; it is also the male and female generative fluids. In terms of the mind, bodhicitta is the support of the mind itself, and its subtle aspect is inseparable from mind's essence.

Unclean Substances

The Buddhist scriptures, from sutra to tantra, classify the components of the physical human body as thirty-two unclean substances. These are listed as follows: head hair, body hair, nails, teeth, skin, flesh, sinew, bone, bone marrow, kidneys, heart, spleen, lungs, entrails, stomach, intestine, colon, bladder, stool, bile, phlegm, joints, blood, sweat, fat, tears, grease, saliva, snivel, lymph, urine, and brain.[58]

However, Yangönpa speaks of the thirty-two constituents that generate these components of the physical body as the thirty-two unclean substances. We must assume that the thirty-two constituents to which he refers are unrefined aspects of the vital essence of bodhicitta that flows in the thirty-two channels branching off from the main chakras. Thus, even the thirty-two unclean physical components of the body are part of the vital essence of bodhicitta, and are aspects of the fundamental nature of the body, the vajra body.

Although Yangönpa employs the same disparaging term, "unclean substances," as is used by Buddhist scholars, he states that, for Tantric practitioners, the thirty-two constituents that produce hair and so on are not impure, but are Tantric heroes; and the thirty-two body components they produce are the thirty-two sacred Tantric places.

Thought

From the mind essence originates the triad of the subtle layer of the body, which in turn produces the coarse layer and the gross consciousnesses. This renders the line of demarcation between body and mind almost imperceptible. This line becomes even more blurred when Yangönpa places "thought" (Tib. *rnam rtog,* Skt. *vikalpa*) within the bodily factors.

By citing the deep interpenetration of body and mind, he tries to prove that thought is a subdivision of body. From the creative energy of the mind essence, the luminous source of everything, the five elements—earth, water, fire, air, and space—come into being. At conception, the qualities of the elements are inherent in the father's semen and the mother's ovum. It is from these qualities that, through the subtle body, the coarse body and the consciousnesses gradually form to completion. Thus, the elements are the prior cause of consciousness, the result.

In this picture, although the elements manifest as the creative energy of the mind essence and are not different from it, we conceive of them as having characteristics of their own. In this way arises the duality of mind as the subject and matter as the object. Yangönpa states that this duality is the causal nexus through which the body gradually comes into being, like a tent supported by its poles.

Thus, the body is a mental manifestation, and at the same time, it appears as it does because it is an embodiment or natural expression of thought. Here we must assume that "embodiment of thought" refers to the Buddhist belief that the ripening of traces left by ungoverned emotions such as anger, jealousy, and attachment can manifest as a body and as an environment.

The Fundamental Nature of the Voice

Yangönpa introduces the fundamental nature of the voice by citing a passage from the *Nondual Victory Tantra:*

> As to the voice,
> By virtue of the five elements, syllables, vocal resonation,
> coordination, and words,
> The phenomenon of voice exists.[59]

In this passage, "five elements" refers to the energy-wind that expresses the functions of the five elements: earth, water, fire, air, and space. And, as mentioned above, in the triad of the channels, energy-wind, and vital essences, energy-wind is the subtle correlate of voice. At the beginning, in the mother's womb, it formed the body and sustained its development; now it keeps the body alive. For this reason, the primal aspect of energy-wind is referred to as life-sustaining: the very life force of the individual.

But what is the nature of energy-wind? In his *Encompassment of All Knowledge,* Kongtrul states that the term *energy-wind* (*rlung;* Skt. *prana*) denotes potency or strength, in the sense that energy manifests as everything, and in the final analysis, everything is of the nature of energy.[60]

But the main characteristic of energy-wind is motion. The energy-wind is present in and governs all the activities of body, voice, and mind that involve motion. Energy-wind performs the various bodily functions: it enables breathing, swallowing, excretion, motor activity, and exertion. It supports the assimilation of the nutritive essence of food by distributing it through the vascular system, thus regenerating the body, and it confers physical strength. Energy-wind plays a key role in cognition and other mental processes. In particular, it sustains memory and awareness, enables the sense faculties to perceive, and provides the sense of physical as well as psychic equilibrium. As it accompanies every state of mind, energy-wind determines our feelings of happiness or sorrow, our overall emotional stability or instability.

When activated through special techniques such as breath control, energy-wind can perform extraordinary functions, producing heightened states of awareness, mystical experiences, clairvoyance, blissful physical sensations, and the emergence of the natural state of the mind.

Energy-wind not only serves as a bridge or means of communication between body and mind, but in the Tantric perspective, it coexists with the mind as an indivisible unity. The relationship between energy-wind and mind or consciousness is described in the *Guhyasamāja* literature, which states that although they have distinct characteristics, they perform the same functions. Consciousness is characterized by awareness and clarity; energy-wind by motion, deception, and matter. For example, it is said that consciousness is like a lame man with excellent eyesight, while energy-wind is like a blind horse: together, they travel everywhere. Similarly, consciousness, driven by energy-wind, flashes through the doors of the senses toward objects. Moreover, all that occurs during the life cycle occurs with consciousness as the primary cause and energy-wind as the secondary condition.

The inseparability of energy-wind and mind is a general concept whose meaning changes at various moments of existence. At the time of death, all gross layers of the mind dissolve, and there manifests the mind of luminosity—the mind essence just as it is—accompanied by its subtle energy-wind. This is "the inseparability of energy-wind and mind" at that time. In the intermediate state, from the mind of luminosity, there manifests the mental body and its consciousness with its inseparable energy-wind. At conception, only the pervasive energy-wind and the mind loaded with karmic imprints are present. The dream state and the waking state each have their own particular inseparability of wind and mind. Thus, although energy-wind and mind are always inseparable, this inseparability manifests differently at different times.

Quoting an array of tantras, received instructions, and his own experiential knowledge, Yangönpa discusses the various names, characteristics, functions, and manners of circulation of energy-wind. He divides the energy-winds into two major categories: coarse and subtle. The coarse winds, which are said to number 21,600, flow through the channels, sense organs, and orifices. This number reflects the 21,600 breaths that a healthy individual is said to take during a twenty-four hour period.

Employing a scheme widely used in the tantras, Yangönpa principally classifies the energy-winds in the body as the ten winds: five root and five branch winds.

The five root winds are known as the life-sustaining, the downward-clearing, the upward-moving, the pervasive, and the fire-accompanying winds. These winds develop in the mother's womb from the moment of conception, and are fully present by the end of the second month of gestation.

Yangönpa describes their locations and principal functions as follows:

The life-sustaining wind is located in the heart and in the life channel. It keeps body and mind united, and gives rise to the notion of "I."

The downward-clearing wind is located in the perineal region. It governs the expulsion and retention of urine, feces, semen, and menstrual blood.

The upward-moving wind is located at the Adam's apple. It enables the swallowing and regurgitation of food. It makes speech and laughter possible.

The pervasive wind is located in the head and in the twelve major joints. It governs the movements of the body, such as walking, rising, sitting, and posing.

The fire-accompanying wind is located at the navel. It governs the digestion, separation of nutrients from waste, transformation of the nutrients into the seven organic components, and the sending of waste downward.

Among these winds, only the pervasive wind is found throughout the entire body. Thus, in terms of the five psychophysical aggregates of the person, this wind has a special connection with the physical body. The fire-accompanying wind sparks up feelings and sensations. The downward-clearing wind confers discernment. The upward-moving wind supports volition that is based on habits. The life-sustaining wind is indivisible from the consciousness.

From the perspective of the psychophysical aggregates in their pure state, these energy-winds represent the five buddhas: the life-sustaining wind represents Akṣobhya; the downward-clearing, Ratnasaṃbhava; the upward-moving, Amitābha; the fire-accompanying, Amoghasiddhi; and the pervasive, Vairocana.

Yangönpa does not spell out the association of the root energy-winds with the five elements. But in Sakyapa works we find the following correlation: the life-sustaining wind is the nature of the water element; the fire-accompanying, of earth; the downward-clearing, of air; the upward-moving, of fire; and the pervasive, of space. In other traditions, however, the association of the five root winds with the five elements is presented differently. And an interlinear note to the text quotes the *Lamp Summary of Tantric Practice*, which states:

The pervasive is the wind that flows in all four mandalas of the elements. This pervasive light, which does not exit [from the body], is the *tathāgata* Vairocana, the very essence equal to space.[61]

Thus we may infer that in Yangönpa's view, the pervasive wind is allied with the space element, and the life-sustaining wind with the water element.

The psychosomatic functions of these winds are more precisely explained and elaborated in Tibetan medicine, but Yangönpa apparently deems this scanty explanation sufficient, and goes no further.

The branch energy-winds are the life-sustaining winds that reach into the nerves of the sense faculties, enabling the individual to relate to the external world. The branch winds each have two sets of names: the Serpent, or Rising and Flowing; the Tortoise, or Wind That Flows Thoroughly; the Lizard, or Wind That Flows Perfectly; the Gods' Gift, or Wind That Flows Intensively; and Victorious with the Bow, or Wind That Flows Resolutely.

Drawing from Sakyapa sources, Yangönpa states that these winds reside in the five major organs of the body. From there, helped by the force of their associated elemental winds, they empower the nerves that enable the perceptual sense functions.

The Serpent wind, residing in the intestines, enables seeing, through the pure essence of the water wind. The Tortoise wind, residing in the liver, enables hearing, through the wind of air. The Lizard wind, residing in the lungs, enables smelling, through the earth wind. The Gods' Gift wind, residing in the heart, enables tasting, through the wind of fire. The Victorious with the Bow wind, residing in the kidneys, enables touch, through the wind of space.[62] By the fifth month, the branch winds are fully present in the fetus.

Here, Yangönpa seems to deviate from the usual way of correlating the branch energy-winds with the elements as found in Sakyapa works, as follows: the Serpent wind is of the nature of earth;

the Tortoise, of water; the Lizard, of fire; the God's Gift, of air; and the Victorious with the Bow, of space.

Yangönpa describes some additional characteristics of the branch winds in an attempt to explain their peculiar names. He states that apart from its beneficial functions, the Serpent wind can cause serious illnesses. The Tortoise wind extends and contracts the arms and legs just as a tortoise does. The Lizard wind can make one angry and upset like a lizard does. The Gods' Gift wind causes yawning and attachment, which are godly attributes. The Victorious with the Bow wind causes sneezing and holds life. By the tenth month in the womb, the power of both root and branch energy-winds is fully developed. The strength of the energy-wind will facilitate birth and provide the child with a strong constitution.

Energy-winds and breathing are closely interrelated. The two flow in synchrony with one another. Energy-winds work like the interlocking gears of a clock. They start to flow from the navel through the channels of the various chakras, up to the nostrils, where their flow unites with the breath. For this reason, the methods for controlling the energy-winds primarily consist of breathing techniques such as the retention of breath. Thus, energy-wind is also classified as inhalation, exhalation, and pause. Several tantras include the statement:

In essence, the energy-winds are [the three phases of] inhalation, exhalation, and pause.

Yet, energy-wind is not identical with breath. At death, when respiration ceases, the energy-wind in its subtle aspect remains in the body for some time. And in the deep calm state of the mind when the breathing stops, energy-wind is still there.

Yangönpa tells us that during youth, inhalation is more forceful, favoring physical growth. During adulthood, inhalation and exhalation are of equal strength, so the body remains stable. And in old age, exhalation is more forceful, so the body declines and ages.

Energy-winds are also classified as male, female, and neuter; energy-winds of vitality and exertion; upper and lower energy-winds; and hot and cold energy-winds. These classifications are also specifically related to breathing. For example, the characteristics of male, female, and neuter winds are reflected and detected mainly in the person's type of breathing: short, rough breathing is the male; long and smooth breathing, the female; and balanced breathing, the neuter type.

The energy-wind of life is said to be inhalation, and wind of exertion is exhalation. The upper wind in the *prāṇāyāma* practices is connected with the breath that is inhaled. The cold wind is connected with inhalation of cold breath, as opposed to the hot wind already present in the body. While these energy-winds are taught mainly as inner winds, each one has a specific connection to breathing. Thus, in order to govern them, the yogin must apply breath control. The following words of Yönten Gyamtso can serve to summarize the important points of our discussion of the energy-winds thus far:

> Consciousness in itself is powerless to move from one place to another. It is only through the operation of the winds that it spreads into different parts of the body. If, by working with the physical body and the channels, one is able to bring the winds under control, consciousness can be harnessed. Control of the wind-energy is therefore extremely important.
>
> The teachings speak of many kinds of wind, but here we will explain only the four characteristics of stillness (*gnas*), movement (*rgyu*), rising (exhaling, *ldang*), and entering (inhaling, *'jug*). At first, when taking birth in a new

existence, the consciousness mounted on the wind enters the womb. Taking support of the mingled essences of the father and mother, the wind remains there in a condition of *stillness,* and the consciousness faints into a state of oblivion. At this time, the wind has the nature of the wisdom wind. Then by degrees, the ten kinds of wind manifest, beginning with the life-wind, and the physical body develops. For as long as the being in question is alive, the body does not rot, and this is due to the moving winds. The winds that *rise* and *enter* generate different thoughts and feelings. It is these last two winds that are used on the path in the practice of yoga.[63]

The Central Role of the Life-Sustaining Wind

In the *Hidden Description of the Vajra Body,* Yangönpa states that the life-sustaining wind possesses five lights that give rise to the potentialities of the five elements, to the inner organs, to the senses, and to the emotions. In particular, the life-sustaining wind is the chief or basis of all other root and branch energy-winds. All other types of energy-wind are extensions of the life-holding wind. Flowing through the pathways of the body, and associating with emotions and thoughts, its extensions reach the recesses of the body-mind complex, where they govern various functions; for this reason, they are known by a variety of names.

To illustrate the primary role of the life-sustaining wind in the context of yogic practice, Yangönpa describes the dynamic interaction of the various winds. When, through breath control, the course of the downward-clearing wind is reversed, the fire-accompanying wind becomes increasingly powerful, the life-sustaining wind is purified, and other winds are balanced. In this way, the karmic wind that feeds discursive thought subsides. And when the fire-accompanying wind is brought downward, the vital essence rises in the body, giving rise to mystical experiences and realization.

One would assume that it is the life-sustaining wind that determines life and death. But Yangönpa asserts that it is the pervasive energy-wind that, through its presence or absence, determines life and death:

> The energy-wind of space flows within the body, pervading all its parts. Except at the time of death, it does not flow outside [the body].

The pervasive energy-wind also accompanies the consciousness in transmigration:

> The consciousness of the intermediate being, accompanied by the karmic pervasive energy-wind, enters through the father's anus, joins with the semen, and enters the mother's womb.

And:

> The so-called "karmic" wind, in general, refers to all kinds of wind [present in the individual] on the mundane and lower paths.... In particular, [it refers to the] pervasive [wind], the karmic wind that accompanies the consciousness of the intermediate being as it enters [the place of conception], and which [then] dwells in the innermost part of the great channel in the center of the half-moon.[64] ... At the time of death, together with the mind, it exits the body.

Later Tibetan authors claim that it is the life-sustaining wind that, accompanying the transmigrating mind, enters at the moment of conception. Kongtrul, in his *Encompassment of All Knowledge*, writes:

> Accordingly, during the formation of this vajra body, the great life wind is the first to come into being. This wind is supported by the ground of all consciousness, which has entered the midst of the white and red [regenerative fluids].... During the course of the life, the life [wind] abides within the central channel as the dominant factor in determining the [cycles of] increase and decrease of the winds.[65]

Yangönpa does not state his reason for settling on the pervasive wind as the wind that accompanies the consciousness principle of the individual from one life to another. Perhaps his choice reflects the fact that the pervasive wind is associated with Vairocana, and Vairocana represents the purity of form; all phenomenal existence is said to be the Body dimension of Vairocana. The wind that creates the physical manifestation of the body is the pervasive wind. From Yangönpa's quotation from the *Vajramāla*, we understand that the pervasive wind is present not only in the body, but in the overall environment:

> The wind that pervades the entire body
> Manifests [as] the three realms,
> And holds the support and the supported.
> Therefore, the pervasive [wind] performs the functions
>   of all [winds].
> It is the Body dimension of Vairocana;
> And in the end, at death, it leaves [the body].

Another related reason may be that, as mentioned above, Yangönpa associates the pervasive wind with the element of space. This would make this wind the suitable vehicle for consciousness during the passage between life and death, in the intermediate state, and from the intermediate state to a new life.

Moreover, in all Tantric literature, Tantric instructions, and in Yangönpa's *Hidden Description of the Vajra Body*, the ten root and branch energy-winds are characterized as karmic winds. This means that they serve as the mount for the ungoverned emotions that become the cause of habitual patterns. Since, according to Yangönpa, this function is performed by the pervasive wind in particular, it makes sense that this wind should be considered the support for the consciousness that, laden with the predispositions generated by actions during an individual's life, crosses over into another life.

Karmic Wind and Wisdom Wind

But what is karmic wind? Yangönpa describes it as follows:

> The [wind] that flows through the solar and lunar [channels]—together with exhalation and inhalation—and [always] circulates as various thoughts, is karmic wind. It is called [karmic wind] because, from the mundane paths down,[66] it performs the ten actions.[67]

Thus, all five root and five branch energy-winds are karmic winds because they flow through the right and left channels that are the basis of duality. Because energy-wind and mind are inextricably united, each movement of karmic wind is essentially discursive thought, conception, and judgment. Yangönpa explains that the ten winds are karmic because, in unrealized beings, they perform the actions related to the five aggregates and the five senses, which comprise all the functions of body and mind.

However, karmic wind may be more easily understood as energy-wind that is associated with emotions. As stated by Longchenpa in *Thorough Dispelling of Darkness throughout the Ten Directions,* "In this regard, that which flows in a coarse manner is the karmic wind, or wind of emotions."[68]

The karmic wind is the mount for the eighty natural concepts, including attachment, anger, ignorance, and so on.[69] These conceptions manifest during the life of the individual, and are like a pattern or cage in which the individual is trapped. At the time of death, when the three lights—the white light of vision, the red light of increase, and the black light of near attainment—occur, the energy-winds lose their power, and the eighty conceptions subside, allowing the real nature of the individual to manifest as luminous clarity. While these conceptions naturally subside at death, yogins attempt to gain freedom from them in this very lifetime by binding the movement of the karmic wind through prāṇāyāma and other methods. Yangönpa specifies:

The so-called "karmic" wind refers in general to all kinds of winds [present in the individual] on the mundane and lower paths. In particular, [it refers to the] pervasive [wind], the karmic wind that accompanies the consciousness of the intermediate being as it enters [the place of conception], and which [then] dwells in the innermost part of the great channel in the center of the half-moon.

In his *Encompassment of All Knowledge,* Kongtrul, after describing karmic wind as inseparable from thought, distinguishes the karmic wind to be relinquished from that which can be provisionally useful:

Concisely stated, everything in cyclic existence and perfect peace was declared by the Buddha to be of the nature of energy-wind. Karmic wind is the wind that is inseparable from thought. All winds fall into the category of karmic wind and the [wisdom] wind.... There are two karmic winds, karmic winds to be relinquished and remedial karmic wind.

Karmic wind to be relinquished [is threefold]. The conception of self that has been present in the ground-of-all is the wind of delusion. Not knowing the five lights (which are the appearance aspect of ... [wisdom]) to be self-manifestation, conceiving [the lights] to be "other," and the craving that develops is the wind of desire. Based on that previous wind, the discrimination of phenomena in terms of what to accept and what to reject and the fixation that develops, is the wind of aversion. The nature of those three poisons is ignorance, the power of which creates cyclic existence.

The second karmic wind is remedial wind, which stops the course of cyclic existence; this is correct thought, such as the view of the absence of the self. Nevertheless, it is still designated as karmic wind.

In short, that which is called karmic wind is [equivalent to] thought in that it stirs [things], [is involved with] the subtle, and moves from one [thing] to the next.[70]

Thus, karmic wind, essentially inseparable from thought, represents the level of mind in which reality is deceptively experienced as the duality of subject and object.

In contrast to karmic wind, there is wisdom wind. While karmic wind represents the mind, wisdom wind represents the mind's nature, the reality in which the subject-object duality is absent and objectifying thoughts cease. The mind's nature is characterized by bliss, clarity, and nonthought.

In his *Encompassment of All Knowledge,* Kongtrul clearly states this point:

> The great wind of wisdom is mind nature, that of bliss, clarity, and nonthought. When the wisdom wind is directly cognized, all the movements of karmic wind are overcome.[71]

And Yangönpa states:

> The wisdom wind that is beyond discursive thought [manifests] when these [ten winds] enter the central channel and their movement comes to a halt.

Likewise, Longchenpa writes:

> In these [seventy-two thousand] channels, in a day, the wisdom wind flows, hidden, the same number of times. If the energy-wind is bound, the energy-wind of emotions itself becomes, and flows as, wisdom-wind, and therefore the positive qualities arise in the yogin. In general, the coarse winds flow 21,600 times daily. In that regard, that which flows in a coarse manner is the karmic wind, or wind of emotions. By binding that energy-wind, the wisdom of clarity and nonthought arise: this is wisdom wind.[72]

In Tantric praxis, the wisdom wind is recognized when the karmic energy-winds are made to enter the central channel. Longchenpa writes:

> Regarding the colors of the energy-wind, the wind of earth is yellow; the wind of water is white; the wind of

fire is red; the wind of air is green; the wind of space, the great wisdom, is blue. These [winds] depend on the five channels of the heart chakra, four in the four directions and one in the center. When these energy-winds enter the central channel, they become wisdom-wind, and therefore the glow (*gdangs*) of these five winds manifest as smoke, mirages, and various empty forms.[73]

In the literature of the *Guhyasamāja* it is said that when, by means of experiential techniques, energy-wind is held in the central channel, like a man without his mount, consciousness deprived of energy-wind's stimulus stops functioning and becomes pliable. Like a blind horse with no rider, the activating wind, lacking consciousness, cannot move, and is thereby self-liberated. In that moment, reality is spontaneously recognized, and with energy-wind and consciousness self-purified, there is enlightenment.

At several points in an individual's life, the energy-wind naturally enters the central channel. Yangönpa quotes the *Summary of the Initiation,* which mentions four such occasions: death, birth, when the energy-wind flows in a balanced way, and during sexual intercourse. An interlinear note to the Beijing edition of the *Hidden Description* specifies that the third occasion is actually the daily shift of the energy-wind from one set of navel channels representing the zodiacal house to another, paralleling the annual shifts of the sun in these houses.[74] For adepts trained in the methods of inserting the energy-wind into the central channel, who are able to remain in the ensuing state of nonthought, these occasions afford the opportunity to recognize the wisdom wind. But for ordinary people, these occasions largely go wasted.

Just as the mind's nature is always present but may be unrecognized, the wisdom wind, too, is always present. It is not constructed by the absorption of the karmic wind into the central channel. This may be understood from descriptions of the wisdom wind's flow that are found in many Tantric sources. While all tantras agree that the energy-wind flows 21,600 time daily, some tantras describe its flow in terms of the four elements: earth, water, fire, and air; and others, in terms of the five elements: earth, water, fire, air, and space. This accounts for the discrepancies in the calculations. Yangönpa offers both explanations.

For each of the elements, the wisdom wind flows from the navel chakra, up through the various chakras, to the nostrils. According to the *Kālacakra* and other tantras as well, the energy-wind flows during the twelve periods of the day. Yangönpa states that at the shifts between one period and another, the wisdom wind flows 11.25 times, or 675 times in twenty-four hours. At that rate, in the course of one hundred years it would flow for three years, one and a half months. In his *Encompassment of All Knowledge*, Kongtrul writes:

> The wind that passes through the right nostril is the solar wind.... The solar wind flows through the right nostril at a rate of 10,462.5 times per day. The wind that passes through the left nostril is the lunar wind.... The lunar wind flows through the right nostril at a rate of 10,462.5 times per day.
>
> Wind flows equally through the center [of both nostrils] at a rate of 650 [times] per day. It is possessed of power resembling that of the external [planet] Rahu and is therefore called "element of Rahu." It creates openness like space and is therefore called "wind of space." Since it enters the central channel, it is also called wisdom wind....
>
> Within [the 21,600 daily energy-winds], there are 675 [movements] of the wisdom wind ... in short, one thirty-second of each breath.

Moreover, half of the wisdom wind flows externally, and half flows internally.... When the external movement [of the wisdom wind] increases, there occur signs of eventual death; when [this wind] is retained internally, immortality is attained.[75]

Just as ordinary channels may be activated to perform extraordinary functions, and thoughts, like ocean waves, can return to the mind's nature from which they surge, karmic wind can indeed become wisdom wind. In his *Encompassment of All Knowledge,* Kongtrul writes:

In (a lifetime of) one hundred years, the total time taken by the movements of ... [wisdom] wind equals three years and three fortnights. If, during that period, one were to transform all karmic wind into ... [wisdom wind], one would attain enlightenment.[76]

The words of a contemporary master, Dilgo Khyentse Rinpoche, clearly sum up the above discussion of the karmic and the wisdom winds:

In fact, the wisdom wind and the karmic wind are the same thing. If this wind is brought under control, it engenders wisdom; if it is not controlled, it gives rise to the ordinary mind, together with its poisons. Thus the most important thing, at the perfection stage, is to work effectively on the wind, since it is by such a means that one will also be able to work with the essence-drop, which the wind conveys. If, as a result, one attains mastery of the essence-drop, the mind, which is supported by it, will also cease to move, thereby giving rise to the experiences of bliss, clarity, and nonthought.[77]

As to the different ways of stopping the movement of karmic wind, Yönten Gyamtso writes:

The movement of the wind-mind may be arrested in various ways. It may be halted indirectly [by realizing the wisdom of no-self], and it may be halted suddenly and forcefully by binding its movement [as in the Anuyoga]. In addition, without having to rely on such efforts, there is the path of the supreme pith instructions [of the Atiyoga], whereby the wind-mind is spontaneously purified. In the final analysis, however, all three ways are geared to the same objective.[78]

The ways of stopping the movement of the karmic wind alluded to in this passage are those of Mahayana, Tantra, and Dzogchen, respectively. The Sutra path of the Mahayana does not provide an elaborate presentation of energy-winds, nor does it teach the yogic method for binding them. Nonetheless, through the direct and nonconceptual understanding of emptiness that is one of the main foci of that path, the karmic wind is naturally brought under control. This also occurs when the primordial state is directly recognized through the methods set forth in the Dzogchen teaching.

The forceful binding of the karmic wind refers to the Highest Tantra's particular methods for inserting the karmic wind into the central channel. In what seems to be a unique explanation, for Yangönpa, the insertion of the energy-wind in the central channel is not simply the retention of the outer energy-wind within this channel. It is a state in which energy-wind and mind are experienced as the essence of open space; a state that arises after the inner and outer energy-winds are integrated as one, and their movements are stilled within the central channel. Yangönpa writes:

As to the so-called wisdom wind, it is the manifestation of energy-wind and mind as the essence of space.

[This occurs] when, having been integrated as one, the flow of the inner and outer winds is severed: this is known as [energy-wind] entering the central channel. [The] inner causal nexus [for the manifestation of energy-wind and mind as the essence of space] is [the wind] entering the central channel.

This does not mean that all outer winds are enclosed in the innermost part of the central [channel] and remain there. Thus, the integration of the inner and outer winds as one is an exclusive essential point.

The integration of the inner and outer energy-winds mentioned by Yangönpa in the above passage is clarified somewhat by Chen Ngawa in his *Advice on the Hidden Description:*

This integration of the inner and outer energy-wind is an extremely profound [point of practice]. Thus, in this regard, the general locale of [energy-wind] is the lungs. The door [of energy-wind] is the nostrils. The essence of energy-wind is vitality and exertion. And the function of energy-wind is to create all faults and qualities of samsara and nirvana. Applying the essential points on the basis of energy-wind and bliss, one passes beyond misery, and all good qualities are produced. In this context, if, having integrated mind and energy-wind, one practices the blazing and dripping [of inner heat], this is the essential point through which all qualities are developed at the extremity of the central channel; all other energy-winds will be inserted in the central channel; and the energy-wind will not flow externally: this is asserted as a nonthought state of crystal-clear luminosity.

In this context, the energy-wind and mind flowing outside or remaining inside is considered to be equally good. For when the energy-wind and mind flow outside, in a state of clear space of the inseparability of wind and mind, the visions of the eight consciousnesses are purified in the unsupported state. When wind and mind remain inside, their movement is purified, and one remains in a state of inseparable bliss-emptiness beyond [the grasping of] subject and object. In this way, the energy-wind is integrated outside and inside. When [this occurs], energy-wind and mind are inserted in the ultimate central channel and become pure like space; they become free from internal and external subject and object [grasping]; and they become one. This is the integration of inner and outer energy-wind and mind.[79]

According to Chen Ngawa, in this process in which the wisdom wind is experienced as open space, having applied instructions on breathing, one practices "inner heat," involving the blazing of the inner fire at the navel and the dripping of the white vital essence from the chakra at the head, to elicit bliss. This will give rise to manifold mystical experiences, and the energy-wind will enter the central channel. The ensuing state is one of utter clarity in which thoughts are either absent or innocuous. At this point, it makes no difference whether the energy-wind is retained inside through the practice of vase-like breathing or allowed to flow with the breath. When energy-wind flows with the breath, perceptions are not grasped as subject and object, but experienced like a vision in space. When the energy-wind and mind are retained with the breath, one dwells in a state of bliss and emptiness. This seems to be the meaning of integration of the inner and outer energy-wind. And when this occurs, Chen Ngawa asserts, wind and mind are inserted in the ultimate central channel, and one perceives the true nature of things.

At the opening of the section on the fundamental nature of the voice, Yangönpa divides energy-wind into two categories: coarse and subtle. He discusses the five root and five branch winds, placing them in the category of coarse winds while specifying that they are also karmic winds. Then he briefly discusses the nature of the subtle energy-winds, and there he mentions the wisdom wind.

To illustrate the nature of the subtle energy-wind, Yangönpa quotes two texts belonging to the *Guhyasamāja* tradition: Nāgārjuna's work on the five steps of the completion stage of that tantra,[80] and the *Prophetic Declaration of Intention*,[81] a tantra belonging to the *Guhyasamāja* literature. He quotes such texts because, as a father tantra, the *Guhyasamāja* places great emphasis on the principle of energy-wind, both in the genesis of the world and its beings and in the yogic practices related to energy-wind.

The subtle energy-wind, Yangönpa contends, is not limited to the physical body, but is inseparable from the basic mind. This basic mind is present everywhere, unbounded by space and time. Thus, everything is the embodiment of basic mind and energy-wind. All is an expression of wind-mind. This might seem to echo the Cittamātra view that all is mind: all outer and inner phenomena are the manifestation of predispositions deposited by past actions on the ground-of-all-consciousness, and are of the same substance as the mind itself. But this is not the case.

The fact that the quotation from the *Prophetic Declaration of Intention* describes the inseparability of energy-wind and mind as the unmanifest subtle energy-wind from which vision is always manifesting leads us to think that here Yangönpa and the sources he quotes are actually speaking of the mind's ultimate nature, which, in the father tantras, is described as the indivisibility of profundity (*zab mo*) and clarity (*gsal ba*), and of the subtle energy-wind that coexists with it.

Vitapada explains that "profundity" denotes that which is free from mistaken concepts and primordially transcends thoughts and words. Within this profound nature—stainless like space and devoid of phenomena—manifests the wisdom of clarity. It is free from ideas and associations held by ordinary beings; thus it is called "profundity beyond scrutiny." The inseparability of profundity and clarity is the nature that is present in everything, without exception.[82]

Thus, the creative energy of mind's ultimate nature and the energy-wind that, according to the tantra, coexists with it, is the underlying basis for the functioning of living beings and of all things that manifest from the ground of emanation. This ground is called bodhicitta, which here denotes the true nature of the individual and the world. It is a reality that, like space, does not exist in any place, and yet is not separate from the psychophysical aspects of the individual and the building blocks of the external world.

The fact that Yangönpa speaks of the wisdom wind in his section on the subtle wind reveals the fact that he considers the wisdom wind to fall into the category of subtle wind.

To sum up the above points, we quote from Yönten Gyamtso's *Commentary* on Jigmed Lingpa's *Treasury of Precious Qualities*:

The winds constitute the support for both the ordinary mind and for primordial wisdom. When the mind is in its impure state, and when circumstances that call forth the five poisons or defilements present themselves, it is on the basis of the five winds that these same defilements automatically proliferate. When, however, the mind is in a state of pure primordial wisdom, the five winds are the foundations for the appearance of the five primordial wisdoms, which directly cognize all things both in their nature and in their multiplicity. Thus the five winds are like the causes from which the ordinary mind and primordial wisdom both proliferate as though they were results. They are the basis for them.[83]

Yangönpa's description of the fundamental nature of the voice presents the energy-wind as the vehicle that takes the mind into the microcosm of the body, making it indivisible from the body. In the body, mind becomes conditioned and restricted by materiality, and its contact with infinite space can unfold only in a limited way through the senses and through thought.

Energy-wind moves as the various thoughts, judgments, concepts, and emotions that stir the ocean-like surface of the mind, causing wave-like pleasure and displeasure, happiness and suffering, and so on to arise. Fortunately, the energy-wind is inextricably connected to the breath. Thus, by controlling and modifying the course of the breath through yogic techniques, energy-wind and mind are brought to a halt within the central axis of one's body. Discursiveness either ceases or becomes innocuous, making space for the arising of manifold mystical experiences and qualities. In this way, the wisdom wind—the subtle wind that is one with the mind's ultimate nature—manifests as liberating, space-like openness.

Energy-Wind as Sound

With regard to the last four aspects of the voice mentioned in the *Nondual Victory Tantra*—syllables, vocal resonation, coordination, and words—Yangönpa explains how energy-wind is also the very nature of the voice as audible and meaningful sound. Energy-wind becomes sound because it is empowered by the net of syllables, vowels, and consonants described in Tantric physiology as being present in the body. The syllables are present in the channels and chakras as the shape of the tips of these channels and as the vital essence contained in them.

The syllables are the root of the names and words that we use in language. The main syllables—OM, ĀH, HŪM—are located within the three main channels of the body: the rasanā, lalanā, and central channel. Their sound is naturally present in the tone expressed by the movement of the three phases of breathing—inhalation, pause, and exhalation—to which the tantras refer as the naturally occurring "vajra breathing." Yangönpa states that the very core of these syllables is the A located at the central channel's lower extremity. As the life force of all sounds and verbal expressions, this A is considered to be the supreme of all syllables, and is often used in the tantras to symbolize the state of emptiness from which everything manifests. Starting from the very bottom of the central channel, circulating through the chakras and infinite channels of the body, the energy-winds bring forth from the mouth the sounds of the syllables they penetrate along their way.

Moreover, the inner condition of channels, energy-winds, and vital essences adapts to the individual's environment. According to Yangönpa, this explains how, after living for six months in a foreign country, one can learn the language; and it explains how, after applying for six months the special practices explained in the tantras, one can achieve enlightenment.

The arising of vocal resonation through the movement of energy-wind within the body depends on several conditions. The first of these is the space in the body's air-filled cavities, including the chest, tracheal tree, larynx, pharynx, oral cavity, nasal cavity, and sinuses, which promote vocal resonance. But by "space" Yangönpa does not simply imply these cavities. He quotes the Buddha's teaching that the source of sound, its nature, and that which it becomes once it has ceased, is emptiness. This emptiness is the reality whose energy is the source of everything: like all phenomena, sound arises, exists, and ceases.

By themselves, the syllables within the body, its energy-winds, and cavities would not be able to produce the sound of the voice. The next condition for speech, states Yangönpa, is coordination. By this he means the combined action of the channels-syllables; of energy-wind and mind as one; and of the movements of the many parts of the body, including the palate, larynx, nose, lips, tongue, and teeth. Here the essential unity of energy-wind and mind provides the conceptual stimuli that activate speech. But such stimuli do not lie only in the mind; they are also the energy-wind that is inseparable from the body.

The last requirement for speech is words. Words are the essential component of speech, and coherent speech is indeed the manifestation of various thoughts as words. But thoughts can only manifest as speech because body, voice, and mind are one and inseparable. This is the principle that Yangönpa stresses at each level of his explanation, and one that is often presented in the tantras—particularly the father tantras and Dzogchen tantras—in the form of cryptic statements pointing to the unity of body, voice, and mind.

Voice has an infinite potential for expression, and when, through yogic practice, the knots of the throat chakra's channels are loosened, this potential is actualized as the extraordinary qualities of speech. When it is fully actualized, one can overcome all language barriers and communicate with all kinds of sentient beings. All this is the manifestation of the above-described requirements for speech—energy-wind, syllables, thoughts, and so on—experienced as the dimension of clear and open space.

THE FUNDAMENTAL NATURE OF THE MIND

As before, Yangönpa opens this section with a quote from the *Nondual Victory Tantra* that mentions five factors that make up the fundamental nature of the mind:

> As to the mind, by virtue of five wisdoms,
> Bliss, vital essence,
> Nonthought, and contemplation,
> The phenomenon of the mind exists.[84]

Yangönpa's treatment of the fundamental nature of the mind is clearly not an abstract discussion of the mind as a space-like, empty, and luminous dimension. He is a yogin and an educator of yogins; thus his main concern is the embodied mind.

Vital Essence

In the preceding sections, Yangönpa stressed that consciousness is produced by the channels, placed thought as a subset of the body, and demonstrated the essential unity of energy-wind and mind. All this points to the fundamental nature of mind being based on and intermingled with both the coarse and the subtle layers of the body.

Thus, instead of discussing the five factors of the mind in the order in which they appear in the above quotation, he tells us that they need to be rearranged, and accords first place to the vital essence that he had previously defined as "the support of the mind." The vital essence is variously referred to as the *thig le* (Skt. *tilaka*); *byang chub sems* (bodhicitta); or as the vital essence of bodhicitta. In his *Encompassment of All Knowledge,* Kongtrul writes, "Since it serves as the seed of great bliss, it is … termed vital essence."[85] He then proceeds to describe four types of vital essence: the vital essence that is the mind's nature; the vital essence of deceptive ignorance, which is the vital essence of the five psychophysical aggregates, including the methods of the Mantra Way; the vital essence of the energy-winds, including the methods for controlling them; and the vital essence of substance, including the methods for controlling it. He also mentions an alternative twofold classification: the vital essence of substance, and the vital essence of wisdom. The term *vital essence* thus has a vast range of definitions. In our text, Yangönpa deals mainly with the vital essence of substance.

In his discussion of this topic, Yangönpa seems to use several terms interchangeably: quintessence (*dwangs ma*), vital essence (*thig le*), constituent (*khams*), and bodhicitta (*byang chub sems*). *Bodhicitta* is a term widely used in Buddhism, with varied meanings ranging from the altruistic intention to attain enlightenment (in the Mahayana), to the pure and perfect consciousness (in Dzogchen). Here, in its Tantric connotation, on the relative level, bodhicitta is *khu ba* (Skt. *shukra*), which in its narrowest sense is the male's semen, but in its broader sense refers to both the male and female reproductive fluids. In its very broad sense, it refers to the white and red vital essences that give the body its strength and radiance.

To follow Yangönpa's treatment of this topic, it may be useful to cite the following words from the *Little Pithy Volume of Many Oral Instructions on Vajrayoginī of the Sakya:*

> Although the nectar constituents are infinite, [they are all] subsumed under the thirty-two constituents. These are subsumed under the nine constituents. These are subsumed under the seven organic components of the body. These are subsumed under the five nectars. These are subsumed under the white and red bodhicitta, and these are subsumed under the white one alone.[86]

In his section on the channels, Yangönpa has described how the thirty-two constituents are present in the thirty-two main channels that branch off from the chakras. The nine constituents, he says, are the pure essences of the four elements and five nectars. In the body, the nature of the four elements—earth, water, fire, and air—is found mainly in bones, blood, warmth, and breath, respectively. Thus, in the body, the pure essences of the elements are correlated with the four bodily components, and described by the following examples: the pure essence of the channels that are the correlate of the most solid bodily constituents (the bones and flesh) is like a white silk tread. The quintessence of the blood is like liquid cinnabar. The quintessence of warmth is like the sun striking a mirror. The quintessence of the breath is like the breath blown on a gem.

Yangönpa next explains the five nectars as the quintessence of the five chakras. Of the various lists of the five nectars found in the tantras, he mentions feces, semen, urine, blood, and great pure essence. The last of these five may refer to brains or human flesh. In Tantric practice, these substances are utilized to overcome the limiting concepts of the clean and the unclean, acceptable and unacceptable. Ritually consecrated, they are then consumed as pills during the Tantric Feast.

"Feces" here refers to the quintessence of the head chakra; "semen," of the throat chakra; "urine," of the heart chakra; "blood," of the navel chakra; and "brains," or human flesh, of the chakra of the secret place.

However, by saying that these substances are the pure essence of the five chakras, Yangönpa clearly does not mean feces, and so on, in their literal sense. In fact, he says that they are pure essences of the chakras that produce the thirty-two vital essences, from whose refined aspects the various consciousnesses, the organs, the senses, and so forth, originate.

As mentioned above, the nine vital essences are subsumed under the seven organic components of the body: nutritive substance, blood, flesh, fat, bone, marrow, and regenerative fluids. These components are produced during the process of regeneration taking place within the body. This process, which is clearly explained in traditional Tibetan medicine and briefly outlined by Yangönpa in his text, starts with the intake of food and the extraction of its nutritive substance. This nutritive substance is conveyed through the intestinal channels to the liver, where blood is produced. The quintessence of blood becomes nutrition for the flesh. The quintessence of flesh transforms into fatty tissue. The quintessence of the fatty tissue produces bones. And the quintessence of bones becomes marrow. The last and seventh link in this process is the regenerative fluid (*khu ba*) that is thus the quintessence of all the elements of the body.

The regenerative fluid exists in two aspects: the white constituent prevalent in men, and the red constituent prevalent in women. These white and red constituents each have two aspects, one coarse and one refined. The coarse aspect of the white constituent is the semen. The course aspect of the red constituent is the ovum. According to Tibetan medicine, which presumably reflects the view of Buddhist Tantra as well, the refined aspect of both spreads from the heart into the body's seventy-two thousand channels, producing its radiance, strength, and vitality.

Thus, all vital essences are subsumed under the white and the red constituents. As we have seen, these two constituents are the last and final link in the process of regeneration of the body, and are thus produced during this process. Yet, the original white and red constituents derive from the intermingling of the father's semen and the mother's ovum in the womb at the time of conception. Until birth, these constituents remain united at the navel. When the umbilical cord is cut, the white constituent ascends to the chakra at the head, where, according to Yangönpa and the New schools of Tibetan Buddhism, it is held in the form of the syllable HAM by the power of the lalanā channel. The red constituent descends to the lower extremity of the central channel, where it is held in the form of the syllable A by the power of the rasanā channel.

Incidentally, these two syllables, A HAM, are also the first ones the newborn baby will pronounce when the energy-winds' outward flow begins. During gestation, these original syllables give rise to a series of other syllables that are the support of the body-mind complex.

From Yangönpa's discussion, we understand that the original red and white vital essences bearing the form of A and HAM serve as the basis and interact with the white and red constituents produced during the body's self-regeneration. Although the vital essences circulate through countless channels in the body, the main pathways of the white and red vital essence number thirty-two. These are also connected to the channels of the genital area.

The condition of the vital essences has a positive or negative impact on both the person's health and spiritual development. When they are unrefined and impure, illness, obstacles, and misfortune arise. Refined and pure, the vital essences confer health and radiance, good fortune, and spiritual realization. Just as karmic wind can be transformed into wisdom wind, unrefined and impure vital essence can be purified to the point that the entire body becomes ambrosia-like, healthy, strong, and blissful.

Yangönpa briefly outlines the meditative process through which, working with the white and red vital essences, one experiences the innate wisdom. This can be affected by the practice of inner heat, which involves breath retention as well as visualization of the chakras, of the white constituent at the head, and of the red constituent at four finger-widths below the navel. Breath control will fan the flames of the red constituent, which will melt the white constituent at the head chakra. The descent of this last, and its union with the red constituent, will destroy mind's discursiveness, and bring about the natural state, innate wisdom.

A parallel process occurs during a qualified sexual union, as explicitly stated by Yangönpa. In that instance, the winds and vital essences spontaneously enter the central channel, giving rise to various extraordinary experiences and to the innate wisdom, space-like and devoid of objects. Success in this practice depends on the yogin's ability to control the energy-winds, and thereby the vital essence, particularly the semen. Yangönpa points out that for ordinary people who are unable to control the energy-winds and vital essence, the semen would be lost; therefore, the innate wisdom would not be recognized, and the person would experience unpleasant consequences for both body and mind.

In Tantra it is widely believed that the retention of the vital essence, and of the semen in particular, is of primary importance for spiritual development. Loss of semen implies not only the exit of vital essence from the body, but also the loss of recognition of the bliss that is the nature of the mind. Thus, a stable state of recognition of bliss can be achieved only when there is no loss of the semen that is the basis for such bliss. Various methods are taught—including breathing, visualization, and physical exercise—to effect the retention of the semen, pull it upward when it has liquefied and descended to the sexual organ, and then spread its essence throughout the body.

Having thus described the vital essence, Yangönpa launches into an interesting explanation of how the white and red vital essences are subject to cycles of increase and decrease. These cycles resemble biorhythms that influence the physical, emotional, and spiritual dimension of the individual's life. They operate daily, monthly, annually, and throughout the entire life.

Before we briefly examine the various cycles, it might be useful to restate that the white vital essence is also known as "lunar," and the red as "solar." Thus, the white vital essence is characterized by the cool qualities of the earth and water elements, and the red by the hot quality of the fire element. In the external environment, these qualities are represented by the sun and moon. Just as in the external environment the sun and moon move in cycles, in the human body the white and red vital essences move accordingly. The external and internal cycles are not just similar but are totally interconnected, for what happens within reflects the external condition; and what happens without reflects the internal condition.

Daily Cycle

In a solar day, the cycle of the red vital essence proceeds during the daytime, and that of the white vital essence during the night. The red vital essence rises from the genitals in the morning as the sun rises; it reaches the apex of its strength at midday as the sun reaches its zenith; it decreases as the sun sets.

The white vital essence begins its descent from the chakra at the head in the late afternoon, in concomitance with the setting of the sun and the appearance of the moon in the sky. It reaches its apex at midnight as the moon reaches the center of the horizon; it decreases as the moon disappears. During the twelve two-hour periods of the solar day, the procession of this daily cycle impacts the degree of digestive heat, the complexion, the moods of happiness and sadness, and the emotions of attachment and anger.

Monthly Cycle

During the first fifteen days of the lunar month, the strength of the white vital essence increases, parallel to the waxing of the moon. During the last fifteen days of the month, the strength of the red vital essence increases, parallel to the waning of the moon. During the monthly cycle, the vital essences shift through various areas of the body. During the waxing moon, in men the white vital essence ascends from the left big toe, and in women from the right big toe. At the same time, the red descends from the head on the other side of the body. Then, during the fifteen days of the waning moon, it is the red vital essence that ascends from the big toe to the head and the white that descends. During the full moon and new moon, the white and red vital essences, respectively, pervade the entire body. Thus, states Yangönpa, during those days it is particularly important not to lose the vital essence through sexual intercourse.

Here, the areas through which the vital essences circulate during the waxing and waning of the moon are identical to those of the monthly course of the protective energy (*bla*) described in Tibetan astrology as well as in the tantras. This protective energy—the power expressed by the totality of one's bodily elements—is considered to be an aspect of the vital essence. Therefore, during the times when the protective energy is present, one is advised not to practice any drastic therapies on these areas of the body.

The cycles of the white and red vital essences during the two phases of the moon affect a person's ordinary life as well as his spiritual life. During the first fifteen days of the month, one feels lighter and happier; during the last fifteen days, heavier and sadder. Moreover, although one may encounter no obstacles in spiritual practice during the waxing phase, the opposite may be true during the waning phase.

Yearly Cycle

In the course of a year, the cycle of the white essence proceeds during the semester extending from the autumn equinox (September 21–23) to the spring equinox (March 21–23). Its apex is at the winter solstice (December 21–23). The red vital essence cycle extends from the spring equinox to the autumn equinox. Its apex is at the summer solstice (June 21–23).

The six months of the cycle of the white vital essence are deemed positive, for it is during this time that people feel predominantly happy. Physically, they have a healthy complexion, they sleep less, and their body strengthens. Material goods abound, and sense pleasures are enjoyed. The six-month cycle of the red vital essence is deemed negative, for it is then that the feeling of unhappiness predominates. Physically, people have an unhealthy complexion, sleep more, and are weaker. Material goods are scarce, and although attachment increases, sense pleasures are few. This is because—in terms of their internal and external function—the white vital essence (expressing the qualities of the water and earth elements) promotes growth and development, while the red vital essence (expressing the power of the fire element) favors drying and withering.

Life Cycle

During the human life, the white and red vital essences develop until age twenty-five; consolidate until age forty-five; and decay from that point on.

Overall, the health and purity of the body's vital essences ensures good health and spiritual accomplishment, while their imbalance and impurity causes illness and creates obstacles to spiritual development. In particular, the vital essence of bodhicitta—known as the "relative" bodhicitta—serves as the basis for recognizing and abiding in the 'ultimate' bodhicitta, the great bliss that is the mind's innate nature. Thus, as stated in the tantras, just as the fragrance of the jasmine flower cannot be produced without the flower, this knowledge cannot arise without the vital essence as its basis.

Great Bliss

Yangönpa's concluding thoughts in the previous section serve to directly introduce the next factor of the mind mentioned in the *Nondual Victory Tantra:* great bliss. As he repeatedly points out in the *Hidden Description of Vajra Body*, ordinary body and mind exist in the nature of the enlightened Body, Voice, and Mind. This inseparability is imbued in the three subtle layers of the vajra body: the channels, energy-winds, and vital essences. This is a reality simultaneously material and immaterial. Thus it is not surprising that vital essence and great bliss are both presented as factors of mind.

Great bliss is a key term in the Highest Tantras. It represents the basis of existence, the nature of everything, the experiential momentum by which this basis is brought into consciousness and is comprehended, as well as the final fruit of Tantric endeavor. As the basis, great bliss is paired with emptiness as the reality that pervades the animate and the inanimate world. It is pure and perfect consciousness (bodhicitta) beyond the range of the rational mind's comprehension. As the experiential momentum, great bliss is that which occurs when, through the practice of inner heat or union with a consort, the energy-winds enter the central channel. As the final fruit, great bliss is the very innate basis that, by the force of contemplation, becomes totally apparent and integrated with oneself.

Thus, far from being a feeling of pleasure as opposed to one of suffering, great bliss is so named because it is beyond all possible concepts of pleasure and pain, happiness and suffering, and so on. Great bliss is not the fleeting experience of sexual pleasure grasped as enjoyable and pleasant by the dualistic mind of attachment. In fact, as Yangönpa explains, it is devoid of any polluting emotion; it does not depend on someone else for its existence; it is always present; it is the reality that pervades everything; it cannot be experienced by the ordinary mind; it is the unique flavor of all experiences; and it is the very natural state of the individual.

This bliss is found within the temple of one's body when the white vital essence at the head chakra is melted by the practices of inner heat or union with a consort. When the vital essence melts, it descends through the chakras, giving rise to bliss of different degrees, the last of which is known as the innate bliss. In this experience there is no subject-object dichotomy and no pleasure tainted by ordinary attachment. Although innate bliss is the very nature of the ordinary consciousness, it remains hidden unless discovered through those powerful experiences.

Wisdom, Nonthought, and Contemplation

Yangönpa states that "the nature of the mind is great bliss." This great bliss has five facets that are only conceptually distinct, known as the five wisdoms: the wisdom of sameness, of the ultimate dimension of phenomena, of discernment, of accomplishing actions, and the mirror-like wisdom.

There are many ways of defining the five wisdoms. Here Yangön-pa explains them in relation to great bliss. Since great bliss is the unique reality equally present in everything, it is the wisdom of sameness. Although it is omnipresent, it cannot be grasped as anything in particular; thus it is the wisdom of the ultimate dimension. Since it manifests as all phenomena that bear distinct characteristics, it is the wisdom of discernment. Since it is the very nature that performs the operations of all the senses and of the mental consciousness, it is the wisdom that accomplishes actions. Since everything reflects in it, although its nature is luminous and without thought, it is the mirror-like wisdom.

The term *wisdom* does not imply knowledge involving subject and object, accumulated through a process of learning. Wisdom is the very source and nature of the phenomena that manifest from the energy of emptiness inseparable from bliss. When this is not recognized, and appearances are taken as the object and mind as the subject, one enters the cloud of unknowing. Although one naturally possesses this bliss, as one might search for a hat that is already on one's head, one begins to search for it elsewhere. When one's endeavors are unsuccessful, anger arises. Fear of losing it brings jealousy. And thinking of oneself as its greatest referent generates pride.

The habits created through these five emotions lead to birth as a sentient being, as a god or demigod, human, animal, tormented spirit, or hell being. Yet these five emotions exist from the beginning as the radiance or energy of the blissful nature of mind of every being.

The fourth factor of the mind mentioned in the *Nondual Victory Tantra* is nonthought (*mi rtog pa*). Yangönpa states that nonthought refers to the natural luminosity of that objectless wisdom that is the mind's essence (*sems nyid*). Thus, when he speaks of nonthought, he is not necessarily using this term as it is commonly understood. Through various meditations, and even spontaneously, one can occasionally find oneself in a state devoid of thoughts, and this state can last for a short or a long time. But the natural luminosity of the mind does not disappear when thoughts occur; it is always present. If one's awareness is awakened to such luminosity, the presence or absence of thoughts makes no difference, for their motion would neither positively nor negatively affect it. This is what Yangönpa means by nonthought. If one is awakened to this luminosity, although thoughts, appearances, perceptions, and so on, may occur, they do not become its objects. To be objectified, the thoughts, and so on, would have to be perceived as separate from the luminosity, but this luminosity contains no such duality, for it is the very nature of everything. Implemented as advice for meditation, this principle is illustrated in Tilopa's six teachings: Do not imagine. Do not think. Do not reflect. Do not meditate. Do not analyze. Stay in the natural condition of the mind.

This leads us directly to the meaning of the fifth factor of the mind, contemplation (*ting nge 'dzin*, Skt. *samādhi*). Here, "contemplation" does not refer to an object-bound meditation or mind training, but to the uninterrupted presence of the mind's essential nature. Although it appears to come instant by instant, this nature never changes. It is no different for an ordinary person than it is for a realized being. Thus in the tantras it is called "causal continuity" or "tantra of the cause," and since everything manifests from its radiance, it is called "base of all" (*kun gzhi*, Skt. *alaya*). This uninterrupted state of the mind's essence is endowed with an inherent disposition that can be called contemplation, for it never strays from itself. When recognized with one's own awareness, in a state devoid of observer and observed, this uninterruptedness itself is the contemplation.

INSEPARABILITY OF BODY, VOICE, AND MIND

Having dealt separately with the fundamental natures of the body, voice, and mind, in the fourth section of the *Hidden Description*, Yangönpa sums up his previous discussion by stating that, by way of the mutual interdependence of their coarse and subtle aspects, body, voice, and mind are an inseparable unity.

The body is the manifestation of energy-wind and mind appearing as it does due to past actions and habitual patterns. Since energy-wind represents the subtle level of the voice that is inseparable from mind, body is completely interdependent with, and inseparable from, voice and mind. Voice arises from the interaction of energy-winds, channels, syllables, thoughts, and coordination of the parts of the physical body involved in speaking. Thus it cannot be separated from body and mind. As for the mind, the gross sense consciousnesses and the mental consciousness are produced by the channels, vital essence, and energy-wind. Moreover, the body, as well as everything else, is the display of the mind essence through whose radiance or energy everything manifests. To support his point, he quotes the *Guhyasamāja Tantra*, wherein the unity of body, voice, and mind is often emphasized as the characteristic principle of the father tantras.

The inseparability of body, voice, and mind is also demonstrated in common experience. In fact, changes occurring in the mind reflect and cause changes in the voice and in the body. For example, when one experiences anger, one's facial expression and voice become altered. This change is not only perceived subjectively, but is also perceived by others. At the subtle level, any changes in the mind affect the energy-wind and thereby the body. And any change in the body affects the energy-wind and thus the mind. This principle has been well known for millennia, not only in Tantra but also in several Eastern medical traditions.

Even at death, although the coarse body becomes a corpse, decays, and is separated from the mind, the very subtle level of body, voice, and mind are never separated and continue to exist during and after the death process. But this very subtle layer of channels, voice, and mind is not the same as the channels, coarse energy-winds, and red and white vital essences described above.

Yangönpa speaks of an ultimate central channel, the wind of space, and the quintessence of the vital essence beyond creation and destruction that is always body, voice, and mind. Ever inseparable and one with the mind essence, they manifest as body, voice, and mind throughout all states of life and beyond: as the ordinary body by day, the dream body by night, the mental body in the intermediate state, and the wisdom body, voice, and mind in the final fruit of the spiritual path. Although these manifestations will vary according to the individual's circumstances and level of realization, their source—or very nature—is always the same: the very subtle body, voice, and mind.

The ultimate central channel, the essential wind of space, and the quintessence of the vital essence, Yangönpa tells us, are inseparable from mind. But mind here is not the same as mind in the triad of body, voice, and mind. Mind here is the mind essence that is the basis of all three, the ineffable reality that underlies and pervades everything. This is present as all the various forms in the universe, as all the various sounds produced and unproduced, and as the invisible quality to which we refer as "mind." Thus we may conclude that the three very subtle aspects Yangönpa describes are in fact the innate potential of reality to manifest as body-form, wind-sound, and mind–invisible force. The ultimate central channel appears to be the innate nonduality; energy-wind, the innate potential from which movement originates; and the quintessence of the vital essence, the very nature of the bliss that is the mind essence.

Overall, from the above discussion we can understand that the category of body, voice, and mind that Yangönpa presents far exceeds the ordinary notions of body, voice, and mind. For him, the meaning of body, voice, and mind ranges from the ordinary body of flesh and blood, voice as sound, and mind as object-bound consciousness to a body, voice, and mind as the single reality that pervades all existence. It shatters the concept of a subjective body, voice, and mind seen as fundamentally real.

This principle of inseparability contains, in a nutshell, the entire content of the tantras, but its implementation, Yangönpa states—avoiding once more the disclosure of specific practices—should be learned orally in the context of a teacher-student relationship.

THE NATURALLY ACCOMPLISHED SPIRITUAL PATH

In this section, Yangönpa explains that the ordinary body, voice, and mind are already the enlightened body, voice, and mind. This is so because the spiritual path that leads to the attainment of the enlightened body, voice, and mind is naturally accomplished in the human embodiment itself through the spontaneous, effortless presence of method and wisdom in the formation, life, and death of the human body.

Method (*thabs*, Skt. *upaya*) and knowledge (*shes rab*, Skt. *prajña*), key principles in both sutra and tantra, are understood differently in different systems. In the context of Mahayana Buddhism, method is primarily the altruistic mind of awakening (bodhicitta), and knowledge, the understanding of emptiness. In Tantric imagery, method and knowledge are represented by the figures of the male and female deities in union. The male deity stands for method and the female represents knowledge. The frequently quoted lines from the tantras are:

Appearances are the male,
Emptiness, the female.

Thus, in Tantra, method comprises all that is perceived, the experience of which—not to be forsaken as in the path of the Buddha's
common discourses—is used to awaken knowledge. Things are
experienced, and when they produce their various sensations, are
recognized to be empty. This union of vision and emptiness is the
union of method and knowledge, the essence of reality and of enlightenment.

But this does not exhaust the layers of meaning attributed to
method and knowledge in Tantra, for everything is represented as
method and knowledge in a variety of paired attributes, including
male and female, right and left, day and night, and so on. Likewise,
here Yangönpa proceeds to distinguish the various paired factors
involved in the formation, life, and death of the body by assigning
them the characteristics of method and knowledge.

During formation, the father is method and the mother is
knowledge; semen is method and ovum is knowledge, and so forth.
During life, the male is method and the female is knowledge; the
energy-winds and vital essences are method and the channels are
knowledge; the six sense organs are method and their six objects are
knowledge; sleep is method and dream is knowledge, and so on. At
death, the dissolution of the four elements is method and the dissolution of the senses is knowledge; the stopping of energy-wind is
method and the cessation of discursive thought is knowledge; death
is knowledge and the intermediate state—or, alternatively, birth—is
method, and so on.

Breaking down method and knowledge into their practical application on the Tantric path, Yangönpa associates conception with
the four phases of the initiation that purifies karmic imprints and
authorizes engagement in Tantric practice. Then he describes gesta-

tion and birth in terms of the enactment of the various steps of the phase of creation, in which one visualizes oneself as a deity within a mandala. And finally, he explains how the living body is the enactment of the five stages and the four mudras (or symbols) of the phase of completion. Similarly, through the channels, energy-winds, and vital essences, and with the fire at the junction of the three main channels in the body itself, the fire-offering ritual spontaneously takes place. Likewise, when food is digested and its nutriment spread to all areas of the body, a natural Tantric Feast takes place. As a result of all this, the body also embodies the final fruit of spiritual practice: death is the reality dimension (Skt. *dharmakāya*); the intermediate state is the enjoyment dimension (*sambhogakāya*); and birth is the emanated dimension (*nirmāṇakāya*).

Moreover, the body itself is both a method and an explanatory tantra, for it reveals enlightenment itself. But if the body exists in such a sublime way and the spiritual path is accomplished solely by being born, living, and dying, why do we need a spiritual path, and why make the effort of following it? Yangönpa points out that the key is recognition. Just possessing a hidden treasure is of no use if one does not know that one has it. The so-called spiritual path consists solely of acquiring the recognition of that which already is innate enlightenment.

THE NATURALLY PRESENT FINAL FRUIT

Mirroring the statement found in many tantras—that one is already enlightened—Yangönpa tells us that the final destination of the spiritual path is innately present when the body forms, when it lives, and also when it passes away.

An enlightened being is the embodiment of the five enlightened families. This means that one's psychophysical aggregates have been recognized as being five aspects of the single state of innate bliss-reality. But the body and mind themselves already possess the nature of the five families. When the consciousness of the intermediate being enters during the union of the future father and mother, the elemental properties (earth, water, fire, air, and space) present during sexual contact—which create the conditions for conception—impress the future being with the marks of the enlightened families, distinguishing him as an enlightened one. Moreover, as explained in the section on the fundamental nature of the body, the process from conception to birth is, in Yangönpa's view, the unfolding of five spontaneous manifest awakenings. Consequently, birth is the divine birth of an emanation (nirmāṇakāya); the ethereal bodies of the intermediate being and of the dream state are the dimension of enjoyment (sambhogakāya); the mind is the reality dimension of awakening (dharmakāya). The indivisibility of these three dimensions is the dimension of great bliss (mahāsūkhakāya). These are the four dimensions of enlightenment, which in the Mahayana are said to be produced at the culmination of a spiritual career in which the bodhisattva traverses the ten levels of realization.

In opposition to the Mahayana view, Yangönpa states that all ten levels of realization spontaneously occur during gestation itself. As soon as the consciousness of the intermediate being enters the mother's womb, it remains in a state of blissful contemplation for seven days; this is the first level of awakening, known as the "joyful." Proceeding from there, the various stages of fetal development reflect each of the remaining levels of realization, until the tenth month, corresponding to the tenth level—the "cloud of teaching"—and finally birth, corresponding to enlightenment.

In Yangönpa's time, and even today, for many Tibetan Buddhists, the archetypal spiritual person is a monk. Following the statements made by tantras such as the *Hevajra*, Yangönpa explains that one is already a monk, for prior to birth, the father is the abbot and the mother is the preceptor who confers monastic ordination. The navel, where fetal development begins, is the monastic residence. The amnion is the robe. The lack of hair is the monk's shaven head. The palms folded at the crown of the head at birth is the prostration to those who conferred the ordination, and so on.

The various characteristics of the body are present in the nature of the enlightened being's qualities of perfection: the syllables of the thirty-two vital essences are the thirty-two excellent marks of a great being. The eighty concepts are the eighty minor signs. The colors of the energy-winds and of the vital essences are the luminous aura. The ten energy-winds are the ten powers and strengths.[87] The chakras and channels are the secret of the body; the energy-winds and syllables, the secret of the voice; the vital essences and thoughts, the secret of the mind; and so on.

Also, the seven features of union that characterize the final fruit of Tantric endeavors—total enjoyment, union, great bliss, lack of self-nature, filled with compassion, unending stream, and uninterrupted presence—are inherent in the body of every being from the beginning.

In his conclusion, Yangönpa states that even death, an event commonly associated with pain and suffering, is in fact a demonstration of innate enlightenment. The spontaneous untying of channel knots, the dissolution of syllables and relocation of the vital essence, and the dawn of luminous clarity are the three dimensions of awakening: emanation (nirmāṇakāya), enjoyment (sambhogakāya), and reality (dharmakāya). The disappearance of coarse and subtle conceptuality, and death, are, respectively, the freedom and the realization that characterize enlightenment.

Yangönpa's aim is to establish that throughout birth, life, and death, there is always a perfect condition that does not need to be sought elsewhere, modified, or improved in any way. This is the ultimate body, voice, and mind, an indivisible unity that represents the real condition of the individual, pure and perfect from the beginning. Although its manifestations as the body, voice, and mind by day; of the dream by night; and of the intermediate state are subject to change and destruction, the ultimate body, voice, and mind are not. This ultimate triad is found within the body, which is its expression. Thus, in essence, this expression is not different from its source. For this reason, Yangönpa considers the mandala of the body to be a perfect enlightened state even amid its changes and transformations.

Since every being is already pure and perfect, one who knows this should never scorn the body or mind of others, however negative their manner of appearance. Reminding us once more that although beings are indeed pure and perfect, they are clouded by adventitious stains, Yangönpa reiterates the necessity of recognizing one's real nature and abiding in it. This will end the cloud of unknowing and fully reveal the essence of the final fruit of spiritual practice that is inherent in the body.

CONCLUDING VERSES OF YANGÖNPA'S *HIDDEN DESCRIPTION OF THE VAJRA BODY*

In his concluding verses, Yangönpa acknowledges the influence of several of his teachers on his composition of the text:

> Here, I have fully condensed the quintessence
> Of the nectar of the unfailing oral instructions
> Of the knower of the three times, Drigung
>   Rinchen;
> Of the powerful being Maha Pandita, versed in the
>   five sciences;
> Of the lord of yogins known as Dorje;
> And of the unwaning standard of perfected merit.

[These] faultless teachings come through a successive
   lineage [of masters].
[In particular], this great treasure of profound and vast
   essential points
Comes through the blessing of the glorious master
   Heruka.

Interlinear notes in the Beijing edition indicate that this Drigung
Rinchen is Drigung Chung Rinchen, the lama who succeeded Drigung Chenga Tragpa Jungne as abbot of Drigung Thil monastery,
and who transmitted the entire body of Phagmo Trupa's teachings
to Yangönpa while he stayed there. However, it seems strange that
Yangönpa would not mention here his most cherished teacher, Drigung Chenga Tragpa Jungne. Thus, the interlinear note's identification remains doubtful.

   Whatever the case may be, the second master that Yangönpa
mentions, "Maha Pandita, versed in the five sciences," is certainly
Sakya Pandita. This is also confirmed by an interlinear note in the
Beijing edition.

   Other interlinear notes in the Beijing version state that "the
lord of yogins known as Dorje" refers to Götsangpa Gönpo Dorje;
"the unwaning standard of perfected merit," to Kotragpa; and "the
glorious master Heruka" to Sakya Pandita. The fact that Sakya Pandita is mentioned twice in the colophon indicates that, although the
teachings received from the other three lamas mentioned certainly
influenced his composition of the *Hidden Description,* it is to Sakya
Pandita that Yangönpa's work owes the most. It was Sakya Pandita
who taught Yangönpa the *Hevajra* and the *Cakrasaṃvara Tantra* as
well as the *Path and Its Fruit* from which he draws heavily in this
particular work. On two or three occasions in the book, Yangönpa
also explicitly states: "This is the view of Sakya Pandita."

YANGÖNPA'S SYNCRETIC APPROACH

From his biography, *The Great Mirror,* we know that Yangönpa had been introduced to the meaning and practice of Dzogchen or Total Perfection by some of his early masters. There, it is written that at age six he heard the lama Pulmar brothers expound the *Unwaning Standard of Victory,* one of the five early translated scriptures of the Mind Series of Dzogchen, also known as the *Total Space of Vajrasattva.* We may infer that Yangönpa learned many other Dzogchen teachings from the Pulmar brothers. In particular, the biography states that when he was nine years old, he received instructions on the Dzogchen Semde practice according to the Aro tradition. At that time, he experienced a vivid realization of the essence of his own mind.

When Yangönpa was ten years old, Latöd Mikyöd Dorje, a well-known Nyingma master and a student of Nyangral Nyimai Wözer, praised him for his knowledge of the Total Perfection and imparted to him the entire cycle of Nyangral Nyimai Wözer's Hidden Treasures. Yangönpa also received the transmission of the Dzogchen teaching from lama Dzimbu, and the rituals of the Nyingma from his uncle, Drubtob Darma. Yangönpa's words are quoted in Sogdogpa's instructions on Dzogchen Semde:[88]

> Yangönpa [himself] said that his understanding arose
>   through the Dzogchen teaching:
> It is through the celebrated Dzogchen Teaching
> That this beggar understood something,
> And the knowledge of simultaneity, too, arose.

Concerning how he meditated, in his songs he states:

> Don't meditate with the mind on what is meditation
>   from the beginning!

Do not correct through fabrications what is in
    its natural state!
Without considering mind and thoughts a defect,
Without meditating with the purpose of finding
    a nonthought state,
Leave the mind in its condition and keep watch
    from afar!
Thus, you will attain the essential point of *Shine*
    meditation
[If you also attain presence, this is the union of *Shine*
    and *Lhagthong*].

And,

Do not lose undistracted presence.
Do not fabricate the real condition beyond meditating.
Do not wish to express the unthinkable *rigpa*.
Undefiled by eternalism and nihilism, continue freely,
And you will realize the union of *Shine* and *Lhagthong*
    meditation.[89]

From these passages we can understand that Yangönpa was not only
deeply influenced by the Dzogchen teachings, but was a master of
them.

As he grew up, he studied mainly with teachers of the New
schools of Tibetan Buddhism, in particular of the Sakya and Kagyüd.
He dedicated himself to the yogic methods of Tantra that brought
him to a high state of realization. But we may infer that in his spiritual
career, Yangönpa integrated the practice of Tantric yoga techniques
with the view and the understanding of Mahāmudrā, a style of
practice that, far from being uncommon, is almost the rule among
Kagyüd and Nyingma practitioners. Moreover, the four yogas of the

Mahāmudrā system devised by Gampopa Sönam Rinchen—forefather of all the Kagyüd subsects—which Yangönpa must certainly have applied, if not identical, bear a close correlation with the four contemplations of Dzogchen Semde.

This is particularly pertinent to this book, because it is clear that in the *Hidden Description of the Vajra Body*, Yangönpa attempts to explain the fundamental nature of things by integrating Tantric explanations with Dzogchen principles. He does this by unraveling the inner structure of the human body—channels, energy-winds, and vital essences—as the basis for yogic practice as presented in the major tantras and in the writings of noteworthy Tibetan masters belonging to the lineage of explanation and application of secret instructions related to these tantras. But borrowing the Dzogchen notion that all beings are already in a state of enlightenment, he argues that, in its very structure, the human body is naturally in such a state.

The fundamental nature of things is not an ultimate reality distinct from and opposed to the ordinary body, voice, and mind, as presented in the common Buddhist teaching. Nor is it split into impure and pure vision, as in the Tantric path of transformation. Yangönpa clearly states: "Nor is there anything negative to be changed into [something] positive."

In the Dzogchen view, all is a manifestation of the creative energy of the primordial state. And just as a piece of gold remains gold despite the various beautiful or ugly forms into which it may be cast, the manifestations of the primordial state are not different from that state. The basis of the manifestations, and the manifestations themselves, cannot be differentiated in any way as relative or absolute; impure or pure, and so on. Likewise, Yangönpa affirms that the ultimate level of body, voice, and mind is reality itself comprising the ultimate central channel, the energy-wind of space, and the vital essence inseparable from bliss. The various manifestations of body, voice, and mind in the shifting circumstances of life and beyond are inseparable from this reality. Although these manifestations have various characteristics and are subject to change and dissolution, they are inseparable from the ultimate body, voice, and mind, and thus cannot be posited as relative, impure, or unenlightened. In fact, they are the enlightened Body, Voice, and Mind. This seems to be the meaning of the fundamental nature of things in Yangönpa's *Hidden Description of the Vajra Body*.

PART TWO
The Great Mirror: The Remarkable
Life of the Shri Mountain Hermit

THE BRIEF PRAISE-BIOGRAPHY
OF THE GREAT GYALWA YANGÖNPA[1]

Oṃ svasti

Having perfected the two accumulations: the most profound
    qualities and an ocean of wisdom,
King of wish-fulfilling gems, mandala of inexhaustible ornaments
    of the three kāyas' activity, crown ornament of gods [and men],
You are the source of all temporal and spiritual happiness
    and fulfillment:
To you, chief of men, leader of beings, omniscient Victorious One,
    I bow.

[You are] the reality dimension, flawless and perfect in all qualities,
The glorious Precious One, sameness of the temporal and
    the spiritual,
And the clouds of Victorious Ones converging in the universe's
    buddha-fields:
To you [who embody] the masters of the three times, I bow.

Unborn, beyond concepts, completely pure from the origin,
Self-perfected, unperturbed, luminous clarity that neither goes
*   nor comes,*
All-pervasive, uncreated essence of mind:
To you, unchanging vajra dimension, I bow.

Indivisibility of bliss and emptiness, innate expanse [of reality]
*   and pure awareness,*
Sovereign of the five enlightened dimensions, Vajradhāra,
*   Lord of the families,*
Magical dancer, eternal dimension of equal taste:
To you, the Heruka of great bliss, I bow.

Your compassion manifests impartially and accords with the
*   condition of sentient beings.*
Through countless emanations in hundreds of millions
*   [of lands],*
And an array of myriad activities,
You liberate living beings: to you, I bow.

In the Snow Land of Tibet, in Jambudvīpa,
You are the one [embodiment] of the enlightened activity of the
*   Victorious Ones of the three times.*
Incomparable Lord of the Teaching, Buddha appearing
*   on earth:*
To you, teacher of gods and men, I bow.

At the glorious Lhadong, the stupa of the Victorious One,
Through the five visions, you took birth as a siddha's son.
As you entered the mother's womb, [she] received prophecy
*   in dreams:*
To you, sublime among humans, leader of men, I bow.

Emanation of the enlightened ones who accomplishes their activity,
From the very moment you appeared [in this world],
All your youthful deeds [reflected] the light of the Teaching:
To you, self-originated buddha, I bow.

With the blossoming of your wisdom that knows the mandala
*   of the knowable,*
Reading, writing, performance of rituals and actions, and
*   contemplation*
Clearly manifested untaught:
To you of flawless intelligence, I bow.

At age five, a constant luminous clarity arose in you;
At age six, you entered the monastery to study and reflect;
At age nine, you proclaimed the Dharma's thundering roar:
To you, known to all as an emanation [of enlightened beings],
*   I bow.*

With a lovely physique, you steal the mind of all living beings,
With a fearless, melodious voice, you turn the wheel of the ultimate,
In the single flavor of mind, you master cyclic existence and its
*   transcendence:*
To you, teacher of living beings, I bow.

Avalokiteśvara who regards all living beings with the eyes
*   of compassion,*
Benevolent to the spiteful, the ungrateful, the lowly, and the poor,
Intent on exchanging your happiness for others' suffering:
To you, great bodhisattva, I bow.

For twenty-two years, you devoutly served the dust at the feet
Of the glorious Kotragpa, savior of beings,

And became a renunciate in the Teaching of the Sage:
To you, golden Blessed One, I bow.

Relying on authentic masters as your crown ornament,
With supreme faith and devotion, you filled the vase of qualities
  to the brim.
Unique son of all spiritual teachers:
To you, matchless mighty one, I bow.

[Though] you're one and inseparable from the wheel of limitless
  ornaments
Of the very Body, Voice, and Mind of the undisputed siddha,
  glorious Götsangpa,
You pretended to invoke one another:
To you, who are no different [from Götsangpa], I bow.

Three masters and the ḍākinīs foretold to you
The chief of all sacred places,
And [you yourself] beheld [its] wondrous signs:
To you who, in that supreme place of practice, achieved the
  two aims, I bow.

Having cut off concepts [held by] worldly beings distracted
  by material things,
For eleven months you sat in lotus posture:
To you who, [to achieve] enlightenment, in a single
  contemplative state,
Brought under your power energy-wind and mind, I bow.

Like sunlight, you illuminated the mandala of the knowable,
And have attained contemplation, visions, and the ten signs.
As foretold by the ḍākinīs, you were satiated by the siddhis' essence:

To you, powerful lord of yogins, I bow.

In an instant, you saw the Gandhavyuha pure realm
  of Akaniṣṭha,
Oḍḍiyāna, Lhasa, Samye, and other places,
And all invisible dimensions:
To you, amazing marvelous one, I bow.
You knew and could describe beyond words and reckoning
The far and near, the past and future;
[That which] goes and comes; the actions and actors in the three
  times:
To you, omniscient one, I bow.

The leading arrogant worldly deities bowed down to you;
The king of nāgas requested teaching; nonhuman local spirits
Respectfully vowed to assist and to obey your orders:
To you, a refuge for all, I bow.

To repel the savage hordes of the Mongol army,
You arranged 3,300 tormas,
And exhibited many displays and emanations:
To you, victorious war hero, I bow and [offer] praise.

Sole friend of beings, embodiment of love, you resolved internal
  conflicts
And [disputes] in village communities [fueled] by hatred,
Nurturing our world with happiness and spirituality:
To you, gracious Lord Avalokiteśvara, I bow.

On the glorious mountain, you met the unborn Shang;
At Lhading monastery [you made] a rain of Dharma fall
  from the sky;

While you dwelled at Yangön, the precious Drigung [master]
   arrived:
To you, inconceivable master, I bow.

Sakya Pandita, undisputed [scholar] of the five sciences,
Entrusted you with the secret instructions on sutras, tantras,
   and treatises,
And foretold and appointed you their holder:
To you, ocean of teachings, I bow.

From the heart and face of the sacred Buddha statue,
An incomparable blessing in this world,
Shone multicolored light rays that dissolved in you:
To you, amazing matchless [one], I bow.

The omniscient master dwelling in the turquoise house
Had foreknowledge of your coming, welcomed you, displayed great
   kindness,
And said: "I invoke you as the joy and happiness of samsara
   and nirvana":
To you, in the unique state of the reality dimension, I bow.

Like swans converging on a lotus lake,
The vast communities of spiritual practitioners of the ten directions—
Prominent persons, learned spiritual teachers, and ordinary monks—
All came to touch their heads to your feet:
To you, whose time to tame disciples has come, I bow.

King of the Teaching, ruler of the spiritual domain,
You revealed the vast, profound meaning of sutras, tantras,
   and treatises,
The state of realization of the Sage just as it is:

To you, Lamp of the Teaching, I bow.

You [joined] the unbroken lineage of enlightened beings,
And the lineage of blessing, transmitted one to one,
Of the undisputed Kagyüd, unrivaled in the world,
And [thus] spontaneously recognized the innate [bliss], the secret path
*   that gives immediate protection:*
To you, who planted the victory banner of the practice lineage,
*   I bow.*

If one invokes you, Body essence of enlightenment, reality dimension,
Inseparable from the mind-mandala of the Four Precious [Masters],
Everything one thinks, needs, and desires will manifest:
To you, jewel-like master, I bow.

In the second summer month of the Tiger year,
For seven days, you remained in contemplation,
[Nourished by] the food of meditation, needing no coarse food,
And to the devotees, gave strict orders:
"Do not come, and do not speak to others."
For nine days, you stayed in one [continuous] meditative state,
As various signs and wondrous magical displays appeared.
On the fifteenth day of the waxing moon, the day of the yogini,
On the earth, in midair, and in the sky,
dākas, dākinīs, local guardians, and nonhumans
Offered incense, butter-lamps, and clouds of offering
With song, dance, and music:
To you, marvelous blessing, I bow.

Glorious Heruka, sovereign of blessing,
With the wrathful deities' nine dance moods, you outshone the three
*   existences,*

With vajra laughter, subjugated the three worlds;
And through various emanations, annihilated vicious beings.
[While] dwelling in the hundred [doorways] of the nondual mind's
    contemplation,
The four motions of the outer, inner, and secret connections aligned,
You eliminated all demonic obstacles and conquered the dark forces.
[Then] a sphere of glorious light blazed all around,
And filled the billion-fold universe, illuminating the three worlds;
Its multicolored rays, infinite and indescribable,
Appeared and reabsorbed, brilliant and luminous,
And long remained for all to see.
To you, inconceivable wonder, I bow.

Glorious teacher, incomparable Master of the Teaching,
I respectfully invoke you, the kind one:
I beg you to care for me with compassion.
From now, until the essence of enlightenment,
Foregoing the extremes of samsara and nirvana,
[Accomplishing] infinite, inconceivable altruistic benefit,
May you liberate all beings in the primordial condition,
And lead them to your pure realm, great benevolent one.

The Praise-Biography
of the Great Gyalwa Yangönpa[2]

Om Swasti

Having perfected the two accumulations: the most profound qualities
  and an ocean of wisdom,
King of wish-fulfilling gems, mandala of inexhaustible ornaments of
  the three kāyas[3] activity, crown ornament of gods [and men],
You are the source of all temporal and spiritual happiness and
  fulfillment:
To you, chief of men, leader of beings, omniscient Victorious One,
  I bow.

Although the inconceivable marvel that is the life story of this Precious
  Jewel
Cannot be comprehended by those of limited intellect [such as myself],
Through [my] long reliance [on him], I have seen and heard a little
  of what is [commonly] perceived,
[Thus,] urged by a friend, for the sake of others, I have written
  it down.

In reality, this master, a fully enlightened buddha, is a friend of
beings who maturates and liberates all living creatures, infinite as
space, by means of the treasure that is the mandala of inexhaustible
ornaments, the essence of wisdom indivisible from the Body, Voice,
and Mind of all tathāgatas of the three times. He sees the mandala
of the knowable of the three times through his knowing wisdom.
He is the embodiment of the freedom[4] and maturation[5] of the [ten]
powers[6] and of the [eighteen] exclusive [qualities][7] of mastery,[8] and
of all the supreme qualities.

In the perception of beings to be trained [during] the last of the five-hundred-year [periods],[9] whose past actions are pure, this sixth buddha, the great Vajradhāra himself,[10] [has appeared] in the form of an ordinary being who is like the light of the Buddha's Teaching; the shelter of all living beings; the third eye and the heart of all creatures; the king of wish-fulfilling gems that fulfills all desires just as they are conceived.

This master was enlightened countless eons ago. Even the buddhas of the three times, recounting his freedoms, wisdoms, knowledge and compassion, inconceivable realization, and blessing; his deeds that evaporate the ocean of suffering of cyclic existence; and the qualities of his enlightened activities, would be unable to arrive at a partial description of just one of these qualities, for they are exceedingly deep in nature, and cannot be fathomed or conceived by ordinary beings of limited perception.

I have composed the following few words of praise from the perspective of the small eye of my own devotion:

[You are] the reality dimension, flawless and perfect in all qualities,
The glorious Precious One, sameness of the temporal and the spiritual,
And the clouds of Victorious Ones converging in the universe's
    buddha-fields:
To you [who embody] the masters of the three times, I bow.

To explain: in the range of experience of noble ones[11] who see the other shore,[12] the great sages who are the tathāgatas of the three times (past, present, and future) [manifesting in] the infinite buddha-fields of the universe; the great bodhisattvas, such as Lord Avalokiteśvara,[13] who dwell on the levels of realization; the great siddhas of the Precious Oral Transmission[14] stemming from Vajradhāra; and all the great teachers of today, such as the Four Precious Lords,[15] and so on, who uphold the Teaching of the Buddha and work for the benefit of others, are all the manifestation or emanation of this master. With this conviction:

To you [who embody] the masters of the three times, I bow.

Unborn, beyond concepts, completely pure from its origin,
Self-perfected, unperturbed, luminous clarity that neither goes
*   nor comes,*
All-pervasive, uncreated essence of mind:
To you, unchanging vajra dimension, I bow.

The indivisible [nature] of the Mind of all buddhas, the self-originated innate wisdom, the genuine Great Symbol[16] is undifferentiated from the mind of embodied creatures. It is the reality of all phenomena, from its origin peaceful, unborn, and devoid of the transitions of birth and death. It is beyond loss and gain, beyond decline and increase. Pure, blissful, and eternal, it is the transcendent sacred Self.

I praise the dimension of reality, the luminous clarity, the vajra that is unchanging in the essence of the one uncreated wisdom:

To you, unchanging vajra dimension, I bow.

Indivisibility of bliss and emptiness, innate expanse [of reality]
*   and pure awareness,*
Sovereign of the five enlightened dimensions,[17] Vajradhāra,
*   Lord of the families,*
Magical dancer, eternal dimension of equal taste:
To you, the Heruka[18] of great bliss, I bow.

Great master, dimension of perfect enjoyment [sambhogakāya],[19] you are the lord of all [buddha] families, principal of all the man-

dalas; the form of wisdom's magic together with the naturally manifesting consort; and are adorned with the light of the major and
minor marks.[20] You individually cognize the phenomena of cyclic
existence and its transcendence; you are the protector of all powerful
lords at the tenth level of realization[21] who are the pure apprentices
of the [dimension] of perfect enjoyment. Through your expertise
in learning and reflecting on the blissful path of the unsurpassable
great secret[22] that swiftly [affords] protection, and through profound
discriminating wisdom, you are unique and superior.

I praise the glorious dimension of perfect enjoyment, the Heruka endowed with the seven facets of great bliss,[23] the Buddha Vajradhāra who teaches the adamantine vehicle of the Secret Mantra.
Thus:

To you, the Heruka of great bliss, I bow.

Your compassion manifests impartially and accords with the condition
of sentient beings.
Through countless emanations in hundreds of millions [of lands],
And an array of myriad activities,
You liberate livings beings: to you, I bow.

Master emanation body,[24] your enlightened activity [unfolds in the
state] in which the Body, Voice, and Mind of all buddhas and the
nature of the body, voice, and mind of all living beings, are indivisible. You are the very embodiment of nonconceptual compassion
and pure aspiration. Having accomplished the deeds of a supreme
emanation,[25] through incarnated emanations,[26] you appear in forms
that accord with [the condition of] those to be trained. You appear
to each of the six types of beings[27] as a separate emanation. With
the Bodies [of these emanations], you train living beings; with their
Voices, you teach the spiritual path; with their light rays, you puri-

fy obstacles; and with their Minds of nonconceptual wisdom, you bring [living beings] to maturity and liberation.

[You] create a fresh breeze and coolness in the abodes of hell. You illuminate [everything] in the darkness between continents, from beings' arm movements, and so on. You accomplish the benefit of others [in the animal world] through the forms of tigers, rabbits, and so on. That is, through the meditative absorption of an unequivocal altruistic resolve to attain enlightenment, and [with boundless] compassion, you swiftly liberate beings [in numbers] limitless as space from the ocean of suffering of cyclic existence, and establish them in the levels of enlightenment and omniscience. This is the very nature of an enlightened one's form-emanation. Thus:

You liberate living beings: to you I bow.

In the Snow Land of Tibet, in Jambudvīpa,[28]
You are the one [embodiment] of the enlightened activity of the
Victorious Ones of the three times.
Incomparable Lord of the Teaching, Buddha appearing on earth:
To you, teacher of gods and men, I bow.

Having attained [the state of] a Victorious Blessed One, king of the Teaching in the infinite and limitless buddha-fields, [you] became fully and perfectly enlightened, and set in motion the wheel of the Dharma. In particular, at the Vajra Seat[29] in hundreds of millions of Dzambu lands, [you demonstrated] the defeat of Mara,[30] the Evil One; the attainment of perfect, full enlightenment; and established the apprentices of the three affinities[31] in the three enlightenments.[32]

Particularly in the kingdom of Tibet—the snowy mountain ranges of the northern lands; the palace of the Three Precious Jewels;[33] the country of the four districts of Tibet[34] that is the pure land of the apprentices to venerable Mahākāruṇika[35]—you are the unique [embodiment] of the qualities and activities of the Body, Voice, and Mind of the buddhas of the three times. You are the second Omniscient One of the five-hundred [-year period],[36] incomparable and unequaled, whose name—Precious One from Lhadong, Master of the Teaching—is difficult to pronounce, and whose fame and renown pervades the world and the god [realms]. [You,] master, are what is referred to as "Buddha appearing on earth."

To you, teacher of gods and men, I bow.

At the glorious Lhadong, the stupa of the Victorious One,
Through the five visions,[37] you took birth as a siddha's son.
As you entered the mother's womb, [she] received prophecy in dreams:
To you, sublime among humans, leader of men, I bow.

Birthplace

The perfect place [of Yangönpa's birth was] the glorious and prosperous region of Shri valley, at the foot of the Seven Nyen Siblings,[38] near the ḍākinīs'[39] natural gathering place called Śrī Parvata.[40] [This was] a place blessed and delightful, where the mind became clear, where special experiences and realizations arose, one that was praised by many masters, and one in which many buddhas' and bodhisattvas' emanations had set foot. Through perfect coincidences, [all] material goods were available; thus, any favorable circumstance one desired fell like rain. It was a place where the five perfections[41] of retinue, all [kinds of] merit, spiritual teaching, and the enjoyment of material things were spontaneously present.

It was in this locale of the glorious monastery of Lhadong, the Great Stupa of the Victorious One, that [Yangönpa] was born [in 1213].[42]

Family

Concerning his ancestry, in the world, [his] was a great family of householders renowned for virtue, and praiseworthy as a great Sal tree.[43] Also, his paternal ancestors had been chiefs and leaders; [thus, his was] a lineage exclusively consisting of capable people.

Of [his father's] two brothers, the eldest was a practicing spiritual teacher. Having studied with various holy masters such as the siddha[44] Ang Phugpa and others, he himself became a treasure trove of all profound oral instructions. Having crossed the threshold of the spiritual path at the age of twenty, he spent the next ten years learning and reflecting on [the teachings], and came to master them. From the age of thirty until ninety, for sixty years he dedicated himself to spiritual practice [seated] on the same mat. Thus, blessed by the meditational deity, he possessed inconceivable blessing and power, and had visions of the Master Padmasambhava,[45] the Brahmin Saraha,[46] the Indian Lord Pha Tampa Sangye,[47] the Lady Lakshminkara,[48] and others. At age ninety, he had eleven small teeth growing in, and had no white hair. Since he possessed many qualities of genuine realization, he was known by the name "Lama Siddha."

The Precious One's [Yangönpa's] father was the great spiritual friend called Lhadongpa who, for a long time and with extraordinary devotion, followed authentic and excellent spiritual teachers such as Palchenpo Kolungpa, lama Nyang Rinpoche, and the great siddha, lama Pulmar Ne Senge Dra.

He learned and constantly reflected on the teachings of the sutras and tantras. Thus, while staying at a monastic college, he would listen to the doctrine twice a day, reflect on it in the morning and afternoon, perform the 100 *torma*[49] ritual and the water offering of Mañjuśrī,[50] write approximately eight [large] cut folios, and recite *Chanting the Names of Mañjuśrī* aloud five times.[51] Then, in the evening, looking directly at the [setting] sun, he would say, "This day has passed in vain."

Moreover, he behaved according to the explanations in the sacred spiritual teachings, and guarded the principle of actions and their consequences as [he would] the pupils of his own eyes. [For example, on one occasion] when he was harvesting [peas] for lama Pulmar [Ne Senge Dra], as he followed the mule [loaded with] the unthreshed crop, a few peas fell off. He ate some, and held the others in his hand. Realizing [what he had done], he thought, "These are the teacher's property!" He spat out the peas he was eating and put the ones in his hand with those loaded on the mule. It is said that, as an act of contrition, he offered the teacher a good set of clothes that he had, and a woolen strap for carrying loads.

One night, the lama invited him to attend to the performance of an offering [ritual, but] thinking that if he went, he would not be able to do many of his daily prayers, he did not go. Later, at about midnight, he thought, "The lama told me to go; since I did not go, I have violated his command." The next day he went [to the lama] to offer his apologies.

He remained in strict retreat in various solitary places and monasteries, sealing off the entrance [of his meditation place]. Thus, for periods of time, he did not enter any village. Feeling disinclined to [engage in] play and games, he would say, "Just like the desirous ones who [spend all their time] harvesting crops, I [spend] all my time practicing the Dharma and engaging in virtue."

Moreover, the students in his presence did not succumb to the slightest laziness in learning, reflecting, and meditating, and he led them to [acquire] spiritual qualities. Also, through their relationship with him, his male and female lay benefactors improved spiritually by means of [the rite of] Amoghapāśa,[52] the various levels of commitments, [the eight] lay precepts,[53] [the casting of] votive images, recitation of the sutras, and so on. Whoever was defiled, he purified.

His teacher, Pulmar [Ne Senge Dra], who was clairvoyant, [once] prophesied to him, "To the right side of the Variegated Monastery, in a raised stupa, many ḍākinīs are building a Dharma throne for you! You will accomplish your own aims, and your activity for others' benefit will blossom." Later, the [lama's] words came true.

In brief, this lama, the great spiritual friend Lhadongpa, endowed with [meditative] experiences and realization, blessings and compassion, whose [actual] name was Chosam, was the father [of Gyalwa Yangönpa].

[Yangönpa's] mother was a wisdom ḍākinī,[54] a hidden yogini who, in the guise of an ordinary woman, worked for the benefit of living beings. Through her extraordinary blessing and power, she was able to clear away outer and inner obstacles.

In a [place called] Pharo there was a female dog called "evil spirit bitch of miserliness" that none could control. Common travelers had to be accompanied by a strong man [as they passed through that place] or [risk] having their way blocked. [Once, when] she went to visit one of her daughters who was staying at Olgong, the bitch came running along the road after her. Unflappable, the mother firmly set the [daughter's] gifts on the ground, and with both hands, held a piece of loosely woven woolen cloth that she had with her as a shield before the bitch's face; and there she stood. The dog came charging [toward her], but got wrapped up in the cloth. With one hand, the mother pressed [the dog] down, and with the other, she punched it. And so, the bitch's [arrogance] was crushed to dust. Then, the mother went off without looking at the people [who had witnessed the event]. The local people [looked upon the mother as a source] of help and, seeing that nothing had happened to her, they began to speak of her as a nonhuman ḍākinī and were all greatly surprised. From that time onward, this dog did not attack anyone, and everyone came to know that [the mother] had tamed the evil spirit bitch.

It is said that [once, when Yangönpa's] mother and her three children were churning curd to make butter, they prayed [for a large quantity of butter to be produced], and simply because [the mother] desired it, a *khal*[55] of butter formed.

It is said that in the [very] session during which she was given the oral teaching on the training in transference of consciousness,[56] as a sign [of success], a bird's egg appeared at the crown of her head.

If she was feeling unhappy or she scolded someone at a ritual gathering, that person would rapidly turn bad. [If] she felt happy and caring toward someone, that person would become noble, important, capable, and possessed of many qualities.

When [Yangönpa's] mother passed away, at the cremation, mercury-colored relics[57] appeared. When these were seen, they were handed to the Precious One [Yangönpa], who said, "She was a woman whose [body] is bound to produce relics. These relics are authentic."

In his own writings, the Precious One stated, "The mother suffices as father, mother, and teacher; she is the kind one who can serve in [all] these roles." Later, at each anniversary of her passing, [Yangönpa] would regularly perform an offering [ritual in her memory], and would say, "I see [in her] the qualities of a yogini possessed of the essence of Vajrayoginī, mother of all buddhas of the three times; or of the venerable Tārā."

While [Yangönpa] was in his mother's womb, she was strong and in good health. Even when she did not eat, she would feel neither hunger nor thirst, and would experience a natural, excellent state of contemplation. She had many amazing dreams. For example, she dreamed that the sun and moon shone within her body, their light illuminating all the world systems; that beautiful women were bringing food, circumambulating around her, and building a bridge that they said would lead to the liberation of many beings.

His father reported the following dreams: "I dreamed there was a huge bird's nest in my bed. [I thought that] this time, a son will be born. What is more, he will be the regent of the Victorious Ones of the three times; the blazing splendor of happiness and joy for himself and others. Thus, he will be called Regent of Blazing Splendor." After leaving this testament, on the eleventh day of the horse month,[58] among countless wondrous signs, [Yangönpa's] father, aged seventy-five, passed into perfect peace.

[Yangönpa] had one brother, and one sister from a different mother. His Presence[59] was the youngest.

At birth, his body was so handsome that one could not tear one's eyes away from it. Because of his radiance and overwhelming presence—superior to anyone in the world—just as his father had named him, he was called [Regent of Blazing Splendor]. From that moment, and throughout his lifetime, the harvests were good; there was no illness; everything was auspicious; the spiritual teachings flourished; and many good omens appeared. Finally, even today, the spiritual teaching flourishes in this area of western Tibet; many spiritual teachers appear; and the region is peaceful and happy. All this is due to the blessing of the Master of the Teaching [Yangönpa].

Childhood and Early Training

To you, sublime among humans, leader of men, I bow.
Emanation of the enlightened ones who accomplishes their activity,
From the very moment you appeared [in this world],
All your youthful deeds [reflected] the light of the Teaching:
To you, self-originated buddha, I bow.

As to the phrase, "Emanation of the enlightened ones who accomplishes their activity," the Precious One himself said, "The abilities to think and recollect the teaching arose in me simultaneously. I never behaved like a small child. I [always] had great mental fortitude, and thought that I could become some kind of great [being]."

As an infant, crawling here and there, [when he reached] the door to the shrine, he bowed three times and touched his head to the doorstep. In the same period, as he was learning to speak, [he] favored words of the sacred spiritual teaching. Thus, from age three, he would recite the four-line teaching[60] and give blessings.

At age four, telling the teacher's spouse, "Ho, lady! When I grow up, I will make a lot of clamor," he would become excited. [His play] consisted solely of laying out the materials and tools required for building monasteries, and building teaching thrones.

From the age of five, he would arrange offerings for the Three Precious Jewels,[61] make the mandala offering,[62] read the *Chanting of the Names of Mañjuśrī* aloud, perform the ritual of one hundred tormas, perform the water offering [known as] "of Mañjuśrī," and only spend his time in virtuous activities.

He made the promise to bow to any representation of the Three Precious Jewels that he saw and to offer them the Sevenfold Prayer.[63] Thus, while traveling to study with Pulmar,[64] he would dismount his horse and bow to any of the eight [auspicious] symbols[65] and stupas that he saw along the road, and offer the Sevenfold Prayer, however long it would take.

Whenever he saw a humble or a poor person, with complete detachment he would give his remaining food and his clothing.

Since he was a small child, whenever he heard the name of a spiritual teacher, such as that of Lama Shigpo Dütsi,[66] he would firmly resolve, "I, too, will become just like them."

Since he did not become mentally engaged in any worldly activity or behavior, he did not know how to flatter or please his friends and relatives, and in his songs of realization he states, "I did not have habitual tendencies toward worldly behavior."

With the blossoming of your wisdom that knows the mandala
of the knowable,
Reading, writing, performance of rituals and actions,
and contemplation
Clearly manifested untaught:
To you of flawless intelligence, I bow.

At age four, when the students in front of him would say, "Master, please learn how to read," and give him a [paper marked] with the alphabet letters: KA, KHA [and so on], he would say, "This is how I read." To the amazement of all, he would clearly and directly pronounce [the letters] without having been taught to read.

The Precious One himself said, "I had no teacher [for] reading and writing; I never did all the so-called spelling exercises. [So] nowadays, when I write, I make a few small errors in the suffixes and prefixes." Moreover, he knew and would effortlessly master all the rituals of the Secret Mantra[67] just by being taught the opening words of the [ritual] acts, mantras, symbolic gestures, and melodies. Thus,

To you of flawless intelligence, I bow.

At age five, a constant luminous clarity arose in you;
At age six, you entered the monastery to study and reflect;
At age nine, you proclaimed the Dharma's thundering roar:
To you, known to all as an emanation, I bow.

At age five, he went to the home of [a lama called] Apa Trokyab. [This lama] had him sing a song whose lyrics brought him to a state of meditation in which he spontaneously experienced a blissful, clear, nonconceptual contemplation. Day and night, he continuously remained in a spontaneous, all-encompassing state of contemplation, a luminous clarity without center or boundary, which persisted when he left it, and which [he] perceived as soon as he looked at it.

Thus, his mother and sister thought, "This child cannot be in a state of meditation without having being taught by anyone. This [unlikely phenomenon] might be an obstacle caused by demons, and, as he is compelled to act in this way, his energy-wind might become disturbed and [his bodily] elements weakened." Having said this, they tried to distract the Precious One in various ways while he was absorbed in contemplation, [intending] never to allow him to meditate. [But] during this period, a genuine yoga of undivided presence[68] arose in his mind. Then [his mother] said, "If he were to be taught by an experienced master, he would [be able] to maintain [this practice] by himself, and that would suffice."

Moreover, at that time, he possessed a degree of clairvoyance, so anything he said about the quality of the harvest, and other [matters], would come true. "Everyone was asking me [to tell the future], and I responded. But in dreams, many angry, displeased women told me, 'Do not make predictions!' Because I had made them, later on, when I grew up, [my clairvoyance] became clouded and [eventually] disappeared."

Also, during that period, [Yangönpa] recognized Mikyöd Sangchö Rinpoche,[69] who had come to collect alms. Thus, later on, [this lama] remarked, "When I went to collect alms at Latöd,[70] a five-year-old boy was the only person who recognized me."

A [few years] later, [Mikyöd Rinpoche] said, "Up in Latöd, there is a child who recognizes his [spiritual] father. Let's go to meet him." Thus, with many attendants and people who venerated to him, he arrived at Langkor and stayed [at a place called] Shochung. From there, he sent someone to [invite Yangönpa]. At that time, the Precious One was eleven years old.

[Yangönpa,] his mother, the other children, and their entourage went there to meet [Mikyöd Rinpoche]. The disciples who had arrived in their presence declared, "Father and son have met." The Precious One curled into the lap [of Mikyöd Rinpoche], who asked, "Noble son, are you happy?"

There, they engaged in much teaching and conversation. [The spiritual father] said, "Noble son, sing a song." [Yangönpa] responded by offering many songs of realization that came to his mind, pleasing [his spiritual father]. [Mikyöd Rinpoche] said, "This boy of ten has fastened the belt of the Total Perfection.[71] He is an amazing child of Samantabhadra."[72] Later [Yangönpa said], "At Langkor, I received the complete teachings [of Mikyöd Rinpoche]."[73]

When [Yangönpa] reached the age of six, the spouse of the teacher [Gyaltsen] who served as caretaker of the monastery, the disciples, and the mother and her three children went to [lama] Pulmar[74] to pursue spiritual studies. The Precious One himself said, "This Pulmar relation, my lama, was a buddha. Another master would not have imparted the sacred teaching to a small child. He showed great kindness in instructing me on spiritual matters when I was small." As to the esteem in which he held [Yangönpa], it is said that at that time there were seventy exemplary monks at Shang Ngön college,[75] and [lama Pulmar,] said, "Of the seventy spiritual teachers of Shang [college], I favor only this noble son."

As to the spiritual teachings he received, [lama Pulmar told Yangönpa's] older brother to learn the tantras, so he earnestly did that. "His Presence is too young," [said lama Pulmar]. "If he studies [the tantras], he will be recalcitrant and unwilling to [continue]. He should not listen to high teachings [now, but] should memorize the Rite of the Peaceful and Wrathful Deities,[76] and other [liturgies]."

One day when the Precious One had caught a cold, afraid that he would fall asleep, his mother took him to the place where [lama Pulmar] was teaching. They arrived just as the lama was explaining a chapter [known as the] *Unwaning Standard of Victory* from the

All-Creating King[77]—a teaching of the Great Perfection—and [lama Pulmar] said that this was an auspicious event.

After he had heard this exposition, on their way home, he directly related to his mother all that the teacher had taught. Very pleased, his mother invited lama [Pulmar], and had [Yangönpa] directly repeat all the teachings [he had heard]. The lama was very pleased, and said, "Now, he should also hear the tantras and be taught any oral instruction he desires."

Thus he heard many sutras, tantras of the Secret Mantra, and oral instructions[78] from the three lama [Pulmar] brothers who were learned spiritual teachers. By receiving the reading transmissions or hearing the [explanations] just once, he perfectly grasped the words and meaning.

From what others could perceive, he did not take [his studies] very lightly; earnestly applied himself to reflection; and seemed increasingly to persevere in getting to the bottom of the subject matter.

One day, [when] the Precious One went on an outing to restore his health, in his sleeping place, the teacher Gyaltsen left a [scolding] note in which he wrote, "Why have we come to this place?" As [Yangönpa] entered the house and saw the note, he laughed and said, "We have come for the spiritual teaching."

[Yangönpa] said that in the winter in which he turned eight, [since] it was not really [the right time] to give guidance [to others], in order to receive instructions, he requested the teaching of the Aro [tradition] on taming the mind.[79] [On that occasion] he felt a sincere desire to earnestly practice meditation, and he meditated vibrantly.

Thus, in the context of this [teaching], when the results—the capturing of the uncaught mind, the stabilization of the captured mind, and the perfection of that which is stabilized, without requiring the pointing-out instructions—were obtained, the teacher said, "Clarity is the characteristic of mind; emptiness is the nature of mind; pure awareness is the essence of mind; union is [the indi-

visibility of] method and knowledge."⁸⁰ And, based on the teacher's
words, he gained a high definitive knowledge. It was like the light-
ing of a lamp in darkness, the dawning of the day, or the removal
of a head-covering. He recognized the essence of his own mind. He
experienced a vivid realization beyond concepts. He experienced
the definite knowledge that innate wisdom is this very state. All
[his] doubts were resolved. This conviction cheered his heart. He
thought, "Now there is no difficulty. Once this [state] is revealed
to all, many Togdens⁸¹ will appear." And he experienced [such an]
exceedingly happy feeling that, lying in his bed, he would wave his
arms and legs in the air, exclaiming, "What joy!" This was how the
realization of direct leap arose in him.⁸²

At times he experienced a naked, clear, and lucid openness. At
times [this state] was slightly dim and hazy. By maintaining this
[realization], he definitely understood that all phenomena of cyclic
existence and its transcendence—all things that exist and appear—
are his own mind.

He thought that in the mind [-essence]—which, from the
very beginning, is a sky-like emptiness beyond concepts—there
is no accumulation of habitual tendencies [generated by] virtuous
or nonvirtuous actions, and he resolved all [his] doubts regarding
emptiness. Thus, he said that at that time, he heard all sounds as
the great sound of emptiness.

He remained there [with lama Pulmar] for three years. At the
age of nine, he returned [to Lhadong monastery and was installed as
its abbot]. In Lhadong, before a large gathering of people, without
fear or hesitation he delighted the wise with the profound and vast
[aspects of the spiritual path], and proclaimed the Dharma's thundering roar, instilling clear faith [even] in deluded ones.

At first, he taught the *Narrative of Former Lives* [of the Bud-
dha]⁸³ that belongs to the Set of Discourses.⁸⁴ [Then] he responded
to the people who introduced themselves to him and dedicated the

offerings they gave him. He overwhelmed all—the great, the average, and the lesser—with the brilliance of his charisma.

As this was happening, people everywhere would say, "The Little Child from Lhadong, a nine-year-old boy, is teaching the spiritual path to the multitudes." His fame and renown as an emanation of the enlightened ones spread throughout all the countries on earth and under the sun.

To you, known to all as an emanation [of enlightened beings], I bow.

With a lovely physique, you steal the mind of all living beings,
With a fearless, melodious voice, you turn the wheel of the ultimate,
In the single flavor of mind, you master cyclic existence and its
    transcendence:
To you, teacher of living beings, I bow.

Spiritual Development, Teaching, and Altruistic Works as a Lay Practitioner

Until age twenty-two, he lived as a lay practitioner,[85] gave up eating meat and drinking alcohol, and with a noble and pure way of life, worked for the benefit of all beings and fostered enlightened activity.

Possessed of measureless qualities of the Path of Method,[86] from the start, he wore only a cotton robe. None could tear their eyes away from his physical form perfected with the two accumulations.[87] Just by being seen, it would steal the mind of all living beings and inspire clear faith.

With your majestic radiance and blessing, you outshone and governed all external appearances. The mandala of your body had all the divine proportions, just as explained by all the tathāgatas, and was superior to anything [in the] world.

This master's speech was endowed with the attributes of Brahmā's melodious [voice]: it was pleasant, clear, and powerful. Thus, when he taught the spiritual path to the mandala of his retinue, [his exposition] was deep; flawless; free from attachment; and virtuous at the beginning, middle, and end.

[His teaching was] profound in meaning, [precise in its] words and letters, [conveyed] in a voice neither loud nor soft, and free from trivialities and errors. Never separate from the equipoise of meditation, in the individual language [of each listener], his voice explained the spiritual pursuits[88] suited to [their level of] understanding; the subject matter of the three divisions [of the Buddha's Teaching];[89] and the four classes of tantra[90] subsumed under the Three Precious Trainings [of ethics, meditation, and knowledge].[91]

He taught all the public and the profound Dharma of the tantras, the means of accomplishment, the secret instructions, the introductions and the steps of guidance, the [methods for] dispelling obstacles, and those for obtaining results. Without depending on even the letter KA[92] from the texts, he publicly presented the vast topics with their citations, logic, secret instructions, essential points of experience, and practical applications. As to the profound teachings, he presented the deep essential points of the above [teachings]. As to the steps of guidance, he presented [the theory] along with its means of implementation.

He realized the essence of the unique nonconceptual wisdom of the buddha mind [that] distinctly and completely [sees] the entire mandala of the knowable. Therefore, in the state of the inseparability of his ultimate and relative aspiring and venturing [mind of awakening] and the bliss and emptiness essence of his mind, through the contemplation of the vision of the profound [reality], with each shift in his internal meditative state, [the elements] of external phenomena—[such as] pebbles or twigs—also changed, and thus he effortlessly overcame all flaws and obtained qualities for himself and others.

In fact, if the disciples around him would indirectly ask, "What if the people of Nagtsang[93] were to have this? They need it," he would say, "What would they do with it? Whatever one happens to have or receive is sufficient." If they would [insist] that it was necessary, he would say, "Okay; it can be done." Having said this, either immediately or within two or three days, [whatever was needed] would spontaneously arrive. This was actually witnessed by all in his presence.

In brief, being the lord of cyclic existence and of its transcendence, the one who enjoys and governs all phenomena of cyclic existence and of its transcendence, you are the teacher of all. Thus,

To you, teacher of living beings, I bow.

Avalokiteśvara who regards all living beings with the eyes
   of compassion,
Benevolent to the spiteful, the ungrateful, the lowly,
   and the poor,
Intent on exchanging your happiness for others' suffering:
To you, great bodhisattva, I bow.

Effortlessly, and [with] inconceivable compassion, he infinitely benefited living beings. Thus, swiftly implementing various skillful deeds, through happiness and goodness he led [them] from the bottomless ocean of suffering of cyclic existence to the dry shore of enlightenment.

Naturally and without any exertion, he gifted his own happiness to others and took on their suffering. He himself said, "If it is for the benefit of all beings, nothing is worthier than actually jumping into the fire-pits of hell, to say nothing of working for the benefit of many beings of the regions and countries [of this world]. If it will surely benefit beings, with this purpose in mind, I can enter the dungeon of hell."

[Moreover,] he said, "I consider the suffering of each of the six types of beings, and also help human beings through concrete acts. I also bring immediate aid to animals by freeing them from cages, traps, and hunters. I immediately benefit the tormented spirits through the dedication of torma and water offerings.[94]

"Out of love, the unbearable thought of the hell [beings'] suffering [makes] tears fall from my eyes. Ho, [sentient beings, my] children! Now I am attaining enlightenment. Once I've swiftly achieved it, I will rescue you from your suffering, so bear up a little longer. If I cannot actually help you right now, I can only [engender] the wish to do so [in the future]."

For one year while he lived as a lay practitioner, the land became ravaged by a great famine. [At that time] he made a promise not to eat more than a third or a half of his lunch [and give the rest to others], and said, "Helping the poor will save many lives."

During that year, for a few days he fed any beggars who showed up, and blessed them by anointing their heads with oil. In particular, in the Bird year, when he performed the Amoghapāśa [rite], a great many beggars gathered, and for several days he fed them all.

At that time, a beggar died of a sudden intestinal colic caused by a bile disorder. [Yangönpa] carried the man's corpse up a mountain, and when he saw the lice swarming in the [corpse's] hair, feeling unbearable compassion, he collected them and put them on his own clothes, and his clothes became white [with lice]. Then, as he descended the mountain, he saw a worn animal skin garment on which no fur but only worms could be seen, and he felt great overwhelming love. Thus, without hesitation, he donned the clothes of the man who had died of intestinal colic and the worn skin garment, even though it smelled of human waste. Over these, he fastened a thick hemp cloth. He said that this gave him the feeling of being pierced by needles all over his body.

In the night, he did not sleep, but trained in meditation, and remarked that he experienced great progress. In fact, he adopted the practice called Exchanging One's Own Happiness for Others' Suffering.[95]

Moreover, at all times he also cared for the people of this degenerate [era] who engage in spiteful behavior, and for malicious people who respond with harm to the help they are given and who, although they are helped with food, clothing, and spiritual teaching, simply continue to in misbehave.

He always took care of people who were "nobody" and who had no protection.

He said, "Since I have unconcernedly dedicated my body and possessions to others, uninfluenced by even a moment's self-interest, may all who enjoy my wealth without having been given it, incur no downfall."

[You are the one who performs the] activity of a great bodhisattva; such is our spiritual master. Thus:

To you, great bodhisattva, I bow.

For twenty-two years, you devoutly served the dust at the feet
Of the glorious Kotragpa, savior of beings,
And became a renunciate in the Teaching of the Sage:
To you, golden Blessed One, I bow.

Meeting Kotragpa and Receiving Monastic Ordination

When he was eleven years old, [Yangönpa] met the Precious Master of the Teaching, the glorious Kotragpa,[96] and from then on, never wavered, even for a moment, from his deep and boundless devotion [to this master]. [Of Kotragpa], he said, "He has been my master in countless lives," and for a long time, he dedicatedly served him in the three ways of pleasing [the master].[97]

Although that Precious Master of the Teaching had unimaginably [great] students who were spiritual masters [in their own right], such as Trophu Lotsawa[98] and Lama Chalpa,[99] he considered the Precious One to be his supreme spiritual son, and while still living, entrusted [Yangönpa] with his monastic seat.[100]

The Lord of the Teaching [Kotragpa] did not fawn over important people, not even the ruler Shakya Wö of Chumig Ringmo. Under no circumstances did he ever engage in flattery or boot-licking, but to the Precious Lord of the Teaching [Yangönpa] he would say, "We are father and son," and whenever [Yangönpa] came to meet him, he would give him magnificent gifts and [show] great reverence.

He [would sleep] in the sleeping room with his head touching the pillow of His Presence [Yangönpa], letting him use his mattress and bedclothes; and all night he would joyfully talk with him. Sometimes, [while] sleeping in his presence, he would cheerfully say, "Is this bedding enough to keep us warm? In the past, the venerable Mila[101] had no more heat than this, either."

At age twenty-two, [Yangönpa] thought of becoming a monk,[102] and said that he had wanted to become a monk from the very beginning. Thus, he held the four ordained monks[103] in high esteem, and even as a lay practitioner, had a large retinue of monks and many disciples.

Moreover, [he thought that] since, in general, the root of the Buddhist doctrine lies in the community of ordained monks, the basis or foundation of all one's own spiritual qualities is to cherish and diligently train in a high standard of ethics. In addition, [after considering] the benefits of being ordained and the disadvantages of the [life of a] householder, he gave up all worldly life and developed a genuine ethical sense, intent on liberation.

Due to many considerations, he firmly resolved to become an ordained [monk], and, entering the presence of [Kotragpa,] the Master of the Teaching, he said, "I request ordination." [Kotragpa] replied, "Ho! This is very good. A great monastic community will grow in Latöd, and my humble self has established the favorable conditions for this; therefore, it can be done."

"Whom shall I ask to act as my preceptor?" asked [Yangönpa]. "You can invite the venerable elder Chowo Lha,[104] a stainless preceptor who has the three qualities of learning, morality, and goodness," replied Kotragpa, and [Chowo Lha] was invited.

[Kotragpa,] the Master of the Teaching himself, served as officiant, and Lama Tröchungpa[105] was invited to serve as the teacher who examines the candidate [for ordination]. The reverend monks were headed by many learned spiritual keepers of the monastic discipline. [In this way,] he was ordained in the presence of eighty pure monks.

As to the [ordination] name [given to Yangönpa, Kotragpa], the Master of the Teaching himself, thought of calling him Gyaltsen Palzangpo, and in these auspicious circumstances, gave him this name and empowered it. Then [Yangönpa] offered three prostrations to each of the reverend monks, without taking a break.

[Yangönpa later] said, "During the ceremony, when the words 'After the Sage of the Shakyas, Lion of the Shakyas, Chief of the Shakyas, was ordained ...' were spoken, I experienced an extraordinary sense of joy, my tears flowed, and the hair on my skin stood up [due to] genuine faith and devotion."

At that time, the Master of the Teaching dreamed that from the place where a pure white sheep stood, a great eagle rose in the sky and flew into the far distance; and also that he was giving instructions on the construction of several gold [representations of the] eight [auspicious] symbols and stupas. He said that these [dreams] were signs related to [Yangönpa's] ordination.

Then, when [Yangönpa] was recounting the extraordinary signs and experiences he had had through his spiritual practice, [Kotragpa] said, "These are like those previously experienced by my humble self while I was pursuing my own spiritual practice. Keep this in mind."

Also, one day, in the month of the horse, [Yangönpa] went to resolve a conflict that had broken out in Nyanam. In Tsade, a frozen place on the Thog pass, although he wore only a cotton garment, he suffered no injury; [on the contrary,] his face and body were more oily and shining than ever. All the worldly people were surprised and amazed. Many of his companions—even those wearing layered clothing and good boots—had frostbitten ears, and some had frostbitten feet. Hearing of these feats, [Kotragpa] was very pleased, and said, "Prior to this, he had a minor obstacle, but thanks to this [trial], it has been cleared away."

On another occasion, when [Yangönpa] was residing at Lhading, a message [from Kotragpa] arrived, stating: "My humble self is resolving a dispute, but I have just a bit less than enough wealth [to cover the compensation]. Therefore, to make up for the shortfall, send someone with six sets of the *Prajñāpāramitā [Sutra] in 100,000 Lines,* and all your most valuable possessions."

Just as he was told, [Yangönpa] sent the offerings of the doctrine and material goods [to the master]. [Kotragpa] said, "For us, father and son, food and wealth are but a magical creation. Can this fit into your mind? Look!" And, greatly pleased, he showed [the people around him] some large chunks of turquoise on the lap of his garment.

Later, while staying in central Tibet, he sent a written command [to Yangönpa] stating: "Since my humble self does not wish to live longer than the eighty-one years I now possess, you should come as quickly as possible."

When [Yangönpa] received the letter, the road was blocked by Mongol troops, so he could not meet [Kotragpa before he died]. But he said, "When it was time to rely [on the master], I relied; when it was time to please [the master], I pleased him. My teacher—the ancestor of all spiritual teachers—is the one who, with his splendor, outshines the three worlds."

To you, golden Blessed One, I bow.

Relying on authentic masters as your crown ornament,
With supreme faith and devotion, you filled the vase of qualities
*   to the brim.*
Unique son of all spiritual teachers:
To you, matchless mighty one, I bow.

He met and pleased nine excellent contemporary teachers.[106] In fact, with faith and devotion devoid of object or attachment, he won the hearts of his masters and received the individually transmitted blessing and benevolence of the profound Dharma, essence of the nectar of spiritual instructions.

The Precious One himself said, "I have relied on many authentic masters, serving and pleasing them. Anything they taught me, I held to be true; and [thus] I made them happy. The opportunity that you now have—to beseech undisputed teachers from a lineage not even momentarily stained by the broken *samaya* of displeasing [the teacher]—is your great fortune, my disciples. Moreover, at first, although I had the desire to meditate, I experienced a lack of spiritual instruction. I went through great hardships just to practice one type of instruction. Thereby, I have realized all the profound essential points that I am now revealing to you; there is nothing vague about this [teaching].

"Without any sense of loss, I have revealed to you only the profound instructions that I have personally practiced and experienced, which I received by offering a single mandala of gold. Immediate experiences and signs will directly arise from half a day's [practice] of even one [of these instructions]. I have nakedly revealed to you all the introductions.

"The essential points of [my] teaching are distinguished from others in that, if one is a meditator and practices in a genuine way, one will experience the benefit [of the teaching]. This is not bragging. Ho, children! Meditate, and see!"

Furthermore, he said, "Those who pile up bundles of wood, those who pile up packages of lac dye,[107] those women who leave things in disarray will not [experience] meditation. Also, there are not many lamas who reveal such teachings. But the teachings I have revealed to you in a natural way, I myself did not receive in this manner."

Like a vase filled to the brim, he attained the qualities [and realization] of many authentic masters, and having considered him as their supreme spiritual son, they conferred on him the blessing of the actualization of the ultimate meaning. Thus:

To you, matchless mighty one, I bow.

[Though] you're one and inseparable from the wheel of limitless
*   ornaments*
Of the very Body, Voice, and Mind of the undisputed siddha, glorious
*   Götsangpa,*
You pretended to invoke one another;
To you, who are no different from [Götsangpa], I bow.

Meeting Götsangpa, the Vulture's Nest Dweller

[Yangönpa] met the Master of the Teaching, Götsangpa,[108] the Vulture's Nest Dweller, whose fame and renown as a great siddha pervades the entire Indian subcontinent, and who is a matchless and undisputed master of the teaching, when, as a lay practitioner with five attendants, and dressed as a beggar, he made a pilgrimage to the monasteries of Shri [mountain].

Upon his arrival, he met Götsangpa, who was in retreat. When [Yangönpa] asked for instruction in order to establish a spiritual connection, [Götsangpa replied], "You are more learned than myself in spiritual matters, but if you wish, we can do [this]," and he gave [Yangönpa] an exceedingly profound instruction.

At that time [Yangönpa] was having doubts about something and was thinking, "Will this come about, or not?" [Götsangpa] understood [Yangönpa's thoughts], and cleared up all his doubts. [When this occurred, Yangönpa] thought, "This master has unobstructed clairvoyance," and he became strongly certain of this.

When [Yangönpa] asked him for blessing, [Götsangpa] said, "I do not know who has the greater blessing; you excel me in this. However, my humble self will give you [the blessing]."

That night, [Yangönpa] slept in the place [where Götsangpa was in retreat]. During the sixth two-hour period of the night,[109] in the first part [of dawn] when it was time to prepare the seat [for meditation], he clearly and distinctly heard the chanting of a lovely invocation. He wondered, "Who is that?" It was the Master of the Teaching, [Götsangpa] himself.

As soon as [Götsangpa] had finished his recitation, [Yangönpa] met with him, and said, "Please show me your face too." Götsangpa replied, "It is not worth looking at, but if it makes you happy, that's fine," and with his hand, he removed the cotton curtain [that concealed him], showing himself. There he sat, wearing an old, long, sleeveless shawl of woven wool fastened with a round sash, and [over that,] an old double-layered blanket with the yellow cotton layer on the outside. His hair was the length of a finger.

At the mere sight of [Götsangpa's] face, [Yangönpa's] ordinary consciousness collapsed from its depths, and there remained a powerful blessing through which he experienced things as insubstantial. Then [Yangönpa] went before the cotton curtain and said, "Please keep me in your mind." "Please come to visit me," said [Götsangpa].

When [he] went [back to his] monastery, the Lord of Dharma [Götsangpa] repeatedly asked the people around him, "Who was that person [who came to meet me] the other day?" They replied, "We have never seen anyone who has more merit than he."

Later on, [Yangönpa] went to Tengdro[110] and requested all the teachings of the Venerable Drugpa [Götsangpa]. [Along with Yangönpa,] the monks living at Tengdro also received many instructions, including the *Instructions on the Path of Method,* and the *Five Points That Dispel Obstacles.*[111]

When [Yangönpa] was living at Shri Namding, he heard that the Lord of Dharma [Götsangpa], who was residing at Tengdro, was slightly unwell. Thus, he created many auspicious occurrences with a miraculous nine-pointed vajra,[112] composed some four-line verses of invocation, and offered them [to Götsangpa]. At that very moment, [Götsangpa] recovered, and his health improved. After that, he invited [Götsangpa] to Lhadong and made infinite offerings and showed him infinite respect.

When the Lord of Dharma [Götsangpa] was staying at Ganden Ling[113] in Nyanam,[114] [Yangönpa] went to meet him. Before [Yangönpa arrived], Götsangpa had been having problems with his legs and was not able to stretch or bend them, but from the night they met, [Götsangpa] could once again stretch and bend his legs. He even stood up and walked around. The next morning when [Yangönpa] went to see him, [Götsangpa] said, "A sick man has risen from his crookedness. You are very kind," and he engaged in conversation with [Yangönpa].

[Götsangpa] also said, "Emanation of the buddhas, [you] took as your master one such as I, a beggar without qualities, from far away, and served me uninterruptedly with great faith and devotion, filling my home with wealth, and enveloping me in brocade. I will keep this in mind; you have great kindness," and he kept his palms joined [in prayer].

"Please do not praise me so," [said] His Presence, at which [Götsangpa] displayed some agitation and repeatedly moved his upper body saying, "This is not flattery. You are a real emanation of the buddhas; even my humble self can understand this. I have equal faith and devotion toward [all] three: Chöje Repa,[115] Chöje Drigung,[116] and Chökyi Gyalpo [Yangönpa],[117] and I also invoke you equally. I have a reason for this."

His Presence [Yangönpa] set his mind on [practicing at the] Shri hermitage. Lhadong was near [his native] village, so first he went to [Lhadong] monastery, but he did not like it [there]. During the time [Yangönpa] was changing his retreat place, the Lord of Dharma [Götsangpa] left Tengro and went to Lhadong with three attendants who were in spiritual retreat at Bhuta hermitage. "The King of the Teaching is not in Lhadong [now]," [said Götsangpa], "but [since] the power of the monastery is alive, and nonhumans are present as densely [as clouds], I will stay here for a while." And that is just what happened.

At a later time, when [Yangönpa was about] to enter the state of peace that is the great transcendence of suffering—the last of the twelve deeds of a buddha—in conversation with each other, they each revealed their wish to pass away. Thus:

To you, who are no different from [Götsangpa], I bow.

Three masters and the ḍākinīs foretold to you
The chief of all sacred power places,
And [you yourself] beheld [its] wondrous signs:
To you who, in that supreme place of practice, achieved the two aims,
*   I bow.*

Experiences in Retreat

As to the amazing and supremely glorious hermitage of Shri Namding, the mountains on its northern [side] have the shapes of vajras and bells; the rocks on its southern part have the forms of the eight [auspicious] symbols and of stupas.

Replete with the substances [required to attain and implement] the *siddhis*, it is a natural gathering place for heroes and ḍākinīs.[118] It is a charming and pleasant environment that [evokes] the clarity of pure awareness and the spontaneous arising of contemplation; [a place] where the mind may rest and be joyful.

It is a cliff resembling Śrī Parvata in the south,[119] widely known as Shri Cliff, a place where realization is attained; where many of the earlier masters—[such as] Togdens—who attained realization, had stayed; and where all spiritual qualities can be realized. This is the place, the chief of all the twenty-four sacred places,[120] where [Yangönpa] wished to dedicate himself to spiritual practice and manifest the fulfillment of all the qualities of the higher paths.

[With this] desire he addressed Kotragpa, the precious Master of the Teaching, asking, "Since I am about to practice, where shall I do it?" Kotragpa replied, "From Mount Kailash downward, there is no [better] place than Shri mountain for the clarity of pure awareness, so practice there."

And he asked Götsangpa, the precious Master of the Teaching, "Since my humble self is going to practice, should I do it in a remote place [such as] Tsari[121] or Kailash, or in a nearby place [such as] Pule[122] or Shri? Which is the most auspicious place?" [Götsangpa replied,] "I like Shri. From Shri there is even a view of [my] house in Tengdro." To this [Yangönpa replied], "Now I will do [my retreat] right in Shri."

He also met Rinpoche Pardrogpa[123] and discussed [his plan to] stay in retreat, asking him about a good retreat place. "I have an idea," he replied. "It would be good for you to stay in Shri."

Then, one autumn, he went to collect alms in Phadrug and examined the region. [There,] he slept in the garden of the king of the west.[124] At around midnight, [he heard] a formless voice say, "I will go to practice at Shri before [you]. If you don't go there quickly, you will not be able to go."

Prior to that, [Yangönpa] had thought: "Where shall I practice? On the way up, I will inspect [the area of] Dzarum, and if I like it, I will practice right there."

He hurried back, and arriving down in Lhadong, he reached Shri. There he remained for three days, searching for a place to build a hut. Then he found a large shelter in the rocks. He thought of building [an adjoining] wall out of earth and stones.

That night in a dream he saw the entire area of Namding as if it were daytime, and in the spot where his [hut] would [eventually] be built, there was a tent of swaying rainbow light. He thought, "What is that up there?" And someone said, "That is the place where you will build your hut."

The next morning, after breakfast, the Precious One thought, "Where could such a place be?" And as he went up [the road], he arrived at a place exactly like the one he had dreamed about, and there he built a hut.

In that place, he earnestly applied himself to the practice of approaching [the meditational deity, including the mantra recitation].

Except for the occasional hunter, there was no one wandering around the area, and it was not [even] possible to make a fire. The area was like an eight-petaled lotus blossom, the sky was like an eight-spoked wheel, and the foot of the mountain [looked like] a heap of thrones. Also, the surrounding rocks naturally appeared as mandalas and deities. At night, the place was cozy and reverberated with the various sounds of small and large drums, conch shells, and cymbals. Nonhumans gathered there like clouds. Thus:

To you, who in that supreme place of practice, achieved the two aims,
I bow.

Having cut off concepts [held by] worldly beings distracted by
material things,
For eleven months you sat in lotus posture.
To you who, [to achieve] enlightenment, in a single contemplative
state,
Brought energy-wind and mind under your power, I bow.

On seven occasions, [Yangönpa] stayed for various periods at the hermitage of Namding in the glorious place of Shri. The first time, once he had finished building the hut, he remained there in retreat. Nobody was able to speak with him or see his face.

[Yangönpa] did not sleep, and even cooked for himself. Every five days, someone would bring him water, and he would [communicate by] writing important matters on a writing tablet. Except for these activities, for five months he remained in one-pointed contemplation.

Then he thought, "To attain enlightenment in this very life, from the core of my heart, I need a spiritual practice [yoga], that is [uninterrupted] like a river's flow. Even attending to my immediate needs—such as cooking—slightly interrupts [my pursuit of] this objective. For energy-wind and mind to enter the supreme place [of the central channel], I must meditate one-pointedly over a long period of time, without body, voice, and mind remaining in their ordinary condition even for a moment. And for a long period of time [I must maintain] a strict practice uninterrupted by even a moment's distraction. This will purify all defects and fulfill all [spiritual] qualities. [Thus,] in my mind, I should generate [this] desired practice."

After these considerations, he decided to [sit] continuously in the vajra posture[125] on the same seat inside his small hut.

Directly facing his bed, he made a small window through which to take in [things that were left for him], and for eleven months he sat without relinquishing the vajra posture.

Ordinary practitioners would have found this difficult [to maintain] for one day, and would not have been able to tolerate it even until midday. [Even] if they were [able to tolerate it by] generating willpower and perseverance, they would have experienced many problems, such as stiffness or swelling. Except for the glorious, great Ga Lotsawa[126] and the Precious One [Yangönpa] himself, I have never heard of anyone performing such a feat.

During that time, he became gravely ill with a fever that brought intense pain to his upper body, and he thought, "This time, I will probably die; I will die in a shining yogic posture, without releasing the full lotus posture, so the great meditator will not make a poor show of himself."

To his helpers, he said, "Bring me a bucket of water, and do not come or send anyone else for three days."

[He did] this not because he wanted the illness to worsen, but [he] exclusively applied the reversing meditation[127] in order to see how much stronger the pain could become, and how much his mind could withstand it.

[Yangönpa] himself said, "Having meditated on many paths of method, my energy-winds have indeed become manageable. Now, when I block them, I can do so in half a day, and the tips of my ears stand up. These are signs that the karmic winds are dissolving in the body. Thus, by the weight of the upper [body], the lower body is unaffected by illness."

Even when, after relinquishing the vajra posture, [Yangönpa] stood up and walked around, he was unchanged.

Once during that period, when he went to Langkor, he experienced no problems with his legs, and arrived much faster than the others.

Then one day, he said, "Today I will present a play and put on a show. [First,] pile a heap of earth in the depression on the surface of this slab." Someone piled some smooth, soft earth there, and [Yangönpa] told him, "Sit there." He showed each one of his fingers in turn, and the [slab] moved straight ahead, then stopped. He said, "These [feats] are nothing to be amazed at. Do not report them to others!" And he gave them a strict injunction of secrecy.

On another occasion, one day a learned teacher brought some refined dark honey and some excellent hot water [to mix with it], but the honey became toxic, and when [Yangönpa drank it,] it blinded him and made his entire body go numb. "Although it is toxic, there is no problem," said [Yangönpa], and he performed a yogic exercise and recovered. Such are the inconceivable liberated qualities [that arise when one has made] the energy-winds and mind manageable. Thus, to you:

[Who] brought energy-wind and mind under your power, I bow.

Like sunlight, you illuminate the mandala of the knowable,
And have attained contemplation, visions, and the ten signs.
As foretold by the ḍākinīs, you were satiated by the siddhis'
*   essence:*
To you, powerful lord of yogins, I bow.

When [Yangönpa] was engaging in spiritual practice at Shri, his realization became constant by day and by night, with no distinction between the meditation session and the interval [between sessions]. All doors to the profound interdependence nondual [from the] real nature of the cause and result of all phenomena were opened, and his wisdom that knows the mandala of the knowable expanded.

[He himself] said, "My realization of the nonconceptual state leapt higher into that of the unique flavor."[128]

To recount this [in detail], even earlier, when performing spiritual practice in the monastery, he had recited some fourteen *lakhs* [of his deity's] mantra, and one night he had a vision of the Bhagavati [Vajravārāhī]. Her swine face[129] was slightly concealed by her hair, and her body was veiled by a black haze resembling smoke or clouds. [However,] her bodily form was quite clear. At the tip of the staff [that she held at her armpit] was a three-spoked, spinning swastika.

[Yangönpa] asked, "Do the slight obstacles [indicated by] the partial concealment of the swine face and the smoke-like [veil reflect] my shortcomings, [such as] interrupting the recitation by [speaking] ordinary words, or my laxity during retreat?"

At that time, he had been experiencing all the signs,[130] including smoke, mirages, and so on, but when he would go for his daily walk on the mountain to refresh himself, without encountering anyone, "Due to this alone," he said, "these [signs] would disappear." Therefore he thought, "If my body can withstand it, I will stay in the strictest retreat possible, in order to fully and rapidly elicit all the signs of progress."[131]

Later, while staying at Namding, he performed the preliminary practices[132] for one month, and thereafter recited [even] more mantras than before.

There, he considered meditating on the Seven Successive Points of Interdependence,[133] [but] that night he dreamed that [the female guardian] called Chomo Tragser told him, "Do not meditate on interdependence; instead, recite the mantra of the Bhagavati [Vajravārāhī] one hundred thousand times."

[Yangönpa] thought that "one hundred thousand times" meant reciting [the mantra] one hundred thousand times for each letter [of the mantra], so combining the recitation in a meditative state with the path of method, he mostly did the recitation while blocking [the energy-winds].[134]

He said that, from time to time, he also practiced vajra recitation.[135] During some of the intervals, he also did the recitation for "sending out and gathering in."[136]

Seated in the vajra posture, he promised daily to apply contemplation while holding the vase-like breath[137]one hundred times. [He later said that] by practicing in this way, "I did not need [to hold the breath] a hundred times; it was sufficient [to hold] the breath five times for half a day each."

As to quantity,[138] he did thirty-six lakhs of repetitions [of the mantra] without interrupting it with ordinary speech.

In between, he trained in the creation phase,[139] and said, "Even now, when I am in equanimous contemplation during the creation phase, when others look, they have the distinct impression that I am invisible."[140]

He had inconceivable signs of experience in such [practices] as the dream[141] and the illusory body.[142] One night while he was doing the [mantra] recitations, he heard the sound, "*si ri ri.*" He thought, "What was that?" Seeing vapor billowing from the special [skull-cup filled with beer used as a] support [for the practice], he lifted the lid and saw that the beer[143] was boiling. He drank the beer without attachment or concepts, and it had the effect of greatly improving his practice: his body was entirely permeated by bliss, and many auspicious circumstances came about.

Then, when he had completed the recitations, he offered a hundred Tantric Feasts,[144] and on the nineteenth day of the last [month] of the year of the Pig,[145] he had a vision of many bodhisattvas holding small cymbals[146] in their hands. Also, [he said,] "In the entire space before [me] I saw flickering letters."[147]

That evening, [when] evidence of obstacles caused by spirits[148] manifested, [Yangönpa] threw a skull cup full of beer that he had empowered. [The beer] hit a boulder in Lhaye, and flames flashed [up from it].[149]

[The next morning,] when he awoke at dawn and was thinking of starting his practice session, in the space before him, he saw the blessed [Vajravārāhī] appearing as a sixteen-year-old girl, with a blue face, holding a curved copper-bladed knife, and [adorned with] her characteristic ornaments and attire. [She] showed him the four examining signs,[150] and when he responded [to the signs], he had the experience of receiving an inconceivable blessing.

At that time, he composed the praise called *The Thundering Sound of the State of Union*. Knowing that all [experiences and visions] are the master's kindness, he wrote down the praise called *The Precious Sound of Thunder*. Then, at daybreak, [he experienced] a naked, clear state inseparable from his own wisdom, and [unpolluted by] conceit and attachment.

In Lhadong, when he was administering the levels of the vows, he had a vision of the eleven-faced Mahākāruṇika,[151] and the understanding that all the activities of the buddhas of the three times are present in the activity of Avalokiteśvara arose within him; thus, he invoked Mahākāruṇika.

[Moreover,] he had visions of both the Wisdom Mahākāla and the Action Mahākāla[152] who immediately accomplish one's necessary activities. He also had visions of countless [other] meditation deities.

Inspiration for the *Hidden Description of the Vajra Body*

The Precious One himself said, "First, I meditated a great deal on the empty enclosure.[153] [Then,] by the power [my] training in the pure illusory body, I actually saw the condition of the vajra body— [with its] stable channels, moving energy-winds, and positioned vital essences—just as it is. This is why I composed the *Hidden Explanation of the Vajra Body*."

Having seen the colors of the energy-winds of the five elements, calculating [the cycles] of the energy-winds, he was able to know the times of the solstices, and so on. [For example, once when] someone conversant in Kālacakra astrology[154] made a calculation, the Precious One knew that the [calculation was] inaccurate, and later [said], "I corrected it accordingly."

Dreams and Visions

One night in Lhaye, five ḍākinīs came to him. Among them, a tall ḍākinī, light blue in color and [wearing] lovely ornaments, sat by him, continuously kneeling.[155] [At a certain point,] she woke him up at his pillow, saying, "Great Being, wake up and sing a song! Offer a Tantric Feast to us ḍākinīs." And the [other] four ḍākinīs who stood there chanted melodiously, "Wonderful! Great Being, Fortunate One …"

On another [occasion], while seated in the vajra posture, in the pilgrimage month[156] of the year of the Pig, he reported having many wonderful dreams, including the following: the Precious One himself was riding a lion up a mountain, holding the sun and moon in his hands, and flying back and forth in the sky performing a variety of miraculous feats.

After that, when he woke up, a ḍākinī came into his presence, and he said, "Give me the *Teaching on the Profound Hūm.*"[157]

Also at this time [he reported], "Five wisdom ḍākinīs from the great charnel ground of Herin [gave me] their blessings." [All this is more than] the mind can conceive. Thus:

To you, powerful lord of yogins, I bow.

In an instant, you saw the Gandhavyuha pure realm of Akaniṣtha,
Oḍḍiyāna, Lhasa, Samye, and other places,
And all invisible dimensions:
To you, amazing marvelous one, I bow.

The Precious One himself said, "I have had great experiences in the dream and illusory body [practices]; I have seen all these pure realms while training in the dream [practice]."

To explain, the Gandhavyuha pure realm of Akaniṣṭha[158] appeared to him in the following way: a divine mansion, square, with four entrances adorned with archways, and many goddesses who, [walking] on the ledges,[159] [were presenting] many offerings.

The five red ruby layers of the [mansion's] walls [were] unmixed, with a distinct exterior and interior. The cornices were made of precious gems, and [on the walls] hung lattice works and tassels of various kinds of silk scarves. [The mansion] had balconies and balustrades. Above [the mansion] was a blazing pinnacle [made] of the precious *doli*[160] gem.

Within [the mansion] hung a canopy of divine multicolored silks, and tassels [strung] with various kinds of white and red pearls.

Beautiful and captivating to look at, it was a totally luminous [phenomenon] with no distinct interior or exterior. By looking at it, it was impossible to measure even a single dimension, [but] to the mind it appeared very distinctly square.

Inside, on a ground of multicolored flowers, there were thrones [supported by] lions, elephants, and so on. It seemed [to Yangönpa] that these thrones were speaking the words of the Dharma, [but] he did not see the buddhas [seated on the thrones].

"Because I saw this divine mansion," he said, "my meditation on the mandala, and all my Dharma activities directed toward others, became distinctly superior."

Also, he said that in the victorious palace, the abode of the thirty-three [gods],[161] he beheld Devendra Śakra [Indra flanked by] the thirty-two gods, [his] retinue of royal vassals, and so on, enjoying a variety of divine pleasures.

Again, in the land of Oḍḍiyāna[162] to the west, he [saw] the chief [ḍākinī], the blessed Vajrayoginī,[163] encircled by ḍākinīs wearing a variety of ornaments and attires. Most wore bone ornaments, but there were also [ḍākinīs] wearing ornaments of both precious stones and of bone; there were also some who wore no ornaments.

He said, "At times, these [ḍākinīs] appeared in my mind to be very numerous, beyond mental reckoning; at [other] times, they were few enough to be counted."

Moreover, in dreams he saw the locale of Lhasa, the Trulnang temple,[164] and the Ramoche temple,[165] as well as the two Lords,[166] the array of butter-lamps, and the other offerings [in these temples], and thought: "Ho, such things exist!" Later, when he visited central Tibet, he saw these things just as described [in his dreams]; it was a great wonder.

Also, he said that when he had a vision of Samye,[167] on the circumambulation path around the temple he [saw] a woman with long hair, wearing a red dress. She was striking various poses with her arms and legs while reciting a particular teaching that, later on, he could not recall.

When he felt a sincere desire to meet the precious master, he would have visions of entering his presence and meeting him. One night, [he dreamed] that he was going to meet him in Langkor, and saw the master [appearing] as if he were ready to go to sleep. The moon was white and bright, and when he ascended from the lower teacher's residence, he encountered a man along the road who approached [him], carrying a beer jug. "This man probably did not see me," he said.

Once, he was staying at Namding during a very wet and humid summer. It rained constantly, day and night, for twenty-five days, and due to the fog that contained droplets of rain and to the absence of sun, he felt slightly unwell. At that time, he was principally [engaged] in the successful practice of the yoga [known as] "the luminous clarity of [actual] realization." Occasionally, by the force of his awareness of the luminous clarity of [meditative] experience, he reported distinctly seeing a subtle brightness [pervading] the interior of his hut, with all the fine details [of the objects clearly visible].

At times, he would see a country as large as Rangön, and at others, an even larger one, [as clearly] as if it were daytime.

Later on, he also said that, by consulting his dreams, he could see the location of the Mongol camp and the Mongol army.

To you, amazing marvelous one, I bow.

You know and can describe beyond words and reckoning
The far and near; the past and future;
[That which] goes and comes; and the actions and actors in the three
*   times:*
To you, omniscient one, I bow.

Just as one equipped with eyes [can] see a form, with the mind that is nondual wisdom, directly and unimpededly, he could see the mandala of all the knowable in the three times. Yet, if someone had asked him to recount [his visions], he would say, "If I were to tell, it would contradict your [experience] and broaden the divide [between your perception and that of] the teacher. This is why I now speak in a rough, indirect manner.[168] If a master were to describe what he sees to the ordinary beings of this degenerate era, they could not be [adequately] held in his care."

"Also, if one were to truly describe one's qualities, including one's previous lives and so on, just as they are, it would be like revealing the fact that one is an incarnation. [Such an] undisguised revelation would displease the ḍākinīs. The authentic masters of this degenerate era are the actual presence of each of the eighty-four mahasiddhas, lords of yogins. But for the reason I just mentioned, I do not explicitly say that I am [an incarnation]."

Once or twice, he said that in the previous life he had been born in central Tibet and had possessed greater qualities and charismatic activity than [he did in the present life].

Once, he said that, in a house belonging to his previous incarnation, there were bundles of felt that he himself had placed side by side to cover the surface of the wall.

Demonstrating Clairvoyance

On one occasion, while he was at Lhading teaching a ritual for auspiciousness called *One Sufficient for All*, he said, "If we [are to] sincerely apply the spiritual teaching [that prepares us] for the moment of death, we need to relinquish [distracting] activities; put an end to our desires; be content with what we have. And, alone, in the seclusion of hermitages, [we must] reflect on the liberation stories of the siddhas of the Kagyüd [tradition]. Having set aside [concerns for] body and life and reduced our need for food and clothing to the barest minimum, we must practice for a prolonged period.

"Previously, while staying at Tramonkar, I made fifteen pounds[169]of mixed barley and wheat suffice [to sustain me] for three months." Then he said, "Gompa Chölo, where are you?" There was a commotion among the crowd [of people] who, overcome with great devotion, had come [to listen to] the conclusion of the teaching. Then, Gompa Chölo, who was right there amid the crowd, declared, "I am that one [Gompa Chölo]."

Once, while explaining the *Mountain Teaching* in the context of the Mahāmudrā to twenty people, [Yangönpa] became excited and said, "Through the kindness of my authentic teachers, I have come to understand this profound reality. But to those of you who say that I don't comprehend it, I tell you that my tongue has become [so] stiff [from] teaching [Mahāmudrā] during three of my previous lives [that I] can no longer speak [properly]. Any mistakes I might make here and there in [my teaching] may be due to this."

While staying at Shri, he said, "To a certain extent, I know the goings and comings of your thoughts. There is no need for you to tell me about your spiritual practice; I know. I know by your countenance."

[Once,] when he saw that a meditator who, feeling somewhat satisfied with his spiritual practice, was becoming distracted by everyday activities, [Yangönpa] told him: "Don't do this. You need to progress by applying methods that advance your wisdom." Also, seeing that [this meditator] was not making the torma offering in a continuous manner, [Yangönpa] told him, "You must not do this. You should avoid bringing harm to sentient beings."

One day, many practitioners [attending] an offering ritual by Lama Tröchungpa[170] came and assembled [outside] the little window [of the retreat hut] of His Presence. [Yangönpa] performed a fine *gaṇacakra* and received many written [explanations] on effectively applying the practice of profound teachings. On that occasion, [before they arrived], he had said: "From below, many people are on their way up; they all are going back to their place."

He [also fore-] saw that eleven people would be coming up from the lower Omphug valley. After a while, eleven yogins sent by lama Omphugpa arrived to pay their respects [to Yangönpa].

Another [time], he reported a vision of Gompa Chökyi Pal emerging from his grass hut, performing three prostrations, and coming to him carrying a sheet of white paper in his hands.

[Yangönpa experienced] these and other inconceivable and utterly indescribable signs of clairvoyance. Moreover, after just giving it some thought, he would make notes for his attendants on whether or not the meditators around at that time were in good health, whether or not they had sufficient food, and whether or not they had everything they needed, and the attendants would act [accordingly]. Thus, it was often evident to all that there was no need to make a specific request to him on such matters.

Again, while he was staying at Lhadong, an important lama was coming to visit the Trin hermitage. One day when the lama and his attendants had reached [a place] between Tomakha and Tragtse, Yangönpa asked, "Are you not going to welcome [those who are arriving]?" The few people in his presence thought this was a joke, but shortly thereafter, [the lama and his attendants] arrived.

On another day, he said, "Today, prepare a seat [and] sharpen the knives; some food is on its way." After a little while, the wife of the master Chöbum arrived, bringing [an offering of] a cooked animal carcass, a bag of roasted barley flour, [a delicacy made with] sweetened butter and cheese, and a bag of yogurt made from the [milk] of a female yak.

One day while he was staying in [the hermitage of] Pule, [an attendant] had prepared a stew of mountain garlic. When he thought of serving it, he noticed that the stew was not quite cooked. He started to cook it some more, but the tripod shifted and the clay pot of stew fell over, spilling [stew] all over the fire and extinguishing it. As a vortex of ashes filled the entire house, [the attendant] became distressed. He threw the [remains of the] fire outside, cleaned the pot, [and prepared the stew again]. He went to tell [Yangönpa] that he had finished preparing the food. Knowing [through clairvoyance] what had happened, [Yangönpa] said, "Don't be sad. This was a trivial obstacle that has [now] been removed."

Also, while he was staying in Lhading, the wife of the [resident] teacher requested to meet him. His Presence was staying in retreat, [but] when she asked, he told [her] to come. When she came inside [Yangönpa's] retreat house, he was nowhere to be seen. [Since] he had not gone anywhere else, she thought: "What, then?" and looked everywhere, but he was not there. Then she performed prostrations to the Three Precious Jewels, and, thinking of reciting the sevenfold prayer, she half closed her eyes. [When she heard a voice] saying, "Has the lady come?" [she saw that] Yangönpa was sitting on his bed. Then again, as she half closed her eyes to do prostrations, he was no longer there. At the end of the third prostration, she opened her eyes. She said that [Yangönpa] was there, exactly as he had been [before].

Moreover, [occasionally] he would say, "Today something unusual will happen"; or, "[Someone] will be bringing such and such food or gift." Everything he said would unfailingly come true. These events were inconceivable and indescribable. Thus:

To you, the all-knowing, I bow.

The leading arrogant worldly deities bowed down to you,
The nāga king requested teaching; and nonhuman local spirits
Respectfully vowed to assist and to obey your orders:
To you, a refuge for all, I bow.

Giving the Dharma to Humans, Nonhumans, Ḍākinīs, and Local Deities

While he was staying at Shri, the five Sister Goddesses of Longevity[171] came to meet him and made outer, inner, and secret offerings to him.[172] Then, in response to their request to establish a profound connection [with him], through the blessing of his teaching, he chanted songs of realization, while among the rocks, hosts of ḍākinīs gathered to listen. To a few of them, he also sang the songs of the five classes of ḍākinīs.

One day, when he was offering the water torma[173] to Jambhala,[174] he thought he heard the squeaking of a mouse, and when he looked in the bowl of the [water] torma, he saw a bubble [resembling] the round bulge of a highland meadow. Inside [the bubble] appeared the protector Jambhala, yellow in color, holding a jewel and a pouch containing a mongoose in his hands, and adorned with precious ornaments. Yangönpa thought, "Of what use is wealth to me?" and he threw away the water. "Although I don't need wealth, when I am in the emptiness of the snows, everything I need descends like rain."

Moreover, at that time, he established a connection with most of the local deities by [giving them] material goods and instruction. One night, together with his retinue [in the form] of five men riding on horses, [the local deity] Chowo Lhase came to [Yangönpa] and performed three circumambulations. Dismounting the horses, they did prostrations. Then they told him, "For three years, the Mongols will not come to [invade] this region," and left. Later, that is just what happened.

When [Yangönpa] was offering torma and reciting the Discourses [of the Buddha] to nonhuman local guardians, they would gather like clouds to listen to his teaching. The nonhumans gained respect for the Doctrine. After hearing his discourses, they would depart without turning their backs to the open pavilion.

The nonhumans also gained a greater desire to listen, and became conscientious. [For example,] a large pavilion had been constructed when [Yangönpa] was performing hundreds of gaṇacakra offerings. Some people recklessly approached, while the [nonhumans] who came to take the torma of the gods and demons did not dare to enter the pavilion.

[Yangönpa reported that] while reciting to a noble-type white nāga[175] who had come down from upper Shri, the words [from the] Sutra Essence of Wisdom[176] "in this way should [all phenomena] be considered …," [and while] teaching [the nāga] to meditate, [the nāga] remained quiet in meditation. But when [Yangönpa] introduced him [to the nature of mind] and checked whether or not the nāga had understood, [he saw that the nāga] had an animal's proclivities and did not wish to be so introduced.

Also, later on, whenever His Presence was giving the Dharma, nonhumans who gathered like clouds to listen could be seen by ordinary diviners, if they looked.

Another time, while [Yangönpa] was staying at the mountain hermitage of Pule, the local deity of Pule came riding on a white horse, holding a flag and a spear. A snake's head protruded from the large top of the flagpole. [The local deity] said, "I will be your patron and give you all the offerings [I receive]." Having proffered these words, he left.

The local deity of Gangmar would welcome and accompany the master whenever he went to Tingri.[177] He also frequently came to visit Yangönpa here [in Pule]. Thus, it is said that His Presence's two powerful local deities were Pule and Gangmar.

Also, at Shelkyung, ordinary diviners observed the local deity of Dringtsam going to and returning from Latöd. When they asked him where he had gone, he replied, "I went to Lhadong, [where] the Precious One was performing a ritual." Later, when Yangönpa went to Dringtsam, he said: "This is where that important deity who came up here resides."

On one occasion, [through his clairvoyance, Yangönpa] saw that a few thieves were stealing a considerable amount of wealth from the temple in Lhading. He exposed the thieves and, through his own power, made them powerless. There [in Lhading], when he was performing the ritual of casting off the torma at the great offering festival in the horse month,[178] the guardian of the Dharma, the Action Mahākāla, [appeared] with his gaping mouth, bared fangs, bulging red eyes, and body hair standing on end, expressing great joy. Then, not long afterward, three of the four thieves died of knife wounds. [Yangönpa] felt much compassion, and said, "I felt no anger toward the thieves. Now, by reciting many prayers and protecting them with compassion, I must make sure that they are not going to the lower realms." Thus:

To you, a refuge for all, I bow.

To repel the savage hordes of the Mongol army,
You arranged 3,300 tormas,
And exhibited many displays and emanations:
To you, victorious war hero, I bow and [offer] praise.

Protecting the People from the Mongol Invasions

The Precious One himself said: "My disciples, when [I knew that] the Mongols would not be coming, I spared you the suffering of having to flee in all directions: to the Slate Mountains, the snow mountains of Ngari,[179] Bhutan, and other regions of the eastern Himalayas. When the Mongols did come, it was a great mercy that you did not have to face them.

"Others, [alarmed by] exaggerated rumors of the Mongols' [immanent arrival] when they were not coming, fled and suffered. And [later,] when the Mongols actually arrived—just as [if] it they had an appointment with them—they stood before them; so some were killed, and some taken [prisoner]."

One day, when [Yangönpa] was staying at Shri, he said, "On the south side of the bluish rock that looks like a curtain hung on a back wall, facing west in lower Shri, many men [of the Mongol army] are assembling."

Then he took up residence at the Glorious Lhadong monastery, and his fame and reputation spread widely. Followers and riches gathered like clouds. The minds of the most meritorious disciples were spiritually moistened by a great rain of Dharma and worldly wealth. In fact, like a wish-fulfilling gem or a wish-granting tree, he effortlessly fulfilled all [his disciples'] wants and needs. And then, when the time came to train the disciples, engaging in the appropriate altruistic activities, he cared for and guided them in the manner described below.

Due to the power of the peoples' shared karma, the Mongol and the Peri[180] armies [invaded,] causing great destruction and turmoil. The Mongols arrived at Dam[181] and killed everyone they saw. They took everything of value that they could find. They burned every house. They destroyed all temples and monasteries. They were particularly aggressive toward monks and nuns. There were a few people among them—perhaps one in a hundred—who could translate Tibetan or who just might [have known] the spoken language, but they knew neither the Mongol's laws nor customs.

Just hearing the name Tartar or Mongol made people lose the ability to stand on their feet. People were as frightened and terrified as if they were caught in the hand the Lord of Death who enforces [the law] of karma.

Since the people had no protection and no source of hope, with boundless great compassion, [Yangönpa] untiringly took up the burden of others' suffering. Reaching every region, day and night, he constantly gave advice and brought happiness.

"We are beings of the degenerate era with inferior merit who, sharing the same karma, have gathered together. Therefore it is said that, for the welfare of beings, masters, buddhas, and bodhisattvas who liberate us with their compassion will manifest through various emanations.

"Thus, invoke the teacher and the Three Precious Jewels that are our protection, refuge, and source of hope. Accumulate merit, the remedy for lack of merit; observe the [eight precepts] for a day;[182] recite the six-syllable [mantra].[183] In each large household, do one recitation of the [*Large Discourse on the*] *Perfection of Wisdom.*[184] In [each] medium-size household, recite the *Twenty Thousand Line Discourse [on the Perfection of Wisdom]*. In households of just one single woman, do one recitation of the *Eight Thousand Line Discourse [on the Perfection of Wisdom*], or *Dharani of Realization*. Let's make a big torma offering; bring a lot of roasted barley flour." [Thus] he gave much advice, and all was followed.

He brought an end to the worries of wartime; everyone became happy and [came to have] faith in him. Thus, they did whatever he told them to do, and thus he relieved [their anguish] by pulling them from the jaws of the lord of death. Thereafter, for any important purpose, they sought no other method, but invoked the infallible refuge, the definitive teacher [who embodies] Three Precious Jewels.

The Great Torma and Other Great Offerings

To marshal the forces and power of the guardians who protect the white Dharma, he made a huge torma offering, using more than three thousand large measures[185] of barley [flour].

He went to the place he described earlier [the bluish rock in the Shri valley], set up many strands of white and black yak hair, and built a large fireplace. The Buddhist monks, laymen, and Bönpos who inhabited the populous villages collected all the flour, butter, and equipment necessary. And there, on a concave plateau resembling a torma tray, he prepared the torma.

To make the dough for the torma, [first,] on a meadow that was as flat as a battlefield, he had the flour piled up. The water [to be mixed with the flour] was conveyed in many copper vessels from a sizable village. After washing their hands and feet, several strong men from a large village kneaded the dough with shafts,[186] shovels, and pickaxes.

After washing their hands and feet, many monks piled up all the torma dough [on the plateau].

In the center, they arranged the large, high torma [dedicated to] the higher supramundane [deities]. Below this, like the terraces on a round stupa, they arranged the tormas resembling a circle of eight auspicious symbols, with broad bases, and with many red and white tormas as tips dedicated to the powerful worldly guardians who protect the Dharma. Below this, they arranged the tormas for the local deities, the local *tsen*,[187] the guardians of Bön, and so on, as above. Even though a high ladder with thirty rungs had been placed on the last terrace, it was not [long enough] to reach the lower level of the torma, so in order to bring things up, [people] had to climb by stretching out their arms.

The dough was piled up in about fifty levels [one above the other], and sitting on top of it was like sitting atop a small hill or slope that was the highest point [in the vicinity].

White, red, and multicolored tassels, and the silk scarves for the Mahākāla and other tormas, resembled the Bön *gyangbu*.[188]

The torma ornaments consisted of several bodies and torsos. First among them were three fresh corpses; several kinds of precious objects such as gold, silver and pearls; many precious gems such as turquoise, copper, and armor; many balls of molasses packed in goat skin; packages of dye; several skins of wild animals including tiger, leopard, and lynx; many white foods such as leather bags full of butter; a mixture of butter, cheese, and sugar; yogurt and milk; many kinds of sweets, such as sugar and honey; various medicines, such as the Six Excellent Ingredients;[189] various kinds of grain; and various kinds of nectar, such as the nectar of immortality.[190] The tormas were arranged and embellished with these substances.

Anyone approaching the torma experienced the blessing as a shift in their ordinary consciousness, an ephemeral mental state like [that which occurs] upon the descent of wisdom [during] empowerment. [Miraculous signs] also appeared on the torma display itself.

[Yangönpa] invited the prominent spiritual teachers of Sutra, Tantra, and Bön from the local monasteries and villages, and gave them countless offerings and [demonstrations of] respect.

As for the [actual] dedication of the torma, [Yangönpa] instructed [each of the various groups of practitioners] to employ the specific ritual of their own tradition to offer the torma.

Therefore, everyone [dedicated the torma] in their particular way. Wearing the [three] Dharma robes and the patched loose mantle,[191] the monks circumambulated in procession, holding parasols, victory banners, and scarves; playing conch shells and cymbals; [chanting verses] invoking the power of truth; and so on.

The Tantric practitioners "opened" the mandalas [by performing the rituals] of their tradition, such as that of the Peaceful and Wrathful Deities. Holding drums, hand drums, a vajra and bell, a skull with a tuft of hair,[192] skull-cups, and sheathed ritual weapons, they perfectly performed their own rituals.

The Bönpos, holding tiger skins, eagle's horn, drums, and flat bells, dedicated the torma according to the proper Bönpo tradition.

The clan leaders, local officials, and so on, and the inconceivably vast crowds of people, wearing [fine] clothes and ornaments, provided various entertainments such as folk dancing[193] and singing, dance dramas, women's left-circling pantomime dances,[194] dances with masks, and the lion [dance].

Through a very powerful meditative state, His Presence personally consecrated and actually dedicated the torma. When it was time to cast off the torma, through the power of the blessing, everyone present could not help but become excited, and when they loudly played their cymbals, the people saw many different manifestations of the Precious One. Some people saw one Avalokiteśvara sitting on each of [Yangönpa's] shoulders; others saw the Precious One as Avalokiteśvara himself; some saw him in a wrathful aspect with bared fangs; and some saw him flying back and forth in various ways in the sky.

A person said [of Yangönpa], "When the torma was being cast off, without his feet touching the ground, he ascended into midair, performing various poses, threatening gestures, and powerful gazes. Wherever [he] went, I too went below [him]."

[Another] person said that during this time [Yangönpa] went nowhere, but remained seated on a throne right before him. Most of the people shared the perception that he was right there [among them] in the huge gathering.

Before the torma was cast off, a huge dust storm arose from the locale of the torma [offering, showering dust] on the guests present, and then departed to the northeast. This torma kept the Mongols away for three years.

The crowd assembled there was the largest single gathering ever witnessed in the area. On that occasion, even though the crowds used [all] the resources borrowed from the [entire] kingdom, [the resources] were never exhausted. This was due to the blessing [of Yangönpa].

After that, at Lhadong [Yangönpa] instituted four practice sessions in which various rituals were performed.

Then, planning to make a great offering to invoke the Three Precious Jewels, he invited everyone from Kala to Kolung who had ritual knowledge. He also had the sacred statues and images from the Shri valley brought [to Lhadong].

[The incense offering ranged from] large incense sticks, the diameter of slender pillars, protruding [from incense holders shaped like] the mouths of crocodiles, and so on, to the smallest, the diameter of bamboo pens. Some 1,100 of these [incense sticks], as long as a writing board, [were offered].

[Also among the offerings were] one thousand butter-lamps, fifteen pounds of flour for [making] tormas, and one thousand ornaments made of butter. With these and other offerings of five types, thrice replenished, he performed offering [rituals] for an extensive period.

Thereafter, he gave instructions to all his disciples, without distinguishing the old from the new, to apply whitewash to the stupas and to the eight [auspicious] symbols. And following this, in many temples and monasteries, he established the offering of [lamps using] large quantities of butter and vegetable oil. In particular, he fully restored old temples that had no caretaker. Through the blessing of these activities, at Dringtsam,[195] the Mongols turned back and did not come to the region [of Shri].

He promised, "Now, for three years, the Mongols will not come here," and put this in writing. And it happened exactly as he had promised.

But then [after three years], he foresaw that the Mongols were coming. He did not announce this, but behaving as if disgusted [by something], he gave away all his possessions.

From statues and images of the Body, Voice, and Mind [of the enlightened ones], to all the material goods in his possession—including cooking utensils, large metal teapots, salt boxes, and fire pokers—he offered the most valuable into the hands of supreme teachers, while donating the remaining items to various monasteries. He gave individual donations to the community of monks, and organized great banquets for the lay people.

After five days, the Mongols came, but [Yangönpa] said: "Now we can stay where we are; we don't have to flee anywhere." On that occasion, [the Mongol army] from Pongshöd galloped to Cheshe, and departed.

Then, during the year in which the official Hurta arrived, [Yangönpa] was staying at Shri in spiritual retreat. At that time, His Presence thought that unless he moved down [to Lhadong], the region would not be accorded [its due] consideration and respect, so he went to Lhadong.

There he advised the chiefs and the people of Latöd on how to conduct themselves in order to gain respect. Everyone heeded his words, and the [improved] conduct appropriate to high, middling, and lesser chiefs was a gift of the Master of the Teaching. Thus, through the kindness of this master [Yangönpa], the entire region of Latöd came under [his] protection. Thus:

To you, victorious war hero, I bow and [offer] praise.

Sole friend of beings, embodiment of love, you resolved internal conflicts
And [disputes] in village communities [fueled] by hatred,
Nurturing our world with happiness and spirituality:
To you, gracious Lord Avalokiteśvara, I bow.

Resolving Conflicts in Troubled Times

In the land of Tibet, a few years before the Mongols arrived, due to the peoples' bad karma, the force of evil actions [spurred by] attachment, anger, and ignorance increased, resulting in the increasing outbreak of conflicts typical of bad times. The whole country became like an island of cannibals.

During this time, [Yangönpa] was impartial to all, with a love for living beings like that of a mother for her only child. Thus, with great compassion and overwhelming loving kindness, he resolved all types of disputes, major and minor.

The Precious One personally resolved major and minor conflicts occurring in the communities of Tsa and Kong; the conflict in Kal; the fight between Nor and Kog; between Gya and Dre; between Dre and Ngog; between south and north Trangpo; between Meu and Mögog; between the peoples of Yoldong and Tsonkhor; the internal conflict in Agtso; the fight between the communities of Töd and Sur; between those of upper and lower Pongshöd; the fight in Khog, Nawa, and beyond; the fight between the peoples of Tagpo and Kong who'd been punished for breaking the law, and so on.

When he resolved the conflict between the communities of Tsa and Kongched, he returned the goods [that had been confiscated] in the lawsuit [against] the inhabitants of Kongched who had been held responsible for beating [the people of Tsa]. That is, [he] returned many scriptures, beginning with two sets of the precious *Prajñāpāramitā Sutra* [written in] gold, and twenty-eight [copies] of the *Prajñāpāramitā Sutra in 8,000 Lines;* large copper cauldrons [for water]; horses; [monastic] cloaks; and so on. He also provided fencing material, restored houses, filled the homes with riches, provided horses for the chiefs and attendants to ride, and gave them cloaks to wear and turquoise to [adorn] their necks. Moreover, he appointed both parties—particularly the people of Kongched—[the task of] restoring seventeen monasteries and sites [belonging to those who had been] beaten.

He provided a [home] place for the three thousand people of Tingri and Nyanam who had been displaced [by the fighting], and compensated the [families] of the 170 people who had died. To make up for the [unpaid] wages owed to six thousand bricklayers, he thanked them with feasts, so the wages did not have to be paid. He took care of those who had been stripped of their armor, and the wounded, by giving them the appropriate goods.

The gifts of food and wealth [that he donated in order to resolve] large and small disputes are inconceivable and beyond reckoning. He pacified the anger that blazed like fire by compensating [the families of] those who had been killed, paying for that which had been stolen by thieves, giving a [home] place to those who had fled, elevating those who had been humiliated, and so on.

In all regions, he prescribed regulations for [promoting] harmony: rules of husbandry, laws concerning theft, prohibitions of the killing of wildlife, and regulations for roads. And he donated goods to the many places where merchants set out their wares, and to the families who had many children. On dangerous and frightening roads, he organized escorts to take people down from the Dridu pass and up from below the Thog pass; thus, he made them safe.

He had inns built for travelers who had no companions; he built bridges [across] rivers where there was no bridge.

When he began to build the dike for the bridge at Ngampa, in order to inspire others [to participate in such works], His Presence himself carried the stones, earth, and so forth.

Later, when he had built the dike for the bridge at Titung, beneath the bridge, the Pong river deviated to one side, leaving not [even] the blood from the river fish. A huge gathering of people carried earth in the bottom of their tunics and filled in the place [where the river had deviated], so that the waters were made to flow beneath the bridge as before. This was understood to be the blessing of the emanation of the buddhas [Yangönpa].

No matter which of these works he was doing, [his mind] was no different from omniscient wisdom; thus, he lacked neither knowledge nor vision. In each undertaking, great or small, he was assisted by the three [types of beings]: gods, spirits, and humans. Therefore, he accomplished all important enlightened activities without effort or struggle.

The various activities in which His Presence was involved—such as consistent observance of the times for doing spiritual practice and instructing the excellent community of monks in learning, reflecting, and meditating; advocacy for the benefit and happiness of the country; and other [activities] relating to law, support, and mediation—did not conflict with one another, for his mental intentions were effortlessly realized. This is called, "opening the doors of enlightened activity." Thus:

To you, gracious Lord Avalokiteśvara, I bow.

On the glorious mountain, you met the unborn Shang;
At Lhading monastery [you made] a rain of Dharma fall
  from the sky;
While you dwelled at Yangön, the precious Drigung [master] arrived;
To you, inconceivable master, I bow.

Meeting Shang Rinpoche in Dreams and Visions

It is said that lama Shang Rinpoche[196] and His Presence have been
master and disciple through many previous lives. In this life as well,
[Yangönpa] was equally devoted to him as a root teacher. Thus, he
never failed to perform offering rituals in his honor on the prescribed occasions.

[Yangönpa said], "I also invoked him when my realization was
not progressing; when I was refining my training in the dream practice; and when [I was engendering] the altruistic mind of enlightenment. Even now, when I invoke him, I meet him [in visions], and
see him often at night in my dreams. Therefore, I have no need to
ask others for the transmission of lama Shang's teachings. This is
because Shang Rinpoche has blessed my mind."

[Yangönpa] said that on one particular occasion he was blessed when a manifestation of lama Shang's body, [emanating] from
the pure realm of Suvarṇadvīpa[197] in the west, dissolved into him.

Another time, while staying at Shri Rangön, one night he invoked Shang Rinpoche, and so in his dream he saw him sitting on
a huge throne, with a silk bandana tied around his head and a white
parasol [above him]. He was supported on the right and left by two
ḍākinīs. Before him was a great assembly of monks, lay practitioners, and mendicants. Feeling great joy and unimaginable devotion,
[Yangönpa] did prostrations and then went before him. Lama Shang
Rinpoche was eating something that looked like a torma. He gave

His Presence something that he could not identify [resembling] a tiny grape, the size of a sesame seed or the seed of the Himalayan mayapple.[198] As soon as Yangönpa put the [seed] in his mouth, in the sweet shell he tasted a hundred different flavors that his tongue had never tasted before. In the morning, while he was still in bed, the taste was still on his tongue and between his teeth, and there it remained for a many days. He said, "Even nowadays, when I am healthy, I have that taste [in my mouth]."

At that time, Yangönpa said, "He gave me the teaching on the *Secret Dream Practice.*"[199]

Yangönpa said that one night when he happened to be sleeping in front of the clay statue of the western direction at Tsal Kungthang,[200] he invoked [Lama Shang] and then, in a dream, he met him and received a great blessing, teaching, and prophecy.

Again, when he was staying at Lhading, one night [these words from] a profound teaching resounded from the sky: "There are no phenomena that are dependent and born," and so on.

Once, people were saying that the Mongols had arrived in Pongshöd, so everyone prepared to flee. But a girl appeared in his dreams, and told him, "You relax; it is alright for you to [continue to] sleep." He told his attendants not to hide the next morning's provisions, and said, "You should continue to sleep." The next day, [the people's talk] revealed itself to be an empty rumor, and just as [Yangönpa] had said, [the Mongols did not come].

Again, he said that one night he received a prophecy from a female [local deity] of Langkor called Majo Shachungma. And one spring, while staying at Lhadong, he dreamed that Drigung Chenga Rinpoche[201] came to his residence in Lhadong and sat in the Precious One's bedroom, wearing fine clothes, and brilliant, with a radiant smile. Moved by the force of intense faith and devotion [Yangönpa] joyfully performed many prostrations to him. And, clutching the mandala dimension of his body, he dreamed that he received from him the blessings through the hands and feet. He reported that the next morning, his meditation practice was greatly enhanced.

The next year, he went to Drigung,[202] and the spiritual father and son met in the turquoise house. The two [events]—his dream and the actual meeting—occurred in the same month and on the same date; this alignment, he said, was a great wonder. Thus:

To you, inconceivable master, I bow.

Sakya Pandita, undisputed [scholar] of the five sciences,
Entrusted you with the secret instructions on sutras, tantras,
*   and treatises,*
And foretold and appointed you their holder:
To you, ocean of teachings, I bow.

Meeting the Great Sakya Pandita

When the lama, Master of the Teaching, the great Sakya Pandita,[203] came to Kungthang, traveling on the lower road to Sakya,[204] he stopped at Menkhar. The Precious One was staying at Lhading, and hearing that [Sakya Pandita] had come, went there with his attendants to meet him.[205] [But] since at that time he had promised not to enter towns and villages, he put up a sleeping tent at the outskirts [of Menkhar], and there he stayed. He invited [Sakya Pandita] to come, and made great offerings, demonstrating great respect. In the evening, they engaged in a long conversation, and [Sakya Pandita] gave him many Dharma transmissions.

That night, the Master of the Teaching dreamed that several girls were circumambulating Yangönpa's sleeping tent; after doing that, some of them were leaving. The Master of the Teaching was holding a thick cloak in his hands. When he thought of putting it [on Yangönpa], the circumambulating girls were happy; those who had finished circumambulating him and were leaving, were sad; thus, he dreamed that [Yangönpa] was wearing [the cloak] pleasingly on his body.

[Sakya Pandita] told [Yangönpa], "Some more auspicious events have occurred, indicating that we have a profound connection. Keep our meeting in mind."

Sometime later,[206] [Yangönpa] went to the glorious Sakya [monastery, where Sakya Pandita gave him] many initiations, such as those of Cakrasaṃvara, Hevajra, and others; the reading transmissions of various sutras and tantras; and many extraordinary instructions. [Yangönpa] also received many oral instructions on the *Hidden Explanation of the Path*[207] that had been entrusted directly by Virūpa[208] to the Great Sakyapa[209] [through visions], and which were unknown to others. He also gave Yangönpa many other authentic teachings.

"I have entrusted all these teachings to their owner," said [Sakya Pandita]. "So bring beings to maturity and liberation by conferring empowerments; explaining the tantras; revealing the oral instructions; and [teaching] the unmistaken profound path of the authentic doctrine whose essential points are flawless."

His Presence asked, "Should I give the empowerment after I complete [the prescribed mantra] recitation?"[210] Sakya Pandita replied, "You may give the empowerment even if you have not done the [mantra] recitation. In many previous lives, you had visions of countless meditational deities;[211] thus, you have already done the recitation. Give the empowerment to all who request it."

[Yangönpa explained to Sakya Pandita,] "Previously, I practiced such and such oral instructions on the Path of Method, and enjoyed such and such benefits and experiences." [Sakya Pandita replied,] "It seems that you have mastered them. Regarding [the path of method,] here are such and such oral instructions," and he taught them to [Yangönpa]. [Sakya Pandita] said, "Keep them in mind. Even the names of these oral instructions are unknown to those who've spent their entire lives practicing the Dharma in the Sakya [monastery]."

The Master of the Teaching said, "Never have I seen in others the wisdom experiences; realization; charismatic activity; and life story such as yours, Precious One. I hope that my [nephew] Phag-pa[212] will become like this."

Whenever [Yangönpa] would enter his presence, [Sakya Pandita] would have a seat arranged for [Yangönpa] and would demonstrate his respect. He would address [Yangönpa] exclusively by the appellation Precious One, and fold his hands. He would also encourage the prominent persons and learned spiritual teachers in his presence to stand up, offer prostrations, and show respect [to Yangönpa]. Exhibiting an esteem unlike that which he accorded anyone else, [Sakya Pandita] entrusted [Yangönpa] with the responsibility of holding the teaching. Thus:

To you, ocean of teachings, I bow.

From the heart and face of the sacred Buddha statue,
An incomparable blessing in this world,
Shone multicolored light rays that dissolved in you:
To you, amazing matchless [one], I bow.

Wondrous Experiences in Lhasa

The Magical Apparition Temple of Lhasa,[213] actually built by the sovereign emanation of the bodhisattva Mahākāruṇika, king Songt-sen Gampo,[214] [houses] the golden statue of Buddha Śākyamuni. Fashioned out of various human and divine precious materials by the divine artist [Viśvakarmā],[215] it was brought to Tibet by [the Chinese] princess [who was an] emanation of the venerable Tārā.[216] This statue, which was consecrated by the Buddha himself, is renowned in our world as an incomparably great sacred object.

[Other sacred objects in this temple include] the Chowo Akṣobhya,[217] a [Buddha statue] consecrated by the Buddha Kāśyapa;[218] the statue of Maitreya turning the wheel of Dharma;[219] and the self-originated sandalwood statue of the venerable Tārā brought [to Tibet] by the Nepalese Princess[220] [who was an] emanation of Bhrikuti Devi.[221] These statues are [considered] self-originated, based on them being divine works of art.

Also [in Lhasa] are the statue of the eleven-faced Lord [Avalokiteśvara][222] into which king [Songtsen Gampo] and his two wives dissolved, the eight divine statues that actually emit light rays, and others.

On his way to Drigung, [Yangönpa] went to Lhasa to make invocations before these amazing sacred objects. The residents of Lhasa gave him a warm welcome, offered hospitality, and asked [him to stay] for a thanksgiving ceremony.

The Drigung Rinpoche told him, "Do not stay in central Tibet, but come straight to Tsang." Since it was such a strict order, and since [if he attended the thanksgiving ceremony] it would postpone his journey for six days, he left without attending.

While staying [in Lhasa], during the day he would do nothing but perform prostrations, circumambulations, and recitations of the sevenfold prayer. At night he slept before the Chowo statue, and the face of the statue became utterly luminous as never before.

After three days had elapsed, the statue [began to] emit many multicolored but predominantly white light rays from the heart, mouth, and tuft of hair between the eyebrows, which dissolved into Yangönpa. All the many visitors in the temple saw this multicolored light, and became exhilarated and amazed. In particular, the people circumambulating outside, including the female devotees and others, were called inside to see [the light]. When the female devotees, various others, and the groups of the faithful [saw the light], they were all very surprised and amazed. Then, the Precious One said, "This event alone made coming to central Tibet worthwhile."

To you, amazing matchless [one], I bow.

The omniscient master dwelling in the turquoise house
Had foreknowledge of your coming, welcomed you, displayed great
*   kindness,*
And said: "I invoke you as the joy and happiness of samsara
*   and nirvana":*
To you, in the unique state of the reality dimension, I bow.

Yangönpa's Spiritual Father: The Drigung Lama

The following describes how [Yangönpa], the spiritual son, met his spiritual father, Drowai Gönpo Chenga Rinpoche,[223] the Victorious One of the three times. [Yangönpa] said that long before he met the Drigung Lama Rinpoche, he felt an extraordinary devotion toward him and was pervaded by the kindness of his blessing.

Later, the hermits of Chuwar made this request [to the Drigung lama]: "In Latöd in Tsang there is a teacher called Lhadongpa. Although he is young, he has great merit. [Please] create the auspicious conditions so that he can come into your presence." They asked [the Drigung Rinpoche] to perform a torma ritual [for this purpose]. [The Drigung lama] replied, "There is no doubt that he will come here at some point."

That year, the hermits asked [the Drigung lama again] to perform the torma rite, and requested that he send a letter to [Yangönpa] inviting him to enter his presence. At this, [the Drigung lama] said, "There is no need for a letter; soon he will come."

A day before [Yangönpa] arrived, a man came to Drigung to search for a hut [and, seeing him], the mountain-dwellers said, "This is probably not he, [but] perhaps it is his chief disciple, his brother, or both." When they offered the torma, the attendants [of the Drigung lama] informed everyone that the man was [Yangönpa] himself. [The Drigung lama told the hermits,] "To meet this great being tomorrow morning you ought to be in good condition, so stay in your homes doing spiritual practice. It will also be good for my humble self to do spiritual practice." Then he placed his seat on the ground, and the practitioners of Tsang joyfully prepared to welcome [Yangönpa]. At Nagtsang, without even taking time for tea, while [Yangönpa] was having breakfast, someone came to call on him to [ask him to] come to meet [Drigung Rinpoche].

In the glorious turquoise house, the palace of Akaniṣṭha, the Precious Teacher rose from his throne and stood on the ground on his tiger skin and [humble] monk's seat of matting, wearing the robes and the patched loose mantle of a monk. [Then] having taken three steps, [he] said, "This is my humble self's welcome to you." Then they exchanged prostrations and symbolic gifts.

His Presence sat on the throne while a seat was being arranged for the Precious One directly before the mandala of the [Drigung Rinpoche's] face. Yangönpa sat on that seat [made of] four mats piled one on the top of the other, and revered [Drigung Rinpoche] with the offering of tea.

[Yangönpa] said that, at that time, he was confident to speak as freely [to Drigung Rinpoche] as an elder son [to his] spiritual father, or a student to his teacher, and their minds merged together [as one]. He said that although on that occasion, there were eighteen thousand students thinking, "I am the lama's heart son," he felt the exultation of being cherished.

"I actually beheld all the qualities of Body, Voice, Mind, and charismatic activity of that master, and my mind received [his] blessing. [At this,] the hair on my body stood on end, and tears fell from my eyes. It was a great joy to meet such a master in this degenerate era. Thinking, 'I am the one who has accumulated the merit for this,' I felt proud."

[Drigung] Chenga also said, "I will keep our dialogue and related conversations in my mind. Thank you. I am most grateful." [Yangönpa replied,] "Thank you. I will keep the answers and related conversations in my mind." Many such [words of mutual] praise were spoken.

The Precious One's heartfelt devotion also overwhelmed the minds of [Drigung Rinpoche's] leading disciples, causing them to burst into tears. They remarked, "With such devotion, how could he not receive the [master's] blessing and acquire the spiritual qualities? We ourselves never possessed such devotion," and they rejoiced in admiration [for Yangönpa].

Then, one day, [the Drigung lama] gave him a meditation hat and a set of clothes, and seated him on a high throne. When he saw [Yangönpa] wearing the meditation hat, he said, "Oh! How beautiful [he looks in] the meditation hat. Here is someone who, having been a great meditator in many [past lives,] is [now] an ultimate [yogin]." When [the Drigung lama] said this, [Yangönpa] took off the hat, but [the master] said, "Do not take it off; wear it while you meditate."

[The Drigung lama] quickly gave all the spiritual instructions and, skipping the [daily] ritual prayer gathering for monks, he gave the profound essential points to Yangönpa alone. [The Drigung lama] said, "[Now] that you have all these profound essential points, it is the same as if everyone possessed them." Having emphatically taught the system of yogic exercises called *yantra*, he said, "You need this. When you will have in your charge an assembly [of students] vast as the ocean, make them practice these yogic exercises."

[The Drigung lama] said that [his exchanges with Yangönpa] were like the many spiritual talks held between the master Phagmo Trupa[224] and Jigten Sumgyi Gönpo[225] when they met.

Furthermore, [the people of] Drigung were stricken with a grave disease transmitted by the [local drinking] water. This disease affected the legs, and remained for years. [Yangönpa's] legs were affected by this illness, causing him great pain. [But once] he remained in retreat for ten days, he was completely cured of the illness. [Drigung] Chenga, very pleased, said, "The ancient masters such as Changtang Repa would be astonished by a feat such as this. He has given an example of asceticism to all 'sealed ones' or great meditators." All eighteen thousand students were delighted, and [Yangönpa's renown] as a great siddha spread.

Because he won over the master's [mind] with his devotion, the teachers and practitioners said that none who had come to Drigung had ever done this, and they regarded him with esteem. He was placed at the head of the eighteen thousand students, was offered prostrations, and was honored by everyone. Each day he attended [the master's] teaching, and each time he revered the master.

Even when [the master] was in secluded meditation and was not seeing anyone, his door was unguarded, and whenever [Yangönpa] came, he was allowed in. [Drigung Rinpoche] gave [Yangönpa] the copious offerings he had received, as well as five gold coins in the evening and in the morning [to use] for his various needs.

One day, while [Yangönpa] was staying at Namkha Ding, he went to meet [the Drigung lama] and received many extremely profound teachings and delightful words. [The Drigung lama] said, "I think that if the precious Jigten Sumgyi Gönpo were alive, he would feel proud of this master's devotion, spiritual practice, and ocean-like qualities." The Precious One [Yangönpa] replied, "I don't need to have water in my mouth thinking [with regret] that I have not met Jigten Gönpo. Precious Master, [you] are the actual Jigten Gönpo." Smiling, [the Drigung lama] said, "Well, that may be. Since my humble self has [received] the authentic teachings of Jigten Gönpo

198878888

and those of the glorious Phagmo Trupa and their spiritual sons, what you say may be so."

Another day, when [Yangönpa] came to attend the teachings, before the explanation of the "vital essence" was complete, [the Drigung lama] felt a desire to get up [and leave]. Thus, he said, "For the teacher [Yangönpa], it suffices to give the vital essence in one session. For this master, one day of meditation yields greater results than many years of meditation would for others. From whichever perspective one regards it, [the life of Yangönpa] is in no way different from the liberation story of the precious Jigten Gönpo as a young man."

Whenever [the Drigung lama] saw that [Yangönpa] was sitting on the ground without a mat, he reprimanded his attendants and ordered, "Prepare a seat quickly! It would not even be too much to arrange a seat supported by lions," [he] said.

Although [the Drigung lama] was usually very strict as far as [giving] the Dharma, he would give the Precious One anything he requested. The Drigung [lama] would get excited and say, "Since the Precious One from Lhadong—who possesses the spiritual eye, who is a holder of the Dharma, and whose mind is like a vase brimming with an ocean of qualities and teachings—is present, I am eager to teach the spiritual way, and I cannot but reveal all the profound [points]." And the monks and nuns would fold their hands and say, "It is due to your kindness that we are receiving such teachings."

[The Drigung lama] privately taught the other profound instructions to Yangönpa alone. He would say, "As a service to the master [Yangönpa], in one year I have given [him] all the teachings—without exception—that I received while devoting myself to Jigten Gönpo for twenty-four years. Omitting nothing, I have thoroughly imparted all the teachings; [now] my mind is content."

One night, after completing [the transmission] of a profound teaching, he folded his hands and said, "Without even the minutest exception, I have given the Glorious Lhadongpa all the teachings of the precious Jigten Gönpo."

From that time on, [Drigung Chenga would say that] the two who possessed all the teachings of the Precious Master[226] without exception, were master Phagmo Trupa[227] and the Precious One from Lhadong. And this was undisputed.

Then, the spiritual father and son sent infinite gifts [to one another], and Gompa Shagrin gave a [farewell] talk. [The Drigung lama] installed [Yangönpa] as the sovereign of all who wore a meditation hat in the region of Latöd.

[Drigung] Chenga said that when [Yangönpa] was leaving, he felt such great fondness for the Precious One that he could not bear his leaving, and felt as if his heart was being split in two; but [Yangönpa] had to leave.

With a big smile, [the Drigung lama] said, "You have a master like me to invoke. You will spontaneously accomplish wondrous benefits for yourself and others. I am the lord Phagmo Trupa as well as the precious Jigten Gönpo. Gompa Shagrin, have I ever boasted like this before? Now that all my auspicious circumstances have been set in place, I feel that, come what may, everything will be accomplished."

Then, when [Drigung] Chenga stood up, His Presence said, "I will go to Namkha Ding." [The Drigung lama] told [his attendants], "Escort him as far as he is [still] within sight of my humble self." But since the attendants escorted [Yangönpa] for only a short distance, [when they returned, the Drigung lama] scolded them.

After [Yangönpa's] departure, every time [the Drigung lama] gave profound teachings, he would say, "The one who perfectly understands all these is the Precious One from Lhadong."

To you, in the unique state of the reality dimension, I bow.
Like swans converging on a lotus lake,
The vast communities of spiritual practitioners of the ten
*   directions—*
Prominent persons, learned spiritual teachers,[228] and ordinary
*   monks—*
All came to touch their heads to your feet:
To you, whose time to tame disciples has come, I bow.

Coming of Age as a Great Spiritual Teacher

The root of the doctrine of the Sage [the Buddha] is the community of spiritual practitioners. Thus, in order to support such [a community] in accordance with this doctrine, [Yangönpa] took care of every [monk and nun], including the most ordinary little monks. Considering them as his supreme spiritual students, he looked after them by giving them food, clothing, and spiritual teaching.

To new students, he provided everything from clothing and food supplies to donations for preceptors and teachers. For senior students too, who were engaged in study, he scheduled study periods, provided books, indicated subjects to be explained, and so on. To the [hermits] who dwelled in the mountains, with great delight, he sent various gifts such as retreat provisions, travel necessities,[229] tea for the road, and flour.

For those men and women spending years practicing in his presence, he would provide necessities for the practice within [the monastery]. To any of the spiritual teachers or prominent people of the region who came to meet him, he would give provisions, money, and hospitality, and during their stay [would provide them with] spiritual teaching and material necessities. With the five excellent certainties[230] he made the act of supporting the spiritual community [of monks and nuns] a priority.

At that time, there was no one of higher, average, or lower status interested in spiritual matters who did not come to meet him or have a profound connection [with him] through devotion.

To you, whose time to tame disciples has come, I bow.

King of the Teaching, ruler of the spiritual domain,
You revealed the vast, profound meaning of sutras, tantras,
  and treatises,
The state of realization of the Sage just as it is:
To you, Lamp of the Teaching, I bow.

This master, king of the Teaching, touched the feet of all the excellent teachers of the central and western Tibetan provinces, received their impeccable spiritual instructions, and, by applying them, became adorned with genuine inner experiences.

Having gained mastery of the wisdom [that knows] all phenomena, and of the words and letters [that communicate such wisdom], he fearlessly assumed the lion-supported throne amid an ocean-like gathering of disciples.

[From that throne,] in one voice, he taught the spiritual ways that accorded with the minds of different types of people, and each one of them heard [what he was saying] in his own particular language.

In the divine voice of Brahmā, his teaching consolidated all three divisions of the [Buddha's] doctrine[231] and four classes of tantras[232] into three precious trainings,[233] which arose instantaneously in his mind along with quotations from scriptures, reasoning, and secret instructions. Even a single word from his voice [of] experience could open the gate to all teachings, [conveying] the extraordinary meaning of the sutras and tantras: the extensive and the profound, the unheard of, the heretofore unexamined, consistent in every respect, and especially exalted.

He turned the wheel of the Dharma [in a way] that left listeners stunned, with a feeling of inner warmth, bringing joy to the learned and awakening faith in the ignorant.

Anyone who heard this teaching, which possessed spiritual vision, would irresistibly feel devotion and develop faith, thinking, "This master really is an omniscient Buddha," and would acquire a definite understanding of the Dharma.

His words [even] reached the minds of any ignorant people who listened, and were understood by all. Some, just by hearing his words, were set free from suffering. Some, just by hearing them, experienced a natural state of meditation. Some, just by hearing them, [banished] impurities from their spiritual vision, causing the lotus of flawless perfect intelligence to bloom.

Even ordinary people would abandon their habitual lifestyle and, inspired with faith, their minds would connect with the spiritual path.

Such an exposition of the doctrine has not often occurred in the [human] and celestial worlds; does not often occur in the present; and will not often occur in the future. [It was an exposition] in which each four-line verse conveyed, in an orderly fashion, the complete and unerring path to the state of omniscience. His teaching was like a great lamp of the Doctrine. Thus:

To you, Lamp of the Teaching, I bow.

You [joined] the unbroken lineage of enlightened beings,
And the lineage of blessing, transmitted one to one,
Of the undisputed Kagyüd, unrivaled in the world,
And [thus] spontaneously recognized the innate [bliss],
*   the secret path that gives immediate protection:*
To you, who planted the victory banner of the practice lineage,
*   I bow.*

If one invokes you, Body essence of enlightenment, reality dimension,
Inseparable from the mind-mandala of the Four Precious [Masters],
Everything one thinks, needs, and desires will manifest:
To you, jewel-like master, I bow.

[Yangönpa received] the unbroken transmission [stemming] from the great Vajradhāra and leading up to the precious Drowai Gönpo,[234] passed from one enlightened being to another enlightened being; the lineage of the siddhas; and the lineage of Togdens,[235] the unbroken close and distant transmissions passed from one individual to the next, uninterrupted by [any] dog [-like individual].

Generally speaking, there were some twenty-four masters with whom [Yangönpa] had a spiritual connection. Among them were four undisputed and incomparable Precious Lords. The essence of the Lord of the Family[236] was the Precious Lord of Drigung.[237]

Through his invocation of this master, father, and son[238]—essence of the sixth buddha Vajradhāra,[239] essence of the five *kāyas*[240]—all the qualities of body, voice, and mind simultaneously came to [fill Yangönpa] like a vase filled to the brim. Through the blessing of the indivisibility of their minds, [Yangönpa] joined the end of the row [as the most recent holder] of the Kagyüd [tradition] that transfers the wisdom of realization, the ultimate transmission. Now we, too, need to train in keeping with, and retain [at least] a fragment of [this master's] life and liberation story.[241]

The predominant theme of his life was that, through intensive practice in the seclusion of mountain hermitages, he became filled with a vast measure of qualities, and then actualized his own and others' benefit.

In the early part of his life, the Precious One devoted himself exclusively to spiritual practice in such places as Lhadong, Shri, Lhading, Tricham, and Pule. Even later on, when he was engaged in great charismatic activity, he would spend four summer months and four winter months in retreat. During these eight months, he would spend the first half of the month in semi-retreat and the latter half in full retreat. If he was unable to do this, he would continually remain in semi-retreat doing only spiritual practice. He would spend the other half of his time teaching.

When he was leaving for some destination, and also along the way, he would always unfailingly pay homage and make offerings to sacred images of the Body, Voice, and Mind.[242] At these times, too, during the pause between formal meditation sessions, he would arrange a sacred image; offer a mandala,[243] light, and incense; and recite the sevenfold prayer.[244] [Thus,] he never skipped his formal meditation sessions.

Wherever he was staying, even if there were various distractions, he would do the following daily practices without missing a day: the [sādhanas of] blessed Cakrasaṃvara male and female in union,[245] of Hevajra, of Vajrakīlaya,[246] of the eleven-faced Mahākāruṇika,[247] of Uṣṇīṣavijayā,[248] of Tārā,[249] [and] of the Profound Meaning Mañjuśrī. [He would recite] the liturgy of the guardians of the Dharma with its mantra recitation, [perform] the torma food offering, [recite] the daily confession, [recite] the taking of the vows, [practice] the receipt of empowerments of meditation,[250] [recite] the Kusulu accumulation of merit,[251] and the extensive verses of dedication and aspiration. [He would] replenish offerings twice each day and night,[252] [perform] the morning Surupa torma offering,[253] the midday water offering to Vasuka,[254] the sixty-four-part [torma offering], the five-part [torma] offering, the ten-part [torma offering], the sessional torma [offering][255] at dusk, the one thousand torma [offerings] on the full and new moon days, the seven inner torma [offerings] during the night, the Cakrasaṃvara offering rite on the tenth day of the waning moon, the inner offering to the Victorious [Vajravārāhī][256] on the tenth day of the waning moon, [the sādhanā] of Uṣṇīṣavijayā on the eighth day of the lunar month, the [sādhanā] of the seven Medicine

Buddhas on the night [of the eighth day of the lunar month], the offering ritual to the earlier masters, [and] the offering on behalf of deceased parents. [He would offer] the twenty-one tormas, [recite] the *King of Meditative Stability* [*Sutra*]²⁵⁷ in one session, annually [perform] the offering of 108 gaṇacakras [at the same time], annually [perform] the108 fire rites²⁵⁸ [at the same time], annually prepare and empower nectar pills,²⁵⁹ [and prepare] 108 votive images daily. During [the astrological conjunction called] Wangpo,²⁶⁰ [he would recite] *The Large Prajñāpāramitā in 100,000 Lines,* the reading of the Buddha's words. During [the astrological conjunction called] *Hari*,²⁶¹ [he would perform] the sādhanā of Amoghapāśa. [He would recite] a level of the vows on each new moon day,²⁶² [and recite] the engenderment of the mind of enlightenment during [the astrological conjunction called] *Chabo*.²⁶³

He gave empowerments and teachings without interruption. He made a promise never to refuse [giving alms] to any beggar he met. Even when seemingly engaged in various [potentially] distracting activities, he never stopped the [above mentioned] practices. In all circumstances, he would spend his time in meditation or spiritual activity. This was the inconceivable lifestyle of this master, Lord of the Teaching.

The Precious One himself said, "From Vajradhāra, the sixth Buddha, to my four great Precious Lords, [all my teachers] belonged to the lineage in which the teaching is transmitted from one person to one person only, and [these teachers] were inseparable from the essence of the unique Mahāmudrā that is the dimension of reality [dharmakāya].²⁶⁴ Thus, if one invokes me fervently each month, those of the highest [ability] will attain realization, those of average [ability] will have [genuine] spiritual experience, and the lowest too will grow somewhat disillusioned by the worldly life or, to some extent, receive my blessing. If this does not occur, I have been telling lies. [Like] a poor sack with an excellent hanging strap, I have had teachers who are siddhas in the Kagyüd [tradition]." Thus, [as] a master, he was like the fabulous wish-fulfilling gem that satisfies [all] who invoke him but once. Thus:

To you, jewel-like master, I bow.

In the second summer month of the Tiger year,
For seven days, you remained in contemplation,
[Nourished by] the food of meditation, needing no coarse food,
And to the devotees, gave strict orders:
"Do not come, and do not speak to others."
For nine days, you stayed in one [continuous] meditative state,
As various signs and wondrous magical displays appeared.
On the fifteenth day of the waxing moon, the day of the yogini,
On the earth, in midair, and in the sky,
ḍākas, ḍākinīs, local guardians, and nonhumans
Offered incense, butter-lamps, and clouds of offering,
With song, dance, and music:
To you, marvelous blessing, I bow.

Glorious Heruka, sovereign of blessing,
With the wrathful deities' nine dance moods,[265] you outshone
     the three existences,
With vajra laughter, subjugated the three worlds;
And through various emanations, annihilated vicious beings.
[While] dwelling in the hundred [doorways] of the nondual mind's
     contemplation,
The four motions of the outer, inner, and secret connections
     aligned,[266]
You eliminated all demonic obstacles and conquered the dark forces.
[Then] a sphere of glorious light blazed all around,
And filled the billion-fold universe, illuminating the three worlds;

Its multicolored rays, infinite and indescribable,
Manifested and reabsorbed, brilliant and luminous,
And long remained for all to see:
To you, inconceivable wonder, I bow.

In the summer of the year of the Tiger, when [Yangönpa] was staying at Shri, he told his attendants and disciples to quickly prepare
some [provisions]. When the [disciples] earnestly did as they were
told, he was pleased, and recited pure prayers of aspiration. At that
time, he spoke to no one. He wrote [a message] to his attendants
[stating] that he had an important matter [to address], and that for
a few days he would do some sacred spiritual practice. Therefore, he
gave a strict order, "During this period, put a lock on the outside
of [my] door, and, until the sound of the gong is heard, even you
should not enter, neither let anyone else enter."

On the second evening at dusk, loud thunder that persisted long
and without interruption, came from the east and traveled to the
west; and from the west, moved to the northeast; and was [heard]
in the south and north. Light, lightning, sounds, and various other magical displays occurred. At dawn, there was a heavy snowfall.

On the ninth day at dusk, the area was surrounded by waves of
incense fragrance, by sounds like the footsteps of a great gathering
of people, and by many indistinguishable humming sounds.

That night, around midnight, there was a droning musical sound
that could not be said to be this or that. When the people went to
see [what it was], above [Yangönpa's] house they saw a sphere of red
light emanating rays of various colors. By the light of that sphere,
one could see the entire area of Namding as if it were daytime, and
the whole interior of [Yangönpa's] house and courtyard was visible.

The longest light rays from the [sphere] radiated very far, while
the mid-length ones [radiated] farther than the range of an arrow.
The shortest [radiated for] one fathom. At times the light appeared

in the shape of a small book; at times, as a vase or clay pot. Wondering if this was an optical illusion, people would look again and again, and it was [always] the same.

The sky resounded with various kinds of music, such as that of large cymbals, drums, conch shells, small cymbals, hand drums, lutes, and flutes. At times the music seemed to be nearby; at times it seemed have gone far away.

There were also sounds of various mantras, such as those of the male and female deities; [the mantras] *Hūṃ Hūṃ, A A Ha Ha Phaṭ Phaṭ,* and *A La La,* and waves of fine incense fragrance.

On the ground and in midair, many beings were performing circumambulations. Indistinct in the details of their forms, these beings whirled up and down. During that time, because of the blessing, I,[267] too, experienced a condition in which my mind was at ease in a state of meditation.

Everyone heard the music, while the light, incense, and sounds were perceived in a similar way by many people.

The next morning, just as it was getting warm, when the sound of the gong was heard, the students entered the presence of [Yangön-pa]. His physical condition was excellent. His body was even more radiant and luminous than before.

He said, "My health and meditative state have greatly improved." They informed him that they had seen such and such [displays] on the previous day. ["Oh, yes,"] he remarked, "Someone must have seen them."

For these nine days, he neither ate nor slept, but remained motionless in a single yogic posture. Within the single state of contemplation of the nonconceptual mind, he crossed many thresholds of meditative absorption.

His body became the body of the glorious Heruka Cakrasaṃvara, powerful lord of the three existences: he manifested ḍākas and ḍākinīs numerous as the sky is vast, and revealed their nature;

he subjugated the three worlds with the nine joyful moods of dance; and he performed the dance that pervades all [the three worlds].

With extreme ferocity, he annihilated all the vicious beings using the implements of the wrathful [deities]; and in order to remove his own and others' obstacles, he made the Dharma protectors serve, in general, as Dharma guardians, and made them enact [specific] deeds. By aligning the motions of the outer, inner, and secret interdependent connections, he turned the wheel that masters and dominates the phenomena of samsara and nirvana.

By manifesting infinite emanations, and from these other emanations, he inspired faith in future generations. And in order to reveal the enlightened beings' deeds and [leave] evidence [of these deeds] in the environment where [they had taken place], he left his footprints in a white rock.

Knowing that, during that period, he had benefited others with countless emanations in inconceivable pure realms, [his attendants and disciples] asked him, "What kind of contemplation were you in at that time?" He replied, "It was an undivided equanimous contemplation not interrupted even for an instant by discursive thoughts."

The disciples asked, "Is this a state in which one always abides in the absence [of a divide between] meditation and post-meditation?" He replied, "In the practice of Mahāmudrā, there is no meditation or post-meditation; it is a contemplation in which each of its infinite doors has a unique quality."

[The disciples again] asked, "What kind of contemplation is it?" [Yangönpa replied,] "Since it is inconceivable, [even] if I were to explain it to you, it would not be comprehensible. It does not come about through mind-made fabrications. Don't listen to vain and foolish talk; it comes of long maintained protracted meditation. But don't ask [any more] questions about it now!" Thus:

To you, inconceivable wonder, I bow.

Yangönpa's Passing

Then he performed the last of the ten deeds of an enlightened being, the great passing away into the state of peace. Thus, in order to broadly benefit the beings of other realms, and to exhort those who think their life will go on forever [to forgo] laziness, he manifested his passing.

[Around that time, Yangönpa said to his disciples,] "From the beginning, I made few promises as to the length of my life; I will not live long; the disciples are more numerous in other [worlds]. Even if [I have] a short life, it does not matter, [as] all my direct disciples—those who have a connection with me—will be liberated presently. It is just as [is mentioned] in the sutras: "Many buddhas, such as the Buddha Purna, became enlightened in the morning; turned the wheel of the Dharma at midday; and passed away in the evening. All who became their disciples were brought to spiritual maturity on the same day."

Moreover, he said: "My life is unobstructed. From age nine, when I became a spiritual teacher, up to now at age forty-six, for thirty-seven years I have worked for the benefit of others; thus I have established a connection with many beings. On some occasions I also brought disciples to spiritual maturity and liberation. May this great moon of the Kagyüd transmission long endure."

While he was abiding by his resolution to remain at Lhadong [in retreat, in a cave] sealed with mud for three years, one evening, [some beings] came from the gods' realms to invite him [there], and it was [agreed that] he would go during his fortieth year. [In his fortieth year, when] he went to central Tibet, he told his disciples, "My students, your intensely devout performance of many rites for dispelling obstacles, and for [my] longevity, has created the auspicious circumstances [for my life to be extended] another six years."

Then one evening while he was staying at Chag Ngur, the [gods] who had invited him came [back, and Yangönpa told them], "The forty [-sixth] year has passed; I must go." [But they] replied, "Since it is said that [one year] as a god equals fifty human years, the time has not yet elapsed." [But,] not acceding to [the request of] the inviters, he said, "This time, I will not stay; I will go [with you]."

Once, while he was staying at Lhadong, he said, "Why feel agitated?" and he gave away all his material possessions. "I will not stay here. By all means, I should leave. I should go to a mountain above this highland."

Since all [his students] insistently requested that he stay at Namding that summer, he departed [Lhadong] monastery, and when he arrived at the Rogpa plain, he looked [back] once at the monastery, and said: "Nice decrepit ruin of a building called Lhadong monastery, I will not return to you."

We often heard [him] remark that he did not wish to remain [at the monastery], but thought only of staying in retreat.

That summer, he said, "If you wish to receive some spiritual teachings, you should ask for them now. The master will not remain forever. And all of you, too, will scatter to mountain hermitages and enter retreat. And, in any case, I will not remain here."

At that time, feeling [no desire] to live [any longer], he wrote down his testament, which [he] left among his books.

Then, he went to Pardrog[268] to meet the Dharma Lord Götsangpa. That year, both spiritual father and son had the same intention not to live [any longer]. But they pretended to make [the customary] reciprocal requests [not to pass away], and engaged in what seemed like a long conversation.

When six of the eight months for which he had said he would stay at Chagnur had passed, he felt as if his health was slightly impaired. Although the [students] requested the performance of rituals to dispel obstacles and [promote] longevity, he did not agree.

Through various means, they made the [same] request to both the spiritual father and son; thus, when he arrived in Shri, they asked him again, and he said, "Please invite Yonten Öd, the attendant of the Master of the Teaching [Götsangpa]." To him he said, "Please tell the Master of Teaching [Götsangpa] that I really must go now. I have left some instructions among my books. Please secretly ask the Master of the Teaching three times, [to make sure that] what is written there [will be implemented]."

Then, when [Yangönpa] took residence in Namding, [the disciples] requested the performance of rituals to dispel obstacles and [promote] longevity, and again he said, "This time, my illness is serious; I will not perform the rites to dispel obstacles, or accept medical treatment. I will remain in the state of one flavor with the illness. To remain in a state of one flavor with illness, three conditions must be present: one must be able to withstand illness in the present circumstances; one must be able [to withstand] death at the end; and one must not, even for an instant, wish to be cured of the illness. These [three conditions] are present in me; thus, I can be in the state of one flavor. In an ultimate sense, this illness of mine does not exist; thus, it is bliss. In a relative sense, it removes obscurations; thus, it is joy. The medicinal *arura*[269] fruit will be of no benefit. Hundreds of words of the ritual to dispel obstacles will be of no use. Although extreme methods and visualizations do exist, I will not apply them. I will remain with this illness, and will not make the slightest attempt to get rid of it. Rituals to dispel obstacles and [promote] longevity will not improve my health. An elephant that has fallen into a quagmire must get out by himself. But since it will help to complete your stock of merit, read and recite the flawless words [of the Buddha], and offer any wealth in your possession to the master and the Three Precious Jewels."

On the eighth day of the lunar month, he granted an audience to everyone, spoke with the students, and gave instructions and vast and profound advice. He would say, "Just as I have previously taught you, everything is transitory, compounded, and subject to death. I too have meditated [on this]. Now, to summarize the essential point: one needs the spiritual teaching. This teaching must not be mixed with worldly [concerns]; therefore, give up the worldly mind, and dedicate yourself to the practice. Purely maintain the three levels of vows.[270] Since we are spiritual practitioners, we should [behave] in harmony with the teachings. Furthermore, it is enough to invoke me once, and you and the people of Lhadong will receive a blessing greater than [you did] before [my passing]. You people of Lhadong will not be less happy [when I die]. I was not boasting before: if one has devotion, the teaching [I have given] will suffice." And he gave many such profound [words of advice].

Then, beginning with the needle and thread he that he held in his hand, he gave everything away. He also divided all his precious books, and gave away the wondrous sacred objects in his possession.

That night he said to those who had taken care of him during his illness, "Now my mind is at peace. I do not own as much as a needle of what is called 'wealth.' Meeting once with my spiritual sons has been meaningful. At the time of death, you must behave similarly. All [of you] should apply the spiritual teaching; you need this. On the morning of [your] death, nothing will be of help.

"I still don't know the state of my health. At the time of [my] death, you should do [just as I told you]. Place the testament that I have left among my books in the box of sacred objects."

Then one day, he summoned ten learned spiritual teachers, headed by the abbot and preceptor, and told them, "My state of health is uncertain. It may improve, or it may worsen. We need to discuss the Dharma, and in particular, a matter [relevant to] today. Should I pass away, there is a [written] testament containing my wishes in the box of sacred objects. Do not transgress it; you are bound to what is written therein. I entrust it to you. Its points are the following," and he roughly explained their general meaning.

Then [they said], "Precious One, do as you wish, but please take care of us; be in good health; and live long." When they made this request, he replied, "It is not that I lack the power [to do this], but [that] the people of the degenerate era only have so much merit."

They asked him, "If our request [for your long life] is not met because the merit of beings is meager and our devotion is weak, when will our request be fulfilled?"

He replied: "[As to your] request, the wisdom indivisible from my body, voice, and mind, and the treasury of the wheel of inexhaustible ornaments of the Body, Voice, and Mind of all buddhas, are inseparable. Their nature is a unity, beyond separation, as the reality of the three vajras that are undifferentiated from the body, voice, and mind of oneself and others. Therefore, invoke [me] from the center of your heart. This [will yield] great blessing."

On another occasion, he said, "In my next life, I will come in four physical manifestations. Even now, in a place called Gothapuri in India, [I am] the *paṇḍita* Jinashri who principally teaches the causal spiritual way of characteristics.[271] In a large charnel ground called Magsha Island, I am the yogin called Yogi Ha who has attained the siddhis,[272] and who, encircled by nonhumans, mainly reveals the supreme quality of the Vajra Way of the Secret Mantra. In the midst of snowy mountains, I am the monk, or the one dressed as the monk called Satasi. At the time of partaking of the gaṇacakra offerings, an emanation of the ḍākinīs manifests in front of each of these three [yogins]. In the future, from now on, I will infinitely manifest countless emanations, and none will be more deserving to become their disciples than yourselves."

One day, without the permission of the abbot and his students, the hermits who were leaving for mountain retreat and those who were arriving, insistently asked where they should pay their respects [in the future]. [In reply, the master] gave the following strict order: "Well, then, build a clay statue of me [adorned] with silk and medicinal substances, but use no precious gems. On the platform for spiritual teaching at Lhadong temple, I taught vast and profound doctrines, and thus [established] a spiritual connection with masses [of beings], human and nonhuman. For this reason, that [place] is very sacred and holds great blessing, so place [the statue] there. Thoroughly clean [the area] up to and including the statues that stand to the right and left. Make a beautiful but small statue [and place it in between the two]. It would not be appropriate [to build] a temple, and so on, in front of it."

"Shall we build a rain shelter above [the statue] so that the face will not get damaged?" they asked. He replied, "If you can, it would be good to do this. When I went to the central regions [of Tibet], I saw many damaged temples in which water was dripping. Do what you can. Also, those who are departing for mountain hermitages should once offer the sevenfold prayer, make an invocation [in front of the statue], and then leave. Those who are arriving should do likewise. The person [who does this] will receive a great blessing."

"Should we also deposit [your] remains and relics inside [the statue]?" asked the [abbot and the students]. "In my testament, there are instructions on the procedure to follow in this regard. Do what you like with one portion [of the relics]," he replied happily.

Concerning the statues of the Four Precious Ones,[273] don't make them any higher than the span from the tip of the thumb to the tip of the middle finger. They should be made by an expert artist. Place the mantra [rolls] correctly within. Place these statues at about the shoulder level of the main clay statue, to the right or left, whichever is easiest, [so that] the golden glow may be visible. This will certainly yield a great blessing."

One day around that time, as he remained in a state of meditation, he asked that excellent offerings be prepared, and said that countless ḍākas, ḍākinīs, and deities of the meditation deities' mandalas—the glorious Cakrasaṃvara principal among them—were present in the posterior section of [his] body.

Again he said, "Quick, prepare fine offerings." [His attendants] told him, "We have prepared them." After a while he said, "Now the exalted master Nāgārjuna has arrived."

Again, he told [them] to prepare some offerings, and remained with his hands folded. "We have prepared them," said [the attendants]. [Yangönpa asked,] "Does each offering bear a flower? Light two incense sticks!" and he emphatically inquired if both were present. Then he said that Drigung Rinpoche and Tagpo Rinpoche[274] had arrived.

One evening, he said, "Prepare a fine torma offering." "We have prepared it; there it is," [said the attendants]. He decided to sit for a while to create an auspicious condition, and said, "All these ḍākas and ḍākinīs have gathered here." At that time, he told [the attendants] to quickly prepare several white and red tormas and good-quality offerings, and to burn incense. On all these occasions, they knew there was a reason behind [his request].

Again, one day he asked, "When is the nineteenth of the month? Common people say that the nineteenth is the day of the spirits; [but] for you it is an auspicious day." Then, in the early morning of the nineteenth, he exclaimed, "Ho! today is a [day of] joy, happiness, and pleasure for us, the father and children. Prepare a good torma offering for this day. Today is the day to prepare good [things]. Today is the occasion for offering your prayers. Also, you should stay alone and practice meditation."

That day,[275] in the morning, as the sun was warming, he passed away in the supreme bliss of the dimension of eternity, and dissolved the mandala of his emanation into the realm of peace, manifesting [nirvana,] the complete transcendence of suffering.

[Yangönpa had] said, "I have arranged things so that my body will not become a sacred object. So since my body will not be preserved, deal with my remains in the way [described in the testamentary letter] that follows."

Then, when his precious body was cremated, flowers fell from the sky, including some with three, some with five, and some with seven petals. Tents of rainbows and countless wondrous signs appeared.

Even afterward, the statue of his body spoke, and relics emerged from the clay of his remains from which the statue was composed. Fearing that it would be too much to write down all these countless wondrous signs here, I did not write them down. They should be learned from those who heard them earlier and later.[276]

Incomparable Master, precious buddha,
Your qualities are beyond my mind's comprehension.
The light of the sun that dispels the clouds,
How can it be seen by the eyes of bees?
In the wheel of inexhaustible ornaments
Of [your] immaculate body, voice, and mind,
The infinitude of samsara and nirvana,
Even if described for eons by all buddhas of the three times,
[Your] wisdom of knowledge, loving compassion,
The vision of the wisdom of freedom and maturation,[277]
All [your] powers,[278] and [your] unique[279] qualities of mastery,[280]
Could not be exhaustively [described] even in part.
Profound and vast, [your qualities] cannot be grasped by the minds of
*   ordinary beings.*
All the authentic masters who were omniscient buddhas,
Made prophecies, granted permission-blessings, praised,
And prayed to you with folded hands.
All who know this [are] fortunate disciples.

These words should also be known.

As requested by several supreme friends, I wrote the contents of this praise in the form of a biography one summer at the glorious monastery of Lhadong.

I beg forgiveness, and apologize for the various distractions to which I had been subject; for the fatigue of body and mind; for my unclear intellect; for the flaws caused by forgetfulness; and for any errors I may have made; and I ask for your blessing.

Through the merit of this composition, may the auspicious [circumstances] arise that I and all sentient beings might never be separate from the incomparable master, and that the goals of the teaching, for myself and others, might be realized.

May enlightened activity endlessly blaze in [all] times
and directions,
May it bring peace to living beings,
And may the community of spiritual practitioners,
Like the sun [that shines] on earth,
Bring happiness and wellbeing everywhere.

Shubham

Lhadongpa's Letter of Testament

Oṃ svasti siddham

To you, Lord, essence of all enlightened ones of the three times,
Precious master, king of the Teaching, and [other masters] of the
Kagyüd lineage,
Three Precious Jewels who are the supreme refuge,
Buddhas and bodhisattvas,
Meditational deities, ḍākas, ḍākinīs, great guardians
of the Teaching,

And to all who are worthy of veneration, I reverently bow,
Recite verses, and with faith, pay homage in a nondual state.
I beseech you, through your great compassion, to uproot the cycle of
*   existences,*
Liberate the three realms in the state of Mahāmudrā,
And empower all the six types of beings, our mothers,
That the nondual wisdom might, right now, arise in their minds.
In particular, I beseech you that my mind of Mahāmudrā,
This fresh and naked state in which all that arises is the reality
*   dimension,*
Might, right now, be transferred to the minds of all the lineage
*   disciples, my followers.*

I am standing directly in the nonduality of self and others, delighted and bright, [yet] all that is compounded is impermanent; all things are surely perishable. The life energy of the individual is subject to birth and death. The composite phenomena of the beggar of this world, the cotton-clad hermit, are taking their course. He plays the game of illusion, and [thereby] brings disciples face to face [with reality]. The imputed material [body] and consciousness having separated, in the immortal state of the mind, he takes hold of the natural dimension of reality.

Thus, you disciples who have actually met me and [have now been] left behind should not overstep the boundaries that I have here set down in writing. This is a secret command!

[Through] the relative altruistic mind of enlightenment,[281] the unceasing radiance of the mandala of samsara and nirvana of all phenomena that appear and exist, I have completed the accumulation of merit; and [through] the ultimate mind of enlightenment,[282] the real state that transcends all definitions, I have completed the accumulation of wisdom. Thus, with regard to the two types of merit, there can be neither decline nor need for increase. The results of this [merit] are the three dimensions of enlightenment in which there is neither coming nor going. The function [of the three dimensions] is the unceasing [accomplishment] of one's own and others' benefit.

In this regard, do not seek the help of any other virtue [through funerary ceremonies]. Thus, even the gathering of two or more persons or four or more monks specifically for my farewell ceremony would be a violation of your sacred commitment with me. You need not [perform a ceremony to establish] any root of virtue. You need not perform a weekly [ceremony] for the deceased. Through my own capacity, I have already done all that is [required].

You should live in unfamiliar [places]. Live in unfamiliar [places]! Eh! Eh! Great joy! Cotton-clad hermits do not need sacred objects of worship. My body is present as the inseparability of the vajra body of all enlightened beings [that comprises all the] phenomena of the entire animate and inanimate universe. Make your outer shrine out of this [inseparability].

My vajra voice is present as the inseparability of the melodious voice of the realized ones and all language. Make your secret shrine out of this [inseparability]. My mind is present as the inseparability of the vajra mind of all realized ones and the mind-essence of all creatures. Make your inner shrine out of this [inseparability].

Know that the body is the innate mandala of the deity; know that the resounding voice is the vajra mantra of emptiness; and offer the uninterrupted offerings emerging from the cocoon of duality of mind's clarity and emptiness.

Apart from this, making even one votive image as an outer support for your faith in me, or one heap of cremation ashes as an inner support, would be a violation of your sacred commitment with me. There is no need to build any sacred representation; thus, there is less to be done. The great sacred representation built from the very beginning contains greater blessing. Great Joy!

Cremate my body on the roof of my house, along with a few good offerings made by a few people of pure commitments. Then, pulverize the handfuls of bone that will remain, and throw half of that pile of powder into the Pong river, and half into the Yaru river.[283] The sentient beings [living in] the places touched by these waters will be liberated from birth in the lower realms, and infinite karma and obscurations will be exhausted. This is another aspect of benefiting others.

Furthermore, there are some other things to be done to generate auspiciousness.

When the body is cremated, instead of weeping, you, my students, should recite fervent invocations. [In this way] you will all be granted great spiritual advancement. The small-minded should not despair at the cotton-clad mountain hermit's performance of the dance of illusion. I am beyond going and coming. I am beyond death. I did not come from anywhere, and I am not going anywhere. I do not abide anywhere. I am inseparable from the mandala of your mind. When you grieve in remembrance of me, look sharply at your mind, and you will meet [the mind] in its nakedness, as clarity and emptiness: remain steady in that condition.

"I am separated from the teacher. I am separated from being with the master. [Yet] I remain in a happy state of mind." If you do not maintain such an attitude, but weep and grieve, you are disobeying my words.

The mountain hermit does not need a monastic residence. I do not have a monastic residence. So there is nothing to look after. My monastic residences are the carefree mountain hermitages. Those who can settle [the mind in] meditation should hold to that residence. My residence is the permanent dimension of the original state. Those who understand the unborn nature of mind should uphold that. My residence is the unconditional benefit of others. Those who have trained in the altruistic mind of compassion, should uphold this. Moreover, if I have spiritual heirs, they will uphold the teaching in the ten directions.

Instead of all those [material sacred objects], you can fashion sacred objects of farewell out of the merit [of your prayers] upon my death. Instead of [staying in] all those monastic residences, I ask that those great meditators who have completed the preliminary practices and beyond should come to the mountain hermitages. The best [should] stay in retreat for nine years; the average, for six years; and the least [able], for three years. This is my view from the tomb.

Practice the water offering.[284] In general, you should practice it as long as you live. Don't take up hierarchical positions. Do not maintain a small place of your own or a monastery. What you need now is self-reliance. To become self-reliant, roam among the mountain hermitages, the monastic ancestral home. My disciples, [my work for] the benefit of others is still stockpiled on your behalf, with my prayers; thereby will both yourselves and others greatly benefit.

Generate patience and perseverance. Female meditators too, living in harmony, after receiving some [instructions], should enter mountain retreats. Remain in solitude [with your meditation place] sealed with plaster, and engender enthusiasm for spiritual practice. If none were to appear who practiced in this way, this would be a major transgression of the master's words.

Do not think that my life has been [interrupted] by an obstacle: for thirty-seven years, from ages nine to forty-six, I worked for the benefit of others, I accomplished the benefit of sentient beings, and I brought many students to maturity and liberation. Some great meditators, practitioners who could meditate, and wanderers in mountain hermitages also appeared [to me]. The great moon of the Kagyüd masters' [work for] others' benefit, which has endured the longest, has fulfilled its mission.

Now, my students, practice all your lives, and ensure that what the Kagyüd fathers have created is not interrupted.

Yangönpa's testament is completed.

Oṃ svasti siddham

Root master and masters of the lineage; Venerable Refuge; Precious Three Jewels; ocean of meditational deities, ḍākinīs, and guardians of the Dharma: I beseech you to empower all followers [of Yangönpa].

Precious king of the Teaching; essence of all goodness, charismatic activities, and qualities of the body, voice, and mind of the buddhas of the three times: you have never experienced death.

The indestructible nature of wisdom indivisible from the body, voice, and mind of you, Precious One, spontaneously present, pervades—without even an instant of separation—the body, voice, and mind of ourselves, your disciples.

Master, by encountering your body, anything seen as an object of the six consciousnesses, manifests as the innate [simultaneity of] vision and emptiness.

Master, by encountering your voice, anything heard [manifests as] the [simultaneity] of sound and emptiness.

Master, by encountering your mind, the myriad movements of the mind manifest as the innate [simultaneity] of pure awareness and emptiness.

Furthermore, when my body is visualized as the illusory body of the deity, this is the encounter with your body, Dharma king.

When the mantra of your invocation resounds, this is the encounter with your voice.

When awareness of various thoughts manifests, this is the encounter with your mind that is inseparable from the two types of wisdom.[285]

Such uninterrupted manifestations are encounters with your qualities, Dharma king.

Whatever we do selflessly and exclusively for the benefit of others is the encounter with your charismatic activity. Whatever we do without departing from the immaculate dimension of reality is the encounter with your goodness. It is sufficient to apply the key point of devotion.

From this point on, our aspiration is to practice according to your teachings and writings. [You] will also help me to accomplish [the goals of] your teachings and writings, and, at any rate, I have your verbal assurance. Also, when the master Gunaprabha came to meet you, [you] placed great emphasis on [following the master's example], so I have acted in accordance with your writings.

Since we have received the master's blessings, siddhas as numerous as the stars in the sky will arrive; benefit as [abundant as] the flowers that bloom in summer will come to beings; and [your] charismatic activity will lead the infinitude of sentient beings to the state of full enlightenment.

It is important that we, the disciples, act in keeping with your mind, and practice as you taught us.

On the basis of this immense root of merit accumulated in the three times, may all sentient beings, infinite as space, become enlightened in one body and in one lifetime.

In particular, may the [residents of] Lhadong enjoy good health and longevity, and may they become like the fabulous wish-fulfilling gem that fulfills all wants and needs. This has been taught for the sake of the disciples, followers of the Master of the Teaching, and his heirs.

At the age of eighty, when the Master of the Teaching Götsangpa was feeling rather unwell, and the teachers Zhonseng, Wangchug Gyaltsen, and others were in his presence, the robes that the Precious Lhadongpa was wearing when he died, and other things, arrived to be offered [to Götsangpa]. The Lord of the Teaching said, "This is a being who is accomplishing the benefit of others." At that time, these words of [Götsangpa] were sent in a letter to Lhadong.

The Master of the Teaching [Yangönpa] said, "In a previous life, [Götsangpa] was born as the venerable Mila,[286] and then he was born into the lineage of lama Ngogpa.[287] Then he was born as the Master of the Teaching himself in Lhodrag.[288] In the future, in the world called Nonattachment, he will be born as the bodhisattva Lotus Without Attachment. Then, in the world called Devoid of Suffering, he will become enlightened as the buddha Dispeller of Misery, and work for the benefit of beings."

During that year, the Master of Teaching Götsangpa also passed away.[289]

Invocation for Pacification of the Age of Turmoil, and for the Welfare of Tibet, by Jamgön Kongtrul Lodrö Thaye

Three roots, three Jewels, infallible refuge;
Especially Avalokiteśvara, Lord of the Land of Snow,
Venerable Tārā, and Guru Padmasambhava: I invoke you.
Fulfill the oath you have taken;
Grant your blessing so that this invocation will be answered.

The misguided intentions and actions of people
    of the degenerate era,
And the causes and conditions of turmoil manifesting without and
    within,
Have spawned epidemics, heretofore unknown, among humans and
    animals.
The rays emanating from negative forces, provocations of za,
    of nāga, and gyalpo spirits,

[Have brought] blight, frost, hail, poor harvests, war, turmoil,
    and conflict;
Uneven rains, heavy snows, bad omens of tra[290] and mice;
Threats of earthquakes, fire, and the enemies of the four elements;
And border wars, in particular, have damaged the spiritual teaching.
May all types of harm befalling this Land of Snow,
Be swiftly pacified, and come to an end.

[May] the precious and sublime altruistic mind
    of enlightenment
Arise spontaneously in the minds of all beings, human and
    nonhuman.
Devoid of harmful intentions and actions,
May they possess a loving mind toward one another,
So that the grandeur of peace and happiness might come
    to all regions of Tibet.

May the Buddha's Teaching flourish and long endure,
And, by the power of the truth of the Three Roots,
Of the enlightened beings, and their heirs,
And of any of root of virtue in samsara and nirvana,
Through the power of our pure intention,
May our invocation's goal be realized.

Lama Jamyang Khyentse Wangpo told me, "Since the outcome of the present time of turmoil is unpredictable, I recite an invocation for the welfare of Tibet six times daily. Thus, this is an important [practice] for you too." In keeping with this command, I, the lazy Lodrö Thaye, at Tsadrag Rinchen Trag, composed this prayer on the morning of the auspicious month of the auspicious constellation Gyal.

PART THREE
The Hidden Description of the Vajra Body

HOMAGE AND INTRODUCTORY REMARKS

Homage to Śrī Vajrayoginī![1]
[Herein is contained] the *Hidden Description of the Vajra Body*.[2]

I salute the indestructible reality (vajra)[3] that is the inseparability of magnificence and great bliss; and the ḍākinīs together with their families.[4]

This [body,][5] the supreme abode of the twenty-four [sacred places[6] where] the ten levels of realization[7] [are attained] is the divine mansion complete with the thirty-seven [factors of enlightenment].[8] It is beautified by the circle of the mandala[9] of the enjoyment of nondual heroes[10] and ḍākinīs,[11] [the wisdom] that performs the dance of illusion.[12]

May this indestructible reality, the essence of the Body, Voice, and Mind of all buddhas;[13] self-originated;[14] conqueror;[15] nature of the union of secrets;[16] net of magical manifestations; sovereign of the four enlightened dimensions;[17] be victorious.[18]

Having relied on [the way of Mantra][19] unknown to Lion, Ravisher, or Essence of Wealth; the disciples, rhinoceri, or children of the Victorious One,[20] I have gained certainty through experience[21] regarding the fundamental nature of the hidden[22] vajra body,[23] the tantra of exegesis that is the method that clarifies all teachings,[24] that swiftly protects one with bliss,[25] revealed to me by the master's kindness.

To benefit others, I will write down the secret words of the ḍākinīs, which are the profound meaning of the stainless tantras.[26]

The great scholar Nāropā,[27] by devoting himself for twelve years to the lord of yogins Tilopa,[28] created the auspicious connection of the profound path of devotion. Oblivious to all [his] earthly suffering, he endured twelve severe trials that brought him [close to] death. At the end, he offered a mandala of blood and his severed ear [to the master][29] and, on that occasion, received the following teaching:

The fundamental nature of things, the path,
And the steps of the fruit come to light.[30]

To explain: there is the fundamental nature of things, which is to be realized; the way of applying the path, which is the method for realizing; and the steps for generating qualities, which is the realization. The sacred master said, "All sublime teachings are included in these three."[31]

That is to say, the inseparability of path and fruit of the tradition of the Way of Indestructible Reality (Vajrayana) is the base. The understanding that the base and fruit are inseparable is the path. And the realization that base and path are inseparable is the fruit.[32]

In this regard, if you do not understand the fundamental nature of things, you will not understand the path and fruit. If you do not become certain about the general idea, you will not realize the specific characteristics. If the understanding does not accord with the object of understanding, the [understanding] will not become the path. For example, even if you meditate for eons thinking that the ear is an eye, [the ear] will not become an eye.

Moreover, if you do not understand the fundamental nature of the body, you will not understand the essential point of meditation.

If you do not understand this, the mind [essence] is not recognized. If you do not understand the fundamental nature of the mind, the meditator's flaws will not be exposed. If these are not exposed, you will pursue concepts and conceptual reality. If you do not understand the fundamental nature of body and mind inseparable, you will not recognize the object of meditation, the ultimate essence. If you understand this, [you will know that] the five enlightened dimensions (kāyas)[33] are present as innate qualities.

The followers of the Way of the Perfections[34] know the fundamental nature of the mind, but do not know the fundamental nature of the body. Therefore, although their knowledge may be profound, they will be ignorant of the method for realizing [this fundamental nature], and consequently they will not attain the final fruit for a long time. The *Samputa Tantra* states:[35]

If you do not know the nature of the body,
All the methods of the eighty-four thousand aspects
   of the Teaching[36]
Will [yield] no fruit.

For these reasons, here I shall write a little bit about the fundamental nature of things as it has come from the masters through a successive lineage of transmissions, and has been learned through my own experience.

The fundamental nature of things [is explained under three headings]: [The Base:] how all phenomena of the world and of its transcendence (samsara and nirvana) exist as the fundamental nature of body, voice, and mind; [The Path:] how the aspects of the path are complete by establishing that body, voice, and mind] inseparable are the method and knowledge; and [The Fruit:] how all qualities of the final fruit are complete by establishing that Body, Voice, and Mind inseparable are the perfect state of an enlightened being.

222 �֍ Secret Map of the Body

The Base: How All the Phenomena of the World and of Its Transcendence Exist as the Fundamental Nature of Body, Voice, and Mind

This is explained in four parts: the fundamental nature of the body that is the Vajra Body of all enlightened beings; the fundamental nature of the voice that is the Vajra of the Voice of all enlightened beings; the fundamental nature of the mind that is the Vajra of the Mind of all enlightened beings; and the fundamental nature of the inseparability of body, voice, and mind that is the Vajra of the wisdom of the inseparability of Body, Voice, and Mind of all enlightened beings.

Introduction

In regard to the term *vajra*,[37] the *Glorious Equal to the Sky Tantra* states:[38]

> In every respect, the Bodies of all buddhas,
> And likewise, in every respect, their supreme
> 	Voices and Minds,
> Are one with all the animate and inanimate;
> Hence, they are called "vajra."

One's ordinary body, voice, and mind are inseparable from the Body, Voice, and Mind of the *heruka*[39] at all [times: at the time of] the cause, path, and final fruit. Therefore, they are the Body, Voice, and Mind of the vajra.

To explain: channels, syllables, vital essences, and the ruler of them all, which is the wisdom energy-wind, are [in order:] the Vajra

Body, the Vajra Voice, the Vajra Mind of all *sugatas,* and the Hevajra of the essence.[40]

Syllables are included in all channels, energy-winds, and vital essences. Thus, there are three [topics]: the stationary channels, the moving energy-wind, and the positioned vital essence.

Moreover, the channels are like a house. The vital essences are like wealth. The energy-winds are like the owner. These three are also body, voice, and mind [respectively].

In fact, the *Tantra of Vajravārāhī Called Vajra Manifestation* states:[41]

> The stationary channels, the moving energy-wind,
> And likewise, the positioned vital essence
>   [of bodhicitta],
> Are [respectively,] the essence of body, the body
>   of voice,
> And the support of the mind.

Hence, the channels are the essence of the body; the energy-wind is the body of the voice; and the vital essence [or bodhicitta] is the support of the mind.

THE FUNDAMENTAL NATURE OF THE BODY, THE VAJRA BODY OF ALL ENLIGHTENED BEINGS

How the Body Is Formed through the Five Manifest Awakenings

Regarding the first topic to be explained—the fundamental nature of the body—the *Vajramāla,*[42] a tantra belonging to the Great Yoga, states:

As to the body, by virtue of the five awakenings,[43]
Channels, vital essences,
Unclean substances, and thoughts,
The phenomenon of the body exists.

The Five Outer Manifest Awakenings

Regarding the formation [of the body] through the five manifest
awakenings—the first of the five [aforementioned] bodily factors—if
we relate it to the five "outer" manifest awakenings that accord with
the Yoga tantra, it proceeds as follows:

When—with the result of one's past actions serving as the primary substantial cause, and the sexual union of father and mother
as the contributory cause—the consciousness of the intermediate
being for which this cause and condition are present [is about to]
enter [the mother's] womb, if the womb is affected by an illness[44]
or if it already contains a fetus, [the consciousness] cannot enter.

Therefore, the empty womb unaffected by illness, and in which
the menstrual period occurs, is the "manifest awakening through
emptiness that is the very nature of things."

The coming together of the father's semen and the mother's
blood is the "manifest awakening from the sun and moon's seats."

The consciousness of the intermediate being, accompanied
by the karmic pervasive energy-wind,[45] enters through the father's
anus, joins with the semen, and enters the mother's womb. This is
the "manifest awakening from the syllable of the Voice."

Then, the [four elements][46] successively form—from the air
element up to the earth element—in a way that parallels the formation of the elements in the external world.[47] In this regard, the
agent of purification of the phase of creation is taught in accordance
with the nature of the being that is the basis of the purification.[48]

To explain: first, the initial [element] basis that supports the body is air. It performs three types of functions: it increasingly integrates the roundish [embryo that] is the union of the vital essences [semen and blood]; it produces the three phases of respiration—exhalation, inhalation, and pause—and it supports bodily movement.

At the same time, the fire element forms, performing three functions: it prevents the rotting of the substances of semen and blood that form [the embryo], ripens its strength and power, generates the warmth of the body, draws in the mother's nutriment, and promotes the growth of the organic components.

At the same time, the water element forms, performing three functions: it prevents the mutual dispersion of the particles constituting the semen and blood [of the embryo]; balances the [aspects of the] subtle and gross sense organs; and produces blood, lymph, and other wet components of the body.

At the same time, the earth element forms, performing three functions: it confers solidity, that is, it hardens and strengthens the body; it produces the coarseness of flesh, bones, marrow, nails, and so on, and hardens them; and it creates and develops the protruding shapes of the sense organs.

In this way, with the space element providing the opportunity, the potency of the four elements gradually forms the entire body.

Moreover, during the first seven days, [the embryo is called] "watery"[49] and resembles curd that is beginning to congeal. During the next seven days, [the embryo is called] "lump" and resembles well-congealed curd.

Then, [during the period when] the embryo is called "hard and oval" and resembles butter produced by the churning of curd, the first [chakra] of the navel forms, which is the first of the four chakras of existence.[50] The consciousness dwells [there] in the form of the syllable A (ॲ) symbolizing the unborn [reality]. This being so, in the body of all creatures, the syllable symbolizing the unborn is present as the life force itself. That is, [this life force] is located at the center of the triangular knot of channels of the navel "emanation" chakra—the king of channels—called "ox eye," resembling the eye of the *enaya* antelope.

The *Tantra of the Manifest Enlightenment of Vārāhī* states:[51]

As to the stages of birth in conditioned existence,
First, the navel forms at the center;
From there the body, too, is said to form.
The channels of the vagina arise from that,
Pervaded with the heat of great bliss.

Therefore, the emanation chakra at the navel is the body's center that develops the body, upward and downward. From this originates the central channel (Skt. *avadhūti*), the channel of the unborn, and on the basis of that, from the navel, all the upper and lower chakras are formed.

The [months of gestation] are associated with the ten incarnations of Viṣṇu[52] as a fish, as a tortoise, as a pig, as the two Ramas [Rama and Pashurama],[53] as Krishna, as a human-lion [Narashima], as a dwarf, as a swan, and as a buddha.[54]

To explain: by the time [the fetus] has completed its second month in the womb, the five root energy-winds, the three main channels, and the channel-knots at the center of the four chakras have been formed. As the upward-moving wind and downward-clearing winds unblock the upper and lower doors of the three main channels, the body is roundish at the center and narrower at the top and bottom. By depending on the emerging and the flowing energy-winds, [the fetus] takes on the form of Viṣṇu as a fish.[55]

During the third month, the petals inside the four chakras are formed, and thus the basis for the limbs is laid out. The upper arms, the thighs, the penis (if the fetus is male), and the form of the head begin to protrude slightly, and [the fetus] takes on the form of Viṣṇu as a tortoise.[56]

At this time, in males, on the basis of the life-sustaining wind, there forms [the penis,] narrow in the middle, resembling a vajra. In females an empty cavity resembling a bell is formed. This is the "manifest awakening through the hand-symbols of the Mind."

Then, in the fourth month, the five branch energy-winds form on the basis of the life-sustaining wind. Thus, first the shoulders and the eyes appear. The lower part of the body is narrow and the upper is wide. Since the head is slightly raised and the eyes clearly appear, the [fetus] takes on the form of Viṣṇu as a pig.

In the fifth month, all of the 360 bones and the joints are formed. Thus, the shapes of the two arms, the two legs, and the head become defined, and the [fetus] takes on the form of the two Ramas.

During the sixth month, the flesh, the skin, and the characteristics of the sense organs appear. The five branch winds are completed; thus, the [fetus] takes on the form of Krishna.

In the seventh month, the eyebrows, hair, and body hair are formed. The completed head resembles [the head of] a lion, and therefore [the fetus] takes on the form of a human-lion [Narasimha].

During the eighth month, the male or female sexual organ becomes clearly defined.[57] Furthermore, the colors [of the various parts of the body], from the black color of the hair to the bluish color of fingernails, clearly appear. The particular features of the sense organs, the limbs, and other minor body parts become distinct; thus, [the fetus] takes on the form of a dwarf.

During the ninth month, the seven organic components of the body[58] are completed, and the sense organs become fully developed. Therefore, [the fetus] wants to exit the womb, and takes on the form of a swan.

During the tenth month, the body is fully developed, and [the fetus] can readily be born. Thus, [the fetus] takes on the form of a buddha that has completed the ten levels of realization.[59]

The *Kālacakra Tantra* states that, starting with the second month after conception, two hundred new channels develop each day.[60] At the end of the twelve months, all seventy-two thousand channels of the human body have entirely formed,[61] and from that time onward, two channels dry each day.

The three, channels, skin, and flesh, are produced by the pure vital essence of the mother, and take form from the bottom upward. The three, marrow, bones, and tendons, and ligaments are produced by the pure vital essence of the father, and take form from the top downward.

During the gestation just described, because energy-wind and mind dwell as one collection in the central channel, [the fetus] does not require coarse food. [Through] the umbilical cord, the essence of the organic components of the mother's body develops the organic components of that of the child.[62]

Even though [the fetus] has excellent contemplation, he or she does not recognize it, and the consciousness remains as if comfortably asleep. The discomfort caused by the mother's movement is just like the fear [experienced] in a dream.[63]

Concerning the position of the fetus in the mother's womb, from the fifth month, the body takes the form of a male or female. If male, the fetus will be crouching on the right side of the mother's womb, concealing its face with its two hands,[64] facing her spinal column. If the sex is female, the fetus is positioned on the left side of the mother's womb in the same way as just explained, [but] facing the belly of the mother.

In the tenth month, when the strengths of the energy-winds are fully present, the energy-wind presiding over movement enters the left nostril, causing [the fetus] to turn upside down and be born from the mother's womb. Therefore, if the power of the child's air element is strong, the child will be born quickly; if the power of the [air element] is weak, birth will be delayed for long time. The quality of the child's bodily constituents can be understood through this [point].

Thus, the process of birth in the form of a male, female, or hermaphrodite is the "manifest awakening through completion of the Body."

The Five Inner Manifest Awakenings

If we relate [this process] to the five inner manifest awakenings that accord with the Highest Yoga Tantra:

First, [the consciousness of the intermediate being] that, having entered through the anus of the father, abides in the channel of the penis below the navel and is propelled by the father's semen [into the womb], is the "manifest awakening through the moon," the "mirror-like wisdom."

Then, the [consciousness of the intermediate being] that, having entered the mother's womb, is enveloped by the pure essence of blood, is the "manifest awakening through the sun," or the "wisdom of sameness."

In this way, the consciousness of the intermediate [being] dwelling in a state of innate bliss between sun and moon, is the "manifest awakening through the seed-syllable," the "wisdom of discernment."

The three factors [semen, ovum, and consciousness] intermingling in the aspect of bliss of wind and mind, becoming the [embryo developing through its] watery, lump, and hard-and-oval [stages] is the "manifest awakening through the intermingling," the "accomplishing wisdom."

Then, upon the gradual completion of the body that has taken form during the [stage] of hardening,[65] birth is the "manifest awakening through completion [of the form]," the "wisdom of the real condition of existence."

The eighth chapter of the *First Examination of the Hevajra Tantra* states:

> The moon is said to be the mirror [-like wisdom];
> The sun, the [wisdom of] sameness;
> One's deity's hand-implement with the seed-syllable
> Is the [wisdom] of discernment;
> All becoming one is [the wisdom] of earnest action;
> The completion is the [wisdom of the] pure,
>   real condition of existence.[66]

This explains how the body is formed through the five manifest awakenings, the first of the five bodily factors.

How the Fundamental Nature of Channels Exists

Introduction on the Channels and the Four Chakras

There are two bodies, one coarse and one subtle: the coarse is the [body] that possesses the physical sense organs' support [of the inner subtle sense faculty]. As for the subtle, since the entire body is [made up of] channels, [the subtle] body is said to be the channels.

As to the number of channels, distinguished in detail, they amount to ninety-five million. The channels containing blood[67] equal seventy-two thousand. The channels through which the winds flow are 21,600. One hundred fifty-seven [channels] pertain to the five chakras, and thirty-seven to the sacred places.[68] The channels in which the vital essences descend are thirty-two. The principal channels are three.

Besides that, the *Kālacakra Tantra* states that [there are] 364 bones; the vital essences [amount] to one *dre* measure of Magadha plus one handful;[69] the hairs [number] 1,600,000; the blood and lymph [amount to the volume of] one curd vessel plus two handfuls;[70] and the channels, ninety-five million. Because flesh is subject to increase and decrease, its measure has not been mentioned.[71]

To summarize all these channels, there are three [main] channels and four chakras.

The chapter of the vajra family from the *First Examination of the Hevajra Tantra* states:[72]

In reply to the question:
Kye! Bhagavān, how many channels are in the vajra
    body?
[The Bhagavān] said:
"The channels are thirty-two.
[Within them] flow thirty-two vital essences
That fall to the place of great bliss.
Among them, there are the three main [channels]:
Lalanā, rasanā, and avadhūti."[73]

And:[74]

Of the four chakras, the chakra of emanation at the
    navel [has] sixty-four radial channels;
The chakra of phenomena at the heart [has] eight radial
    channels;
The chakra of enjoyment at the throat [has] sixteen
    radial channels;
The chakra of great bliss at the crown of the head [has]
    thirty-two radial channels.[75]

The *Cakrasaṃvara Tantra* speaks of five chakras, including the "chakra that sustains bliss" at the secret place. The *Kālacakra Tantra* instead describes six chakras, including that at the forehead, called the "chakra of the innate."[76] The *Path and Its Fruit* explains eighteen chakras: four mobile; two immobile; and the chakras of the twelve continents, making eighteen, or twenty if we include the two chakras that perform actions.[77]

As to the fundamental nature of these channels, at the genital chakra the channels are like a tree whose branches extend [upward]; at the navel chakra they are like ropes being pulled horizontally; at the heart chakra they are like a ball of yarn; at the throat chakra they are like a coiled snake; at the head chakra they resemble an inverted umbrella; at the chakra of the twelve continents they are like intertwined strands of hair.

Concerning the shape of the four chakras, the *Saṃpuṭa Tantra* states that the head and navel [chakras] are said to have the shape of E, and the heart and throat [chakras], of VAṂ.

The *Two Examinations [of the Hevajra Tantra]* states that the four chakras have the shape of the four [syllables] E, VAṂ, MA, and YA.[78]

The form of E [the navel chakra] is said to be
Lochana,
The form of VAṂ [the heart chakra], the Sovereign
Lady.
MA [the throat chakra] is said to be Paṇḍāravāsinī.
The form of YA [the head chakra] is Tārā.[79]

There are two reasons—outer and inner—why the four chakras are known by the names of the four enlightened dimensions.[80]

The Second Examination of the Hevajra[81] states:

[That which] produces and emanates

Is said to be the dimension possessing emanations
    [nirmāṇakāya].
The mind is the nature of phenomena,
Thus, the dimension of reality [dharmakāya] is the heart
    [chakra].
Eating that which has the form of the six tastes is actual
    enjoyment [*sambhoga*];
[Thus,] at the throat there is the enjoyment chakra.
[At] the head, [the chakra] dwells [as] great bliss
    [*mahāsukha*].

According to the outer reasons, since the body emanates [or develops] from there, it is called the "navel chakra of emanation." Since it serves as the support [for the manifestation of] phenomena that are of the nature of mind, it is called the "heart chakra of phenomena." Since it enjoys the six tastes, it is called the "throat chakra of enjoyment." Since it exists as the essence of bliss of the vital essence, it is called the "crown [of the head] chakra of great bliss."

According to the inner [reasons, the names of the four chakras are related to] the four times.

To explain: during sleep, the mind dwells at the heart, and since the earth element is dense [at that time], we fall asleep.[82] With the [manifestation of] the three lights of appearance, increase, and attainment [white, red, and black] serving as the link [leading] to sleep,[83] the energy-winds flow in the central channel and we then experience the state of the reality dimension, the total freedom from concepts. For this reason, the heart [chakra] is called the "chakra of reality."

When a fragment of the energy-wind strays into the rasanā and lalanā, hazy dream images manifest in waves. At that time, the consciousness dwells at the throat, and we experience the state of the enjoyment dimension, the vision that is insubstantial. For this reason, the throat [chakra] is called the "chakra of enjoyment."

[When the mind reaches] the crown of the head, we wake up, and then the energy-winds start to move as the two energy-winds of vitality and exertion. During that time—that is, the daytime—the mind dwells at the navel, and we experience the state of the emanation dimension, the arising of various discursive thoughts. For this reason, the navel [chakra] is called the "chakra of emanation."

At the time of sexual union, the consciousness dwells at the crown of the head and, since body and mind are [then] entirely permeated by pleasure, we experience the state that is the dimension of great bliss. For this reason, the [chakra at the] crown of the head is called the "chakra of great bliss."

For those who have no knowledge, these [experiences] are just a similitude [for the real enlightened dimensions].

Extensive Explanation of the Fundamental Nature of the Channels

The Central Channel

[Some] claim that the central channel is imaginary.[84] If this were the case, all the qualities related to the central channel would be mere imaginings, and one would not be able to traverse the path of the Secret Mantra.

Some allege that [the central channel] is the life channel. When the energy-wind and mind collect in the life channel, this leads to insanity or seizures. But the central channel gives rise only to excellent qualities, and cannot reward harm. Therefore, [the central channel] is not [the life channel].

Some say that [the central channel] is the spinal cord. [However, because] the spinal cord does not fulfill the four characteristics of the central channel,[85] [and because it would] distort the essential points of the [practice involving] channels, the [central channel] is not the [spinal cord].

Few people [correctly] identify the central channel. To meditate on the path of method[86] without identifying [the central channel] would be ridiculous.

The way the central channel exists is as follows, as stated in the *Tantra of the Extraordinary Secret*[87] that belongs to the Great Yoga:

> It abides within the life-pillar,
> Having thirty-two knots.
> It is the perfect sublime one, the subtlest
>   of the subtle.
> It is neither outside nor inside.[88]

In regard to this, located at the center of the body, the [central channel] that sustains life extends from the crown of the head to below the navel, and has knots at the centers of the six chakras.

The *Catuḥpīṭha Tantra* states:[89]

> In relation to the life-staff of body and mind,
> There is the secret teaching on the six unions.[90]

Alternatively:

> Withdrawal; meditative absorption;
> Prāṇāyāma; retention; subsequent recollection;
>   and contemplation.[91]

[These six] are the secret instructions for the practice based on the six unions, and on the central channel.[92]

The great brahmin Saraha stated:[93]

When the great energy of wind and movement
    is inserted in the life channel,
The ordinary consciousness automatically ceases.

These passages also relate [to the central channel].

From [the central channel] branches off a particular life channel
of three varying lengths that connects to the heart. Called "supreme
central [channel]," it serves as the support for the supreme organ
of the central channel's interior space. Its upper tip inserts in the
crown of the head above the bone and below the flesh. Its lower tip
inserts in the long [abdominal] crease.[94]

The glorious Kotali stated:[95]

Like a lotus's stamen in form,
It dwells above and below.
It is called "knowledge,"
The very consort of all buddhas.

From that [supreme central channel] branches off another channel
called "lesser" that extends from the left ear to the A (ཨ) of knowledge.[96] When wind and mind collect in this [channel], one hears
the sounds of the three realms.[97]

These two [the supreme central and the lesser channels] are also
called the "supreme and lesser bell-possessing channels." They are
also called the "central channel of the male" and the "central channel of the female."

At the upper tip of the supreme central [channel] dwells the
inverted syllable HAM (ཧཾ).[98] From that [tip] branches off a channel-
possessing the power to hold the vital essence, and which produces
the inclined syllable HAM in the [area] of the tuft of hair between
the eyebrows.[99] Its [upper] extremity splits into two [channels], one

of which inserts in the tip of the nose. The other, called the "flow of nectar of immortality," inserts in the uvula.

The central channel's own nature possesses four characteristics: it is straight like the trunk of a plantain tree, slender like a lotus stem, luminous like a sesame oil lamp, and red like the lacquer tree's flower.

The *Samputa Tantra* states:[100]

The channel located at the center of the [body]
Is of a distinct and an indistinct nature.[101]
Lacking parts, and most subtle,
It is has the light of great pure essence,
And always dwells at the center of the heart.[102]
From this very beautiful channel originates[103]
The so-called "liberator from the demon."[104]

These words indicate that the power of the central channel increases in the heart region and that, through concepts, the central channel gives rise to the nonconceptual state possessed of fabrications.

[But the channel called] "liberator from the demon" gives rise to a nonconceptual state that is free of all fabrication. [Thus, the liberator from the demon] is [called] the "spring vital essence."

One may wonder, if the central channel is straight, why does it have thirty-two knots? As for the knots, the channel stands in the middle of the four chakras with the lalanā and rasanā [forming] knots by entwining it.

The chapter on wisdom from the *Kālacakra Tantra* states:[105]

The sound, and a part of the vital essence;
The places [to which] the wisdom's nectar has gone;
The channel bound with chains;
The three paths of the life, and downward-clearing
    [winds];

The lotus with the vajra;
And the vajra with the lotus.
When energy-winds meet at the center,
Through the objects and the senses,
There is arising and entering.[106]

The [lower] extremity of the central channel terminates at the great [abdominal] crease. From there, it divides into two extensions, anterior and posterior.

The anterior extension connects to the "crow-faced" [channel][107] that inserts in the anthers of the secret place where it discharges the lunar element [semen].

The posterior extension connects to the "fire of the eon" [channel] whose function is to discharge feces.

The Right and Left Channels: Rasanā and Lalanā

The chapter of the vajra family in The *Hevajra Tantra* states:[108]

Lalanā exists as the nature of knowledge
Rasanā, by virtue of the method.
Avadhūti, at the center,
Is totally beyond subject and object.[109]

Lalanā, white in color, dwells in the left side [of the body], facing downward. Rasanā, red in color, dwells in the right side [of the body], facing upward.

The upper tips of these two channels insert into the nostrils. Up [in the head] they bend, thus, [there] they are [known as] the "two channel nails of the brain."

[Where they] extend down [to the neck] they are [known as] the "two channels, waves of enjoyment." They run [entwining] the four chakras like chains. Having come [along] the two armpits and breasts,[110] they bend inward over the kidneys, and converge above the long abdominal crease toward the central channel, almost inserting into its opening.[111] Their extremities end right there.

From that point, the rasanā connects to [the channel called] "fire lady" that discharges the solar element [blood]. Lalanā connects to [the channel called] "sleepy" that discharges musk[112] [urine].[113]

Regarding this, the *Hevajra Tantra* states:[114]

Lalanā discharges Akṣobhya,
Rasanā discharges blood.
That which discharges wisdom, or the
    lunar element,
Is known as "all-shaking."[115]

In both men and women, the lower tip of the lalanā is elongated, and thus discharges urine.

In women, the lower tip of the rasanā is elongated, and thus discharges the solar [element: menstrual blood] once a month when the red vital essence has reached its apex.

In men, the lower tip of the [rasanā] is curved. Thus, bleeding occurs from the right nostril when the body is unbalanced.[116]

In men, the lower tip [of the central channel] is elongated, and thus discharges semen when this [element] has reached its apex.

In women, the lower tip [of the central] channel can be of four types: fine and coiled like a conch shell, closed like the gland of the musk deer, folded like the trunk of an elephant, or opening and closing like a lotus flower.[117]

On the basis of the causal nexus of the two channels lalanā and rasanā, the various phenomena of duality—such as male and female, right and left side [of the body], sun and moon, east and west, sleeping and waking, going and coming, and so on—manifest.

The *Saṃpuṭa Tantra* states:[118]

The two channels known as "solar" and "lunar"
Are described as the dual [phenomena]
Of going and coming, east and west,
Sleeping and waking, and right and left sides.

In this way, the three channels of the upper [part of the body], from
the lower door downward,[119] split into four extension channels. The
Path and Its Fruit[120] speaks of "four channels of existence, and the
chakras" in consideration of the fact that they expel the nectars.[121]
   The *Summary of the Initiation* states:[122]

The lunar path is the channel of feces,
[In] the solar [channel], urine descends.
At birth, death, when [the energy-winds flow is] balanced,
And [during] sexual intercourse,[123] the seed descends
   in the [channel] of Rahu.

The three upper doors are known as sun, moon, and Rahu,[124] respectively. It is said that in the three lower doors, feces, urine, and
semen descend.
   The *Saṃpuṭa Tantra* states that all the channels of the body
branch off from these three principal channels:[125]

From the feet to the head, [all channels]
Originate from the two threads.[126]

Each of the four chakras has eight channels that govern the phases
of increase and decrease [of the vital essence]. [Thus,] from these
[chakras] branch off thirty-two main channels in which the vital es-

sence descends. Among them, eight originate from the head chakra of great bliss.

The *Saṃpuṭa Tantra* states:[127]

Among the 120 channels,
Differentiated in terms of the four chakras,
Thirty-two channels have the nature of bodhicitta,
And are said to be supreme.

The Eight Channels That Branch Off from the Head Chakra of Great Bliss

The channel [called] "inseparable"[128] branches off from the central channel at the anterior fontanel[129] [known as] Pullīramalaya, one of the twenty-four sacred places. [Its tip] has a knot shaped like [the syllable] PHUṂ (𑀧). It generates the constituents of teeth and nails. Connected and branching off from this channel is the channel [called] "friend" that splits into numerous extensions.

The channel [called] "subtle form" branches off from the central channel at the crown of the head, the sacred place of Jālandhara. It has a coiled tip that resembles the shape of the syllable DZEṂ (ཛེཾ). It generates the constituents of the hair and body hair.

The channel [called] "kind lady"[130] branches off at the crown of the head where the three channels [lalanā, rasanā, and avadhūti] converge. At the right ear, [the sacred place of] Oḍḍiyāna, this channel has a knot in the shape of the syllable UṂ (ཨུཾ). It generates the constituents of skin and sweat.

The channel [called] "left"[131] branches off from lalanā. Its tip inserts in the nape of the neck—[the sacred place of] Arbuda—where it has a knot in the shape of the syllable AṂ (ཨཾ). It generates flesh and lymph, and produces most of the constituents of the left side of the body.

The channel [called] "tamer"[132] branches off from that [channel, the lalanā] at the left ear, [the related sacred place of] Godāvarī. It has a knot in the shape of the syllable GHAṂ (घं). It generates tendons and ligaments.

The channel [called] "tortoise's generator"[133] branches off from the central channel and inserts in the HAṂ (हं) at the point between the eyebrows—[the related sacred place of] Rāmeshvara—where it has a knot resembling the syllable RAṂ (रं). It generates the bones.

The channel [called] "existence"[134] branches off from the junction of the three channels at the crown of the head. It has two tips that insert into the eyes—[the related sacred place of] Devikoti—where their knots have the shape of the syllable DHEṂ (धें). It generates the constituents of the kidneys and spleen.

The channel [called] "empowering"[135] branches off from the life channel that is [located] outside the central channel. Its two tips insert into the shoulders—[the related sacred place of] Mālava—where their knots have the shape of the syllable MAṂ (मं). It generates the constituents of the heart and heart cavities.

The Eight Channels That Branch Off from the Chakra of Enjoyment at the Throat

The channel [called] "angry lady"[136] branches off from the junction of the three main channels [at the throat chakra]. It has four extensions that insert into the two armpits, and into the two depressions above the kidneys—[the field of] Kāmarūpa—where their knots have the shape of the syllable KHAṂ (खं). It generates the constituents of the eyes.

The channel [called] "standing"[137] branches off from the lalanā. It has two extensions that insert into the breasts—[the field of] Odra—where their knots resemble the syllable OṂ (ओं). It generates the constituents of the liver and bile.

The channel [called] "mother deity"[138] branches off from the central channel. It has two extensions that insert into the navel—[the field of] Trishakuni—where their knots have the shape of the syllable TRIM (ဌ). It generates the constituents of the lungs.

The channel [called] "night"[139] branches off from the rasanā. At the tip of the nose—[the field of] Koshala—the knot has the shape of the syllable KAM (ཀཾ). It generates the constituents of the small intestine.

Where this channel extends into the upper palate—[the close field of] Kalinga—it is called "soother."[140] There, the knot at its tip has the shape of the syllable KAM (ཀཾ). It generates tendons and ligaments, and the tissue [covering] the ribs.

Where this channel reaches the cavity of the Adam's apple—[the close field of] Lampaka—it is called "warmer."[141] There, the knot at its tip has the shape of the syllable LAM (ལཾ). It generates the constituents of the stomach.

The channel [called] "grove" branches off from the back of the central channel and inserts in the heart—[the close field of] Kanchi—where the knot at its tip has the shape of the syllable KAM (ཀཾ). It produces feces.[142]

The channel [called] "twisted"[143] branches off from the lalanā. It reaches the pubic region—[the close field of] Himalaya—where the knot at its tip has the shape of the syllable HAM (ཧཾ). Its function is the formation of the clitoris in the female and the testicles in the male.

The Eight Channels That Branch Off from the Chakra of Phenomena at the Heart

At the chakra of the heart there is a channel that is a part of the central channel, known as the "channel of qualifications," which resembles a sleeping female dog.

From this [channel], like external petals, there branch off eight channels correlated to the eight consciousnesses. Their extensions, whose tips have the shape of the long syllable HŪM ($\frac{3}{5}$), insert into the nine orifices, [the sacred places] known as "abstinence from drinking" and "close abstinence from drinking."[144]

In this regard, one of these channels, [called] "beautiful," has the power to move and stabilize the jasmine [or lunar] constituent[145] of the central channel and to generate the pure essence of the consciousness ground of all.[146]

The channel [called] "essence of taste" has the power to move and stabilize the solar constituent[147] of the rasanā and to generate the constituent of the emotional consciousness.[148]

The channel [called] "all-pervading" has the power to move and stabilize the [urine or] musk of the lalanā channel and to generate the constituent of the mental consciousness.[149] The tips of these three channels insert into the two orifices at the secret place.

The channel [called] "three circles"[150] inserts in the two eyes and generates the constituent of the visual consciousness.

The channel [called] "desirous"[151] inserts in the ears and generates the constituents of the auditory consciousness.

The tip of the sixth channel, called "householder,"[152] inserts in the base of the nose[153] and generates the constituent of the olfactory consciousness.

The channel [called] "fierce"[154] inserts in the middle of the tongue and generates the constituent of the taste-consciousness.

The channel [called] "liberator from the demon"[155] inserts in each of the pores of the skin and thus generates the constituent of the tactile consciousness.[156]

The tips of the channels that insert into the five sense organs have the shape of the five syllables[157] and are filled with the liquid of the pure essence of the elements. [Thus,] the collection of these channels, vital essences, and winds constitute the five sense organs.

The organ of the eye resembles an open flax blossom.

The organ of the ear resembles the swirl on birch [bark].

The organ of the nose resembles two spoons placed next to each other.

The organ of the tongue resembles a half-moon.

The organ of tactile sensations resembles the soft plumes of a bird.

[The unity of] energy-wind and mind that relies on [the senses] existing as support and supported inseparable, is the consciousness.

The Eight Channels That Branch Off from the Chakra of Emanation at the Navel

The channel [called] "beautiful color"[158] branches off from the triangular junction of the three main channels at the navel. It inserts in the genitals, [the meeting place of] Pretāpurī, where its knot has the shape of the syllable PREM (ह्रें). It produces the constituent of phlegm.

An extension of that channel, called "ordinary,"[159] inserts in the anus—[the meeting place of] Gṛhadeva—where its knot has the shape of the syllable GHRIM (घ्रीं). It produces the constituent of mucus.[160]

The channel [called] "bestower of the cause"[161] branches off from the rasanā and inserts in the two thighs—[the related meeting place of] Saurāṣṭra —where its knot has the shape of the syllable SAUM (सौं). It produces the constituent of blood.

An extension of this channel known as "separator"[162] reaches the two calves—[the related meeting place of] Suvarṇadvīpa—where its knot has the shape of the syllable SUM (सुं). It produces the constituent of sweat.[163]

The channel [called] "friendly"[164] branches off from the central channel and its tip inserts in all the fingers of the hands and the toes of the feet[165]—[the gathering place of] Nagara—where it has the shape of the syllable NAM (स्). It produces the constituents of fatty tissue and marrow.

An extension of this channel, [called] "accomplished,"[166] is located at the tops of the feet and the backs of the hands—[the related gathering place of] Sindhu—where it has the shape of the syllable SIM (स्). It produces tears.[167] It is connected to the channels [called] "angry lady" and "existence," mentioned above.

The extension of [the previous channel], known as "fire lady,"[168] reaches the thumbs and the toes—[the charnel ground of] Maru—where it has the shape of the syllable MAM (स्). It produces saliva and mucus.[169] It is connected to the channel called "soother," mentioned above.

An extension of the previous channel, known as "attractive,"[170] inserts in the knees—[the charnel ground of] Kulutā—where it has the shape of the syllable KUM (कुं). It produces mucus and snivel. It is connected to the channel called "night," mentioned above.

At the tip of these channels, there is either bodily hair or an itching sensation: this indicates the presence of the [vital essence] constituent.

These [thirty-two channels] are, in order, the twelve levels of awakening that are here indicated by names of the following places:[171] sacred places, related sacred places, fields, related fields, meeting places, related meeting places, gathering places, related gathering places, cemeteries, related cemeteries, places called "abstinence from drinking," and places called "related abstinence from drinking."[172]

The *Saṃpuṭa Tantra* states:[173]

Being more secret than a secret,
The ten levels of the perfections
Are the forms of channels that are the sacred places,
        and so on.

Wind and mind that are present in these places [that is, the chan-nels,] are the heroes and ḍākinīs.

These [places and channels] have been described by presenting, without contradiction, the viewpoints of the *Hevajra* and *Cakras-aṃvara* tantras. "Such an explanation," said Sakya Pandita, "is an oral instruction on the *Hidden Explanation of the Path*."

The Fundamental Nature of the Channels of the Four Chakras

The Channels of the Crown of the Head Chakra

Apart from the above, there is the fundamental nature of the chan-nels of the four chakras.

The chakra at the crown of the head is formed by thirty-two radial channels. In their center is the upper tip of the central chan-nel that has the form of the vital essence [in the shape of the] syl-lable HAṂ (ཧཾ).

All thirty-two radial channels are filled with vital essence, but do not have syllables.[174] Most of the radial channels branching off from their root[175] face downward. Their long extensions run from head to feet:[176] Most of them are connected to the thirty-two [chan-nels explained above].

Moreover, the arterial system[177] originates from the channels called "waves of enjoyment."[178] Four of the eight [peripheral] arter-ies run on the surface of and deep within the arms and legs, then emerge between the index finger and the thumb, the big toe and the first toe, at the palms, and at the soles of the feet, where they coil for a finger-width. Two of the other four [arteries] terminate in the ring fingers, and two in the third toes of the feet.[179] At the center of the body, [all the arteries] merge into two. Branching off from these are the two arteries of the vajra of the secret region.

The Channels of the Throat Chakra

At the chakra of enjoyment of the throat, the knotted junction of the three [main] channels has the shape of the syllable OM (ॐ).

At its center, within the central channel, is the red vital essence in the form of the syllable OM (ॐ).

The knots of the four radial channels of the cardinal directions have the forms of the four syllables YA (ཡ), RA (ར), LA (ལ), and WA (ཝ).[180] These [channels] bind all the channels [descending from the chakra] of great bliss, and the tips of these channels insert into the palate, lips,[181] tongue, teeth, glottis, crown of the head, and ears.[182]

All these channels face upward, and most of them are narrow. Their tips are short,[183] particularly in persons having an unpleasant voice. The longest of these channels insert into each of the knees.

The Channels of the Heart Chakra

At the center of the chakra of phenomena at the heart, the knot of the three main channels has the form of the syllable HŪM (ཧཱུྃ).

The four inner petals [or channels] encircle and lightly entwine the tips of the channels [descending from] the [chakra of] great bliss and from the [chakra of] enjoyment [that is shaped like a rolled-up shuttle].

The knots of these [four] petals or channels, in the four directions, have the form of BHRUM (ྦྷྲུྃ), OM (ༀ), KHAM (ཁཾ), and DZIM (ཛིཾ).[184]

The [channel] in the middle [has the form of] HŪM (ཧཱུྃ). These five [syllables] are the seed-syllables of the five poisons.[185]

These [channels] are called the "five hidden channels" whose pure aspects are the buddhas of the five families.[186]

The *Saṃpuṭa Tantra* states:

Within the heart of beings
Are five types of channels.[187]

And the *Vajramāla* states:[188]

The flow of the actual five indestructible wisdoms—
Whose nature is that of the five buddhas—
Through the five channels,
Is the manifest indestructible state of emptiness.

The four radial channels in the intermediate directions, within which
the energy-winds of the four elements flow, are filled with vital essence. [These channels] are slightly open, and [the vital essences
within them] have the form of the four [syllables] MĀṂ (ঌ), LĀṂ
(ঌ), PĀṂ (ঌ), and TĀṂ (ঌ).

The *Saṃpuṭa Tantra*[189] states that YA, RA, LA, and WA are in
the four cardinal directions, while A (অ), U (উ), I (ই), and E (এ) are
in the intermediate directions.

[Moreover,] there is the channel of qualities called "liberator
from the demon," which is the posterior of the central channel [at the
heart chakra]. [This channel] resembles an open Sichuan pepper.[190]
In ordinary beings it faces downward, and is closed. In bodhisattvas
it is horizontal, and half open. In buddhas it faces upward, is open,
and has the nature of the central channel. It is called "spring."

At the center of the ["liberator from the demon,"] inside the
central channel is the pure essence of the white [constituent in the
form of the syllable] HŪṂ, of the nature of vital essence, the size of
a mustard seed,[191] the color of mercury, luminous with five-colored
light, and on the verge of melting. [This vital essence] brings joy to
the hearts of all beings.[192]

In regard to this, the *Saṃpuṭa Tantra* states:[193]

The lotus that is the heart's center
Has eight petals and a corolla.
The channel in the center
Has a flame-like form,
And the shape of the flower of the plantain tree.
Its mouth hangs, facing downward.
At its center is the hero,
The mere size of a mustard seed,
The indestructible syllable HŪṂ
That descends like snow:
This is called "the spring"
That brings joy to the hearts of all beings.

Accordingly, the potentiality of this channel's constituent gives rise to every joy and happiness of body and mind.

When [this channel] faces downward and is closed, it creates predominantly painful feelings and manifold sorrow.

When it faces upward and opens, the vital essence [within it] becomes clearly manifest, and this produces inconceivable qualities: the body and mind are pervaded by joy and happiness, wisdom arises, and so on. [The channel] will [come to] face upward through yogic meditation.

The *Vajramāla* states:[194]

Just by knowing it,
The changeless state is attained.
In the hollow of the lotus of the chakra of phenomena,
It perfectly abides, just like sound.

That is, the heart [chakra] is the essential birthplace of realization. Therefore, all essential points [of practice] boil down to this. Therefore it is said:

I bow to the sacred supreme being
Who has opened the lotus of the heart.

If the energy-winds and mind dwell [in this channel] while it faces downward and is closed, one falls asleep. [Then] at first, when—due to the potentiality of the vital essence—the energy-winds slightly enter the central channel, there occurs the state of deep sleep totally devoid of thoughts. As the energy-winds cannot enter any farther into the central channel, they disperse into the rasanā and lalanā, flowing into the channels of the throat, and dreams are experienced.

The *[Lamp] Summary of Tantric Practice* states:[195]

When aggregates, constituents of experience, sense
     organs, sense objects,
And the consciousnesses[196] gather in the [central
     channel],
For the one whose earth element thickens,
     sleep occurs.
[Then] by the force of the energy-winds, dreams
     are experienced.

If energy-winds and mind dwell in this channel [while] it faces upward and is open, the luminous clarity arises. That is, through the essential point of the [practice involving the] channels when the *karana* [posture][197] is adopted during the day, the presence of the heart [chakra] between the lungs and chest is nakedly revealed,[198] and the channel ["liberator from the demon"] will face upward and will open.

The [method of] A, NU, TA, RA, HŪM[199] for recognizing the luminous clarity of sleep is related to this.[200]

The *Guhyasamāja Tantra* states:[201]

Through yoga, always meditate with perseverance
On the precious five-colored gem,[202]
The mere size of a mustard seed,
At the nose's tip.

The above passage also relates to this [topic].

The *Dialogue with the Four Goddesses; Continuation of the Gu-hyasamāja Tantra; Vajramāla;* and other tantras as well describe this [channel], presenting their view in the context of the explanation of the energy-winds. In the *Catuḥpīṭha Tantra* [the "liberator from the demon"] is called "bunch from the plantain tree."

Accordingly, [the same tantra] states:[203]

The flower of the plantain [tree]
That stands erect from navel to heart
Is always the door of emptiness;
The wise always invert it.

The master Krishna[204] describes it by calling it "spring"[205] and explains how to apply [the related] key points [of practice].

The master Vajraghaṇṭapa[206] calls it "yoga of the vital essence"[207] and [also] teaches the application of essential points.

In the *Path and Its Fruit* there are many practices for applying essential points related to this.

Below the ["liberator from the demon," at the heart,] is "the channel of qualities," which resembles a sleeping female dog, into which the channels of the eight consciousnesses insert. Below this is a channel knot in the form of HRĪḤ (ཧྲཱིཿ).

All the radial channels of the heart face slightly downward.[208]

The Channels of the Navel Chakra

At the center of the emanation chakra at the navel, the junction of the three [main] channels is shaped like a triangular channel knot pointing upward, whose root is called "ox eye [channel]." In its center is the syllable A (ས), symbolizing the unborn.

In the middle of the [knot], inside the central channel, there is the pure [or red vital] essence in the form of the syllable A (ས).[209] From there until four fingers below the navel is the channel called "mare's face."[210]

Accordingly, the *Samputa Tantra* states:[211]

The form of the fire of the mare's face
Is called "vital essence of selflessness."

At the lower tip of this channel is the so-called "vital essence of Vārāhī," or "mare's face fire-crystal," which is the support for the fire-accompanying [wind] in the shape of the syllable A (ས).[212]

[This fire-like vital essence] that separates the nutrients from the waste [in food], resounds with the sound PHEM, and produces warmth throughout the entire body. The potentiality of the "fire of time,"[213] it resides at the lower tip of the central channel.

In regard to this, the *Kālacakra Tantra* states:[214]

Moving evenly and unevenly,[215]
The fire of time of the central channel operates.

Because the potentiality [of the fire-like vital essence] rises, human beings walk erect. Because the inner fire blazes upward, humans are able to walk erect, have a large head, and thus have a lot of cerebral matter. Because of the great pleasure [of this vital essence], the opening of the "mare's face" channel is soft. Because consciousness is the primary factor [for a human being], his positive or negative actions are potent; thus, the human existence is superior to that of other beings.

The "mare's face" channel reaches up to the "spring" channel [the "liberator from the demon"]. The two [channels] are called "spring" and "vital essence." Since the "spring" [or "liberator from the demon"] and the "vital essence" [or "mare's face"] are now separated, various desires and thoughts arise from the navel chakra. This is because the potentiality of fire [or red vital essence] increases, diminishing that of the [white] vital essence.

Through the meditation [of the inner heat, and so on], the yogin unites the two so that one is empowered by the other.

In regard to this, Krishna's *Vasantatilaka* states:[216]

Aroused by karmic winds,
[The fire] blazes from the mandala of the navel,
And having reached the spring, content,
[They] dwell perfectly in union.

At the chakra of the navel there are eight inner channels called "misty." The vital essence is present in these channels in the form of A (ཨ), KA (ཀ), TSA (ཙ), ṬA (ཊ), TA (ཏ), PA (པ), YA (ཡ), and SHA (ཤ). From these [channels] branch the twelve radial channels of the winds of the twelve time junctures.[217]

From those twelve radial channels branch the sixty-four outer radial channels [of the navel], and from those, many other channel-petals that extend to the upper and lower parts of the body. This is why [the human body] is narrow at the waist.

Various ramifications of these channels branch off from the hollow and the solid organs,[218] and [from other] viscera. These branches are more numerous in the lower part of the body.

The Channels of the Chakra
of the Secret Place

At the chakra of the secret place that sustains the great bliss, there are thirty-two channels. To explain, down from the long abdominal crease is the chakra of the secret place with the triangular shape of E (ཨེ).

In the [chakra of the secret place] are the fourteen syllables of the womb.[219]

At four fingers below the navel, at the terminus of the [lower] extremities of the three [main] channels,[220] from the lower extremity of the rasanā branches off the channel [called] "fire lady" whose knot has the shape of OM (ཨོཾ), [symbolizing] meditative absorption.

From the lower extremity of lalanā branches off the channel [called] "sleepy" whose knot has the shape of HŪM (ཧཱུཾ), [symbolizing] the state of union.

At the lower extremity of the central channel there is the A (ཨ), [symbolizing] the essence.

The knots of the two extensions [one in men and one in women] of the [lower] extremity of the central channel [are shaped like] an inverted KṢA (ཀྵ) [in men]; in women, [like the syllable] BHRUM (བྷྲཱུཾ).

Below this, at the base of the vajra,[221] that is, the penis, the extension of the central channel has the shape of the HŪM (ཧཱུཾ) of strength.

The tip, the extremity of the "crow-face" [or anterior] extension [of the central channel has the form of the] A (ཨ) of the outer shape, *and* of PHAṬ (ཕཊ) inside the hole of the vajra.[222]

Below the HŪM [of the lower extremity of the lalanā] there is the A (ཨ) of knowledge.

An extension branching off above the A of essence at the central channel's lower extremity inserts in the right eyebrow, where its knot [has the shape] of A (ཨ), the seed-syllable of the [realm of the] gods. Another extension branching off below [the A of essence] inserts directly into the beating heart, where its knot has the shape of NRI (ཧྲྀ), seed-syllable of the human [realm].

An extension branching off above the OM at the lower extremity of the rasanā inserts in the left eyebrow, where its knot [has the shape] of SU (སུ),[223] the seed-syllable of the [realm of] demi-gods.

Another extension, branching off below [the OM], inserts in the pubis where its knot [has the shape] of TRI (ཏྲི), the seed-syllable of [the realm of] animals.

An extension branching off above the HŪM at the lower extremity of lalanā inserts in the navel, where its knot [has the shape] of PRE (པྲེ), the seed-syllable of the [realm of] tormented spirits.

A tip branching off below [the HŪM] inserts in the soles of the feet, where its knot has the shape of DU (དུ),[224] the seed-syllable of [the realm of] hell beings.

Thus, since the seed-syllables of the six realms of existence are present in the body as energy-wind, mind, and channels inseparable, it is possible to accumulate actions [leading to birth in the] six realms of existence.

The energy-wind and the vital essence present in these channels serve as the substantial cause of karmic predispositions for the six realms. The many thoughts that arise, the accumulation of karma, and so on, are the outer, inner, and secret coincidences [for birth in the six realms].[225]

When, through meditation, the yogin has exhausted the karma and purified the predispositions for [birth in] the six realms, the syllables of the knots of the channels are destroyed.[226] At that time, there manifests the purification of the realms [of existence]. Once these channels have been purified,[227] the visions of the six realms of existence that succeed the karma no longer manifest. At the time of the fruit, these [six syllables] are the six teachers [buddhas].

In this way, these syllables-channels of samsara and nirvana and of the three realms[228] converge at the secret place, because the secret place is the space of the womb, the palace of the great mother,[229] and the source of all phenomena.

Such explanations accord with the teachings of the *Path and Its Fruit*. Thus, they represent the viewpoint of the great glorious Virūpa[230] that has been transmitted through Sakya Pandita.

Apart from this, some tantras assert that these seed-syllables are located in the head; some assert that they are at the heart chakra; others assert that they are spread throughout all parts of the body. All these [assertions are made] in consideration of the inconceivable fundamental nature of the vajra body.

The secret vajra [that is, the male organ] is equipped with four channels. At the base [of the penis] there is a round channel shaped like a hearth.[231] At a distance of three grains of barley from this is a triangular secret channel. At a distance of three grains of barley from that, there are eight channels of the "palace of the blazing jewel."[232]

At the center of these channels, there is the lotus channel with three openings.[233] From the right side flows the bodhicitta [that is, semen]. From the left side, urine [descends]. In the lower part, there is "fire of time" [the potentiality of fire]. In the upper part is the "fire lady" [channel that discharges blood].

At the tip of the gem of the vajra [the penis,] there is a channel shaped like a large bow.

In these channels [of the secret place] gather [the channels] that branch off from the thirty-two channels in which the bodhicitta descends. In fact, through the condition of the channels and the function of the energy-winds and mind, the [sexual] organ is either aroused or pacified.

To know the fundamental nature of the channels of the woman's secret place, its many channels, and so on, one should consult the secret instructions [on this topic].

In this way, since the thirty-two channels of the secret place are connected to the thirty-two channels of [the chakra of] great bliss and to the thirty-two [channels where the vital essence flows], the pure essence gathers [at the chakra] of great bliss, and then descends to the chakra of the secret place.

Thus, since the five chakras are present within [the body], in the external [world] there manifests all the multiplicity of fivefold phenomena such as the five elements, five classes of beings, five emotions,[234] and so on.

In regard to this, the *Glorious Samputa Tantra* states:[235]

As it is externally, so it is internally;
The binding principle has been well elucidated.

The petals [channels] that branch off from the three chakras,[236] and the three [main] channels, subsumed, are eight, sixteen, four, and so on.[237] Subdivided, they are sixty-four, thirty-two, and so on.[238]

The master Tsami Sangye Tragpa[239] stated:[240]

Regarding the three [channels and chakras],
By subsuming and dividing,
There are five and six [chakras], respectively.

Thus, if summarized there are five chakras; if divided, six.[241] It is said that these chakras are separated from one another by 12.5 finger-widths.

In the *Path and Its Fruit*, eighteen chakras are mentioned. Of these, the two called "unmoving chakras" refer to the HAM at the head chakra, and to the short A at the navel chakra.

The four "moving chakras" refer to the head, throat, heart, and navel chakras.

There are various chakras at the twelve joints, such as the "collection of channels," "intersection of channels," and "holder of channels" that branch off from the channels associated with the sacred places, such as the "undivided." The [chakra] called "small holder of channels" resembles strands of coarse hair. The channels of the skin are like soft paper and resemble lines or strings of ants.

Other Peculiar Channels

The Channels of the Provocations

Concerning the channels of the provocations, at the lungs there is the channel of the tsen;[242] at the heart, that of the gyalpo;[243] at the liver and kidney, that of the *mamo*;[244] at the stomach, that of the *therang*;[245] and at the small intestine, that of the *lu*.[246]

When these channels are opened [by concepts and negative actions],[247] [one will] receive a provocation. Their main critical points are the ring fingers,[248] while the secondary critical points are the fourth toes of the feet [to which] the extensions of these channels [reach].

The Channels of Sorrow

As to the "channels of sorrow," the principal one is located at the big toes and the tops of the feet.[249]

An extension of this channel reaches the thumbs of the hands. Another extension reaches the back of the knees [where] it is called "channel of fear"[250] and is connected to the channel [called] "grove."[251]

This extension [that reaches the knees] encircles the kidneys laterally, where it is called the "channel of yawning." Its extremity is the coiled channel of the eyes, for it is the channel [that produces] tears, and it is connected to the channel called "accomplished."

Another extension [of the channel that reaches the knees] passes medially to the kidneys, arriving at the neck. The trembling of this channel produces hiccups.

[Another channel] that branches off from the channel [called] "night" inserts in the lungs and the heart. When stimulated, it produces sneezing and brings mental clarity.

These are the channels of the twelve chakras [of the joints]. If, in addition to the [eighteen] chakras mentioned above, we add the two chakras of action, that is, the energy-wind of the anus and the fire at the convergence of [the three main channels], we arrive at [a total of] twenty chakras.

The Six Undesirable Channels

Moreover, the following six kinds of undesirable channels are present in the vajra body: "reclining," "lame," "bulky," "pit," "tangled," and "twisted."

If the "reclining" channels are numerous in the body, it will be very stout and short, and in the meditative experience one will have the sensation of being distended or reclining.

If the "lame" channels are numerous in the body, it will be very emaciated, and in the meditative experience one will have the sensation of being pressed between two rocks.

The "bulky" channels are those in which any amount of constituent [that is, the vital essence] that has entered, will fall out.

If these channels are numerous in the body, there will be sterility, and even if one meditates, the vital essence will not increase.

The "pit" channels are those in which the constituent does not enter. If these channels are numerous in the body, there will be hermaphroditism and leakage [of vital essence],[252] and even if one meditates, bliss will not arise.

If the "tangled" channels are numerous in the body, there will indeed be illnesses and poor health. When one meditates there will be much pain [caused by the] channels and energy-winds.

If the "twisted" channels are numerous in the body, it will become curved, and even if one meditates, there will be only hindrances, and no qualities will arise.

If these channels are present in the body, it cannot possess the perfect leisure and endowments of a [body] support for tantric [practice].

The Male, Female, and Neuter Channels

Furthermore, [there are] the so-called "male," "female," and "neuter" channels:[253]

The male channels are thick, knotty, and emerge or rise at the surface of the body.[254]

The female channels are linear, without knots, and disappear internally.[255]

Neuter channels are uniform.[256]

The longest of these channels is one arm-span and two fingers in length. The shortest is half a finger-width, and the others are of varying [lengths].

The identification of these channels and the related essential points [of practice] must be learned from oral instructions.

The [above] description of the fundamental nature of the channels is approximate. It should be known that, [if] explained in detail, their [nature] is inconceivable and can never be fully put into words.

The Vital Essence of Bodhicitta

Now the third factor of the body is indicated by the words, "[the vital essence] of bodhicitta." Whichever channels are present, the [vital essence of] bodhicitta is [also] present.

Concerning this, being the essence of the body and the support for the mind,[257] the vital essence comes as both a physical and mental factor, and will thus be extensively explained below.

The Unclean Substances

The fourth factor of the body indicated by the words "unclean substance" refers to the thirty-two constituents[258] that produce hair, body hair, and so on.

Scholars call these the "thirty-two unclean substances" [of the body]. Secret Mantrins assert that they are the twenty-four heroes, and so on, of the thirty-two sacred places.

It is said that the body contains eighty thousand microorganisms.[259]

Thought

Concerning thought, the fifth factor of the body, when the mind, in the manner of a result, mixes with the five elements that are present in the manner of a cause, the five elements manifest forward and consciousness grasps them from the opposite side.

From the arising of the causal nexus of these two—the pole and tent-like cause and effect—the body is produced.

Since the mind manifests itself as the body, which is the natural expression of thought, this is how it happens that body and mind are inseparable.

The third chapter of the secret seat of the *Catuḥpīṭha Tantra* explains [this] in detail:[260]

> Since the water element comes from mind,[261]
> Consciousness is the water element.
> If water were something else,

Why, after death, does [the body] not become water?
Since consciousness arises as fire,
There is heat in the body.
[If not,] why, in the body left by wisdom,
Is heat not perceived?
Since consciousness is the energy-winds,
      in the bodies [of beings],
The inhalation and exhalation of the breath
      is like smoke.
[If not, why,] in the bodies deserted by wisdom,
Is there no breath?
Since mind manifests as earth,
It manifests as heavy.
[If not, why do] the bodies deserted by wisdom
Float on water?
Although the body has five validating proofs
      [of the five elements],
All five are the essence of a single [mind];
Knowing them to be one,
The yogin examines the dimension
      [of the mind].[262]

When the mind essence manifests as the five elements that are thought's embodiment, the body forms as the expression of past actions and habitual tendencies. Therefore, mental events—thoughts—are also explained as a bodily factor.

THE FUNDAMENTAL NATURE OF THE VOICE, THE VAJRA VOICE OF ALL ENLIGHTENED BEINGS

The fundamental nature of the voice comprises five factors. The *Vajramāla* states:[263]

As to the voice,
By virtue of the five elements, syllables, vocal resonation,
     coordination, and words,
The phenomenon of voice exists.

The Energy-Winds of the Five Elements

[Regarding the] first [factor], the words "five elements" refer to the energy-winds of the five elements.

The Coarse Energy-Winds

To explain, the energy-winds are twofold: coarse and subtle. Among these two, there are the ten kinds of coarse winds: [five root and five branch], and 21,600 winds of the nine orifices.
     The *Mahāmudrātilaka* states:[264]

First, the exhalations and inhalations
Number 21,600,
And flow by day and by night.

Thus, [the energy-winds] flow pervasively from every part of the body and from the nine orifices.
     Subsuming them, there are upper and lower winds; the three [phases of] exhalation, inhalation, and pause; and the male, female, and neuter winds.

The Ten Energy-Winds (Root and Branch)

In regard to that, the tantra of the Great Yoga, called the *Prophetic Declaration of Intention,* states:[265]

The *bodhicitta* is the energy-wind[266]
That abides in space.[267]
It is the life force of all beings.
Of the nature of five,[268] [it has] ten names,[269]
And is known as "twelve links."
In essence, it is threefold.[270]
The so-called energy-wind is bodhicitta:
This is the principal of all consciousnesses.

That is, all winds have the nature of the five elements, and have ten different names. They transit in the twelve houses, and in essence are the three [phases of] exhalation, inhalation, and pause.

As to the ten different winds, the tantra of the Great Yoga called *Vajramukha*[271] states:

The following ten winds have been taught:
The [root] life-sustaining wind, downward-clearing
    wind,
Upward-moving wind, fire-accompanying wind,
    and pervasive wind;
The [branch] winds that rise and flow,
That flow thoroughly, perfectly, resolutely,
    and intensely.
The five [root] winds, beginning with the life-sustaining
    wind,
On the basis of the five aggregates,
Perform the functions of the five aggregates.
The five [branch] winds, beginning with the wind
    that flows,
On the basis of the sense organs,
Perform the outer functions.

266 ❀ Secret Map of the Body

The root winds, on the basis of the condition of the five aggregates, are responsible for the functioning of the [five] aggregates, in the following manner:

The pervasive wind is responsible for the functioning of the form aggregate.

The fire-accompanying wind is responsible for the functioning of the aggregate of sensations.

The downward-clearing wind is responsible for the functioning of the aggregate of discernment.

The upward-moving wind is responsible the functioning of the aggregate of volition.

The life-sustaining wind is responsible for the functioning of the aggregate of consciousness.

These energy-winds are the five buddhas.[272]

The branch winds dwell in the five sense organs, are responsible for the apprehension of the five [sense] objects, and are functions related to the external [world].

These [energy-winds] are the five bodhisattvas.[273]

The wisdom wind that is beyond discursive thought [manifests] when these [ten winds] enter the central channel and their movement comes to a halt.

The [wind] that flows through the solar and lunar [channels], together with exhalation and inhalation, and [always] circulates as various thoughts, is karmic wind. It is called [karmic wind] because, from the mundane paths down, it performs the ten actions.

Moreover, the *Prophetic Declaration of Intention* states:[274]

Then, all the tathāgatas[275] and all the bodhisattvas[276]
Will enter [the central channel][277]
In order to please the lord of tathāgatas.[278]
[These are the] life [-holding], the downward-clearing,
    upward-moving,

Pervasive, [and fire-] accompanying,
The nāga, tortoise, lizard,
Gods' gift, and victorious with the bow [winds].
They are considered as the form of oneself,[279] of the
    woman,[280]
And of the further emanation.[281]

The life-sustaining energy-wind—the basis [of the five root energy-winds]—is located in the heart and in the life channels. It prevents the separation of body and mind, and causes one to cling to the notion of "I" or "self."

The upward-moving wind resides in the Adam's apple, at the OM of the neck. It enables the swallowing of food and vomiting, and makes speech and laughter possible.

The downward-clearing wind resides in the perineal region between the anus and the urinary tract. It is responsible for expelling and retaining frankincense [menstrual blood], camphor [semen], musk [urine], and four equal tastes [feces].

The fire-accompanying wind resides at the navel. It is responsible for the digestion of food, separation of nutrients from waste, transformation of nutrients into the seven organic components, and for sending the waste downward.

The pervasive wind abides at the head and at the center of the twelve main joints. It governs all bodily movements such as walking, rising, sitting, posing, and so on.

[As to the branch energy-winds],[282] the wind that rises and flows resides in the eyes. It enables the cognition of different forms: best, middling, [and inferior].

The wind that flows thoroughly resides in the ears. It enables the cognition of different sounds: best, middling, and inferior.

The wind that flows perfectly resides in the nose. It enables the cognition of the three types of smells: best, middling, and inferior.

The wind that flows resolutely abides in the body [as a whole]. It enables the cognition of tactile sensations: best, middling, and inferior.

The wind that flows intensely abides in the tongue. It enables the cognition of three types of taste: best, middling, and inferior.

These [branch energy-winds] are the potency of the winds of the five elements. In fact:

Through the pure essence of the water wind, forms are seen.

Through [the pure essence of] the earth wind, odors are smelled. Through [the pure essence of] the wind of air, sounds are heard. Through [the pure essence of] the wind of fire, tastes are experienced. Through [the pure essence of] the wind of space, tactile sensations are felt.

The *Prophetic Declaration of Intention* states:[283]

The nāga, tortoise, lizard,
Gods' gift, and victorious with the bow.

The life-sustaining winds flowing in each of the five sense organs are [said to be the] five branch winds.

Regarding this, the nāga, or wind that [rises and] flows, resides like a snake in the intestine, and from there connects the eye to visual forms.

The tortoise, or wind that flows thoroughly, resides like a tortoise in the liver. It connects the ear to sounds.

The lizard, or wind that flows perfectly, resides like a lizard in the lungs. It connects the nose to odors.

The gods' gift, or wind that flows intensely, resides like a gift of the gods in the heart. It connects the tongue to tastes.

The victorious with the bow, or wind that flows resolutely, resides like a bow in the kidneys. It connects the bodily organ to tactile sensations.

These [winds] are connected to the five sense organs and the five solid organs [such as the] heart, and perform their functions through their respective energy-winds.

These energy-winds are also so-named in terms of that which the life-sustaining wind can cause:

Since it provokes all dangerous illnesses and belching, it is [called] "nāga" [wind].

Since it is responsible for the extension and contraction of the limbs, it is [called] "tortoise" [wind].

Since it makes one angry and upset, it is [called] "lizard" [wind].

Since it causes yawning and attachment, it is [called] "gods' gift" [wind].

Since it causes sneezing and does not cast away the life force, it is [called] "victorious with the bow" [wind].

The *Glorious Tantra of Kālacakra* states:[284]

The [wind] that fastens the life force moves in the solar
    and lunar paths;
The downward-clearing moves downward; the [fire-]
    accompanying gathers all tastes;
The upward-moving develops the body, enables the
    mouth to sing, and the arms to dance;
The pervasive provokes all illness, and likewise,
    by virtue of its natural quality, pervades the body;
The nāga causes belching; the tortoise is the wind that
    contracts the arms and legs;
The lizard causes all types of anger and upset; the gods'
    gift causes yawning;
And victorious with wealth[285] is the wind that is the lord
    of man until the body is separated from these five.

The *Eight Vajra Verses* of the Great King Indrabhuti states:[286]

The nāga differentiates the four gates;
The tortoise causes movement;
The lizard causes the traversing of the six gates;
The gods' gift strengthens;
And the victorious with the bow [causes] clinging
        to desires.

The main point of these words also relates to the five [branch] energy-winds.

In the *Buddhasamāyoga Tantra*,[287] a tantra of the Cakrasaṃvara [cycle], the ten winds are referred to with a coined terminology:[288]

Kotaksha [upward-moving wind]; kotabha [life-
        sustaining wind]; kota [fire-accompanying wind];
        kotabhashcha [downward-clearing wind]; kotarika
        [pervasive wind].[289]
Kolabhaksha [rising and flowing]; kolabha [flows
        thoroughly]; kola [flows perfectly]; kolabhashcha
        [flows resolutely]; kolabhastatha [flows intensely].[290]

The Types of Energy-Winds

The ten winds are [associated with] exhalation, inhalation, and pause.

In this regard, until age twenty-five, the force of inhalation is strong, so the body grows and develops.

Between the ages of twenty-five and forty-five, the force of pause is strong, so the body too is complete and stable.

Past the age of forty-five, the force of exhalation is strong, so the body ages and decays.

The [ten energy-winds] are of male, female, and neuter [types].

The male wind is short and coarse.

The female wind is long and smooth.

And the neuter wind is balanced.[291]

In [an alternative classification, the energy-winds are categorized in terms of the] energy-wind of life and the energy-wind of exertion. As to upper or lower, the so-called wind of life is an upper [wind]. As to exhalation or inhalation, it is inhalation. It flows in the left [nostril].

As to upper or lower, the wind of exertion is a lower [wind]; as to exhalation or inhalation, it is exhalation. It flows in the right [nostril].

As to the upper and lower winds: the upper wind flows 21,600 times [daily] from the navel up, based on the thirty-two channels [of the navel chakra].[292]

The lower wind flows in the channels from the forehead down, performing the functions of the lower [part of the body]. When these [two winds] arrive at the mouth, they [produce the sounds] HA and HŪM.

Concerning the [classification of energy-winds as] cold and hot winds, the cold winds resemble a horse, and the hot, a yak. When these two [winds] are balanced, they promote the development of the body. When they are unbalanced, many illnesses and other problems occur.[293]

When yogins first mix the hot and cold winds through their practice, they [experience] many difficulties, but once the two have been mixed, infinite qualities arise.

Regarding this, the *Samputa Tantra* states:[294]

The supreme doors of inhalation and exhalation
Are principally known as upper and lower.
At the lower door there is consciousness,
At the upper door there is the constituent.
Through inhalation and exhalation
Qualities and faults increase.

Moreover, the energy-winds flow in a very subtle way through the nine orifices, penetrating every part of the body. They also flow in a very subtle way through each pore of the skin.

Therefore,[295] when the practice with the energy-winds is successful, with a single application, one can seize all ten kinds of energy-winds at once. Once one is familiar with this [practice],[296] one can direct the energy-winds wherever one wishes, as well as integrate the outer and inner [winds], and so on. There are exceptional oral instructions on these [practices].

The Flow of the Energy-Winds

In a day and night, 21,600 energy-winds flow. In the *Net of Magical Manifestations of Mañjuśrī* of sixty-one thousand chapters; in the *Kālacakra Tantra*; the *Glorious Guhyasamāja Tantra*; the *Prophetic Declaration of Intention*; and elsewhere, it is asserted that [this flow consists of either] twelve two-hour periods,[297] twenty-four transits,[298] forty-eight *ghaṭikā*,[299] or sixty-six *daṇḍa*.[300]

The *Net of Magical Manifestations of Mañjuśrī* and the *Kālacakra Tantra* describe this as the flow of the winds of the five elements.

During each two-hour period [the winds flow approximately] 1,800 times: 360 times for the wind of each of the five elements. During a "transit" [the winds flow] 900 times: 180 times for each of the five elements.

[The flow] through the right nostril begins with the wind of the earth [element], followed by that of water, fire, and air, and concludes with the wind of the space [element].

[The flow] through the left nostril begins with the wind of the space [element], followed by that of air, fire, and water, and concludes with the wind of the earth [element].

Moreover, at the moment when [the wind of] each element of the twelve two-hour periods [of the day and night] changes, the wisdom wind flows 11.25 times.[301]

Thus, during each two-hour period, the wisdom wind moves, flowing 56.25 times in the central channel. In a day and night, the wisdom wind flows 675 times. At that rate, in a month it flows for 56.25 ghaṭikā. In a year it flows for eleven days and six hours. In the course of four years it flows for one and a half months. At that rate, in the course of a hundred years it flows for three years, one and a half months.

Even [for one] in an ordinary condition, it is said that the winds enter the central channel during four[302] or eight occasions.

Moreover, the *Prophetic Declaration of Intention* and some commentators of the treatises assert that the energy-winds of the four elements flow during twenty-four transits. In this case, during one transit, the winds of the four elements flow 225 times each, that is, they flow 900 times [relating to] method through the right [nostril], and 900 times [relating to] knowledge through the left [nostril], for a total of 1,800 times per two-hour period.

In regard to this, the *Prophetic Declaration of Intention* states:[303]

The recitation of Paṇḍāravāsinī, and the other[304]
    [goddesses]
Is said to involve 225 [winds].
Multiplied by the four [elements],
This amounts to nine hundred [winds] included in
    four applications.
These nine hundred that have been explained,
Gradually, through twenty-four [transits]
And from the individual elements,
[Flow a total of] 21,600 [times].

The energy-wind of space[305] flows within the body,[306] pervading all its parts. Except at the time of death, it does not flow outside [the body].

The *Vajramāla* explanatory tantra states:[307]

The wind that pervades the entire body
Manifests [as] the three realms,
And holds the support and the supported.[308]
Therefore, the pervasive [wind] performs the functions
    of all [winds],
It is the Body dimension of Vairocana;
And in the end, at death, it leaves [the body].

To explain, when the pervasive [wind] exits [the body], the life ends.[309]

Since the pervasive [wind] pervades the entire body, the mind also pervades the entire body. [This is why] one dies when an artery is severed; it is also why the channels dissolve at the time of death.

The so-called "karmic" wind refers in general to all kinds of wind [present in the individual] on the mundane and lower paths.[310]

In particular, [it refers to the] pervasive [wind], the karmic wind that accompanies the consciousness of the intermediate being as it enters [the place of conception], and which [then] dwells in the innermost part of the great channel in the center of the half-moon.[311]

Due to several conditions, [the pervasive wind] recedes without overflowing from its place. If it were to move upward, it would give rise to countless problems. At the time of death, together with the mind, it exits the body.

In the *Catuḥpīṭha*, the *Hevajra*, and the *Cakrasaṃvara* [tantras], it is asserted that the energy-winds of the four elements flow during eight two-hour periods, sixteen transits, thirty-two ghaṭikā, and sixty-four daṇḍa.[312]

Accordingly, the *Saṃpuṭa Tantra* states:[313]

The mandalas of fire, air,
Earth, and likewise, of water,
Sustain the mind; [they flow] in the upper and
    lower [parts],
On the walls, and straight [in the center of the
    nostrils].[314]

Moreover, in each [of the sixteen] transits, the winds flow 1,350 times. Dividing this by the four elements, [each element] flows 337.5 times. In a ghaṭikā, the wind of each element flows 675 times; in a daṇḍa, 337.5 times. In this way, the winds of the sixteen transits flow in the thirty-two channels 675 times [for a total of 21,600].

Moreover, the winds flow 225 times for each [of the three modes of] beginning, experience, and dissolution in the following way:[315]

[First,] in the "inseparable"[316] channel, [the winds flow in the mode of] dissolution.[317] In the "subtle form"[318] channel, [the winds flow in the mode of] experience.[319] In the "kind lady"[320] channel, [the winds flow in the mode of] beginning.[321]

[Then,] in the "subtle form" channel, they [flow during the phase of] dissolution; in the "kind lady" channel they [flow during the phase of] experience; and in the "left"[322] channel they [flow during the phase of] beginning.

This process takes place in a similar pattern up to the "attractive"[323] channel. Then again [the winds move during the phase of] beginning in the "undivided" channel.

[In this way,] the path is traversed in sets of three.

The master Krishna, in his *Four Stages,*[324] correlates [the flow of the winds in the channels] with the twenty-four sacred places, but the meaning is similar.

In any case, whatever the winds' modes of flowing, regarding the 21,600 [flows], some assert that between one day and the next, one month and the next, and one year and the next, the winds always flow in the lunar channel; hence, in those periods, the winds reverse their flow from the solar channel.

Vagishvarakirti[325] and others [instead] assert that they flow alternatingly [in each of the two channels].

To explain, during the Rohita time, that is, from the first day of the waxing moon and for three consecutive days, the winds start their flow from the lunar [channel]. During the three following days, they flow in the solar channel. For the three successive days, they again start their flow from the lunar channel.

Then, during the Rohita time, from the first day of the waning moon and for three consecutive days, they start their flow from the solar channel. For the three following days, they flow in the lunar channel, and so on, as above.

The glorious Sakya Pandita asserts that, during the day, the winds [begin their] flow in the solar channel, and during the night, in the lunar channel. During the waxing moon, they start their flow in the lunar channel; during the waning moon, in the solar channel. At the winter solstice, they start their flow in the solar channel and at the summer solstice, in the lunar channel.

The Colors and Spans of the Energy-Winds of the Four Elements

As to the colors and flow spans of the winds of the four elements: the wind of the earth element is light yellow. It flows from the navel chakra of emanation, pervading [the body], and exits [the nostrils] for [a span of] twelve finger-widths. [Then it returns] within, for [a span of] sixteen finger-widths, touching the base of the nostrils. At that time, [when] the energy-wind [is within], it arrives at [a point] four fingers below the navel. Thus, this is [a favorable] time for the practice of inner heat. This is a profound key point.

The wind of the water element is light blue. It flows on the basis of the heart chakra of phenomena, and exits [the nostrils] for [a span of] thirteen finger-widths. [Then it returns] within, for [a span of] fifteen finger-widths, touching the flesh in the center of the nose.

The wind of the fire element is light red. It flows from the throat chakra of enjoyment [the wind of fire], and exits [the nostrils] for [a span of] fourteen finger-widths. [Then it returns] within, for [a span of] fourteen finger-widths, touching the upper part of the nostrils.

The wind of the air element is light green. It flows from the chakra of great bliss [the wind of air], and exits [the nostrils] for [a span of] fifteen finger-widths. [Then it returns] within, for [a span of] thirteen finger-widths, touching the right side of the nostrils. Each of these winds flow for rounds of 270 times.

The wind of the space element lacks any color. It flows out [of the nostrils] for [a span of] sixteen finger-widths. [Then it returns] within, for [a span of] twelve finger-widths at the center of the nostrils. This is the view of the *Kālacakra* [*Tantra*], which states: "The limit of sixteen, and the limit of twelve."

In consideration of the fact that the [winds of the space element] do not [really flow] outside, but [only] inside, it is said that they "flow slowly, as if dissolving, and as if not flowing [at all]."

Apart from the above explanation, there are many discrepancies as to the [energy-winds' colors, the area [of the nostrils] in which they flow, and the span [of their flow].

In some versions, the wind of fire flows in the right side [of the nostrils], water in the left, earth below, air above, and [the wind of] space in the middle.

As to their span, the earth wind flows outside for four finger-widths, and inside for twenty.

The wind of water flows inside for sixteen finger-widths, and outside for eight.

The wind of fire flows outside for twelve finger-widths, and inside for twelve.

The wind of air flows outside for sixteen finger-widths, and inside for eight. The wind of space flows outside for twenty [finger-widths], and inside for four.

The [description provided in this book] is [based on] the understanding I gained when I personally saw the colors and spans of the energy-winds.

The Variation in Flow of the Energy-Winds by Day and by Night

The variation in the rate of [the energy-winds'] flow by night and by day is determined by the increase and decrease of the winds of the solar day.

To explain, during the summer solstice, the daytime [flow of the winds] increases by 2,160. In fact, at that time, by day the winds flow 12,960 times, while by night they flow 8,640 times.

For a period of three months after the summer solstice, for each solar day, twenty-four winds are subtracted from the day and added to the night. In the third month, for one solar day, the night and day [flows] are equal: by day, the winds flow 10,800 [times] and by night, 10,800. Then, for the next three months, each day [the flow] decreases by twenty-four winds, and each night it increases [by the same amount].

During the winter solstice, the [flow by] night is 2,160 [winds] greater than by day. In fact, at that time, the winds flow 12,960 times by night, and 8,640 by day. Then again, as before, for [the next] six months, [the winds of] the day increase, and those of the night decrease. To explain: each day, one night wind is subtracted from the twenty-four sacred places [or channels], and added to the day.

The varying rate of the [winds of] the day are related to the cycles of the constituents [of the vital essences].

In the external [world], in a solar day, the sun and moon traverse the four continents.[326] [Paralleling this,] in the internal body, in a solar day, the solar and lunar energy-winds transit the four chakras.

The sun traverses the twelve houses in a year; [similarly] in the body, the energy-winds transit the twelve channels of the time junctures[327] in a solar day.

Twelve years make up a cycle of years,[328] and each year comprises four seasons, two solstices, and twelve months. Each month comprises fifteen days of the waxing, and fifteen of the waning moon. Each year has 360 days. Each solar day is made of day and night, comprising the six two-hour periods,[329] dusk, and so on. Each year is made of six seasons, [including] the first part of the summer, and so on.[330]

[For] all these, [it is said,] "As it is externally, so it is internally." This must be learned from the oral instructions.

In this way, by shifting at the right time, the flow [of the energy-winds] strengthens the body; and by shifting at the wrong time, health is lost, and [likewise,] good and bad signs manifest.[331]

The Chief of All Energy-Winds

The chief of the ten winds is the life-sustaining wind. Why?

The *Saṃpuṭa Tantra* states:[332]

It pervades all beings,
The animate and inanimate.
Brahmā[333] and so on,[334] the gods,[335]

And the demigods[336] depend on this.[337]
The place of enjoyment of the chief wind[338]
Is called *bhāga*.[339]

It is taught that realization arises when the life-sustaining [wind] has been purified of its residue by the fire-accompanying [wind], and has merged with the pervasive [wind].

[To explain,] by turning the course of the downward-clearing wind upward, the power of the wind of fire increases. Thereby, the life-sustaining [wind] is purified; the upward-moving wind is stabilized; and the pervasive wind is balanced. Because of this, the karmic wind is pacified, and one will not be beset by obstacles. [And] by turning the power of fire downward, the vital essence is uplifted, resulting in the arising of inconceivable qualities.[340]

At the time of death, the course of the karmic winds turns upward and as a result, the five [root] winds disappear [as follows]:

When the downward-clearing wind disappears, urine and feces are spontaneously lost.

When the fire-accompanying wind disappears, food is no longer digested.

When the life-sustaining wind disappears, consciousness becomes dim.

When the upward-moving wind disappears, food cannot be ingested, nor speech articulated.

When the pervasive wind disappears, the body becomes wretched.

Whenever the karmic wind looses its functions, this gives rise to many problems.[341]

In this way, the potentialities of the five elements are produced by the life-sustaining wind. In fact, the five elements, the five emotions, the five sense organs, and the five solid organs such as the heart are produced from within the center of the body[342] by the five colors of the [life-sustaining] wind.

The *Continuation of the Guhyasamāja Tantra* states:[343]

> The breath that has the nature of the five
>   wisdoms
> Is the very essence of the five elements.
> That which emerges in the form of a sphere
> Is imagined[344] at the tip of the nose.[345]
> [This] gem of five different colors
> Is called "vitality and exertion."[346]

And the *Vajramāla* states:[347]

> The heart closely exists as the fivefold,[348]
> And emerges at the five doors.
> Associated with the dream-wind,[349]
> It enjoys the five objects of desire.

The life-sustaining wind is the chief of the five energy-winds. If recognized, [one knows it to be] the energy-wind that flows in a manifest way through the door of the nose.

In this regard, the *Mahāmudrātilaka* states:[350]

> In a stream, from the nostrils,
> It flows as life and [as] exertion.
> That which always flows
> Is said to be the life [-holding wind].

These are descriptions from the perspective of the coarse energy-winds.

The Subtle Energy-Winds and the Wisdom Energy-Wind

As for the subtle energy-wind, to the extent that space pervades, mind pervades, and since mind and wind are inseparable, everything, external and internal, is the embodiment of energy-wind consciousness.

[Nāgārjuna's] *Five Stages* states:[351]

> The subtle form of the winds,
> Perfectly mixed with consciousness,
> Arises through the paths of the senses,
> And determines the perception of various objects.

Moreover, the *Prophetic Declaration of Intention* states:[352]

> It is said that from the unmanifest subtle [energy-winds],
> [Vision] is always manifesting.
> The functioning of beings, and objects
> Depend on it.
> For as long the world is imagined,
> And likewise, [for] other imaginings,
> These will always arise from energy-wind.
> This essence of bodhicitta
> Is the nonduality of the aggregates, and so on,
> And is equal to space.
> It is neither outside nor inside.

As to the so-called wisdom wind, it is the manifestation of energy-wind and mind as the essence of space.

[This occurs] when, having been integrated as one, the flow of the inner and outer winds[353] is severed: this is known as "[energy-wind] entering the central channel." [The] inner causal nexus [for the manifestation of energy-wind and mind as the essence of space] is [the wind] entering the central channel.

This does not mean that all outer winds are enclosed in the innermost part of the central [channel] and remain there. Thus, the integration of the inner and outer winds as one is an exclusive essential point.

All the essential points of the inseparability of wind and mind; inseparability of vision and mind; inseparability of body, speech, and mind; and so on should be understood by way of this [explanation]. No one else possesses this key point; thus, it is extremely secret.

The Syllables

The second factor of the voice is the syllables.

You may think, "If voice is energy-wind, nothing but a whisper will come out, so how can [wind] be uttered as various names and words?"

[It is possible] because, in the body, there are the syllables of the vajra Voice of the enlightened ones, which are the root of names and words.

To explain: at the lower extremity of the three [main] channels are the three syllables[354] whose nature is that of the three—exhalation, inhalation, and pause—that is, the vajra recitation.[355] Now, these are the life force of all [expressions of the] voice.

From among these [syllables], since—regardless of whether they flow from the solar or the lunar [channel—the energy-winds] move from the [lower] extremity of the central channel, the [syllable] A [located there] is the foundation, or life, of all vocal expressions.

In this regard, the root of words are vowels and consonants. The root of these is the three syllables. The root of these [three] is the short A.[356] This A exists as the life force of all [expression] of the voice. If there were no A, verbal utterance would not be possible.

With regard to this, the *Net of Magical Manifestations* states:[357]

A is the supreme of all syllables.
It is the sublime syllable of total reality
That comes from within, and it is unborn.
Beyond verbal expression,
It is the supreme source of all expression,
And it manifests every word.[358]

Moreover, the *Mother of the Buddhas* states:[359]

A is the unborn state.
Thus, it is the door [from which] all phenomena
    [manifest].

The *ali kali*[360]—vowels, consonants, and syllables—are present, |without exception, within the body. Therefore, any word can be spoken.

Indians, Tibetans, Nepalese, Kashmiris, and Mongolians each have their own syllables;[361] therefore, their languages differ.[362]

If you go to another country, in six months your constitution and senses have adjusted to the place. As your inside changes, so your outside changes, and you learn the language [of the country].

This is also why, by practicing for six months,[363] you can attain the realization.

Thus, in the three [main] channels, in the four chakras, and in the infinite minor channels there are syllables in the form of channel knots and vital essence. Therefore, you can speak various words. The short syllables [present] in the middle of the chakras are of one life force with the syllable A, and therefore they become the life of all words.

The *Prophetic Declaration of Intention* states:[364]

All the short [syllables] become speech;
They are neither one, nor are they many.

In this way, when words originate from the causal nexus of the gathering of syllables or channels and energy-winds, vocal utterances clearly manifest as sounds.

Vocal Resonation

The third factor of the voice [is known as] vocal resonation.[365]

In this regard, sounds that manifest externally arise because space provides an opportunity for such occurrences. And voice—as utterances of sound—arises from the channels, the larynx, and the emptiness within the body.

The *Discourse Requested by the King of Kinnaras* states:[366]

The voice of sentient beings arises from space.
The essence of sound is space, the cessation
    of the perceptible.

This means that the vocal resonation arises from emptiness, and this gives rise to utterances as audible language.

In this regard, if the belly is big and too full, the voice does not project loudly, but this can be improved through practice related to the wind-energies.

Coordination

The fourth factor of the voice is coordination.

Now, you may wonder, if words originate from the causal nexus of syllables and winds, and speech arises from emptiness, why are words not uttered when we blow air from the nose?

This does not occur because the coordination needed for the articulation of speech is incomplete.

To explain, speech is articulated through the coordination of syllables-channels, energy-wind, and mind made one by virtue of the essential point of the single identity of energy-wind and mind; and through the secondary condition of the movements of the palate, larynx, nose, lips, tongue, teeth, and so on.

Words

The fifth factor of the voice is words.

From the combination of various syllables, names arise. From the combination of various names, words arise. From the combination of various words, speech arises.

Coherent, meaningful, unconfused speech is the verbal manifestation of any movement of thought by virtue of the essential point of the oneness of body, voice, and mind, [occurring] through the action of mental discursiveness. [Thus] it is said: "Voice resembles mind."

Since thoughts have no end, there is also no end to that which can be expressed in words. Thus, by working on the essential points [of the syllables] while [practicing] the path, the throat channels open and the treasure of the enlightened Voice bursts forth; the mastery of speech is realized, and a limitless confidence in composition or writing manifests.

And at the time of enlightenment, the inconceivable secret of the Voice; the proclamation of the [Buddha's] Teaching in the language of each of the six classes of beings; and the melodious Voice endowed with sixty qualities,[367] are the energy-winds, syllables, and thoughts manifesting as the essence of space.

THE FUNDAMENTAL NATURE OF THE MIND, THE VAJRA MIND OF ALL ENLIGHTENED BEINGS

The fundamental nature of the mind is explained with five factors. The exegetical tantra, the *Vajramāla* states:[368]

As to the mind, by virtue of five wisdoms;
Bliss; vital essence;
Nonthought; and contemplation;
The phenomenon of the mind exists.

The Vital Essence of Bodhicitta

Rearranging the disarrayed order [of the above passage], the first factor explained is the fundamental nature of the vital essence of bodhicitta, the support [of the mind].

The Pure Essences

In relation to the nectar-constituent that is the Mind of all the enlightened ones, infinite pure essences are explained [such as]:
  [the pure essence of] the solar and the lunar [constituents];
  [the pure essence] of the five nectars;
  [the pure essence] of the nine constituents;[369]
  [the pure essence] of the sixteen constituents;[370]
  [the pure essence] of the thirty-seven constituents.[371]
  In terms of the nine constituents, there are the quintessences of the four elements, and the pure essence of the five nectars.
  As for the four elements [in the body], flesh and bones are the earth [element]. Blood and liquids are the water [element]. Warmth, in its various forms, is the fire [element]. The aspect of breath is the air [element].

The pure essence of the channels is like a white silk thread or the silken thread of a spider.

The pure essence of heat is like the sun striking or hitting a mirror.

The pure essence of blood is like powdered cinnabar.

The pure essence of air is like breath blown on a gem. These pure essences are present like dewdrops on the tips of [blades of] gray grass.

The five nectars are the pure essence of the five chakras, [as follows]:

Feces are the [pure essence] of the head [chakra].

Camphor [or semen, is the pure essence] of the throat [chakra].

Musk [or urine, is the pure essence] of the heart [chakra].

Frankincense [or blood, is the pure essence] of the navel [chakra].

Great pure essence [is the pure essence] of the secret place chakra.[372]

In regard to this, the *Saṃpuṭa Tantra* states:[373]

The body [is of the] nature of five nectars:
Feces, urine, phlegm,[374] blood,
And likewise, the fifth, semen.
Hence, it is called, "possessor of the vajra."

The five nectars[375] produce the thirty-two [bodily] constituents,[376] and the pure essence of these produces the eight consciousnesses, the five sense organs, and so on, as explained in detail [above] in the context of the channels.

The waste[377] [from the thirty-two constituents] is phlegm,[378] bile,[379] areas devoid of blood,[380] and so on.[381]

The Seven Organic Components

Internally, these [substances are included in] the seven organic components of the body,[382] the principal of which is the jasmine flower constituent: this the called "seventh internal birth."

To explain, food is first swallowed by the upward-moving [wind] and then descends into the recesses [of the body]. There, the potency of the bile channels that make [organic components] appear as yellow, gives [the ingested food] a yellow color. The fire-accompanying [wind] separates the pure essence from the waste. The waste is directed toward the colon, from which it is expelled by the downward-clearing [wind].

The pure essence becomes phlegm.[383] The pure essence of this [phlegm][384] that comes from the separation from the waste becomes blood inside the *mesarige* channel of the liver. The pure essence of this becomes flesh. The pure essence of that becomes fat. The pure essence of that becomes marrow and bones. The pure essence of that becomes red marrow, spinal cord [fluid], and brains. The pure essence of that, separated from the waste, becomes vital essence.[385]

That which in the *Net of Magical Manifestations of Mañjuśrī* is referred to as "the supreme sublime son of the enlightened ones" is this [vital essence]. Lesser [in importance among the five nectars] is the great essence;[386] lesser than that is blood; lesser than that is urine; and lesser than that is feces.[387]

The Fundamental Nature of the White and Red Constituents

The fundamental nature of the white and red [constituents] that are among these five nectars is as follows:

At the time of the formation of the vajra body, the consciousness of the intermediate being that, accompanied by the pervasive wind, has entered [the womb] in the form of the syllable A, is enveloped by the pure essence [or semen] of the father. [Then, further] enveloped from the outside by the pure essence [or blood] acquired from the mother, it settles above the triangular channel knot at the navel.

Since this [embryo] is connected to the mother's navel, it will develop [into a] body.

When the umbilical cord is severed, the three [that is, the white and the red vital constituents, and consciousness] separate, and since the blood [of the child] is that of both the mother's and the child's hearts, the mother is strongly attached to a male child and, due to that causal nexus, less attached to a female child.

At birth, the two [the white and red vital essence] separate. The white vital essence goes to the upper tip of the central channel. During the lifetime, it is held at the crown of the head by the strength of the left [channel,] lalanā.

The red vital essence descends to the secret place. During the lifetime, it is held at the lower tip of the central channel by the strength of the right [channel,] rasanā.

As to the winds, from within the major channels, the pervasive [wind] spreads to each and every part of the body. The other winds start to flow out through both nostrils with the sound of the syllables A HAṂ.[388] The mind goes to the navel or to the heart.

Therefore, the potentiality of HAṂ produces the HŪṂ at the heart [chakra] that is the support for the mind of bliss of the indestructible vital essence.

[The potentiality of] A produces the A at the navel [chakra] that serves as the support for the fire-accompanying [wind].

The potentiality of this [A at the navel] produces the HAṂ at the chakra of the secret place, that is the support for the radiance of the downward-clearing wind.

The potentiality of the syllable HŪṂ at the heart produces the syllable OṂ at the throat [chakra], where the upward-moving wind that is the support for the [seven] organic components of the body [performs its functions].

The vital essence of HAM is the essence of the entire body. Therefore, it produces the twelve chakras [of the twelve joints where] the pervasive wind [performs its functions].

Since all these [syllables] are the support of the mind, it is said, "Their domain resembles [that of] a universal emperor." [This means that] in the four pivotal states[389] and so on, [the vital essence] dwells in turn at the four chakras or in all the parts of the body.

It is on the basis of [these syllables] that the three poisons, the five poisons, and all subtle and coarse discursive thoughts arise.

In an ordinary body, the constituents within the channels are—for the most part—pure, and are thus present as blood, lymph, and fat.

The syllables at the four chakras, plus HAM, A, HŪM, and so on, are present as this pure essence.

The potentiality [of the pure essences] develops the body and produces the teeth, nails, eyes, and the body's radiance. The impure essences, on the other hand, cause various illnesses.

In persons possessing a good constitution and good organic components, the pure essence is preponderant. In those with a weak or poor constitution and weak or poor organic components, waste is preponderant, [and thus] their bodies are weak, and have little radiance.

Yogins, through meditation practice, gradually separate the pure essence from the waste, and increase the pure essence. [Then,] from the point of their attainment of the levels of realization onward, their constituents become entirely of the jasmine [-like] essence,[390] and their blood transforms into a stream of "milk." Having attained enlightenment, their body becomes like a polished golden bolt, adorned with supreme signs: it is transformed into an indestructible essence.

During sexual intercourse, the fire of the passion [aroused by] the downward-clearing [wind] reversing upward generates the power of the fire at the navel. Its heat melts the constituents, and the potentiality of the syllable HAM trickles [down].[391]

To explain, [during sex,] as the [course] of the downward-clearing [wind] is turned upward, the power of the fire-accompanying [wind] grows, and the life-sustaining [wind] is purified. By the power of this, the energy-winds enter the central channel [where] their movement ceases, and the innate wisdom devoid of any object vividly dawns.

Then, with the loss of semen, the constituents weaken. The power of the fire-accompanying [wind] deteriorates. And, as the functioning of the [life-] holding [wind] diminishes, one immediately[392] falls asleep, the body becomes cold and weak, and discontent [sets in].

[But in] yogins who have gained control over the vital essence,[393] qualities swiftly arise. Furthermore, the essential point of the swiftness of the messenger as the path is related to this.[394]

Cycles of the Vital Essences

Due to the increase and decrease of the solar and lunar [constituents or vital essences] that exist in that way, in the external [world], too, things manifest in the same manner.

Thus, there is the cycle [of the vital essences] during a solar day; the cycle during the lunar month; the cycle in the course of the year; and the cycle in the [course of] a human life.

The Vital Essence Cycle during a Solar Day

In the [twelve periods] of the solar day, during the daytime, the solar [vital essence] increases [as follows]:

[7 a.m. to 9 a.m.] In the early morning, the power of the short A[395] arises. Thus, the sun rises, and the strength of the energy-wind of the fire [element] increases. In the external [environment], warmth flashes forth, and any kind of food that is eaten is digested.

[9 a.m. to 11 a.m.] Then, in mid-morning when the sun is warm, [the solar vital essence] reaches the navel [chakra]; thus, attachment arises. As an external related factor, the desire to chant, dance, and laugh manifests. The prevalent feeling is one of happiness.

[11 a.m. to 1 p.m.] At midday, [the red vital essence] reaches the heart [chakra], so digestion is slightly weaker, the mind becomes somewhat heavier,[396] and one falls asleep. The predominant sensation is one of fogginess.

[1 p.m. to 3 p.m.] After midday, [the red vital essence] reaches the throat [chakra];[397] thus, one experiences sadness and unhappiness. The prevalent mood is one of aggression.

Because the [white] vital essence of the secret place [chakra] is deprived of the red [vital essence, externally], the intensity of the heat subsides. [But internally,] the strength of the fire [element] increases, drying up the [white] vital essence.

[3 p.m. to 5 p.m.] In the afternoon, [the red vital essence] reaches the crown of the head [chakra]; the body becomes cold; digestion of food is difficult; and the power of the energy-wind of the fire [element] is exhausted.

[5 p.m. to 7 p.m.] At sunset, the [white] vital essence is melted by [internal] heat, and sixteen [of its parts] descend to the throat [chakra]. [Externally] there is moonlight, and the stars glow [in the sky]. Internally, the pure essence of the constituents [present] in the channels flow and converge. Thus, it is only at night that heroes and ḍākinīs gather in the external [world].[398] All kinds of spirits gather as well.

[7 p.m. to 9 p.m.] In the evening, because the vital essences of other parts of the body are weak, threats to one's life-force emerge.

[9 p.m. to 11 p.m.] Then, eight parts of the white vital essence] go to nurture the organic components of the body, while the remaining eight descend to the heart [chakra].

[11 p.m. to 1 a.m.] Therefore, at midnight of the fifteenth lunar day, the moon reaches the center of the horizon. One falls into a deep sleep.

[1 a.m. to 3 a.m.] Then, four [parts of the vital essence] go [to nurture] the organic components of the body, while four descend to the navel [chakra].

[3 a.m. to 5 a.m.] At dawn, when the sensation of cold is stronger, two [parts of the] vital essence go to nurture the body, and two descend to the [chakra of the] secret place. Thus, at dawn, the semen of meditators seeps, the vajra [penis] is aroused, and ordinary people have sex.

[5 a.m. to 7 a.m.] Then, [in the very early morning,] two parts of the [white] vital essence generate the power of the red vital essence of the genitals; therefore, in the morning, the sun rises. This is also the reason why, in early morning, people have a good complexion, while in the evening their complexion is poor.

Moreover, the *Saṃpuṭa Tantra* states:[399]

> At dawn, in the afternoon, and at sunset,
> At midday, and at midnight, always,
> [Knowledge] should be realized through union
> with the consort.

Therefore,[400] during the day it is warm, food is digested, and sleeping causes illness; the sun rises, the moon does not appear, and the stars are not seen. At night it is cold, sleep restores one's physical condition, and food is not digested; the moon appears,[401] and the stars glow.[402]

The Vital Essence Cycle during a Lunar Month

The increase and decrease of the vital essence during a lunar month is described in the *Saṃvarodaya,* the *Vajraḍāka,* and other [tantras].

On the first day of the waxing moon,[403] the pure essence of white bodhicitta abides at the toes of the left foot in the form of the syllable A (ཨ).

On the second day it abides at the [left] calf in the form of the long Ā (ཨཱ).

On the third day, it abides at the [left] thigh in the form of the syllable I (ཨི).

On the fourth day, it abides at the genitals in the form of the long syllable Ī (ཨཱི).

On the fifth day, it abides at the navel in the form of the syllable U (ཨུ).

On the sixth day, it abides at the heart in the form of the long Ū (ཨཱུ).

On the seventh day, it abides at the breast in the form of the syllable RI (ཪྀ).

On the eighth day, it abides at the larynx in the form of the long syllable RĪ (ཪཱྀ).

On the ninth day, it abides in the palm of the [left] hand in the form of the syllable LI (ལྀ).

On the tenth day, it abides at the lips in the form of the long syllable LĪ (ལཱྀ).

On the eleventh day, it abides at the cheeks in the form of the syllable E (ཨེ).

On the twelfth day, it abides at the eyes in the shape of the long syllable Ē (ཨཻ).

On the thirteenth day, it abides at the ears in the form of the syllable O (ཨོ).

On the fourteenth day, it abides in the brain in the form of the long syllable Ō (ཨཽ).

On the fifteenth day, it reaches the crown of the head where, during the day, it dwells above the lalanā, on the left side, in the form of the syllable OṂ (ཨོཾ). At night [it dwells] at the [crown] aperture of the central channel, in the form of the long syllable Ā (ཨཱ).

In these places, the vital essence gradually develops more and more, and [as it reaches] the crown of the head, [it is like] the full moon.[404] The solar [vital essence] goes to the toes.

On that day [of the full moon], the white vital essence pervades the entire body.

From the first until the thirtieth day of the waning moon, the lunar [vital essence] gradually decreases, and on the night of the thirtieth day it reaches the big toe [of the right foot].

[During this time], the solar [essence] increases. That is, on the first day of the waning moon, [the solar essence] abides at the big toe of the right foot.[405]

On the second day, it arrives at the top of the foot, and on the third day it arrives at the calf. Then, it gradually increases in the manner explained above until, on the night of the thirtieth day, it arrives at the crown of the head.

At that time, the red vital essence pervades the entire body, and since the solar [essence] has increased, the lunar [essence] is not manifest,[406] [but] stars are glowing.

Then, from the first day of the waxing moon until the full moon, the red essence gradually decreases, and the white one increases, as before.

In this regard, the [*Tantra of*] *the Primordial Buddha*[407] states:

Through the fire of vitality and exertion, the "bearer
of the rabbit"[408] melts, and the water [from this
becomes] an intoxicating liquid.[409]
Because of the lunar days when the moon is at its fullest,
from the joints of the toes, one's mind arrives at the
crown of the head.
During the dark phase,[410] having left the crown of the
head, the lunar [essence] arrives at the toes.
To the yogin who practices at the right time every
day, the attainment of the desired goal is certainly
bestowed.[411]

The *Net of Magical Manifestations* states:[412]

> With the sole of one foot,
> You press the span of ground of the earth's mandala;[413]
> And with the span of a toenail,
> You press the tip of Brahmā's shaft.[414]

In this way, there are right and left, sun and moon, waxing and waning, increase and emptiness, and full moon and new moon when the sun and moon are eclipsed.[415]

Through the upward increase and downward decrease, the solar [vital essence] does not vary in size,[416] [because] this vital essence is stable at the [chakra] of the secret place, and [because] during the day, its potentiality always blazes upward.

In the waning phase, the lunar [vital essence] becomes smaller, and on the thirtieth day it is imperceptible because the solar [vital essence] has invaded its space.[417]

These two [the fifteenth and thirtieth of the lunar month] are particular occasions on which one should guard the vital essence; for this reason, the Buddha taught that [on these days] lay people too should observe the eight precepts.[418]

The ascetics of the past, knowing the principles [of the monthly cycle of the vital essence], would not perform moxabustion or blood-letting on [certain] areas of the body on the days when [the vital essence was present in these areas], and stated, "There is the energy that protects life." This also relates to that [which has just been explained].

When the lunar [vital essence] increases[419] during the waxing moon, people's predominant feelings are of joy and happiness. This is why the first part of the month is called "short period."

When the solar [vital essence] increases during the waning phase of the moon, people's predominant feelings are of sadness and slight unhappiness. This is why the second part of the month is called "long period."

Practitioners of inner heat should know that the increasing course [of the white] vital essence occurs during the waxing moon, and the course when bliss is greater occurs during the waning moon.

During the period in which the solar [essence] is on the rise, obstacles are more exuberant. This is why, during the waning moon, the great Tagpo Kagyüd masters[420] dedicated themselves to solitary retreat.

The Vital Essence Cycle during a Year

For a period of six months after the summer solstice [June 21], the lunar [vital essence of] bodhicitta increases and expands in the left [channels], entering many areas [of the body].

[At the same time,] the solar [essence] increases in the right [channels]. It [moves] swiftly, [but] enters fewer areas [of the body].[421]

Thus, one energy-wind [flowing in] the twenty-four places [or channels] is subtracted from the day and added to [the energy-winds of] the night. So the night becomes longer, and the day shorter. [During such periods,] people have a good complexion, sleep little, and their bodies grow stronger.

In autumn, when the lunar and solar [essences] enter the [areas of the body] in equal measure, the crops ripen. Since this is [the period of] the increasing course of the white [essence, people's] prevalent feelings are those of happiness. Everyone, beginning with children, can sing [loud enough for the sound to project] into the distance. People predominantly experience abundance[422] and enjoy sense pleasures.

Then, when [the weather turns] slightly cold, the lunar [essence] expands and the power of the solar [essence] lessens; thus, [the climate] becomes extremely cold and freezing.

When the six left houses of the left time junctures have passed, the winter solstice [December 21] occurs.

Frankincense, the inner-fire [or solar vital essence] that moves in the right [channels] increases, and slowly enters many areas [of the body].

[At the same time,] the lunar [essence] from the left [channels] [moves] swiftly and enters fewer areas [of the body]. Therefore one energy-wind of the twenty-four places [or channels] is subtracted from the night and added to [the day]. The day becomes longer and the night shorter.

Since the power of the solar [essence] expands, the external [environment] becomes warm, ice melts, people's bodies become thin, the constitution weakens, and sleep increases. The constituents move, and attachment arises. People predominantly experience less abundance, and rarely enjoy sense pleasures.

In spring, [the solar and lunar essences] move equally. That is, since this is [the period of] the expanding course of the solar [essence, seeds] sprout, and the prevailing feeling among people is that of unhappiness.

Then, when the six left houses of the right time junctures have passed, the summer solstice occurs as before. In this way, with the sun passing through the twelve houses, there are the twelve months.

The six months in which the solar [essence] increases are negative months and negative periods; the six months in which the lunar [essence] increases are positive months and positive periods.

In this regard, the *Saṃpuṭa Tantra* states:[423]

When the water's current [flows] at the opening
  of the nose's tip,
This is called the "good time."[424]
When there is movement by the power of fire,[425]
This is clearly [known as] the "bad time."

Moreover, during the day, the solar [essence] increases and its power grows. During the night, the lunar [essence] increases and its power grows. Both are the potentiality [expressed by] the fire [located] below the navel.

The *Saṃpuṭa Tantra* states:[426]

The nectars of day and night are trickling.
This is because the fire brings joy:
By this too are the names distinguished.[427]

The Vital Essence Cycle in the Course of a Human Life

Until age twenty-five, [both vital essences] increase together, but principally the lunar [essence] increases.

[From age twenty-five] until forty-five, they [both] become stable together, but principally, the solar [essence] stabilizes.

After that [age], they both decrease together; principally, the lunar [essence] decreases.

When the two [vital essences] are unbalanced in an ordinary person's body, they cause various illnesses. When they are unbalanced in [one who is on] the yogin's path, they cause many obstacles.

For an ordinary person, their balance produces good health. [For one who is] on the yogin's path, their balance and purity produce good qualities.[428]

Like a flower and its perfume, this nectar of the constituents is the relative bodhicitta that serves as the support for the ultimate bodhicitta.[429]

Accordingly, the *Two Examinations of the Hevajra Tantra* states:[430]

Just as a flower's fragrance
Would not be perceived in the absence of the flower,

Similarly, in the absence of form, and the rest,
Bliss too would not be seen.

This [essence of the constituents] is thus the vital force of the body,
the support of the mind, the syllables of voice, and the pure essence
that produces the sense organs.

The chapter on the initiation of the *First Examination of the
Hevajra* states:[431]

This itself is the life force of living beings.
It is the sacred syllable,
Sentient beings' very nature.
It is the pervader of everything
That abides in the body of all:
Things and non-things arise from it.

Great Bliss

The second factor of the fundamental nature of the mind is bliss,
that is, the mind that depends on the support [of the vital essence]
is also great bliss.

In this regard, the second chapter of the *Second Examination of
the Hevajra Tantra* states:[432]

The bhāga of the vajra queen
Has the form of the syllable E.[433]
The precious receptacle of all buddhas
Always exists as great bliss.

Great bliss has [the following] seven aspects:

It is uncontaminated bliss and thus free from all negativities;

It is autonomous bliss and thus not dependent on other conditions;

It is uncompounded bliss and thus unceasing;

It is nondual bliss and thus pervades all things;

It is inconceivable bliss and thus its flavor has never been experienced by worldly people;

It is bliss devoid of self-nature and thus is the unique flavor of pleasure and suffering, beyond concepts;

It is natural bliss and thus nonartificial. The *Two Examinations of the Hevajra Tantra* states:

> In this way, it is the great bliss essence of bodhicitta that
>   is endowed with seven aspects.

The *Two Examinations of the Hevajra Tantra* states:[434]

> Generate the relative [bodhicitta]
> That embodies the absolute bodhicitta.
> The relative, like the jasmine flower,
> Embodies the absolute bliss.

The relative bodhicitta, the support,[435] is also bliss. The absolute bodhicitta that depends on it is bliss. Bliss is also the path for realizing [the absolute bodhicitta]; and the fruit that is realized is also bliss.

The *Tantra of the Arising of the Vajra Vision* states:[436]

> Vajradhāra [comes] from bliss.
> Through bliss, bliss is attained.
> The result of bliss as the cause is bliss.
> At the time of the cause, it is supreme,
> And at the time of the fruit too, it is supreme.

[In brief,] the nature of the mind is great bliss.

The Five Wisdoms

The third factor of the mind is the five wisdoms.

The radiance of this very bliss manifests in all possible ways [as follows]:

At the time of the cause, when one is a sentient being, [it manifests as] the five emotions. The embodiment of these are the five classes of beings.[437]

At the time of the path, when one is a yogin, [it manifests] as the five contemplations.[438] The embodiment of these are the 1,200 qualities of the path,[439] and so on.

At the time of the fruit, when one is enlightened, [it manifests as] the five wisdoms. The embodiment of these are the buddhas of the five families.

The *Equal to the Sky Tantra* states:[440]

These five classes of beings are the five tathāgatas.
They exist in the manner of dancers and fine paintings.
The so-called great bliss is the unique state.
Through the grandeur of this state proceeds the
        multitudinous dance.

To explain, when one is a sentient being, the great bliss is not recognized and therefore manifests as ignorance. As one seeks [the bliss] for oneself and others, there is desire. Thus, there is the torment of anger. Fearing others' gain, there is envy. Holding oneself as superior, there is pride.

Within each of these five emotions, all five [emotions] are present. Depending on the stimulus of the object, the appropriate [emotion] clearly manifests.

The true nature of great bliss is wisdom.[441] [Since] it pervades all and is nondual, it is the wisdom of sameness.

[Since] it is the reality that does not exist as anything, it is the wisdom of the ultimate dimension of phenomena.

[Since] it arises as anything whatsoever due to conditions, it is the wisdom of discernment.

[Since] it performs the functions of the eight groups of consciousness, it is the wisdom that accomplishes activities.

[Since] it is luminous and nonconceptual, it is the mirror-like wisdom.

Thus, the mind essence is great bliss devoid of the affliction of conceptual constructs, and the specific characteristic of bliss is the five wisdoms.

Since even the five emotions are not beyond it, the things to be abandoned and their antidotes are inseparable, and the cause and the result are inseparable.

Since, depending on whether or not they have been governed by the method, it is uncertain whether or not [emotions] accumulate karma; and since [it is uncertain] whether or not they become the path, the five emotions [are regarded as] neutral.

Nonthought

The fourth factor of the mind is the characteristic of wisdom that is natural luminosity that does not conceive of a subject or object.

Having called upon Nāropā, Tilopa said:[442]

Ah! This is self-disclosing wisdom,
Beyond the ways of speech and the objects of mind.
I, Tilopa, have nothing to teach!
Know that this itself points to itself.

The method to apply this in practice is Tilopa's six teachings:

Do not imagine. Do not think. Do not deliberate. Do not meditate. Do not to analyze. Stay in the natural state of the mind.

Thoughts related to subject and object are mental projections. The essence of mind is a natural clarity without any object. Thus, its nature is nothing whatsoever, its radiance is totally unconfined, and its essence is totally nonconceptual.

Contemplation

The fifth factor of the mind is contemplation.

In this context, [contemplation] means uninterruptedness. In fact, since the mind essence does not change throughout the three times and is free from formation and dissolution, it has a continuum of instants.

From the condition of a sentient being through the condition of enlightenment, the mind essence—pure awareness—is continuously present. Therefore it is called the "causal continuum of the base of all."[443]

THE FUNDAMENTAL NATURE OF THE BODY, VOICE, AND MIND AS INSEPARABLE: THE VAJRA OF THE WISDOM OF THE INSEPARABILITY OF BODY, VOICE, AND MIND OF ALL ENLIGHTENED BEINGS

As to the fourth [part of the] general outline—the fundamental nature of body, voice, and mind as inseparable—in the first introductory chapter of all Great Yoga tantras, the Bhagavān says:[444] "The essence of Body, Voice, and Mind of all tathāgatas resides in the bhāga of the vajra queen."

Thus, the body is like a pole-tent arrangement of the consciousness and the activities of the energy-wind. The consciousness-energy-wind manifests as the body, which is the embodiment of past actions and habitual patterns. Therefore, [the body] is inseparable from voice and mind.

The voice arises from the assemblage of the body's channels, syllables, the mind's thoughts, energy-wind-mind, and physical coordination. Therefore, [voice] is inseparable from body and mind.

The mind's eight groups of consciousness arise from the causal nexus of the pure essences of channels, winds, and vital essences. The animate and inanimate [worlds], body, and voice are all the self-display of mind. Therefore, [mind] is inseparable from body and voice.

In this way, body, voice, and mind are inseparable like water and earth in mud; or like the color, taste, and scent of sandalwood.

Regarding this, the *Glorious Guhyasamāja* states:[445]

Mind is produced as body,
Voice, as mind,
And mind, as the utterance of words.

Even now, if the body changes, voice and mind also change. If our appearance changes, others' perception [of us] also changes. If voice and mind change, the body also changes. For example, when anger arises in the mind, our speech immediately becomes harsh and our body takes on an angry aspect, which others also perceive. Thus, when oneself changes, others' [perception] changes as well. In this way, until death, body, voice, and mind exist inseparably.

At death, the body, [now] a corpse, is left behind, and the voice ceases. If [at that time] we think of going [somewhere], this is a deluded notion. Even though there is a body, it will not move simply by the mere [thought of moving. This is because] when the mind has just transferred [to another life], all the senses cease. [This proves that body, voice, and mind] are inseparable. If this were not so, it would be possible even for a dead body to speak and to function.

The ultimate, body, voice, and mind are beyond formation and dissolution.

In fact, since the ultimate central channel[446] is inseparable from mind, the channel-body continuum is not interrupted.

Since the essential energy-wind of space is inseparable from mind, the continuum of energy-wind-voice is not interrupted.

Since the pure essence of vital essence is inseparable from the mind whose essence is bliss, the continuum of the vital essence-mind is not interrupted.

Therefore, the natural expression of these always manifest as body, voice, and mind.

In fact, in the daytime, they are inseparable as the body, voice, and mind of the fully ripened fruit of karma.

In the dream state, they are inseparable as the body, voice, and mind of habitual tendencies.

In the intermediate state, they are inseparable as the mental body, voice, and mind.

At the time of enlightenment, they are inseparable as the wisdom body, voice, and mind.

Also, in [the expression] "union of secrets" (*guhyasamāja*), "secret" means that since the nature of the vajra of Body, Voice, and Mind is difficult to understand for those who have unwholesome views, it is hidden. And since all three are inseparably present in each of [the three: Body, Voice and Mind], all enlightened beings are one, and thus, a "union."

Regarding this, the eighteenth chapter of that tantra states:[447]

The three aspects of Body, Voice, and Mind,
Are taught as secrets.
That which is called "all buddhas,"

Is said to be a union of many.

Thus, the fundamental nature of the inseparability of body, voice, and mind is exclusive to the tradition of the Way of Indestructible Reality (Vajrayana).

It is through this inseparability that you should know and understand the principles of the Mother tantras that emphasize channels, of the Father tantras that emphasize energy-winds, and of all [tantras] that emphasize mind.

The inseparability of body, voice, and mind is the mode through which one should know: how all phenomena of conditioned existence and of its transcendence exist; what is the basis for the delusive vision of the six realms; how the doors [of birth in these realms] are to be closed; how the unique state creates the various visions of oneself and others; what are the essential points of the two phases of the path;[448] how to master the energy-winds through the key points of the physical postures; how to master body and mind by training in breathing [methods]; what are the essential points in the methods for mastering body and mind through meditative focus; and [what are] the essential points for dispelling obstacles.

If one does not understand this crucial point, all essential points will become erroneous. Therefore, it is very important. The secret words of these [instructions] should be learned orally.

In regard to this, the fundamental nature of the body is the vajra Body of all enlightened ones; the [fundamental nature of the] voice is the vajra Voice of [all] enlightened ones; and [the fundamental nature of the] mind is the vajra Mind of all the enlightened ones. These three, inseparable, exist as the essence of great bliss: [this is the meaning of] "Dwell in the bhāga of the vajra queen."

THE PATH: HOW THE ASPECTS OF THE PATH ARE COMPLETE BY ESTABLISHING THAT BODY, VOICE, AND MIND INSEPARABLE ARE THE METHOD AND KNOWLEDGE

Having conclusively established the inseparability of body, voice, and mind as method and knowledge, [one knows that] all aspects of the path are complete.

This is explained under three headings: during formation, forming as method and knowledge; while living, living as method and knowledge; while dying, dying as method and knowledge.

During Formation, Forming as Method and Knowledge

A body is taken with the previous karma as the primary cause, the mother and father's sexual intercourse as a secondary condition, and the intermediate [being's] energy-wind forming the connection.

When this occurs, the father is method. The mother is knowledge.

The white vital essence is method. The red vital essence is knowledge. The energy-wind of the intermediate being is method. The consciousness of the intermediate being is knowledge.[449]

Pleasure is method. [Pleasure] devoid of self-nature is knowledge.

Entering the father's path is method. Being conveyed to the mother's womb is knowledge. From the coming together of all these [factors], the body is formed.

The mother's womb is knowledge. Birth is method.

Method accomplishes knowledge. From knowledge, method manifests.

While Living, Living as Method and Knowledge

Men are method. Women are knowledge.

The right [side] is method. The left [side] is knowledge.

The day is method. The night is knowledge.

Energy-wind and vital essence are method. The channels are knowledge.

Also, with regard to the energy-winds, the upper wind and exertion are method. The lower wind and life-force are knowledge.

With regard to vital essence, the pure essence of the five nectars is method. The pure essence of the four elements is knowledge.

The upper chakras are method. The lower chakras are knowledge. Body and voice are method. Mind is knowledge.

Vision is method. Emptiness is knowledge.

The six sense organs are method. Their six objects are knowledge. Arms and legs are method. Going and staying are knowledge.

Sleep is method. The dream [state] is knowledge.

Among these and all other outer and inner phenomena, there is nothing that is not method and knowledge. In fact, one should know that method accomplishes knowledge and from knowledge, method manifests.

While Dying, Dying as Method and Knowledge

The dissolution of the four elements is method. The dissolution of the senses is knowledge.

The dissolution of coarse vision is method. The dissolution of subtle [vision] is knowledge.

The freeing of the knots in the channels is method. The movement of vital essence is knowledge.

The stopping of energy-winds is method. The ceasing of discursive thought is knowledge.

The dissolution of the coarse and subtle body and voice is method. The dawning of the luminous clarity is knowledge.

Thus, knowledge is accomplished by method.

Death is knowledge. The intermediate state, or [alternatively,] birth is method; thus, method manifests from knowledge.

In this way, death, formation, and life all exist as method and knowledge. Since the essence of the path is method and knowledge, all paths are complete [in these three].

In fact, all paths of the Secret Mantra are included in the two [stages] of maturation and liberation. First comes the initiation—the path of maturation—that is the preliminary [stage]. When the body is first formed, one receives the four initiations [as follows]:

The father's semen striking the consciousness of the intermediate being is the vase initiation.

The coming together of the white and red vital [constituents] in the womb so that [the consciousness] is coated with the mother's vital essence is the secret initiation.

The [experience] of the joy of innate knowledge is the initiation of knowledge through the consort.

The consciousness swooning in the state of no-thought by way of that bliss is the fourth initiation.

Thus, once the intermediate being's impurities of body, voice, and mind are purified, it obtains the fortune of a fully ripened body, voice, and mind.

Formation of the Body as the Creation Phase

Following this, the path of liberation has two phases. The first is the phase of creation, that is, the gradual formation of the body through the watery,[450] the slippery,[451] and the other [stages].

This is creation of the deity by such means as the five manifest awakenings[452] that purify the four modes of birth.[453]

Then, when the body is born, the completion of the aggregates [and] constituents of experience, with their branches, are the male and female [buddhas] of the five families; the bodhisattvas; and the wrathful deities.

The channels and constituents are the heroes and heroines.

The thirty-seven sacred places [of the body] are the celestial palace [encircled by] the cemeteries,[454] and the protection circle.[455]

In this way, a perfect creation phase is actualized.

The *Two Examinations [of the Hevajra] Tantra* states:[456]

By way of the perfectly pure mind,
There is natural nirvana.
The body of the deity
Exists as form, shape, and color,
Just by being born.
However, [this arises] through ordinary habitual
    tendencies.

In this way, the formation of the body is the phase of creation.

Living as the Completion Phase

[After birth,] the exhalation and inhalation are the "vajra recitation."[457]

The thoughts pertaining to the three lights[458] are the "focusing on the mind."

The dream state is the "illusory body." Sleep is "luminous clarity." The waking state is "union."

Thus, in the mode of the five stages,[459] the phase of completion too is complete.

The body existing as the deity's body is the symbol of the pledge. The union of the fire of the A at the navel and the HAM [at the crown of the head] is the symbol of the action of the inner heat.

The ceasing of all coarse and subtle thoughts related to the three times, and so on, is the symbol of the teaching.

The true nature of these is the great symbol of innate wisdom. Thus, in the mode of the four symbols,[460] the two phases are naturally present.

Also, the branch [practices] of the path are complete [in the body] in the following way:

The junction of the three [channels] is the fire pit.

The short A is the fire god.

Rasanā and lalanā are the implements [used in the fire rite].

Winds and vital essences are the fire-offering substances.

Thus, a natural fire-offering rite [is performed in the body].[461]

Any food that is eaten is the offering for the Tantric Feast.

The fire-accompanying wind is the yogin.

The separation of nutrients from waste is the ritual.

Channels and constituents are the circle of deities of the mandala.

The nutrients reaching the vital points of the channels is the offering.

Thus, a natural Tantric Feast [takes place in the body].

Hence, as soon as one takes a body, one receives the four initiations. Then, when the body has been fully formed, one trains in the [practices] of creation and completion, together with their branch [practices].

Sleep is the completion phase. The waking state is the creation phase.

Death is the completion phase. Birth is the creation phase, and so on. In this way, there is a natural path [that is traversed].

[As to] the result of this [path]: death is the reality dimension of awakening (dharmakāya).

The intermediate state is the enjoyment dimension of awakening (sambhogakāya).

Birth is the emanated dimension of awakening (nirmāṇakāya). In this way, the fruit is naturally present [as the three dimensions of awakening].

That is, in the natural course of the vajra body, the path, and its final fruit are spontaneously perfected through possessing an innate cause, an innate path, and an innate fruit.

Thus, the reason why, in the Secret Mantra, enlightenment is achieved in one life, as well as all the contents of the phases of creation and completion, called "basis of purification" and "purifying agent," should be understood from this.

Because the body does not lack a single aspect of the path, [the body] is the tantra of method. Because, on the basis of the body, all phenomena of samsara and nirvana are clearly revealed, the body is [also] an exegetical tantra.

The glorious Virūpa's *Vajra Lines* state:

> The body is the tantra of method, and so on.[462] [Having
>   arranged] the seats, and so on, through the third
>   and fourth, the causal initiation [is conferred].[463]

And:

> Because, relying on the body, the impediments to great
>   bliss are purified,
> And because it reveals enlightenment, [the body]
>   is an exegetical tantra.[464]

We may wonder, "If [the body] primordially exists in this way, why does [the path] need to be pointed out by the master, and why [must one] practice?" When it is not recognized, and when we are not governed by the method, it is like the wrestler's jewel.[465] Although one has it, it is of no benefit.

Regarding this, the *Two Examinations of the Hevajra Tantra* states:[466]

Look, O goddess, at this gem,
Shimmering in a garland of blazing splendor.
As a gem uncut it is useless,
But once cut, it brings forth joy.
Likewise [this body], this gem of samsara,
Possessed of five desirable qualities,
In its impure state, becomes poison.
When purified, it becomes like nectar.

The natural course of the essential path stirs samsara from its depths, and one cannot help but become enlightened.

THE FRUIT: HOW THE QUALITIES OF THE FINAL FRUIT ARE COMPLETE BY ASCERTAINING THAT BODY, VOICE, AND MIND INSEPARABLE IS THE PERFECT STATE OF AN ENLIGHTENED BEING

Having conclusively established that the body is enlightenment, how then are the qualities of the fruit complete [in the body]?

[This is explained under three headings]: during formation, forming as a perfect enlightened being; while living, living as a perfect enlightened being; and while dying, dying as a perfect enlightened being.

During Formation, Forming as a Perfect Enlightened Being

The body forms as the five buddha families and the five manifest awakenings.

As to the first, when the primary causes and secondary conditions have gathered, the [consciousness of the] intermediate being enters the womb.

[At that time,] the solidity of the earth element of the contact of the [father's and mother's] organs [during sexual intercourse] becomes the [buddha] family of Vairocana.

The wetness of the water element [becomes the vajra family of] Akṣobhya.

The heat of the fire element [becomes the lotus family of] Amitābha.

The element of air represented by the movement of the vital essences [becomes the action family of] Amoghasiddhi.

The element of space represented by the bliss [becomes the jewel family of] Ratnasaṃbhava. The sixth family that includes all five families is that of Vajradhāra.[467]

In regard to this, the *Two Examinations* states:[468]

With the union of *bola* and *kakkola*[469]
The solidity of contact is formed,
And since solidity is the characteristic of ignorance,
Ignorance is said to be Vairocana.

In these and other words, [the *Hevajra Tantra* provides] extensive [teaching on] this point.

The second point, formation as the five manifest awakenings, has been explained [above] in the context of the bodily factors.

Thus, all womb-born beings, by means of the five manifest awakenings, are born from a divine womb. All miraculously born beings have a divine miraculous birth. Therefore, the fully ripened body is the emanated dimension of awakening (nirmāṇakāya).

The mental body of the intermediate being and the dream body of habitual tendencies are the enjoyment dimension of awakening (saṃbhogakāya).

The mind is the reality dimension of awakening (dharmakāya).

The inseparability of the three dimensions is the dimension of great bliss (mahāsūkhakāya).

Moreover, [the body] is an enlightened being that has perfected the ten levels of realization.

To explain, the [intermediate being] enters the mother's womb in the presence of innate joy. Then it remains for seven days in the contemplation of intense joy. Thus, this is the "joyful," the first [level of realization].

From the second month [of gestation], the central channel forms, and on that basis, the chakras at the navel and crown of the head, the faultless channels, energy-winds, and the vital essences [form]. This is the "faultless," the second level of realization.

In the third month, the knots of channels at the four chakras form, and the bases of the four limbs are laid out. Thus, this is the "radiant," the third [level of realization].

In the fourth month, the forms and colors of the body become clearer than before. Thus, this is the "brilliant," the fourth level of realization.

In the fifth month, the mouth, eyes and the [other] sense organs appear, making it difficult for medicines and mantras to manifest or bring forth their power.[470] Thus, this is the "difficult to conquer," the fifth level of realization.

In the sixth month, the doors of the senses are extremely clear. Thus, this is the "manifest," the sixth level of realization.

In the seventh month, the body hair and nails take form; therefore [the fetus] has gone far beyond [being affected by] the power of mantras and interdependent coincidences. Thus, this is the "gone far," the seventh level of realization.

In the eighth month, all sense organs, limbs, and other smaller parts of the body are fully developed, and therefore the gender can no longer be changed from male to female by spirits or other [beings]. Thus, this is the "unshakable," the eighth level of realization.

In the ninth month, the seven organic components and the outer and inner sense fields are fully developed. Thus, this is the "good intelligence," the ninth level of realization.

In the tenth month, through the energy-wind that causes movement, the [fetus] is turned upside down and is delivered. This is the
"cloud of Teaching," the tenth level of realization. Thus, [the body]
is a buddha who has perfected the ten levels of realization.

The *Two Examinations* states:[471]

By these conditions, all beings
Are undoubtedly buddhas.
The ten months are the ten levels of awakening.
Thus, beings are the lords of the ten levels.

While Living, Living as a Perfect Enlightened Being

While living, the body lives as a fully enlightened being. This is explained under two headings: the body lives as an emanation monk;
and [the body lives] as a fully enlightened being.

As to the first, the father is the abbot. The mother is the preceptor.

The navel is the residence. The walls of the womb are the monk's
robe. The lack of hair and beard are the shaven head and bare feet.
The palms folded at the crown of the head is the prostration.

The sounds of A HAM are the mantra recitation. The ten
months are the full ordination.

The act of going forth or moving is the discipline.

Thus, [the body] comes forth as an emanated monk. This is
taught extensively in the *Two Examinations*.

With regard to the body living as a fully enlightened being, the
body is Vajradhāra of the sixth buddha family, the inseparability of
the three dimensions of awakening. Therefore, the qualities of great-
ness of that buddha are as follows:

The syllable-vital essence and the constituent of the thirty-two
channels, [where descends the] bodhicitta present [in the body] as
the thirty-two vowels, are the thirty-two excellent major marks.[472]

The eighty natural concepts[473] and the form of the syllable-vital essence that exist as the two sets of forty consonants, are the eighty excellent minor marks.[474]

The colors of the energy-winds and of the vital essences are the mass of light and light rays.

The ten energy-winds are the ten powers, and the ten strengths.[475]

The chakras and the multitude of small channels are the inconceivable secret of the Body.

The energy-winds and the syllables are the inconceivable secret of the Voice.

The vital essence and all the individual discursive thoughts are the inconceivable secret of the Mind.

The OM and the other [syllables A and HŪM] are the lords of the three realms.[476]

The upper, lower, and middle parts of the body are the protectors of the three planes.[477]

The infinite small channels are the knowledge of the variety of things.[478]

The central channel is the knowledge of the real nature of things just as they are.[479]

The innate clarity of one's own pure awareness—the true essence of body, voice, and mind that is nothing in and of itself—is the knowledge of the real nature of things just as they are.

The unconfined radiance [of this true essence] that manifests in all possible ways is the knowledge of the variety of things.

Ignorance, deception, karma, and emotions—the base accomplished as the path—are the perfect freedom.

The essence of all these, existing as the wisdom that is the nature of all things, is the perfect realization.[480]

The five chakras, the energy-winds of the five elements, the five nectars of the constituents, and the five emotions of the mind are the five [buddha] families.

The actions of the body are the final buddha, the supreme emanation.[481]

The seeds of the six realms are the Six Teachers.[482]

The energy-winds and thoughts based on these are the incarnated emanation.[483]

Syllables and energy-winds are the giving of the Teaching in the individual languages of the six classes of beings.

These and the others qualities of [the body] exist in the nature of all the perfect qualities of fully enlightened beings.

The *Root Tantra of Cakrasamvara* states:[484]

> The great king, the glorious Blood Drinker,
> Chief sovereign of all desires,
> Always endowed with hands and feet,
> Possessed of [the supreme] learning,
> Dwells in the world, enshrouding all. [485]

The Dimension Endowed with Seven Features

Moreover, the special final fruit of Great Yoga is the dimension endowed with seven features. In fact, since the cause exists endowed with seven features, the path that is applied is endowed with seven features, and the fruit that is realized is [also] endowed with seven features.

Vagishvarakirti stated:[486]

> Total enjoyment, union, great bliss, lack
>   of self-nature,
> Filled with compassion, unceasing stream,
>   and uninterrupted presence:
> The goal endowed with these seven features,

Which I assert, established as ideal,
Is praised by the wise.

At the time of the cause, the seven features are present in the following way:
The feature of "total enjoyment" [refers] to the major marks, minor signs, and the light and light rays whose bases exist in the body.

The *Saṃpuṭa* states:[487]

Since all channels are united,
This is the binding net of the ḍākinīs.

The feature of "union" refers to the upper and lower channels existing as a union, to the energy-winds [existing as] the union of the flow of method and wisdom, to the vital essences [existing as the union] of A HAṂ, and to the mind existing as the union of vision and emptiness.

The feature of "great bliss" refers to the fact that at first, [the body] is born with innate joy; that is, it is born in a state of bliss. While living, the essence of body and mind exists as great bliss. While dying, [the body] dies in a state of innate joy; that is, it dies in a state of bliss. Therefore, [the body] is bliss throughout the three times: all feelings are great bliss.

The feature of "lack of self-nature" refers to the inseparability of body, voice, and mind. [This inseparability] is neither true nor false: it is nothing in and of itself, and is beyond all concepts.

The feature of being "filled with great compassion" refers to the mind's unobstructed natural radiance that manifests in all possible ways. Nondual with this, the causal nexus of the channels manifests as the various characteristics [of things] whose essence is nondual.

The feature of "unceasingness" refers [to the fact that], for example, as long as there is ice, there is [also] water. Likewise, as long as mind exists, there are also body and voice. Therefore, the ultimate body, voice, and mind are unceasing: they are ever-present.

The feature of "uninterrupted presence" refers to the very nature of all phenomena that manifest in every possible way, devoid of the limitation of being only emptiness. No secondary conditions can destroy it or make it nonexistent.

All of the [above] essential points and the seven features should be known as one profound teaching.

While Dying, Dying as a Perfect Enlightened Being

When the lifetime is over, at the time of death, the untying of the channel knots is the manifest dimension of awakening.

The destruction of syllables and the movement of the vital essences is the enjoyment dimension of awakening.

The dawn of luminous clarity is the reality dimension of awakening.

The dissolution of coarse and subtle conceptuality is the perfect freedom.

Death is the perfect realization.

The dissolution of the five elements and five senses are the five buddha families.

The luminous clarity is Vajradhāra, the sixth family.

Death is the reality dimension of awakening, and the intermediate state is the enjoyment dimension of awakening.

In this way, birth, living, and dying are the state of an enlightened being. Therefore, all the aspects of the final fruit are present [in the body], with nothing lacking and no need to seek elsewhere. Nor is there anything negative to be changed into [something] positive.

Being unchanging throughout the three times, at the time of the
cause, as a sentient being, [the body] is the very enlightened being.
The *Two Examinations of the Hevajra Tantra* states:[488]

> There is not a single sentient being
> Who is not buddha.
> Therefore, a person who possesses yoga
> Does not scorn or dash the pride of [others].
> These [beings] who live embodied in the relative,
> Are the families of the tathāgatas.

Well then, if this is asserted, one might ask: "If [beings] are enlightened from the beginning, why do [we] need to tread a spiritual path?
The *Saṃpuṭa Tantra* states:[489]

> Though sentient beings are buddhas,
> They are obscured by temporary stains.
> When these are cleared away, they are actual buddhas.

In this way, the existence of [every being] from the beginning as
the innate buddha—Body, Voice, and Mind—is the fundamental
nature of things.

Not knowing this [fundamental nature] is ignorance. [Igno-
rance] is an erroneous construction, a deception. Knowing [the
fundamental nature] for what it is and getting accustomed [to it]
is the path.

Eliminating the imaginary deception from its root and actual-
izing the inherent characteristics of the way things are is the fruit.

324 ❀ Secret Map of the Body

CONCLUSION

Concluding Verses

Having taken the dust at the feet of supreme [masters] on the
    crown of my head,
And definitely comprehended the principles of the unsurpassable
    way to realization,
[I,] the yogin known as Vajra of the Mind,[490]
By the force of familiarizing myself over a long period of time
    with the supreme path of method,
Saw the forms of the channels and the energy-winds of the
    vajra body.
By this realization, I gained the certainty of experience.
Having confirmed this reality through the content of the
    unsurpassable tantras,
And the valid comprehension of consistent citations
    [from scriptures],
Here, I have fully condensed the quintessence
Of the nectar of the unfailing oral instructions
Of the knower of the three times, Drigung Rinchen;[491]
Of the powerful being Maha Pandita,[492] versed in the five
    sciences;
Of the lord of yogins known as Dorje;[493]
And of the unwaning standard of perfected merit.
[These] faultless teachings come through a successive lineage
    [of masters].
[In particular], this great treasure of profound and vast essential
    points
Comes through the blessing of the glorious master Heruka.

By the merit of this writing, may all beings, equal to space,

With the waxing moon of great bliss [rising] in the sky of the
two merits,
Dispel the torment of attachment and illuminate the darkness
of ignorance,
And thus freed from the limits of the four demons,[494] become
sovereign lords of the teaching.

Colophon

This *Hidden Description of the Vajra Body*, which reveals the exceptional tradition of the Secret Mantra, the profound teaching, was
written without impediment by the Sakya monk, yogin of the supreme way to realization, Gyaltsen Pelzang,[495] by assembling, with
no omissions, the teachings of earlier masters, in the glorious hermitage of Lhading during the waxing moon of the Bird year.

May the practitioners on earth spread out like the sun and moon.

This is the pith of all teachings; the sublime inmost heart of all
realizations; the sublime lamp that dispels all beings' darkness. It is
a tantra of the unsurpassable secret endowed with seven greatnesses;
moreover, it is the highest peak of all ways to realization; the king
of all tantras; the universal connection of all crucial teachings; the
root of all secret instructions; the source of all doctrine; the mirror
of all phenomena; the conclusion of all principles.

May it be virtuous![496]

APPENDIX ONE
Collected Works of Gyalwa Yangönpa

These three volumes are found in the *rta mgo chos dbyings pho brang* (Thimphu, Bhutan: Kunsang Tobgey, 1976). They are the original manuscripts used for the edition of the same text printed in Delhi.

Volume 1

1. *dkar chag* (Contents) 1–4.
2. *ri chos brgyud tshul gyi lo rgyus* (*History of the Lineage of the Mountain Teaching*) 5–12.
3. *ri chos phyag len gsal ba'i sgron me* (*Clear Lamp of the Mountain Teaching Tradition of Practice*) 13–22
4. *rin po che lha gdong pa'i rnam thar bstod pa ma* (*Praise Biography of the Precious One from Lhadong*) 23–96.
5. *dpal yang dgon pa'i chen po'i nang gi rnam thar* (*Inner Biography of the Glorious and Great Yangönpa*) 97–104.
6. *lha dgong pa'i zhal chems bka' shog ma* (*Lhadongpa's Letter of Testament*) 105–112
7. *mnyam med rgyal ba yang dgon pa'i gsang ba'i rnam thar* (*Secret Biography of the Incomparable Gyalwa Yangönpa*) 113–34.
8. *mnyam med rgyal ba yang dgon pa'i rnam thar gsang ba ma* (*Secret Biography of the Incomparable Yangönpa*) 135–46.
9. *ri chos bskor gsum du grags pa zab chos brgyan pa bzhi'i dkar chag* (*Index of the Profound Teaching and Ornaments Called the Mountain Teaching*) 147–58.
10. *phyag rgya chen po lhan gcig skyes sbyor* (*Innate Yoga of Mahāmudrā*) 159–84.
11. *khor yug ma'i khrid dpe* (*Manual of Teaching on the All-Encompassing [Contemplation]*) 185–202.

Volume 3

14. *bar do 'phrang sgrol gyi 'khrul 'khor zin bris* (*Notes on the Yantra Exercises of the Liberation from the Narrow Passage of the Intermediate State*) 277–84.

15. *rgyal ba yang dgon pa'i mgur 'bum* (*Songs of Realization of Gyalwa Yangönpa*) 285–314.

16. *dpal rgyal ba yang dgon pa'i bka' 'bum yid bzhin nor bu'i phreng ba* (*The Glorious Yangönpa's Teachings [Entitled] Garland of Wish-Fulfilling Gems*) 315–442. Some discrepancies exist between the original 164-page printed manuscript of these *Songs of Realization* labelled *Ka*, and another consisting of more than 128 pages that is labelled *A*. These require further examination.

17. *bdun tshigs zla ba sgron me* (*Moon Lamp of the Weekly Virtuous Acts [for the Deceased]*) 443–68.

APPENDIX TWO

Unpublished Works and Spoken Words of Yangönpa

1. *dkyil 'khor gyi cho ga thams cad la 'jug pa gsang ba'i gru bo che zhes bya ba yang dgon pas dpal rtsibs ri'i ri khrod du bkod pa* (*Rite of the Mandala Applicable to All, Entitled the Great Secret Ship*, written by Gyalwa Yangönpa at the Tsibri mountain hermitage), 102 pp.

2. *sems bskyed kyi cho ga byang chub spyod pa'i gter mdzod* (*Rite for the Generation of the Altruistic Mind of Enlightenment [Entitled] Treasury of the Bodhisattva Conduct*), 131 pp.

3. *drag rlung gnad lnga ma* (*Five Key Points on Fierce Breathing*), 9 pp.

4. *'phrang sgrol gyi gleng gzhi'i gtam* (*Introductory Remarks on the Liberation from the Narrow Passage [of the Intermediate State]*), 5 pp.

5. *yang dgon pa'i gsung sgros las mnyam bzhag skyong lugs dang sgom la nye bar mkho ba'i mangala'i ming can gyis zin bris su mdzad pa sogs* (*Notes, and so on, Entitled, The Requirements for the Manner of Practicing in the Aftermath and for the Meditation; Mangala's notes from Yangönpa's talks*), 12 pp.

6. *ri chos rin po che'i klad don gsal bar byed pa spyan mnga' ba sgom rin gyis bkod pa* (*Clarification of the Introduction to the Precious Mountain Teaching*, by Chen Ngawa Gomrin), 7 pp.

7. *gnas kyi lhan thabs gsal byed sgron ma rin ldan gyis mdzad pa* (*Lamp That Illuminates the Supplement of Key Points*, by Rinden), 7 pp.

8. *ri chos kyi phyag len gzhon nu grub kyis mdzad pa* (*The System of Practice of the Mountain Teaching*, by Shönnu Drub), 67 pp.

9. *nad gdon hUM chos ma*[1] (*Healing HŪṂ Teaching on [Dispelling] Illnesses and Provocations*), 3 pp.

10. *'dzag srung bka' rgya ma rin chen lnga ldan gyis mdzad pa* (*The Sealed Teaching on Preventing Loss [of Vital Essence], Entitled "Possessing Five Jewels,"* by Chen Ngawa Rinchen Den), 3 pp.

11. *bar do 'phrang sgrol gyi khrid rim sgom rin gyis yi ger bkod pa* (*Gradual Instructions on the Liberation from the Narrow Passage of the Intermediate State* by [Chen Ngawa] Gomrin), 5 pp.

12. *lha gdong ngo sprod bdun ma'i 'grel pa* (*Commentary to the Seven-Point Introduction of Lhadongpa*), oral teaching of Karmapa Mikyöd Dorje.[2]

13. *rgyal ba yang dgon pa'i ngo sprod bdun ma mgur gyi 'grel pa chos rje tsong kha pas mdzad pa* (*Commentary to the Song of Realization of the Seven-Point Introduction of Gyalwa Yangönpa,* by Venerable Tsongkhapa),[3] 28 pp.

14. *yang dgon pa'i gsung sgro las mnyam bzhag skyong lugs sogs dwags po bkra shis rnam rgyal gyis zin bris su byas pa* (*The Manner of Practicing in the Aftermath, and so on, Extracted from the Teachings of Yangönpa;* Tagpo Tashi Namgyal's notes), 6 pp.

The above are manuscripts written in the cursive Tibetan script and preserved at the Library of Aphu Rinpoche, the Lord of Siddhas,[4] in Manali.

APPENDIX THREE

Five Outer and Five Inner Manifest Awakenings

FIVE OUTER MANIFEST AWAKENINGS

	awakening through emptiness	awakening through the sun and moon seats	awakening through the syllable of the Voice	awakening through the hand-symbol of the Mind	awakening through the completion of the Body
Manifest Awakening					
Gestation and Birth	empty womb	mingling of the father's sperm and mother's ovum	consciousness of the intermediate being entering the womb with the father's sperm	gestation until emergence of the gender	complete formation and birth

FIVE INNER MANIFEST AWAKENINGS

	awakening through the moon	awakening through the sun	awakening through the seed-syllable	awakening through the mixing	awakening through completion
Manifest Awakening					
Gestation and Birth	intermediate being's consciousness propelled by father's semen into the womb	intermediate being's consciousness enveloped by the ovum	intermediate being's consciousness dwells between semen and ovum	intermediate being's consciousness dwells in bliss between sun and moon; embryonic development	upon completion of fetal development, birth
Wisdom	mirror-like wisdom	wisdom of sameness	wisdom of discernment	action-accomplishing wisdom	wisdom of the real condition of existence

APPENDIX FOUR

Stages of Embryonic and Fetal Development and Birth

Period	Coarse Body Development	Incarnations of Viṣṇu	Analogy	Subtle Body Development
1st week	embryo is watery		curd beginning to congeal	
2nd week	embryo is a lump		well-congealed curd	
3rd week	embryo is hard and oval		butter from churning curd	- formation of navel chakra
1st month	embryo becomes elongated			- formation of central channel, and all chakras along the central channel
2nd month	embryo is roundish in the center and narrow at the extremities	Fish		- formation of five root winds - formation of three main channels - formation of channel knots at chakras' centers - initial formation of 200 channels each day
3rd month	- formation of basis of limbs, head, and genitals as protrusions	Tortoise		- formation of petals-channels of the four chakras
4th month	- emergence of shoulders and eyes - enlargement of upper body and head	Pig		- initial formation of the five branch winds

5th month	- formation of joints the 360 bones - definition of limbs and head	Two Ramas		
6th month	- development of flesh, skin, and characteristics of the sense organs	Krishna		- complete formation of the five branch winds
7th month	- formation of hair of eyebrows, head, and body - complete formation of head	Human-Lion	head resembles that of a lion	
8th month	- clear definition of gender - clear appearance of body parts' colors - distinct appearance of head, limbs, and smaller body parts	Dwarf	fetus resembles a dwarf	
9th month	- full development of the seven organic components and sense organs - fetus wants to exit womb	Swan		
10th month	- full formation of the body	Buddha	child resembles a Buddha that has traversed the ten levels of realization	-full formation of the body's 72,000 channels
10th month–birth	- winds that cause movement enter left nostril - inversion and birth of fetus - initialization of energy-winds' flow from nose with the sounds A HAM			- apex of energy-winds' strength - ascent of white vital essence to crown of the head - descent of red vital essence to genitals

APPENDIX FIVE

Five Root and Five Branch Energy-Winds

FIVE ROOT ENERGY-WINDS

Name of Wind	Life-sustaining	Upward-moving	Downward-voiding	Fire-accompanying	Pervasive
Aggregate	consciousness	perception	volition	feeling	form
Buddha	Akṣobhya	Ratnasambhava	Amitābha	Amoghasiddhi	Vairocana
Location	- heart - life channels	Adam's apple	perineal region	navel	- head - center of twelve main joints
Function	- prevention of body and mind's separation - causation of clinging to notion of "I"	- facilitation of swallowing of food and vomiting - facilitation of speech and laughter	- expulsion and retention of menstrual blood, semen, urine, and feces	- digestion - separation of nutriment from waste - transformation of nutriment into the seven organic components - downward voiding of waste	- governance of all bodily motion: walking, rising, sitting, pausing

FIVE BRANCH ENERGY-WINDS

Name of Wind	rises and flows	flows thoroughly	flows perfectly	flows resolutely	flows intensely
Alternate Name	*nāga*	tortoise	lizard	gods' gift	victorious with the bow
Area of Activity	eyes	ears	nose	bodily organs	tongue
Sense Function	enables form perception	enables sound perception	enables smell perception	enables tactile perception	enables taste perception
Elemental Wind Potency	water	air	earth	space	fire
Location	intestines	liver	lungs	heart	kidneys
Reason For Alternate Name	provokes all dangerous illnesses	extends and contracts the limbs	causes anger and agitation	causes yawning and attachment	causes sneezing and does not cast away life-force

APPENDIX SIX
Classification of the Energy-Winds

ENERGY-WINDS		
Coarse		**Subtle**
root winds	branch winds	mind wind
karmic wind		wisdom wind
winds of the five elements		
exhalation, inhalation, pause		
male, female, neuter		
wind of life, wind of exertion		
upper wind, lower wind		
cold wind, hot wind		

APPENDIX SEVEN

Colors and Spans of the Energy-Winds of the Five Elements

Energy-Wind	Chakra Where Flow Begins	Color	Outflow Span in Finger-Widths	Inflow Span in Finger-Widths	Area of Flow in Nostrils
Earth Wind	navel	yellow	12	16	base of nostrils, close to the lips
Water Wind	heart	light blue	13	15	touches septum
Fire Wind	throat	light red	14	14	touches front side of nostrils
Air Wind	crown of the head	light green	15	13	touches right side of nostrils
Space Wind		colorless	16	12	center of nostrils

APPENDIX EIGHT
The 32 Channels of the Four Chakras and Sacred Places

CROWN OF THE HEAD CHAKRA				
Channel Name	**Channel Terminus**	**Shape of Channel Knot**	**Sacred Place**	**Constituent Generated**
Undivided (*mi phyed ma*)	anterior fontanel		Pullīramalaya	teeth, nails
Subtle Form (*phra gzugs ma*)	crown of head		Jālandhara	hair, body hair
Kind Lady (*bzang mo ma*)	right ear		Oḍḍiyāna	skin, sweat
Left (*g.yon pa ma*)	nape of neck		Arbuda	flesh, lymph, constituent on left side of body
Tamer (*'dul byed ma*)	left ear		Godāvarī	tendons, ligaments
Tortoise's Generator (*rus sbal skyes ma*)	point between eyebrows		Rāmeśvara	bones
Existence (*srid pa ma*)	eyes		Devīkoṭṭa	kidney, spleen
Empowering (*dbang skur ma*)	shoulders		Mālava	heart, heart cavities

THROAT CHAKRA				
Channel Name	Channel Terminus	Shape of Channel Knot	Sacred Place	Constituent Generated
Angry Lady (sdang ma)	armpits, region above the kidney	ཕ	Kāmarūpa	eyes
Standing (gshang ba ma)	breasts	ཨཾ	Oḍra	liver, bile
Mother Deity (ma mo ma)	navel	ཧཱུྃ	Triśakuni	lungs
Night (mtshan mo ma)	nose tip	ཨཾ	Kośala	small intestine
Refresher (bsil ster ma)	upper palate	ཨཾ	Kaliṅga	ligaments, ribs
Goer ('gro ba ma)	Adam's apple	ཝ	Lampīka	stomach
Grove (nags tshal ma)	heart center	ཨཾ	Kāñcī	feces
Twisted (mchu ma)	pubis	ཏྲ	Himālaya	clitoris, testicles

HEART CHAKRA					
Channel Name	Channel Terminus	Shape of Channel Knot	Sacred Place	Function	Consciousness and Sense Generated
Beautiful (mdzes ma)	genitals	ཨཾ	Abstinence from Drinking	governs white vital essence in central channel	consciousness ground-of-all
Essence of Taste (ro bcud ma)	vagina	ཨཾ	Abstinence from Drinking	governs red vital essence in the rasanā	emotional consciousness
All-Pervading (kun khyab)	urethra	ཨཾ	Abstinence from Drinking	regulates urine in lalanā	mental consciousness

Three Circles (*sum skor ma*)	eyeballs		Abstinence from Drinking	seeing	eye consciousness
Desirous ('*dod pa ma*)	ears		Close Abstinence from Drinking	hearing	ear consciousness
Householder (*khyim ma*)	base of nose		Close Abstinence from Drinking	smelling	nose consciousness
Fierce (*gtum mo*)	tongue		Close Abstinence from Drinking	tasting	tongue consciousness
Liberator from the Demon (*bdud bral ma*)	point between eyebrows, pores of skin		Close Abstinence from Drinking	feeling	tactile consciousness

NAVEL CHAKRA				
Channel Name	**Channel Terminus**	**Shape of Channel Knot**	**Sacred Place**	**Constituent Generated**
Beautiful Color (*mdog mdzes ma*)	genitals		Pretāpurī	phlegm
Ordinary (*thun mong ma*)	anus		Gṛhadeva	mucus
Bestower of the Cause (*rgyu ster ma*)	thighs		Saurāṣṭra	blood
Separator (*bral ba ma*)	calves		Suvarṇadvīpa	sweat
Friendly (*mdza' bo ma*)	fingers, toes		Nagara	fatty tissue, marrow
Accomplisher (*grub pa ma*)	feet, hands		Sindhu	tears
Fire Lady (*me ma*)	thumbs, toes		Maru	saliva, mucus
Adorable (*yid du 'ong ma*)	knees		Kulutā	mucus, snivel

APPENDIX NINE
The Channels of the Five Chakras

CROWN OF THE HEAD CHAKRA			
Number of Channels	**Shape Simile**	**Syllable at Center**	**Orientation**
32	inverted umbrella	HAM(ह्ं) at upper tip of central channel	facing downward

THROAT CHAKRA				
Number of Channels	**Shape Simile**	**Syllable at Chakra Center**	**Syllables of the Channels of the Four Directions**	**Orientation**
16	coiled snake	OM (ཨོཾ)	YA (ཡ) RA (ར) LA (ལ) WA (ཝ)	facing upward

HEART CHAKRA					
Number of Channels	**Shape Simile**	**Syllable at Chakra Center**	**Syllables of the Four Cardinal Channels and of the Channel in the Middle**	**Syllables of the Four Intermediate Channels**	**Orientation**
8	ball of yarn	HŪṂ (ཧཱུྃ)	BHRUM (བྷྲཱུྃ) OM (ཨོཾ) KHAṂ (ཁཾ) DZIM (ཛིཾ) HŪṂ (ཧཱུྃ)	*Hevajra Tantra*: MĀṂ (མཱཾ) LĀṂ (ལཱཾ) PĀṂ (པཱཾ) TĀṂ (ཏཱཾ) *Saṃpuṭa Tantra*: A (ཨ) U (ཨུ) I (ཨི) E (ཨེ)	facing downward

NAVEL CHAKRA				
Number of Channels	Shape Simile	Syllable at Chakra Center	Syllables of the Eight Root Channels	Orientation
64	ropes pulled horizontally	A (ས)	A (ས) KA (ཀ) TSA (ཙ) ṬA (ཊ) TA (ཏ) PA (པ) YA (ཡ) SHA (ཤ)	facing upward

CHAKRA OF THE SECRET PLACE AND THE 14 SYLLABLES OF THE WOMB			
Origin	Channel Name/ Terminus	Channel Knot Shape	Symbol/Realm of Existence
end of rasanā	Fire lady	OM (ཨོཾ)	meditative absorption
end of lalanā	Sleepy	HŪṂ (ཧཱུྃ)	state of union
	end of the central channel	A (ས)	essence
central channel	end extension of the central channel (men)	KSHA (ཀྵ) inverted	
central channel	end extension of the central channel (women)	BHRUṂ (བྷྲཱུྃ)	
	base of penis	HŪṂ (ཧཱུྃ)	strength
central channel	end of *kākamukha* channel	A (ས) of the outer shape	
	inside of penis	PHAṬ (ཕཊ)	
	end of lalanā	A (ས)	wisdom
branch off from end of central channel	right eyebrow	A (ས)	gods
branch from end of central channel	beating heart	NRI (ནྲི)	humans

branch off from end of rasanā	left eyebrow	SU (སུ)	demi-gods
branch off from end of rasanā	pubis	TRI (ཏྲི)	animals
branch off from end of lalanā	navel	PRE (པྲེ)	tormented spirits
branch off from lower end of lalanā	soles of feet	DU (དུ)	hell beings

Notes

Part One: Introduction

1. *'gos lo tsa ba gshon nu dpal, deb ther sngon po,* vol. 2, 806–9. The entry appears in Gendun Chöpel and G. N. Roerich, trans., *The Blue Annals,* 2nd ed. (Varanasi: Vajra Vidya, 2002), 688–91.

2. *dpa' bo gtsug lag phreng ba, chos 'byung mkhas pa'i dga' ston,* vol. 1(Varanasi: Vajra Vidya Library, 2003), 852.

3. *padma dkar po, chos 'byung bstan pa'i padma rgyas pa'i nyin byed.* (Lhasa: Bod ljongs bod yig dpe rnying dpe skun khang, 1992), 444.

4. shel dkar chos 'byung. History of the White Crystal: Religion and Politics of Southern La stod, vol. 252. Veröffentlichungen zur Sozialanthropologie; Bd. 1 (Wien: Verlag der Österreichischen Akademie der Wissenschaften, 1966).

5. *rgyal ba yan dgon pa rgyal mtshan dpal, dpal yang dgon pa chen po'i nang gi rnam thar.*

6. *ma rgan g.yu lo* and *spyan snga ba rin chen ldan, mnyam med rgyal ba yang dgon pa'i rnam gsang ba'i rnam thar.*

7. *rgyal ba yan dgon pa rgyal mtshan dpal, mnyam med rgyal ba yang dgon pa'i rnam par thar pa gsang ba ma.* This latter account was likely written by Yangönpa himself, although not mentioned in the colophon.

8. *seng 'brag rin po che* and *mkhan po shes rab chos 'phel, stod 'brug bstan pa'i mnga' dpal rgyal ba yang dgon pa'i rnam thar gsol 'debs 'gyur med rdo rje'i sgra dbyangs kyi 'grel ba skal bzang rna ba'i bdud rtsi* (Kathmandu: Nub lung bkra shis phun tshogs, 2001).

9. *pha jo ldings.* This is a handwritten manuscript of 39 folios, in the headed Tibetan script (*dbu chen*), contained in the *Collected Works* of Yangönpa, published in Thimphu, Bhutan, by Kunsang Topgey, said to be based on an original preserved at Phajo Ding monastery in Bhutan.

10. *rta mgo.* This is a handwritten manuscript of 33 folios, in the headed Tibetan script, contained in the *Collected Works* of Yangönpa, published at Tago monastery, Thimphu, Bhutan, in 1982. This version appears to be

347

identical to the Phajo Ding one, and is also available through the Tibetan Buddhist Resource Center website.

11. This volume is available through the TBRC website.

12. *mkha' 'gro ma*, Skt. *ḍākinī*. Translated as "sky-farers," this term refers to female manifestations of enlightened beings; yoginis at various levels of realization on the path; and ordinary women who have particular qualities that make them especially suited for tantric practice.

13. *ma ni bka' 'bum*. See Matthew Kapstein, *The Tibetan Assimilation of Buddhism: Conversion, Contestation, and Memory* (Oxford and New York: Oxford University Press, 2000), 146.

14. In *The Great Mirror*, their name appears as *bla ma bul dmar;* in the biography composed by Sengdrag Rinpoche, as *bla ma phul dmar.*

15. See Cyrus Stearns, *Hermit of Go Cliff: Timeless Instructions from a Tibetan Mystic* (Boston: Wisdom Publications, 2000).

16. *sbyor ba yan lag drug:* withdrawal; meditative absorption; energy-wind yoga; retention; recollection; and contemplation. See Jamgön Kongtrul, *Elements of Tantric Practice*, trans. Elio Guarisco and Ingrid McLeod, Kalu Rinpoche Translation Group (Ithaca, NY: Snow Lion Publications, 2008), 154–61.

17. Śāvaripa, the hunter, figures among the eighty-four mahasiddhas of ancient India.

18. *bar do*. Figuring among Yangönpa's *Collected Works* are several works on the Intermediate State that probably contain Machig Shama's instructions; his text has since been lost.

19. *shri ri* is an ancient name for Tsib mountain (*rtsib ri*), a pilgrimage site in the area of Tingri. It is the home of many monasteries, including the important Drugpa monastery of Tsibri Gon. Lhadong, Yangönpa's home monastery, and Lhading, one of his favorite meditation hermitages, are also located in the vicinity.

20. See E. Gene Smith, *Among Tibetan Texts: History and Literature of the Himalayan Plateau* (Boston: Wisdom Publications, 2001), 44.

21. *gegs sel gzer lnga'i man ngag,* in Jamgön Kongtrul, ed., *gdams ngag mdzod,* 259–80.

22. *na ro'i chos drug: gtum mo; sgyu lus'; od gsal; rmi lam; bar do; 'pho ba.*

23. This is according to the *Inner Biography of the Glorious and Great Yangönpa. The Great Mirror* speaks of fourteen lakhs, or fourteen million.

24. *lnga rig.* The five sciences include all the fields of knowledge studied in Tibet: arts and crafts (*bzo rig*), medicine (*gso rig*), linguistics (*sgra rig*), logic (*tshad ma rig*), and inner knowledge (*nang don gi rig*).

25. *lam sbas bshad.* Referred to in the interlinear notes as "The nectar of the teaching of Sakya Pandita." There are two works by Sakya Pandita called the *Hidden Description of the Path.* The first, unsigned, is a three-folio commentary on a verse drawn from *The Vajra Lines of the Path and Its Fruit (lam 'bras rdo rje tshig rkang)* by the eighth-century Indian siddha Virūpa. The second, which is probably the text Yangönpa is alluding to here, was written by Sakya Pandita while he was in China toward the end of his life. It contains a description of the inner vajra body that is to be used in the practices related to the teachings on the *Path and Its Fruit.* This work, as well as *Root Text of the Path and Its Fruit (lam 'bras rtsa ba),* are translated by Ronald M. Davidson, *Tibetan Renaissance: Tantric Buddhism in the Rebirth of Tibetan Culture* (New York: Columbia University Press, 2005) 183–95, and by Cyrus Stearns, *Taking the Fruit as the Path: Core Teachings of the Sakya Lamdre Tradition,* 1st ed. (Boston: Wisdom Publications, 2006).

26. See Deshung Rinpoche, *The Three Levels of Spiritual Perception: An Oral Commentary on the Three Visions of Ngorchen Konchog Lhundrub,* trans. Jared Rhoton (Boston: Wisdom Publications, 2003).

27. *gdan sa mthil:* the monastery founded by Phagmo Trupa (*phag mo gru pa*) in 1158, some 93 miles from Lhasa, not far from the northern banks of the Tsangpo (*gtsang po*) river that separates the regions of On (*'on*) and Yalung (*yar lung*).

28. Our information on Drigung Chenga Tragpa Jungne was drawn from the following sources:

    1. Drigung Konchog Gyamtso (*'bri gung dkon mchog rgya mtsho*), *'bri gung chos 'byung,* 351–58. TBRC W27020.
    2. Drigung Tendzin Padme Gyaltsen (*'bri gung bstan 'dzin pad ma'i rgyal mtshan*), *'bri gung gdan rabs gser phreng,* 110–12.
    3. Konchog Gyamtso (*dkon mchog rgya mtsho*), *gdan rabs grags pa 'byung gnas* (b. 1175). In *'bri gung chos 'byung,* 351–57. TBRC W27020.
    4. Kunga Rinchen (*kun dga' rin chen*), *spyan snga grags pa 'byung gnas kyi rnam thar 'khor ba'i g.yul las rnam par rgyal byed.* In *gsung 'bum kun dga' rin chen,* vol. 1, 177–82. TBRC W23892.

5. Minyag Gönpo (*mi nyag mgon po*, et. al.), *spyan snga pa grags pa 'byung gnas kyi rnam thar mdor bsdus*. In *gangs can mkhas dbang rim byon gyi rnam thar mdor bsdus*, vol. 2, 89–93. TBRC W25268.

6. Roerich, *Blue Annals*, 609–10.

7. *tshe dbang rgyal, lho rong chos 'byung*, 368–70.

29. *rigs kyi bdag po*: the chief deity of the family to which one's particular medi-
     tation deity belongs. In this case, the term is used as an appellative for one's
     master.

30. For Barawa's activities in Bhutan, See Michael Aris, *Bhutan: the Early History
     of a Himalayan Kingdom*, vol. 1 (Warminster, UK: Aris & Phillips, 1979),
     180–84.

31. *stong ra*. This refers to a method of meditation that serves as a preliminary for
     many practices related to channels, energy-winds, vital essences (*rtsa rlung*),
     and for yogic exercises known as *'phrul 'khor*, Skt. *yantra*, which consists
     of visualizing one's body as being internally empty (*stong*) but having the
     outer shape or "enclosure" (*ra*) of a body.

32. *rdo rje lus kyi sbas bshad*, Pha jo ldings, 496/5:
     rdo rje lus kyi sbas bshad lags lha gdings su sbas bshad 'di thugs la 'khrungs
     phyag yig la 'debs par mdzad pas gnyug kha 'thor nas brir ma btub pa la
     brgyud pa'i bla ma la drag tu btab pas (amended to par) gda' nyen (amended
     to nyan) bshad kyi dus na gsol 'debs re mdzad cing gda' bas de phyis kyang
     rje su 'brang nas gsol 'debs re cis kyang mdzad par zhu lags.

33. *Commentary on the Difficult Points of the Hidden Description (sbas bshad kyi
     dka' 'grel)* written by Chen Ngawa Rinchen Den (henceforth called *SMC*),
     2a–4b3.

34. *dngos po'i gnas lugs*.

35. Tilopa's *Perfect Words: Esoteric Instructions of the Ḍākinīs (bka' yang dag pa'i
     tshad ma zhes bya ba mkha' 'gro ma'i man ngag)*, as preserved in Kongtrul's
     Treasury of Precious Key Instructions (gdams ngag rin po che'i mdzod), vol. 7,
     35a4–5; also in Dg. T. rGyud, vol. Zhi, 271–83, Toh. 2331.

36. For an exhaustive discussion of the phases of creation and completion in
     the Highest Tantras, see Kongtrul, *Elements of Tantric Practice*.

37. Tilopa's *Perfect Words: Esoteric Instructions of the Ḍākinīs (bka' yang dag pa'i
     tshad ma zhes bya ba mkha' 'gro ma'i man ngag)*, TBRC W20877, vol. Ja,
     69/4–5.

38. See Jamgön Kongtrul Lodrö Thaye, *The Treasury of Knowledge, Book Six,
     Part Four: Systems of Buddhist Tantra: The Indestructible Way of Secret Man-*

tra, trans. Elio Guarisco and Ingrid McLeod, Kalu Rinpoche Translation Group (Ithaca, NY: Snow Lion Publications, 2005), 154.

39. *ri chos yon tan kun 'byung gi lhan thabs chen mo,* 28/2–4.

40. *'bri gung bka' brgyud chos mdzod las gnyis med rnam rgyal gyi rgyud rje mar pas bsgyur ba.* TBRC W00JW501203, vol. 57, Shi. This scripture, whose content at a superficial reading seem to be connected to the *Guhyasamāja Tantra,* is somewhat controversial. It is considered to be spurious by Putön, the compiler of the Tibetan canon. Others considered it to be altered or partially composed by Tibetans.

41. *Perfect Words: Esoteric Instructions of the Ḍākinīs (bka' yang dag pa'i tshad ma zhes bya ba mkha' 'gro ma'i man ngag).* TBRC W20877, vol. Ja, 69/5.

42. Longchen Yeshe Dorje and Kangyur Rinpoche, *Treasury of Precious Qualities, Book 2: Vajrayana and the Great Perfection,* trans. Padmakara Translation Group (Boston: Shambhala, 2013), 155.

43. Kongtrul, *Systems of Buddhist Tantra,* 171.

44. A more literal translation of the Tibetan term, *srog 'dzin kyi rlung,* would be "life-sustaining wind."

45. *srog pa rtsa:* the channel that, according to traditional Tibetan medicine, is the basis for life. It includes the white and black life channels. The black life channel is connected to the heart, and the blood flows within it. The white life channel is connected to the brain, and wind flows within it. According to some Tibetan doctors, the black channels are the vena cava and the aorta taken together, and the white life channel is the spinal cord. However, the identification of the life channel has been the subject of discussion.

46. Jamgön Kongtrul, *Phrase-by-Phrase Commentary to the Hevajra Tantra* (henceforth, PCH), 2a1–2b1.

47. Kongtrul, *Systems of Buddhist Tantra,* 37.

48. Kongtrul, *PCH,* 21b2–6.

49. *rdo rje lus kyi sbas bshad kyi zhal gdams,* 3/5–6/1.

50. *sbas bshad zhal gdams,* 5/5–6.

51. *Refulgence of the Sun (yon tan rin po che'i mdzod kyi 'grel pa zab don snang byed nyi ma'i 'od zer).* In Dudjom Rinpoche, *bdud 'joms jigs bral ye shes rdo rje,* ed., *rnying ma bka' ma rgyas pa* (expanded edition of the Nyingma Kahma in 58 volumes). Kalimpong: Dupjung Lama, 1982–1987, vol. 40 (Thi). Translation extracted from Longchen Yeshe Dorje and Kangyur Rinpoche, *Treasury of Precious Qualities,* 407, n. 261.

One of Paltrul Rinpoche's main disciples, the nineteenth-century Khenpo Yönten Gyamtso was an abbot and teacher at Gemang monastery, a daughter house of Dzogchen monastery in eastern Tibet. He composed a two-part commentary on the root text of the *Treasury of Precious Qualities* based on Paltrul Rinpoche's *Structural Outline and Explanation of Difficult Points.*

52. Kongtrul, *Systems of Buddhist Tantra,* 37.

53. For example, in his *snyan brgyud bring bo bar do 'od gsal rang snang* (A 'Dzoms edition, 378), a text from the *bla ma yang thig* collection, the great Dzogchen master Longchenpa (1308–1364) states that *ro ma* is associated with the lunar energy and the syllable HAM. The *rkyang ma* is associated with the solar energy and the syllable A.

54. *phyogs bcu mun sel.* Longchenpa's commentary to the *Guhyagarbha Tantra,* 195.

55. Longchen Yeshe Dorje and Kangyur Rinpoche, *Treasury of Precious Qualities,* 155–57.

56. Ibid., 408, n. 264.

57. See Kongtrul, *PCH,* 23b6.

58. *shes rab sna tshogs.* W4CZ5369, vol. 34, 553.

59. *rnam rgyal gnyis med rgyud,* as found in the *Grand Dharma Treasury of the Glorious Drigung Kagyüd Tradition (dpal 'bri gung bka' brgyud kyi chos mdzod chen mo),* 111b2–3.

60. Kongtrul, *Systems of Buddhist Tantra,* 177.

61. *Lamp Summary of Tantric Practice,* 192/20–193/3.

62. Kongtrul, *Systems of Buddhist Tantra,* 177. However, the tantras as well as the works of various Tibetan authors contain different descriptions of the associations between the elements and the branch energy-winds.

63. Longchen Yeshe Dorje and Kangyur Rinpoche, *Treasury of Precious Qualities,* Appendix 6, 359.

64. The "half-moon" may refer to the lunar constituent that is joined with the red constituent as the two halves of a sphere, in the heart region within the central channel.

65. Kongtrul, *Systems of Buddhist Tantra,* 179.

66. *'jig rten pa'i lam.* In my opinion, this refers to the paths of preparation and accumulation that, in the Sutra teaching, are considered mundane because one who pursues them has not gained a direct understanding of emptiness. It also refers to other spiritual paths pursued by ordinary beings.

67. *las bcu:* the action of governing the functions of the five aggregates, and of the senses.

68. Longchenpa, *phyogs bcu mun sel,* 195.

69. *rang bzhin brgyad cu'i rtog pa.* See Kongtrul, *Systems of Buddhist Tantra,* 264.

70. Kongtrul, *Systems of Buddhist Tantra,* 180.

71. Ibid., 180.

72. Longchenpa, *phyogs bcu mun sel,* 195.

73. Ibid.

74. The interlinear note identifies these as the "twelve transits" (*'pho ba bcu gny-is*). These are the twelve transits of the energy-winds in the twelve principal channels of the navel chakra, which parallel the transits of the sun in the houses of the zodiac.

75. Kongtrul, *Systems of Buddhist Tantra,* 179–80.

76. Ibid., 180.

77. *dil mgo mkhyen brtse rin po che,* oral communication, Bumthang, Bhutan, 1983. In Longchen Yeshe Dorje and Kangyur Rinpoche, *Treasury of Precious Qualities,* 414 n. 293.

78. Longchen Yeshe Dorje and Kangyur Rinpoche, *Treasury of Precious Qualities,* Appendix 6, 360–61.

79. *sbas bshad zhal gdams,* 5/1–5.

80. Nāgārjuna's *Five Stages* (*rim pa lnga;* Skt. *panchakrama*), Dg. T. *rgyud,* vol. Ngi, 45a–57a (Toh. 1802).

81. *dgongs pa lung bstan pa zhes bya ba'i rgyud.* Dg. K. *rgyud 'bum,* vol. Ca, 168b6–169a1 (Toh. 444).

82. Vitapada (*sman zhabs*), *Commentary on the Liberating Essence (grol ba'i thig le'i 'grel pa),* (Toh. 1870), vol. Ni, 49b4–50a1.

83. Longchen Yeshe Dorje and Kangyur Rinpoche, *Treasury of Precious Qualities,* Appendix 6, 359.

84. *rnam rgyal gnyis med rgyud,* as contained in the *Grand Dharma Treasury of the Glorious Drigung Kagyüd Tradition,* 111b4–5. However, the *Nondual Victory Tantra* has *snang ba gsum* (the three lights) instead of *ting nge 'dzin* (contemplation).

85. See Kongtrul, *Systems of Buddhist Tantra,* 30. In the tantras, the substantial vital essence (*thig le*) is often referred to as bodhicitta (*byang chub sems*) to stress the fact that the relative vital essence (and also, in its coarse form, the semen) is the basis for the arising of the bliss embodying the bliss that is

ultimate bodhicitta. Just as, in the Mahayana tradition, relative bodhicitta—understood as the resolve to attain awakening—is the seed of enlightenment, here, too, the bodhicitta as relative vital essence is the seed of the bliss whose nature is enlightenment.

86. *sa skya'i mkha' spyod be'u bum.* W3JT13384:016:0014; TBRC W1PD5284.

87. *stobs bcu.* The ten powers of an enlightened being consist of knowledge of: (1) what is possible and what is not possible; (2) the results of actions; (3) the aspirations of men; (4) the elements; (5) the higher and lower human powers; (6) the paths that lead everywhere (samsara and nirvana); (7) the origin of emotions, which leads to liberation, samādhi, and equanimity; (8) one's previous lives; (9) the transference of consciousness at death; and (10) knowing that defilements are exhausted.

88. *rdzogs chen sems sde'i khri yig,* according to the *nyang lugs* tradition, written by Sogdogpa. Found in *snga 'gyur bka' ma,* 54a3–5, 393.

89. These three verses were translated by Adriano Clemente in *The Ati Treasure of Contemplation, First Level of the Santi Maha Sangha Training (Santi maha sangha' bslab rim dang po a ti bsam gtam dgongs mdzod ces bya ba),* 257–58.

Part Two: The Great Mirror

1. *rgyal ba yang dgon pa chen po'i rnam thar bstod pa mdor bsdus pa.*
2. *rgyal ba yang dgon pa'i rnam thar bstod pa ma 'am me long chen mo.*
3. *sku gsum,* Skt. *trikāya.* Vimalamitra explains in a nutshell how the three enlightened dimensions should be understood:

From a common perspective, within the dimension of reality (*chos sku,* Skt. *dharmakāya*), the sky-like unborn nature, there arises the dimension of perfect enjoyment (*longs sku,* Skt. *sambhogakāya*), the cloud-like Vairocana, and from that, Śākyamuni, the rain-like dimension of emanation (*sprul sku,* Skt. *nirmāṇakāya*) that works to benefit living beings.

From a special perspective, pure awareness (*rig pa*) that is by nature luminous clarity, is the dimension of perfect enjoyment. The appearance of pure awareness as the variety [of phenomena] is the dimension of emanation. Regardless of how this variety [of phenomena] may appear, in reality, it is not beyond the unborn [nature] that is the dimension of reality. Dg. T. *rgyud 'bum,* vol. Tshi, 2b6–3a1 (Toh. 2062).

Thus, from the common Mahayana perspective, the three dimensions are attributes of enlightened beings. The dimension of reality is the enlightened being's mind, which is inseparable from emptiness. The dimension of perfect enjoyment is the subtle manifestation of that enlightened being residing in the pure realm of Akaniṣṭha, endowed with the five perfections, and accessible to bodhisattvas at the tenth level of realization. The dimension of emanation is the appearance of that enlightened being in a particular realm of beings destined to be spiritually uplifted.

From the uncommon perspective of the Highest Tantra of the Mahāmudrā and Dzogchen systems, the three dimensions are the very reality that pervades everything, and therefore are also attributes of all beings: the mind's empty nature is the dimension of reality; the mind's luminous clarity is the dimension of perfect enjoyment; and the mind's potential for uninterrupted manifestation as thoughts and so on, is the dimension of emanation.

4. *bral ba,* or *bral ba'i yon tan:* the quality of being free from emotional conditioning.

5. *rnam par smin pa, or rnam par smin pa'i yon tan.* The quality of having manifested one's innate wisdom.

6. *sa skya'i mkha spyod be'u bum.* W3JT13384:016:0014; TBRC W1PD5284.

7. *ma 'dres pa bco brgyad.* The eighteen exclusive qualities of an enlightened being are of three categories. Those pertaining to behavior are: (1) perfect behavior; (2) perfect speech; (3) unimpaired presence of mind; (4) constant meditative equanimity; (5) relinquishment of clinging to concepts; and (6) freedom from indifference and carelessness. Those pertaining to understanding are: (7) unwavering intention; (8) unflagging exertion; (9) unfailing intelligence and memory; (10) undiminished understanding; (11) unaltered liberation; and (12) perfect discriminative wisdom. Those pertaining to deeds are: (13) physical actions preceded and followed by discriminative wisdom; (14) speech preceded and followed by discriminative wisdom; (15) mental events preceded and followed by discriminative wisdom; (16) accurate perception of the past; (17) accurate perception of the future; and (18) accurate perception of the present.

8. *dbang phyug phun sum tshogs pa.* There are various lists of the qualities of mastery, including the eight qualities of mastery (*dbang phyug gyi yon tan brgyad*), both common and uncommon. The uncommon ones are: mastery of body, of voice, of mind, mastery of miraculous powers, mastery that is ever-present, mastery of place, mastery with regard to whatever one wishes, and mastery in activities. In his *Commentary on the Summary of the*

Initiation, Nāropā explains that mastery (*dbang phyug*) consists of the ten qualities of an enlightened being: the ten powers of a buddha; beauty; the major and minor marks of a buddha's body; wealth; the buddha realm, replete with infinite enjoyments; renown; praise, since a buddha is worthy of being venerated by all beings; wisdom; the eighteen exclusive qualities; and diligence in spontaneous, fortuitous, and unmistaken altruistic activities of a buddha that are not based on conceptual motivation. (Toh. 1351) vol. Na, 221b6–7.

9. *lnga brgya pa tha ma.* The last of the ten five-hundred-year periods of persistence of the Buddhist doctrine.

10. *sangs rgyas drug pa rdo rje 'chang chen po.* The primordial buddha of the Kagyüd tradition—the embracing principle of the five Buddha families, and of the five male and female buddhas of the five families—Vajradhāra is often referred to as the sixth buddha. In the Nyingma tradition, he is the fifth of the twelve primordial teachers of Dzogchen, and a figure in the transmission of the Dzogchen teaching.

11. *'phags pa.* Those who have direct cognition of reality.

12. *pha rol gzigs pa.* Those who see the side of liberation beyond conditioned life.

13. *spyan ras gzigs dbang phyug.* Avalokiteśvara, the deity embodying the principle of compassion, is Tibet's patron deity. Occasionally he is represented as a bodhisattva on the path of self-realization.

14. *bka' brgyud rin po che.* The lineage of the teachings of the Kagyüd school.

15. *rje rin po che rnam bzhi.* The four main masters of Yangönpa: Kotragpa Sönam Gyaltsen (*ko brag pa bsod nams rgyal mtshan,* 1170–1249); Götsangpa Gönpo Dorje (*rgod tshang pa mgon po rdo rje,* 1189–1258); Sakya Pandita Kunga Gyaltsen (*sa skya pandita kun dga' rgyal mtshan,* 1182–1251); and Drigung Chenga Tragpa Jungne ('*bri gung spyan snga grags pa 'byung gnas,* 1175–1255).

16. *phyag rgya chen po.* The term Great Symbol (Mahāmudrā) generally refers to the final fruit of the Tantric path. However, in the Mahāmudrā system developed by Gampopa and adopted by the Kagyüd school, as the original condition of the individual or base, Mahāmudrā is the very nature of the mind as well as the underlying reality of everything. The meditation process to access and realize such nature is also called Mahāmudrā.

17. *sku lnga.* The five enlightened dimensions are the three explained above—reality (*chos sku,* Skt. *dharmakāya*), perfect enjoyment (*longs sku,* Skt. *samb-*

hogakāya), and emanation (*sprul sku*, Skt. *nirmāṇakāya*)—plus the essence dimension (*ngo bo nyid kyi sku*, Skt. *svābhāvikakāya*) and the vajra dimension (*rdo rje'i sku*, Skt. *vajrakāya*).

18. *he ru ka*. Sometimes rendered in Tibetan as *khrag 'thung* (blood drinker), Heruka is a general name for the main male figures of the mandala, as well as for wrathful deities. It does not refer only to Tantric deities in a wrathful mood, but also to those in a joyful or peaceful mood. Atiśa explains the four syllables of *shri he ru ka* in this way: *shri* means nondual wisdom, and indicates that beings' mind-streams are indivisible from wisdom; *he* means the dispelling of confusion concerning birth from no cause, and so on, and indicates that everything arises from emptiness; *ru* means the overcoming of death through the knowledge of the ultimate reality that cannot be ana- lyzed or examined; and *ka* means that there is no inherent reality, material or immaterial, either of cyclic life or of its transcendence. This being said, the meaning indicated by the four syllables is the ultimate Heruka (Atiśa's *Vajra Song of the Vajra Seat,* Dg. T., *rgyud 'grel,* vol. Zha, 209a5–7, Toh. 1494). Here, it is used as a term of praise, comparing Yangönpa to the main deity of the mandala.

19. *longs spyod rdzogs sku.* See note 17 above on the three enlightened dimen- sions.

20. *mtshan dang dpe byed.* The thirty-two major and eighty minor marks of an enlightened being's body that result from the performance of specif- ic wholesome deeds. For example, as a result of his generosity, a buddha's palms and soles are marked by wheels; as he has not used slander to destroy others' friendship, his fingers and toes are connected by a web; and so on. See Jamgön Kongtrul, *Treasury of Knowledge, Books Nine and Ten: Journey and Goal.*

21. *sa bcu'i dbang phyug.* Bodhisattvas on the tenth level of realization.

22. *gsang chen bla na med pa.* The Vajra Way of Secret Mantra.

23. *yan lag bdun dang ldan pa,* or *kha sbyor yan lag bdun.* The seven facets of union are qualities of the sambhogakāya aspect of an enlightened being. They are: (1) complete enjoyment; (2) union; (3) great bliss; (4) lack of self nature; (5) presence of compassion; (6) uninterruptedness; (7) ceaselessness.

24. *sprul pa'i sku,* Skt. *nirmāṇakāya.* See note 17 above on three enlightened dimensions.

25. *mchog gi sprul pa.* An emanation of an enlightened being in a particular realm, endowed with the major and minor marks of enlightenment.

26. *skye ba'i sprul pa.* The various forms that buddhas and bodhisattvas can take in order to spiritually uplift beings. These include appearing as humans to humans, as animals to animals, and so on.

27. *rigs drug sems can.* The beings of the six realms of existence: gods, demigods, humans, animals, tormented spirits, and denizens of hell.

28. *'dzam bu gling.* The Indian subcontinent.

29. *rdo rje'i gdan.* The vajra seat is Bodh Gaya, the village located in the present state of Bihar in India, where the historical Buddha Śākyamuni and the other buddhas of our era manifested, and will manifest the attainment of enlightenment.

30. *bdud.* Demonic influences that create obstacles to the attainment of enlightenment. In the life story of Buddha Śākyamuni, Mara is a powerful god dwelling in the highest abode of the realm of desire, a master of illusion who tried to prevent the Buddha from attaining enlightenment at Bodh Gaya. For spiritual practitioners, Mara symbolizes the causes of interruption to spiritual development, and thus the four obstacles to be cut off in the the practice of Chöd (*gcod*): the demons of form, the formless demonic influences, the demon of ego-clinging, and the demon of complacency.

31. *rigs gsum.* Here, the "three affinities" refers to the affinities of *shravakas, pratyekas,* and bodhisattvas.

32. *byang chub gsum.* The three degrees of enlightenment achieved by shravakas, pratyekas, and the full enlightenment achieved by bodhisattvas.

33. *dkon mchog gsum.* In general, the three precious jewels are the Buddha (*sangs rgyas*); his teaching (*chos,* Skt. *dharma*); and the community of practitioners (*dge 'dun,* Skt. *sangha*). In the inner sense, in Tantric practice, they are the teacher (*bla ma*), the meditational deities (*lha*), and the ḍākinīs (*mkha' 'gro*), who are, respectively, the source or root of blessing, of powers, and of enlightened activity. In the secret sense, in the Dzogchen teaching, they are the view (*lta ba*) that is the recognition of one's primordial enlightenment; the meditation (*sgom pa*), being established in that knowledge; and the behavior (*spyod pa*) that is beyond acceptance and rejection. See Chögyal Namkhai Norbu, *The Precious Vase.*

34. *ru bzhi.* Four areas of central Tibet.

35. *thugs rje chen po.* An epithet of Avalokiteśvara. See note 13 above.

36. See note 9 above.

37. *gzigs pa lnga.* The five visions in which Buddha Śākyamuni manifested in our world: the vision of the birthplace, Kapilavastu; the vision of the family

lineage, the Shakya; the vision of the mother, Mahamaya; and the vision of the degenerate era.

38. *lha gnyan mched bdun.* This may refer to seven mountains associated with the Nyen class of spirits.

39. *mkha' 'gro.* Lit. "sky-farers," refers to different kinds of female beings, including: (1) fully realized manifestations such as Tārā or Mandarava; (2) yoginis at various levels of spiritual realization; and (3) ordinary women with a special potential for spiritual development.

40. *shri par ba ta.* Shri mountain, an ancient name for Tsibri (*rtsib ri*), is an important pilgrimage area in the vicinity of Tingri (*ding ri*) in the Latöd (*la stod*) region of Tsang (*gtsang*). This mountain range is the site of some important monasteries and meditation caves, including Tsibrigön (*rtsib ri mgon*), a major Kagyüd monastery cited in this biography as Shrigön (*shri mgon*). Judging from various passages in this biography, it appears that Lhadong was close to Shri mountain. The main caves where Yangönpa resided—such as Namding (*gnam sdings*) or Shri Namding, where he composed the *Hidden Explanation of the Vajra Body,* and Lhading (*lha sdings*)—were located on this mountain.

41. *phun sum tshogs pa lnga,* or *nges pa lnga.* The five perfections, which characterize both the dimension of perfect enjoyment and the dimension of emanation, include those of teaching (*chos*), time (*dus*), teacher (*ston pa*), place (*gnas*), and retinue (*'khor*).

42. *lha gdong.* The monastery was located in Lhadong in Kungthang (*gung thang*), the central plain of Ngari. Yangönpa was born when Götsangpa, one of his great masters, was twenty-five years old. See the commentary to this work, by *seng 'brag rin po che* and *mkhan po shes rab chos 'phel,* titled *stod 'brug bstan pa'i mnga' dpal rgyal ba yang dgon pa'i rnam thar gsol 'debs 'gyur med rdo rje'i sgra dbyangs kyi 'grel ba skal bzang rna ba'i bdud rtsi,* henceforth shortened to *sgra dbyangs kyi 'grel ba,* 28.

43. *shing sa la.* Shorea robusta, a species of tree belonging to the Dipterocarpaceae family, native to the Indian subcontinent.

44. *grub thob.* An accomplished adept of Tantra who has realized ordinary powers or enlightenment.

45. *slob dpon chen po pad ma 'byung gnas.* Popularly known as Precious Guru (Guru Rinpoche), he was the principal protagonist of the first diffusion of Tantric Buddhism in Tibet during the reign of king Trisong Detsen (*khri*

srong lde btsan, 742–797). From his spiritual activities emerged the Nyingma (*rnying ma*) or ancient tradition, the first school of Tibetan Buddhism.

46. *bram ze sa ra ha.* Born in eastern India to a Brahmin family, Saraha is considered the progenitor of all the Tantric adepts in India. His *Treasury of Songs of Realization (Dohakosha)* is the source of inspiration for the practice of Mahāmudrā in the Kagyüd school. For his life and work, see: H. V. Günther, *Ecstatic Spontaneity: Saraha's Three Cycles of Doha* (Fremont, CA: Asian Humanities Press, 1993), and H. V. Günther, *The Royal Song of Saraha* (Boston: Shambhala Publications, 1973).

47. *rje dam pa rgya gar ba,* often known as Pha Tampa Sangye (*pa dam pa sangs rgyas*), was an Indian siddha who transmitted many teachings based on both Sutra and Tantra in Tibet in the late eleventh century. He journeyed to Tibet more than five times. It was on his third journey that he met Machig Labdrön. Because Tampa Sangye figures in many of the lineages of Chöd, in Tibet he is known as the Father of Chöd. But perhaps his best known teaching is the Pacification of Suffering (*zhi byed*), which became integrated into the Chöd lineages founded by Machig Labdrön.

48. *lcam legs smin ka ra.* Sister of king Indrabhuti of Oḍḍiyāna, princess Lakshminkara figures among the eighty-four great Tantric adepts of India. For her life story, see Keith Dowman, *Masters of Mahāmudrā: Songs and Histories of the Eighty-Four Buddhist Siddhas* (Albany, NY: SUNY Press, 1985), 372.

49. *gtor ma brgya rtsa.* Torma are ritual cakes of offering prepared with roasted barley flour, colored, and decorated with butter.

50. *chab gtor 'jam dpal ma.* A ritual involving the offering of water and dough pellets and their dedication to the tormented spirits, composed by Terdag Lingpa (*gter bdag gling pa 'gyur med rdo rje,* 1646–1714).

51. *mtshan brjod.* The *Mañjuśrīnamasangiti,* a most revered Tantra and the first listed in the Collected Buddhist Tibetan Canon. For a translation of this Tantra, see Alex Wayman, *Chanting the Names of Mañjuśrī: The Mañjuśrī-Nāma-Samgīti* (Boston: Shambhala, 1985).

52. *don yod zhags pa.* The Amoghapāśa Scripture is a Kriya Yoga tantra. See *don yod zhags pa snying po'i mdo.* Dg. K. *rgyud 'bum,* vol. Ba, 278b–284a (Toh. 682).

53. *bsnyen gnas.* This set of eight vows or precepts for lay practitioners, usually maintained for one day on special occasions, includes refraining from killing; stealing; engaging in sexual conduct; lying; drinking alcohol; occupying a

large or high seat; singing, dancing, or using perfume and ornaments; and eating after noon.

54. *ye shes gyi mkha' 'gro ma.* The mother of Yangönpa was called Chöthong (*chos mthong*). See *sgra dbyangs kyi 'grel pa*, 27.

55. *khal.* A standard ancient Tibetan measure of volume.

56. *'pho ba.* The transference of consciousness to a pure land, or to the dimension of reality itself, to be applied just as the signs of imminent death fully manifest.

57. *ring bsrel.* Relics that fall from the cremated corpse or from the preserved remains of a highly realized being.

58. *rta ra.* The first month in the Tibetan calendar.

59. *spyan snga ba.* An appellative often used in this book to refer to Yangönpa but also, at times rather confusingly, to other teachers.

60. *chos tshig bzhi pa.* This may refer to the four lines, found in the Vinaya, that summarize the essence of the Buddha's Teaching:

> To do no evil,
> To practice excellent virtue,
> To control one's own mind:
> [This] is the Teaching of the Buddha.

61. See note 33 above.

62. *mandal 'bul ba.* Usually, an offering of the entire world envisioned with all its land, important elements, and riches.

63. *yan lag bdun pa.* The seven-branched practice: paying homage to the Three Precious Jewels, confessing negative actions, making offerings, rejoicing in the virtue of others, requesting the buddhas to set in motion the wheel of the Teaching, beseeching them to not not pass into nirvana, and dedicating the merit to the enlightenment of all sentient beings.

64. *'bul dmar.* In *sgra dbyangs kyi 'grel pa*, the spelling is *phul dmar.*

65. The text reads *rtsa brgya*, amended to *rtags brgyad* for *kra shis rtags brgyad*, the eight auspicious symbols: excellent umbrella, paired golden fish, treasure vase, lotus, white conch shell coiling to the right, knot of eternity, victory banner, and wheel of the Teaching.

66. *bla ma zhig po bdud rtsi.* This may be a reference to the master of the Extended Transmitted Teachings of the Nyingma (*bka' ma*) lineage who lived 1149–1199.

67. *gsang sngags.* The way of the Tantras.

68. *rtse gcig.* The first of the four stages of Mahāmudrā practice formulated by Gampopa; the others being "beyond concepts" (*spros bral*), "one flavor" (*ro gcig*), and "nonmeditation" (*sgom med*).

69. *mi bskyod sangs spyod.* However, in the account of this event found in the *Blue Annals* (404), this person is called Sangye Mikyöd Dorje (*sangs rgyas mi sbkyod rdo rje*). In the *sgra dbyangs kyi 'grel pa* (34), he is called Dzogpa Chenpo Rinpoche Mikyöd Dorje (*rdzogs pa chen po rin po che mi bskyod rdo rje*). This may refer to Latöd Mikyöd Dorje (*la stod mi bskyod rdo rje*), a well-known twelfth century Nyingma master and a student of Nyangral Nyimai Wözer (*nyang ral nyi ma'i 'od zer,* 1138–1204), known for his transmission of the Avalokiteśvara teaching from the Mani Kabum (*ma ni bka' 'bum*). See Kapstein, *Tibetan Assimilation,* 146.

70. *la stod.* The western part of central Tibet (Tsang).

71. *rdzogs chen.* Dzogchen refers to the total perfection that is the primordial nature of every being. The Dzogchen teaching reveals the way to discover this primordial nature. It is considered by many in Tibetan Buddhism to be the peak of spiritual pursuits.

72. *kun tu bzang po.* The buddha figure representing the state of total enlightenment spontaneously present in all sentient beings. In *sgra dbyangs kyi 'grel pa* (34) it is stated that Mikyöd Dorje wept as he spoke these words.

73. The *sgra dbyangs kyi 'grel pa* (34) states that Yangönpa, among others, received the transmission of the *terma* cycle of Nyangral Nyimai Wözer. The *Blue Annals* (690) adds that he also received the teaching on the Pacification of Suffering (*zhi byed*).

74. *bla ma bul dmar* or *bla ma phul dmar,* according to the *sgra dbyangs kyi 'grel pa* (31). This may refer to the great siddha *bla ma bul dmar seng ge sgra,* who was one of the teachers of Yangönpa's father.

75. *zhang mngon grwa sa.* This may be a reference to a college dedicated to the study of epistemology (*mngon pa*).

76. *zhi khro.* This refers to the cycle of teachings known as *Peaceful and Wrathful Deities: The Profound Teaching on Natural Liberations through Recognition of the Primordial State (zab chos zhi khro dgongs pa rang grol)* revealed by Karma Lingpa (*kar ma gling pa*) in the fourteenth century.

77. *mi nub pa'i rgyal mtshan.* The *Unwaning Standard of Victory* is one of the five early translated scriptures of the Mind Series of Dzogchen (Dzogchen Semde, *rdzogs chen sems sde*). Also known as the *Total Space of Vajrasattva*

(*rdo rje sems dpa' nam mkha' che*), it is part of the source scripture *The All-Creating King (kun byed rgyal po)*.

78. The *sgra dbyangs kyi 'grel pa* (32) states that, during this time, Yangönpa received the empowerment of the *Guhyagarbha (sgyu 'phrul)*, the transmission of the Dzogchen tantras with their oral instructions, the teachings of the Kadampas (*bka' gdams*), the Pacification of Suffering (*zhi byed*) of Chöd (*gchod yul*), and the oral teachings on the essence of the *Path and Its Fruit (lam 'bras)* of the Sakyapas.

79. *A ro.* The teaching referred to here appears to be related to the practice of the Mind series of Dzogchen as taught in the tradition of Aro Yeshe Chungne (*a ro ye shes byung gnas*, tenth century) of the Eastern Tibetan Tradition (*khams lugs*).

80. *zung 'jug thabs dang shes rab.* The paired terms *method* and *knowledge* are the main principles effecting evolution on the spiritual path. Their connotation changes according to the three Buddhist spiritual paths: the Hinayana, Mahayana, and Tantra or Vajrayana. In this context of the instructions on the definitive meaning, they seem to indicate the indivisibility of the emptiness, clarity, and awareness nature of the mind, with "method" representing the clarity that is the basis of vision, or manifestation of things; and "knowledge," the mind's emptiness, whose energy becomes the vision or manifestations.

81. *rtogs ldan.* A title attributed to the yogins of the Drugpa school, but more correctly, one denoting a high level of spiritual realization.

82. *thod rgal.* The practice of the Secret Instructions Series of Dzogchen, by which all deceptive vision is ended in one's own primordial state.

83. *skyes rabs*, Skt. *jatakamala*. One of the twelve divisions of the Buddhist scriptures.

84. *mdo sde*, Skt. *sutrapitaka*. The class of the Buddhist teachings that provide training in meditation.

85. *dge bsnyen.* The conduct of the lay Buddhist practitioner is based on respecting five vows: to refrain from killing, stealing, sexual misconduct, lying, and taking intoxicants.

86. *thabs lam.* The aspect of the Tantric path that works with the vajra body of channels, energy-winds, and vital essences. It is twofold: the method of using one's body (*rang lus thabs*) in conjunction with the chakras above the navel, and the method of working with a consort (*gzhan lus thabs*) in conjunction with the chakra of the secret place.

87. *tshogs gnyis.* The accumulations of merit and of wisdom that, according to the Mahayana, are indispensable prerequisites for the attainment of the dimensions of form (*gzugs sku,* that is, those of perfect enjoyment and of emanation), and of the formless reality dimension of enlightenment (*chos sku*).

88. *theg pa, yana.* Lit. "vehicle" or "conveyance," as in Hinayana, Mahayana, and Tantra- or Vajrayana. However, more importantly, a "vehicle" is not a teaching or system, but an inner condition of the mind.

89. *sde snod gsum.* The three divisions of the Buddha's Teaching: the Vinaya (*'dul ba*), which offers training in ethics; the Sutra (*mdo sde*), which offers training in meditation; and the Abhidharma (*chos mngon pa*), which offers training in knowledge.

90. *rgyud sde bzhi.* The four classes of the Tantras: Kriya, the Action Tantra; Charya, the Conduct Tantra; Yoga, the Union Tantra; and Anuttara, the Highest Union Tantra. Such a classification became popular with the New schools of Tibetan Buddhism: the Sakya, Gelug, and Kagyüd, but previously in India the tantras were categorized in a number of different ways, ranging from two to seven classes. See Kongtrul, *Systems of Buddhist Tantra.*

91. *bslabs pa rin po che gsum.* The training in superior ethics, superior meditation, and superior knowledge.

92. KA is the first letter of the Tibetan alphabet.

93. *nag tshang pa.* This may be a reference to the people of a nomadic area to the west of Sakya Monastery and south of the Yeru river (*g.yas ru gtsang po*).

94. *chu sbyin.* An offering of water to the tormented spirits who, unable to drink, constantly suffer from thirst.

95. *bdag gzhan bde sdig brje ba.*

96. *ko brag pa bsod nams rgyal mtshan* (1170–1249) was the founder of Kotrag monastery in the upper Nyang (*myang*) area of Tsang province, central Tibet. He practiced the *Path and Its Fruit* teachings of the female teacher Machig Shama (*ma gcig zha ma,* 1055–1153), and was instrumental in bringing the Six-Branched Yoga of the *Kālacakra Tantra* to Tibet. He seems to have been an early nonsectarian master, and was unaffiliated with any particular school. For details of his life, see Cyrus Stearns, *Hermit of Go Cliff.*

97. *mnyes pa gsum.* Pleasing the master through one's spiritual practice, with one's body and voice, and with material offerings.

98. *khro phu lo tsa ba byams pa dpal* (1173–1225) was the nephew of Gyaltsa Rinchen Gön (*rgyal tsha rin chen mgon,* 1118–1195), who was a student

of Phagmo Trupa and Kunden Repa (*kun ldan ras pa,* 1148–1217). Trophu Lotsawa founded Trophu Monastery in Shab Zhung (*shab gzhung*) in Tsang, from which came the name of the Trophu Kagyüd school (*khro phu bka' brgyud*). This school maintained an independent identity only prior to the seventeenth century.

99. *bla ma dpyal pa.* This may be the translator Chözang (*lo tsa ba chos bzang*) of the Chal (*dpyal*) clan.

100. The *sgra dbyangs kyi 'grel pa* (35) states that Yangönpa listened to countless teachings from Kotragpa, such as the Thirteen Root Indications of Mahāmudrā (*phyag rgya chen po brda rtsa bcu gsum*); The Cycle on the Essence (*snying po'i skor*); the *Path and Its Fruit* (*lam 'bras*); The Pacification of Suffering (*zhi byed*); and The Path of Method (*thabs lam*).

101. *rje btsun mi la ras pa.* The famous poet and yogin Milarepa (1040–1123), great ancestor of the Kagyüd school.

102. The *sgra dbyangs kyi 'grel pa* (36) states that as a lay practitioner, until age twenty-two, Yangönpa neither ate meat nor drank alcohol.

103. The presence of four ordained monks (*dge slong bzhi*) in a particular place is considered to be the presence of a Buddhist monastic community.

104. *jo bo lha.* This lama was also a teacher of Yangönpa.

105. *bla ma drod chung pa.* Another teacher of Yangönpa.

106. The *sgra dbyangs kyi 'grel pa* (40) mentions that Yangönpa studied with nine excellent contemporary teachers, including Chowo Lhatsun Sokhawa (*jo bo lha btsun so kha ba*), lama Phulmar (*bla ma phul dmar*), Trangso Trawopa (*grang so khra bo pa*), Kyese (*kye se*), and Khenchen Tsultrim Nyingpo (*mkhan chen tshul khrims snying po*).

107. *rgya skyegs. Laccifer lacca,* an ingredient used in Tibetan medicine.

108. *rgod tshang pa mgon po rdo rje* (1189–1258). Foremost disciple of Tsangpa Gyare Yeshe Dorje (*gtsang pa rgya ras ye shes rdo rje,* 1161–1211), the first Gyalwang Drubchen head of the Drugpa school, Götsangpa founded the Upper Branch of the Drugpa tradition (*stod 'brug*) in western Tibet, a lineage that eventually claimed Yangönpa as a principal figure.

109. In Tibetan tradition, nighttime is divided into six periods, including three in the first half of the night and three in the latter half (from midnight until dawn). Dawn is the sixth period.

110. *steng 'gro* (spelled *steng gro* in the *Blue Annals,* 402). Tengdro, Pungtra (*spung dra*), Changling (*byang gling*), Dechen Teng (*bde chen steng*), Pardrog Dorje Ling (*bar 'brog rdo rje gling*), and others are monasteries founded by

Götsangpa in western Tibet. In the *Blue Annals* (402) it is said that each of these monasteries produced many thousands of adepts.

111. *gegs sel gzer lnga.* This text might be the *gegs sel gzer lnga'i man ngag,* authored by Nāropā, and contained in the *gdams ngag mdzod,* Jamgön Kongtrul, ed., 259–80.

112. *rdo rje rtse dgu pa.* A vajra or ritual scepter with nine prongs that are said to symbolize the nine vehicles to realization described in the Nyingma school of Tibetan Buddhism: Shravakayana, Pratyekabuddhayana, Mahayana, Kriya Tantra, Ubhaya Tantra, Yoga Tantra, Mahayoga, Anuyoga, and Ati yoga.

113. *dga' ldan gling.* For nine full years, from from age fifty-nine to sixty-seven, Götsangpa resided at Dechen Teng (*bde chen steng*) and Ganden (*dga' ldan*) in Nyanang (*gnya' nang*). See *sgra dbyangs kyi 'grel pa,* 24.

114. *gnya' nang.* Present-day Nyalam town in the Nyalam prefecture of Tibet's Shigatse province, near the Nepalese border.

115. *chos rje ras pa.* Possibly Tsangpa Gyare Yeshe Dorje, the master of Götsangpa.

116. *chos rje 'bri gung.* Possibly Drigung Jigten Gönpo.

117. Occasionally, Yangönpa is called Yangön Chökyi Gyalpo (*yang dgon chos kyi rgyal po*).

118. *dpa' bo* and *mkha' 'gro.* Male and female high-level practitioners dwelling in the sacred places.

119. *dpal gyi ri.* Usually refers to Śrī Parvata, a mountain in southern India (or, according to some, in Sri Lanka), where the great philosopher Nāgārjuna lived. It is now largely submerged by Nāgārjuna Sagar reservoir.

120. This refers to the twenty-four power places of Tantrism in the Indian subcontinent. A replica of these is said to be found in each region of our planet.

121. *tsa ri.* A sacred mountain in what was formerly southeastern Tibet, but that now largely belongs to the Indian state of Arunachal Pradesh.

122. *bu le.* One of the twenty mountain ranges in Ngari (*mnga' ris*) province of western Tibet.

123. *rin po che bar 'drog,* alias *bar 'grog man lung pa,* one of Yangönpa's teachers.

124. *nub kyi rgyal po.* Virūpaksha is the king of the western direction, one of the great protector kings of the four directions.

125. *rdo rje skyil krung.* Full lotus posture.

126. *rgwa lo.* Namgyal Dorje Galo (*rnam rgyal rdo rje rgwa lo*), the translator of Ga.

127. *zlog sgom*. The meditation consisting of training in the equal "taste" of all experiences.
128. *ro gcig*. See note 68 above, on the four stages of Mahāmudrā practice.
129. *phag zhal*. Vajravārāhī, a major female meditational deity in many Tibetan Buddhist traditions, is depicted with a swine's face perched above her head.
130. *rtags*. These are the signs indicating the purification and control of the energy-winds associated with the various elements.
131. *drod rtags*. Signs indicating meditative experience.
132. *sngon 'gro*. The preliminary practices usually include those of taking refuge and engendering bodhicitta, recitation of the mantra of Vajrasattva, offering the mandala of the universe, and the guru yoga.
133. *rten 'brel rab bdun ma*. *A Secret Teaching of Drogön Tsangpa Gyare,* one of the four special contemplative methods of realization of the Drugpa Lineage.
134. *'gog pa'i bzlas pa*.
135. *rdo rje'i bzlas pa*. The yogic practice in which the three phases of breathing: inhalation, pause, and exhalation, are integrated with the sounds of OṂ, ĀḤ, and HŪṂ.
136. *spro bsdu'i bzlas pa*. This may refer to the recitation in which light is spread and reabsorbed from the mantra syllables.
137. *rlung bum pa can*, Skt. *kumbhaka*. The practice of the retention of the breath, in which the energy-winds are drawn into the central channel.
138. *lhus che*.
139. *bskyed rim*. The gradual imaginative creation of the environment as the mandala and of oneself as the deity. In the praxis of the Highest Tantra, meditations similar in aspect to ordinary death, the intermediate state, and rebirth serve as the basis for the manifestation of the attainment of the three dimensions of enlightenment—reality, perfect enjoyment, and emanation—respectively. Such a transformation also counteracts grasping to ordinary vision as real. However, the praxis of this stage is not confined to such imaginative creation, but also includes a range of other methods, such as the visualization of spheres of light, and secret practices with a consort.
140. This is one of the signs of successful practice of the creation phase of the Highest Tantras.
141. *rmi lam*. One of the six yogas of Nāropā.
142. *sgyu lus*. One of the six yogas of Nāropā.
143. *chang*. A typical alcoholic drink of Tibet and the Himalayan regions, prepared by fermenting cooked barley or another grain.

368 ❋ Secret Map of the Body

144. *tshogs 'khor,* Skt. *gaṇacakra.* Here, *gaṇa* means the variety of thoughts, and *chakra,* the wheel that crushes these thoughts through the experience of pleasure beyond limit, in a state of recognition of the mind's nature, or Mahāmudrā.

145. The *sgra dbyangs kyi 'grel pa* (48) states that when Yangönpa had performed nineteen gaṇacakras, on the ninth day of the *smal* month, the eleventh month of the year of the Pig, he had the vision that is described in the text.

146. *phya lang.* Possibly, a misspelling of *cha lang* (cymbals).

147. The *sgra dbyangs kyi 'grel pa* (48) states that on that day, Yangönpa's practice developed greatly and became all-encompassing.

148. The sg*ra dbyangs kyi 'grel pa* (48) states that there was a malevolent female spirit of the rocks (*brag srin mo*) somewhere nearby who tried to create obstacles for [Yangönpa], but because Yangönpa's practice was so exceptional, she did not succeed.

149. The *sgra dbyangs kyi 'grel pa* (49) states that Yangönpa remained in a state of clear light throughout that night.

150. *sad pa bzhi'i brda'.* Signs used by ḍākinīs to communicate among themselves, and with highly developed practitioners.

151. *thugs rje chen po bcu gcig zhal.* Avalokiteśvara with eleven faces.

152. *las kyi mgon po.* Three classes of Mahākāla are spoken about: the Wisdom Mahākāla (*ye shes kyi mgon po*), usually referring to the six-armed Mahākāla whose *sādhanā* is practiced chiefly in the Shangpa Kagyüd school; the Action Mahākāla (*las kyi mgon po*), usually referring to the two-armed Panyjaranatha whose sādhanā is practiced mainly in the Sakya school; and the mundane Mahākāla (*'jig rten pa' i mgon po*), usually referring to the male and female figures that form the entourage of the principal Mahākāla.

153. See note 31 in Part One.

154. *dus 'khor rtsis.* The so-called "white astrology" (*rgya rtsis*) imported from India, as opposed to the astrology of the elements, or "black astrology" (*nag rtsis*).

155. *tsog pu.* Usually, the position used in various meditative practices in which the knees are drawn close to the chest. But here it may just mean kneeling.

156. *bya co.*

157. *zab mo'i hUM chos.* In other contexts, *chos* is spelled *bcos,* meaning healing.

158. *'og min.* At times Akaniṣṭha is identified as the highest realm in cyclic existence, and at others, as a pure land beyond the cycle of existence, or even as the dimension of enlightenment manifested in and by itself; the essential

reality that is without location, size, limits, and direction. Here, it seems to stand for the pure land where the sambhogakāya form of the buddhas reside.

159. *'dod yon.* Probably a misspelling of *'dod snam,* "ledge" or "streamer," a kind of raised platform on the exterior walls of the divine mansion, where offering goddesses are positioned.

160. *rdo li.*

161. *sum cu rtsa gsum gyi gnas.* One of the six abodes of the Realm of Desire (*'dod khams*).

162. *U rgyan.* No one really knows the precise location of Oḍḍiyāna. Some modern scholars believe that it was centered around the Swat Valley in present-day northern Pakistan. In any case, from what we read in histories and biographies, Oḍḍiyāna has been seen as a very special place where the tantras were practiced and their teachings preserved. It is from this land that many siddhas brought many tantras, explanations, and secret instructions back to central India, which were later disseminated throughout India and beyond, into the Land of Snow.

163. *rdo rje rnal 'byor ma.* A major meditational deity of the Highest Tantras.

164. *'phrul snang gtsug lag khang.* A famous temple in Lhasa built by king Songtsen Gampo (*srong btsan sgam po*) (605–649), now known as Jokhang. It houses a famous statue of Buddha Śākyamuni brought to Tibet by Pal Zatri Tsün (*bal bza' khri btsun*), the Nepalese wife of Songtsen Gampo.

165. *ra mo che gtsug lag khang.* A famous temple in Lhasa housing a statue of Buddha Śākyamuni brought to Tibet by the Chinese wife of Songtsen Gampo.

166. *jo bo.* The two statues of Buddha Śākyamuni housed in the two aforementioned temples.

167. *bsam yas.* The first monastery built in Tibet, probably between 775 and 779, under the patronage of king Trisong Detsen (*khri srong sde btsen*) (742–797). It was supposedly modeled after the ancient Odantapuri monastery in what is now Bihar, India.

168. The meaning of the sentence that follows this one is unclear, and thus has not been translated. The Tibetan reads:
   skya ba'i mdung kha yog pa'i ral kha sad de byed pa.

169. *khal phyed.* Roughly 15 pounds.

170. *grod chung pa.* Probably a misspelling of *drod chung pa,* one of the masters of Yangönpa.

171. *bkra shis tshe ring ma mched lnga.* Five Pramoha deities who protect Tibet and its spiritual teaching. They are Tashi Tseringma (*bkra shis tshe ring ma*), Tingi Shalzangma (*mthing gi zhal bzang ma*), Miyo Lozangma (*mi g.yo blo bzang ma*), Chopen Drinzangma (*cod pan mgrin bzang ma*), and Talkar Trozangma (*gtal dkar gro bzang ma*).

172. *phyi nang gsang gsum gyi mchod pa.* This threefold offering usually implies the outer offering of the sense objects, the inner offering of the five types of flesh and five nectars, and the secret offering of bliss.

173. *chu gtor.* According to legend, when Buddha Śākyamuni taught the *Prajñāpāramitā* sutras, the jealous Devadatta threw rocks at him. But the rocks only struck Jambhala on the head. When the Buddha came over to Jambhala and blessed him with his hand, a stream of nectar flowed from Buddha's hand and healed Jambhala's wounds. Then, the Buddha told him: "As I have healed you and poured this nectar on you, in the future, bestow spiritual and material wealth to any of my students who invoke your powers and pour water on your head." Jambhala promised to do as Buddha said. This story became the impetus for the tradition of pouring water over statues of Jambhala.

174. *dzam bha lha.* The God of Wealth. He belongs to the Vajra family, and is considered an emanation of Avalokiteśvara charged with removing the poverty of beings. In Hindu mythology, Jambhala is known as Kubera.

175. *klu.* A half-snake, half-human class of beings said to rule the underworld and waters.

176. *shes rab snying po. The Sutra Essence of the Perfection of Wisdom,* or *Heart Sutra* of the *Prajñāpāramitā.*

177. *ding ri.* A district in western Tibet, bordering Nepal.

178. *rta ri.* Usually, the horse month is the first month of the Tibetan year.

179. *gangs brag.* Possibly the twenty snow mountains in Ngari province (*mnga' ris skor du gangs nyi shu*) in western Tibet.

180. *be ri.* A district in Chamdo.

181. *'dam.* The first Mongol invasion occurred in 1240, when Yangönpa would have been twenty-seven years old. Another invasion occurred in 1252, when Yangönpa was thirty-nine.

182. See note 53 above.

183. *yi ge drug pa.* OṂ MAṆI PADME HŪṂ, the mantra of Avalokiteśvara.

184. *The Prajñāpāramitā Sutra in 100,000 Lines.*

185. *bre.* A variable measure of volume used in ancient Tibet.

186. *dbang pa.*

187. *(yul) btsan.* One of the eight classes of gods and spirits.

188. *rgyang bu.* Ritual objects made of thread, used in the Bön rites of ransom.

189. *bzang drug.* The six excellent ingredients are nutmeg, bamboo pith, safflow-er, cloves, cardamom, and the larger cardamom.

190. *'chi med bdud rtsi.* This may refer to a medicine prepared from several in-gredients, including relics.

191. *snam sbyar.* A monastic mantle made with thirty-two patches of cloth.

192. *ma ral.*

193. *bro.*

194. *shon.*

195. *'bri mtshams.* Probably a misspelling for *'bring mtshams.*

196. *bla ma zhang rin po che.*

197. *gser gling.* Generally speaking, Suvarṇadvīpa is the ancient name for the island of Sumatra. Here, however, it appears to be a name for a pure dimension.

198. *'ol zi. Podophyllum hexhandrum,* an endangered perennial herb of the Ber-beridaceae family that was used in traditional Tibetan medicine.

199. *gsang spyod mnal lam.* This practice is contained in the famous *Six Mothers (ma drug),* teachings of advice accompanying the three cycles of the *Mountain Teaching (ri chos)* of Yangönpa. See the section on Yangönpa's writings in the Translator's Introduction, above.

200. *tshal gung thang.* The Tsalpa Kagyüd temple in the central plain, part of Ngari province, and seat of the Tsalpa Kagyüd school.

201. Drigung Chenga Rinpoche (*'bri gung gi spyan snga rin po che*) or Drigung Chenga Tragpa Jungne (*'bri gung spyan snga grags pa 'byung gnas*) (1175–1255). See the Translator's Introduction, "His Most Cherished Teacher," above.

202. *'bri gung.* A place to the north of Maldro Gunkar (*mal gro gung dkar*) dis-trict north of Lhasa.

203. *sa skya pan di ta,* alias Kunga Gyaltsen (*kun dga' rgyal mtshan*) (1182–1252). Eminent master, abbot of the Sakya monastery in Tsang, and one of the five patriarchs of the Sakya School who also exercised political power in Tibet on behalf of the Mongols. See the Translator's Introduction, "Visionary Encounters with Lama Shang," above.

204. *sa skya.* A place of the "white earth" seat of the Sakya school.

205. This meeting must have occurred sometime around 1243, when Yangönpa was thirty years old.

206. One year later.
207. *lam sbas bshad.* This probably refers to instruction bearing the name of the Great Sakyapa Sachen Kunga Nyingpo (*sa chen kun dga' snying po*) (1092–1158), received from Virūpa in a vision.
208. Known in Tibetan as *bir va pa,* Virūpa was a ninth-century Indian master who is one of the eighty-four Buddhist mahasiddhas, and an important source of the teachings set down in the *Path and Its Fruit* of the Sakya school. See Dowman, *Masters of Mahāmudrā,* 43–52.
209. Probably Ngachang Chenmo Kunga Rinchen (*ngags 'chang chen mo kun dga' rin chen*).
210. *bsnyen pa.* This term not only implies recitation of the mantra but, in a broader sense, the process of approaching the condition of the body, voice, and mind of the deity.
211. *thugs dam gyi lha.* The manifestations of enlightened beings as the dimension of perfect enjoyment (sambhogakāya) with which various cycles of Tantric teaching are associated.
212. *'phags pa.* Chögyal Phagpa (*chos rgyal 'phags pa*) (1235–1280) was an influential Sakya master and nephew of Sakya Pandita, who became the personal preceptor to Kublai Khan.
213. *lha sa 'phrul snang gi gtsug lag khang.* The main temple in Lhasa that houses the Chowo chapel.
214. *srong btsan sgam po.* The king of Tibet in the seventh century.
215. Patron deity of artists and craftspeople in India.
216. *sgrol ma.* The Chinese princess was considered an emanation of the white Tārā.
217. *jo bo mi bskyod pa.* The principal statue in the Ramoche temple in Lhasa.
218. *sangs rgyas 'od srungs.* The buddha who preceded Śākyamuni in our fortunate era.
219. *byams pa chos kyi 'khor lo.* A silver statue of Maitreya with hands in the gesture of turning the wheel of the Teaching, venerated by king Kikri in the time of Buddha Kāśyapa, and housed at the Jokhang temple in Lhasa.
220. *jo mo bal mo bza' khri btsun.* The Nepalese princess, first wife of the Tibetan King Songtsen Gampo.
221. *lha mo khro gnyer can.* The "frowning one," a wrathful manifestation of Tārā.
222. *bcom ldan 'das bcu gcig zhal.* The eleven-faced Avalokiteśvara.
223. *'gro ba'i mgon po spyan snga rin po che.* See the Translator's Introduction, "His Most Cherished Teacher," above.

224. *rje phag mo gru pa*, alias Phagmo Trupa Dorje Gyalpo (*phag mo gru pa rdo rje rgyal po*, 1110–1170), was one of the four main disciples of Gampopa, and also a disciple of Sakya Kunga Nyingpo (*sa skya kun dga' snying po*, 1092–1153), the forefather of the Sakya tradition. His main disciple was Lingrepa (*gling ras pa*), who became the teacher of Tsangpa Gyare (*gtsang pa rgya ras*).

225. *'jig rten gsum gyi mgon po*. Also known as Kyobpa Jigten Sumgyi Gönpo (*skyob pa 'jig rten gsum gyi mgon po*), Jigten Sumgön, or Drigung Chöje Jigten Gonpo (*'bri gung chos rje 'jig rten mgon po*, 1143–1217). A disciple of Phagmo Trupa and the founder of the Drigung Kagyüd tradition.

226. *bla ma rin po che*. Unclear to whom this title refers.

227. This probably refers to Drigung Chung Phagmo Trupay Wontog Dug (*'bri gung gcung phag mo gru pa'i dbon thog rdugs*), Drigung Chengawa's successor as abbot of that monastery, from whom Yangönpa received the *Cycle of Profound Teachings of Phagmo Trupa*.

228. *gnyan* amended to *gnyen*, for *dge ba'i bshes gnyen*.

229. *'gro chos* amended to *'gro cas*.

230. See note 41 above.

231. See note 89 above.

232. See note 90 above.

233. See note 91 above.

234. *'gro ba'i mgon po*. The Drigung master of Yangönpa.

235. See note 81.

236. *rigs kyi bdag po*. The chief deity of the family to which one's particular meditation deity belongs. In this case, it is used as an appellative for one's master.

237. *rje 'bri gung rin po che*. A reference to Drigung Chenga Rinpoche, the Drigung master of Yangönpa. See note 201 above.

238. "Father and son" refers to Drigung Chenga Rinpoche and Drigung Chung Rinchen (*'bri gung gcung rin chen*), who was the former's successor as abbot of Drigung Thil monastery.

239. *rdor rje 'chang*. See note 10 in Part One.

240. See note 17 above.

241. *rnam par thar pa*. Lit. "the liberation."

242. *sku gsungs thugs kyi rten*. Images and statues of deities representing the Body, sacred books representing the Voice, and stupas or reliquaries representing the Mind.

243. On the mandala offering, see note 62 above.
244. On the sevenfold prayer, see note 63 above.
245. *'khor lo bde mchog yab yum lhan cig skyes pa.* A main meditational deity of the so-called Mother Tantra.
246. *rdo rje phur ba.* A main meditational deity in the Nyingma school.
247. See note 151 above.
248. *gtsug gtor rnam rgyal.* Uṣṇīṣavijayā, with three faces and eight arms, forms the triad of deities of longevity with the White Tārā and Amitayus.
249. *sgrol ma.* One of the most popular meditational deities found in all classes of Tantra, Tārā is also the consort of Amoghasiddhi.
250. *ting nge 'dzin gyi dbang bskur.* The empowerment taken by oneself through visualization.
251. *ku su lu'i tshogs gsog.* Possibly, the visualization of offering one's body.
252. This refers to bowls of water and other offerings placed on the altar.
253. The nature of this torma-offering is unknown.
254. *ba su ka' i gtor ma.*
255. *thun gtor.* Also called "daily torma" (*rgyun gtor*), this is occasionally used as a gift at the close of certain enjoyed activities.
256. *bcom ldan 'das ma.*
257. *ting nge 'dzin gyi rgyal po,* Skt. *samādhiraja.* The name of a famous Discourse of the Buddha, *The King of Meditative Stability Sutra.*
258. *sbyin sreg.* Rite in which the fire deity is visualized in the flames, and offered various items, for the sake of purification, development, domination, and destruction.
259. *bdud rtsi ril bu.* Usually, pills prepared with the so-called five nectars and five kinds of flesh.
260. *dbang po.* One of the twenty-seven influential astrological conjunctions.
261. *ha ri.* Another of the twenty-seven influential astrological conjunctions.
262. *nam mthong.* A misspelling of *gnam stong,* the new moon day.
263. *bya rbo.* Altair, the brightest star in the constellation Aquila.
264. See note 68 above.
265. *gar dgu.* The nine moods of dramatic art: coquettish (*sgegs pa*), heroic (*dpa' ba*), ugly (*mi sdug pa*), wild (*rgod*), furious (*drag shul*), terrifying (*'jigs su rug*), compassionate (*snying rje*), awesome (*rngam*), and peaceful (*zhi ba*).
266. *phyi nang gsang gsum 'gros bzhi'i rten 'brel.* The "four motions" (*'gros bzhi*) generally refer to the quick, slow, crooked, and arising course of planets through the sky. This would be the outer (*phyi*) interdependent connection.

Here, a parallel motion is possibly being ascribed to the body—channels, energy-winds, vital essences—the inner (*nang*) interdependent connection; and to the mind, the secret (*gsang*) interdependent connection.

267. "I" refers to Chen Ngawa Rinchen Den (*spyan nga ba rin chen ldan*), the author of this biography.

268. *bar 'brog.* This refers to *bar 'brog rin chen gling,* the monastic seat of Götsang-pa.

269. *a ru ra. Terminalia chebula,* a fruit with curative properties, here symbolizing Tibetan medicine in general.

270. *sdom gsum.* The Hinayana vows of individual liberation, the Mahayana commitments of the bodhisattvas, and the Tantric pledges of mantra adepts.

271. *rgyu mtshan nyid theg pa.* A reference to the way taught by the Buddha in his Discourses, which comprises both the Hinayana and Mahayana. It is referred to as the "causal way," because its followers apply themselves to the causes conducive to the attainment of enlightenment. It is the "causal" as opposed to the "resultant" way of Tantra, where the fruit (enlightenment) is imaginatively taken as the path. It is referred as the way "of characteristics," because, in this path, the characteristics of conditioned life (samsara) and of its transcendence (nirvana) are explained in great detail.

272. *grub pa thob pa.* Can refer to one who has attained either the ordinary powers or the supreme realization of enlightenment.

273. The four main teachers of Yangönpa.

274. *dwags po rin po che.* Gampopa, one of the chief disciples of the great yogin Milarepa.

275. The nineteenth day of the fourth month (*sa ga zla ba*) of the year 1258, the year of the earth tiger.

276. The *sgra dbyangs kyi 'grel pa* (68–69) states:
Just as they had insistently requested and received the permission, after his passing away, Yangönpa's students built a statue of Yangönpa the size of a boy of seven, and a man-sized statue, with medicines and with the clay from his cremation. They put the remains and the relics inside these statues. And the Togdens—the great disciples who had merged their minds with his mind—evoking the master's mind with an infinite devotion, consecrated the statues so that the wisdom-being and commitment-being could remain forever indivisible, and scattered flowers over them. Afterward, the statues spoke, and relics formed from the clay from which the statue was made. In the *Secret Biography,* it is stated: "Four years after the passing away, in the

year of the water male pig, seven manifestations [of the master] arrived, [and] one of them was absorbed into the precious statue." Later, as soon as [a yogin] called Kunpang Rechen (kun spang ras chen) encountered [the statue], he recognized the state of Mahāmudrā just as it is; and it is well known that the statue spoke to old and young pilgrims from eastern Tibet. The statue was thus a great shrine [associated] with countless wonders.

277. *bral dang rnam smin ye shes gzigs pa*. See notes 4 and 5 above.

278. *stobs*. See note 86 in Part One.

279. See note 7 above.

280. *dbang phyug yon tan*. See note 8 above.

281. *kun rdzob byang chub sems*. The wish to attain enlightenment for the benefit of all beings.

282. *don dam byang chub sems*. The understanding of reality, imbued with compassion, attained by bodhisattvas on the path of seeing.

283. *g.ya' chu*, according to the *sgra dbyangs kyi 'grel pa* (65); *g.ya' ru*, according to this biography.

284. *a rgham*.

285. The wisdom that is knowledge of all existing phenomena (*ji snyed pa'i mkhyen pa'i ye shes*); and the wisdom that is knowledge of the unreality of all existing phenomena (*ji lta ba mkhyen pa'i ye shes*).

286. *rje btsun mi la*. See note 101 above.

287. *bla ma rngog pa*. Possibly, a reference to a disciple of Marpa.

288. *lho brag*. A province of southern Tibet and the birthplace of Götsangpa.

289. The *sgra dbyangs kyi 'grel pa* (65) states that Yangönpa's clothes were immediately sent to Götsangpa, and that Götsangpa died within 13 days of Yangönpa's passing.

290. *bra ba*. A rodent.

Part Three: The Hidden Description of the Vajra Body

1. *dpal rdo rje rnal 'byor ma*. A major deity of the highest class of tantra. Here it refers in particular to Vajravārāhī. These words form the customary homage made at the beginning of a text. *The Commentary on the Difficult Points of the Hidden Description* (*sbas bshad kyi dka' 'grel*) written by Chen Ngawa Rinchen Den, states:

The Precious One [Yangönpa] saw in a vision the glorious Vajrayoginī, and received the empowering blessing and prophecy from this
meditational deity. Thus, in order to fulfill the gathering of the two
merits and purify obscurations, [Yangönpa] pays homage to his own
favored deity, the venerable Vajravārāhī, the mother who generated
all the buddhas of the three times. (2a2–4).

2.   Here, an interlinear note written in small point size (*yig chung*) in the Tibet-
      an text states: "This presents the title of the text." Henceforth, such notes
      will be referred to as YC.
      Chen Ngawa explains the two parts of the title as follows:

      In the [title] *Hidden Description of the Vajra Body*, "vajra body" should
      be understood as the fundamental nature of the channels, syllables,
      energy-winds, and mind. If you do not know this, you will not un-
      derstand the meaning of meditation. If you do not understand this,
      good qualities will not arise. Those who do not understand the real
      nature of the body will not achieve the fruit. As to the hidden fun-
      damental nature of the body, it is "hidden" because people of lesser
      intellect—that is, those of the lower spiritual pursuits—have difficulty
      understanding the extraordinary points of the inseparability of body
      and mind. From one perspective, it is hidden for those who, without
      relying on a teacher, wish to practice [these points] that are locked
      by means of the six parameters and four modes [of explanation], by
      hidden instructions, by twisted quotations, and by tantras in dis-
      array. From another perspective, it is secret because it is hidden, in
      the sense that the great innate wisdom is difficult to realize. (SMC,
      2a4–2b2).

      Notes interspersed in this *Commentary* specify the six types of parameters,
      general and specific, and the four modes to follow:

      [The six general parameters consist of the] literal meaning, nonliter-
      al meaning, provisional meaning, definitive meaning, interpretable
      meaning, and uninterpretable meaning. The [six] specific [parameters
      are those concerned with the] practice of the Mantra [way].... The
      four modes are: to expound the general meaning, the meaning of a
      text, the extensive meaning, and the six parameters (SMC, 2b2–3).

For an explanation of these, see Jamgön Kongtrul, *Systems of Buddhist Tantra*, 286–90. Regarding the title, Chen Ngawa continues:

> In what way [does Yangönpa] provide his *Description*? The Precious One himself directly saw the fundamental nature of the vajra body's channels, the colors and spans of the energy-winds, the numbers of flow [of the energy-winds], and the manner of controlling the constituent of great bliss. He taught this by validating it with ideal scriptural references and citations from various classes of tantras, [both] father and mother. [Moreover,] he distinguished the details of the essential instructions of the Four Precious [teachers], incomparable in this world, and explained them, bringing forth their clarity. (*SMC*, 2b3–5).

3.   *rdo rje*, Skt. *vajra*: lit. "prince of stones," or diamond, denoting the indestructible reality that is the very nature of the individual and of the universe. It is characterized by seven qualities: incorruptibility (*sra ba*), invulnerability (*mi chod pa*), indestructibility (*mi shigs pa*), authenticity (*bden pa*), stability (*brten pa*), unobstructibility (*thogs pa med pa*), and invincibility (*ma pham pa*).

4.   This paragraph contains the salutation (*phyag 'tshal ba*) (*YC*). Chen Ngawa comments as follows:

> As to [the lines], "I salute the vajra that is the inseparability of magnificence and great bliss; and the ḍākinīs together with their families," through the vajra that is the inseparability of knowledge (of the emptiness of all phenomena of existence; the great knowledge of the glory of realization) and method (the great bliss that is the method that actualizes this); since such inseparability possesses all the supreme aspects, the nirvana that does not abide is actualized. "Ḍākinīs" refers to the wisdom that moves unobstructed in the space of emptiness, the real condition of existence. "Together with their families" is a salutation to the master who retains the "family" of the realization of the reality dimension of awakening (dharmakāya); and who, as the great lord of the family, reveals without errors the pure and ultimate [reality].

In another explanation, "the vajra inseparable from magnificence and great bliss" refers to one's mind, the self-originated innate wisdom that is directly experienced as nondual bliss and emptiness. "ḍākinī" means that [this wisdom] moves swiftly in the space of emptiness, accomplishing the benefit of beings through magical powers. ["Together with their families"] refers to the five families [of the ḍākinīs] among whom the vajra ḍākinī is the most important; thus, it is a salutation to the *vīras* and the ḍākinīs who are the custodians of the teaching. (*SMC*, 2b5–3b2).

5.   Chen Ngawa comments: "The words 'the one who,' (*gang zhig*) [rendered here as 'this body'] are those that lead, that connect, that open the reverence. In the qualified [human] body that has no faults with regard to freedoms and endowments, that does not have undesirable channels, and so on, all the attributes of the divine mansion are present." (*SMC*, 3a2–3).

6.   Chen Ngawa comments:

"Twenty-four" refers to the twenty-four sacred places. These [places] are present in one's own body: the head is Pullīramalaya, the crown of the head is Jālandhara, the right ear is Oḍḍiyāna, the nape of the neck is Arbuda, the left ear is Godāvarī, the point between the eyebrows is Rameshvari, the eyes are Devikoti, the shoulders are Mālava, the armpits are Kāmarūpa, the tip of the nose is Koshala, the mouth is Kalinga, the neck is Lampaka, the breasts are Odri, the navel is Trishakune, the heart is Kanchi, the pubis is Himalaya, the sexual organ is Pretapuri, the anus is Grihadeva, the two thighs are Saurashtra, the two calves is Survarṇadvīpa, the sixteen fingers and toes are Nagara, the top of the feet are Sindhu, the four thumbs and [big] toes are Maru, and the knees are Kuluta. The channels are present in the shapes of the twenty-four sacred places. (*SMC*, 3a3–5).

7.   Chen Ngawa comments:

"the supreme abode of the ten levels of realization" means that in the Vajrayana tradition, the levels of realization and the path are tread only in relation to the body. The ten levels of realization consist of: sacred places and related sacred places (*gnas dang nye ba'i gnas*), fields and related fields (*zhing dang nye ba'i zhing*), meeting places and related meeting places (*tshan dho ha dang nye ba'i tshan dho ha*), gathering places and related gathering places (*'du ba dang nye ba'i 'du ba*), and charnel grounds and related charnel grounds (*dur khrod dang nye ba'i dur khrod*). These are the inner ten levels of realization. The mandala of the body that is not a mandala of colored powders, or an outer mandala, is said to be the supreme sacred place. The ten levels of realization of [the way of] the perfections, that is, the sacred places and so on, are said to be the forms of the channels. (*SMC*, 3a5–7).

8.   Chen Ngawa comments:

"the divine mansion complete with the thirty-seven" means that in the divine mansion [of the body] all thirty-seven factors of the path to enlightenment are present. It is said that in this [mansion], the Body, Voice, and Mind [that are the nature] of the thirty-seven are fully present. By way of its four arm-spans or four cubits, and so on, [the body] is complete with all the attributes of the divine mansion, and this divine mansion of the three pure realms is beyond mental evaluation, measurement, and concepts. Since it is the abode of the deity, it is called "mansion." This is the meaning of the statement, "the body is said to be the mandala itself." (*SMC*, 3a7–3b2).

9.   Chen Ngawa comments: "Although the three, and the other mandalas are taught, in its etymological definition, 'mandala' has the meaning of taking the essence of the dimension of reality (dharmakāya) and of the dimension of form (*rūpakāya*). For this reason it is [called] 'mandala.'" (*SMC*, 3b5–6). Small notes interspersed in Chen Ngawa's commentary explain the three mandalas:

The [first mandala is] the coarse body mandala with its internal support; the subtle is the forms of the channels. As to the second [mandala], the coarse is the dimension of the secret space of the consort; the subtle, the forms of syllables. The third [mandala] is the dimension of the bodhicitta whose two aspects—the white and red constituents—are the coarse [mandala]; the subtle [mandala] is the five nectars, the sixteen constituents, and the thirty-two constituents. (*SMC*, 3b6–7).

"Circle" means that the support and supported [mandala] that is the uninterrupted wheel of inexhaustible ornaments of Body, Voice, and Mind are not different; that the main deity and the [deities] of the retinue, and the body and mind, are inseparable; and that, like a clean golden vessel filled with excellent nectar, the good qualities are spontaneously arising in the mind; thus [the text states,] "adorned." (*SMC*, 3b5–7).

10. *dpa' bo,* Skt. *vira:* male tantric practitioners at different levels of spiritual realization.

11. Chen Ngawa comments:

> "Enjoyment of nondual heroes and ḍākinīs" means that the channels that are present as the shapes of the twenty-four sacred places, and so on, are of the nature of the ḍākinīs; and that the constituents dwelling in these [channels] are of the nature of the heroes (vira). Since channels and constituents are inseparable and [are] the heroes and ḍākinīs that enjoy the great bliss, the heroes and ḍākinīs of these places are brought under one's power; the phenomena of samsara and nirvana are dominated; and the unalloyed bliss is experienced in a nondual state. (*SMC*, 3b3–5).

12. Chen Ngawa comments:

> "performs the dance of illusion" means that the wisdom that is of the nature of compassion manifests, yet is nonexistent; while nonexistent, it manifests as everything; manifesting, it has no reality; therefore, it is "illusion."

> "performs the dance" means that in order to accomplish the benefit of sentient beings [that are of the nature] of Body, Voice and Mind, [one] performs the dance that tames whoever needs to be tamed, in the appropriate way as skillful means to tame disciples through the nine moods of dance or through various miracles. (*SMC*, 3b3).

13. Chen Ngawa comments:

> "essence of the Body, Voice, and Mind of all the buddhas" means that the vajra of the Body; the vajra of the Voice; the vajra of the Mind of all tathāgatas; the Hevajra of the essence; and the very Body, Voice, and Mind of enlightened beings that are the result, are inseparable from the body, voice, and mind of sentient beings that are the cause. This is the meaning of the statement [from the tantras]: "The essence of the Body, Voice, and Mind of all buddhas resides in the *bhāga* of the vajra queen." "Vajra" refers to inseparability, that is, [a state]

that does not obstruct anything and cannot be harmed by anything; since it is inseparable and beyond union and separation, it is [called] "vajra." The *Vajra Peak* [*Tantra*] states: "Indestructible, incorruptible, insubstantial, imperishable, invincible, not consumed by fire, and impossible to cut. Thus, emptiness is called 'vajra.'" (*SMC*, 3b7–4a3).

14. Chen Ngawa comments: "[This state] does not arise from a cause; it is not produced by conditions; it is not created by the intellect; and its nature exists like that by itself. Thus, it is 'self-originated.'" (*SMC*, 4a3).

15. Chen Ngawa comments:

[As to the term] "conqueror," (*bcom ldan 'das*), "to conquer" (*bcom*) means that it has conquered the four demons: the demon of the godly son, the demon of the aggregates, the demon of the emotions, and the demon of death. "To possess" (*ldan pa*) refers to the eight [qualities] of mastery or to the six [qualities] of glory, renown, wisdom, mastery, beauty, and excellent enthusiasm: these are what is possessed. "Transcendent" (*'das*) means that [this state] is a nirvana that remains neither in conditioned existence nor in [a state] of peace, and it transcends the misery and suffering of samsara. (*SMC*, 4a3–6).

16. Chen Ngawa comments:

"Union of secrets" (*gsang ba 'dus pa*) means that the real nature of Body, Voice, and Mind is the total wisdom of the innate that is difficult to realize, and thus it is "secret" (*gsang ba*). In each of these, all three [Body, Voice, and Mind] are present and inseparable; therefore, all tathāgatas are one, a "union." [The tantras state:] "The three aspects of Body, Voice, and Mind are called 'secrets.' [The words,] 'all the buddhas' express [the fact] that they are a union of many."

"Nature" (*bdag nyid*) means that everything—oneself and others, the animate and inanimate world—has the nature of the three vajras [of Body, Voice, and Mind], and that apart from this nature, nothing exists. With regard to this innate nature, there are no causes, [yet it] appears as delusive. All dualities—such as vision and emptiness—are not contradictory, [being] an inseparable union. Therefore, [the tantras] speak of "true nature" (*yang dag nyid*). In the vajra body, channels, energy-winds, and vital essences are present without any imperfection; thus [they are] the true nature. (*SMC*, 4a5–7).

17. Chen Ngawa comments:

> "Sovereign of the four enlightened dimensions" means that the shapes of the channels represent the dimension of emanation (*sprul sku*); the vital essences within the syllables represent the dimension of enjoyment (*longs sku*); the secret nectar represents the dimension of reality (*chos sku*); and the energy-winds having six limits represent the essential dimension (*de kho na nyid kyi sku*). In this way, the four dimensions (*sku bzhi*) are the spontaneously present sovereign (*dbang phyug*). (*SMC*, 4a7–b2).

18. Chen Ngawa comments: "'be victorious' is the final pronouncement of auspiciousness." (*SMC*, 4b2).

19. Chen Ngawa comments:

> If even these gods and beings] do not know, on what does one rely? "Relying on," means relying on a realized holder of the Mantra [way] that reveals the method for attaining, in one life, the wisdom of the thirteenth level of realization. Who relies on such a [master]? One who has the highest capacities relies on him. What is the manner of reliance? It is to rely on the Vajra way of the Secret Mantra. [The tantras state:] "By not relying on this method, but on other methods, one will not become enlightened."(*SMC*, 4b5–6).

20. The words in this paragraph express the author's commitment (*bshad par dam bca' ba*) to write the text to its completion. (*YC*). Chen Ngawa comments:

> The line beginning with "the Lion" indicates that non-Buddhist fundamentalists, those of the lower spiritual pursuits, as well as the followers of the [way] of characteristics, do not comprehend. Regarding this, "Lion (*seng ge*), Ravisher ('*phrog byed*), the Essence of Wealth (*dbyig gi snying po*)" refers to the non-Buddhist [gods] Brahmā, Viṣṇu, and Maheśvara, and to worldly people. These, and also the "disciples" (*slob ma*), that is, the shravakas, disciples of the Buddha; the "rhinoceri" (*bse ru*), that is, the pratyekas; and the "children of the Victorious One" (*rgyal ba'i sras*), that is, the bodhisattvas, do not

comprehend the state of enlightenment of the great secret that has actualized the thirteen levels of realization in a single life. The tantras state, "Non-Buddhist fundamentalists do not know the state of enlightenment." (*SMC*, 4b2–4).

A note in parentheses in the Beijing edition states: "*Seng ge* is Brahmā (*tshangs pa*); *'phrog byed* is Maheśvara (*dbang phyug*); *dbyig gi snying po* is Viṣṇu (*khyab 'jug*)."

21. Chen Ngawa comments:

As to [the words] "gained the certainty of experience," in general, [Yangönpa] was renowned as a great lord of yogins who had attained realization of inconceivable qualities of the path and the fruit. His paternal uncle understood him to be Vajradhāra himself. Also, in our perception, he was abiding, in particular, in the infinite qualities of the path of method, and regarding the fundamental nature of the vajra body, when he was in the equipoise of contemplation of the empty enclosure (*stong ra*), he perfectly saw the condition of the channels, energy-winds, and vital essences; and the colors, and so forth, of the energy-winds as one whose eyes are looking at form. (*SMC*, 5a4–6).

22. Chen Ngawa comments:

The hidden explanations of the fundamental nature of the stationary channels, of the interdependence of channels and syllables, of the manner of formation of the nectar of the constituents, of the wisdom energy-wind that is the essence of their actualization, and of the hidden [topics] locked by means of the six parameters and the four modes [of explanation], are kept secret from those who wish to engage [in Tantric practice] by themselves, without knowing the nature of the vajra body. (*SMC*, 5a2–3).

23. Chen Ngawa comments: "As to 'vajra body,' the reason why the ordinary body is said to be [the vajra body] is that the ordinary body, voice, and mind and the Body, Voice, and Mind of Heruka are inseparable at all [times: at the time of] the cause, path, and result. This [inseparability] is the vajra." (*SMC*, 5a1–2).

"The [nature of the vajra body] is realized through the master's kindness. It is taught unerringly and understood by once listening to the [teacher's] words. [Yangönpa said:] 'Through the teachings of the Four Precious Ones, my mind was satisfied.'" (*SMC*, 5a3–4).

24. Chen Ngawa comments, "[The hidden nature of the vajra body] is revealed as the method that clarifies all the turnings of the wheel of the teaching of self-originated innate wisdom. Being connected and continuous, difficult to scrutinize, and real, it is a 'tantra of excellent exegesis.'" (*SMC*, 4b7–5a1).

25. Chen Ngawa comments:

> "Bliss" refers to the bliss that is spontaneously present; the unalloyed bliss; the bliss that is not a sensation; the bliss that is all: the cause, the path, and the result. [As is stated,] "At the time of the cause it is supreme, and at the time of the result, too, it is supreme." The great secret of skillful means and profound wisdom is special in that it protects swiftly and through bliss, taking as its path the nonduality of the things to be discarded and their remedies and antidotes, and the liberation from the causes of bondage." (*SMC*, 4b6–7).

26. On Yangönpa's qualities as conveyer of these teachings, Chen Ngawa comments:

> He was not subject to the shortcomings of personally fabricating [the teachings] or of not understanding the principles of the faultless tantras. With [an intention] as white as the moon, he requested [permission] to communicate the master's teaching, his own personal experience, and the secret words of the ḍākinīs, and to make the secret methods known to others. Without self-interest, for the benefit of others, he wrote down [this text on the vajra body]. (*SMC*, 5a6–b1).

27. For an account of the life of Nāropā, see H. V. Günther's translation of Lhatsünpa Rinchen Namgyal's (*lha btsun pa rin chen rnam rgyal*, 1473–1557) work, *The Life and Teaching of Nāropā* (Oxford, UK: Clarendon Press, 1963).

28. Tilopa was one of the most renowned accomplished tantric masters of ancient India. He was the master of the saintly Nāropā from whom, through Marpa the Translator, stems the Kagyüd tradition of Tibetan tantric Buddhism.

29. See Günther, *Life and Teaching of Nāropā*, 54–55.

30. Nāropā's account of his master Tilopa's teaching is recorded in *Perfect Words: Esoteric Instructions of the Ḍākinīs,* preserved in Jamgön Kongtrul's *Treasury of Precious Key Instructions (gdams ngag rin po che'i mdzod)* vol. 7, 35a4.

31. The entire contents of the Highest Yoga Tantra are included in the base (*gzhi*) or fundamental nature, the path (*lam*), and the fruit (*'bras bu*). In his *Systems of Buddhist Tantra,* Kongtrul explains:

> The "fundamental nature" denotes the nature, or way of being, of all phenomena, inclusive of everything from form to omniscience. The fundamental nature is also called "the total symbol of the base stage"; "primordial reality"; "original lord"; "affinity for enlightenment"; and "essence of enlightenment." On that basis of division, there are two fundamental natures of things, that of the body and that of the mind, when distinguished in terms of the way the fundamental nature manifests (154).

In the Highest Tantras, the path consists mainly of the phases of creation and completion that are practiced after receiving the appropriate initiation; the fruit consists of the dimensions of awakening (*kāya*).

32. Chen Ngawa gives a lengthy commentary on these words, as follows:

> To explain: the realization of the buddhas of the three times, the way of existing of the fundamental nature of things, the way of existing of the originary thing to be known, the unborn nature, is the reality devoid of self-nature that has never been experienced in the three times. The uninterrupted creativity that is the natural expression [of this reality] manifests as every objective appearance. The two—reality and appearances—have never existed in the three times. They are nothing whatsoever; therefore they appear as anything whatsoever. And because they appear as anything whatsoever, they are nothing whatsoever. The two stand as a union.

> This is ornamented by the teaching of sublime [masters], and when one obtains the light of discriminating intelligence, all the unmistaken [aspects] of the three trainings of the exceptional spiritual pursuit, the four noble truths of the distinguished path of the shravakas, the twelve links of interdependent origination of the pratyekas, the two accumulations—method and knowledge—of the [way of the]

Perfections, the two truths of the Madhyamika, and the two stages
of the Secret Mantra, are perfectly fulfilled in relation to the mind's
appearance as any object of the eight consciousnesses, in any behavior in which one happens to engage, and in all varieties of thoughts
that occur.

Moreover, unlike in the causal vehicle [in which the eighty-four
thousand aspects of the teachings are taught as antidotes to the three
poisons of the emotions, here], the emotions are not abandoned separately because the emotions flare up as antidotes to themselves. When
the three poisons manifest, they self-liberate as they manifest. When
they are [seen as] empty, the three poisons self-liberate as emptiness.
In pure awareness, the three poisons self-liberate as pure awareness.
Therefore, since the eighty-four thousand aspects of the teaching too
are wholly present simultaneously with the instantaneous consciousness, one speaks of "path." This path is neither denigrated by being
considered nonexistent, nor reified by being considered existent. It is
not born of causes; it does not arise from conditions; it is not created
by the mind; and since reality itself is present in this way, it is said
to be self-originated. Therefore, through this [reality], the natural
course of the essence of the self-originated path takes place.

All of the above-mentioned vehicles are wholly and unmistakably
present as the natural course of the self-originated essence that is
the path, in relation to any appearance of mind, any action, and any
thought. Just then, the true nature of reality whose real character is
nothing whatsoever; which has no "before" or "after"; whose essence
is neither "good" nor "bad"; which is undifferentiated in terms of
location; and whose nature is devoid of an inherent essence, is the
reality dimension of awakening (dharmakāya). The nature of the unobstructed radiance [of this dharmakāya], the characteristic that manifests as everything, is the dimension of emanation (nirmāṇakāya).
The essence that is spontaneously present as the identity of the pure
awareness of appearance and emptiness, is the dimension of enjoyment (sambhogakāya).

The path and the fruit are inseparable from these three [dimensions],
and insofar as they exist as the natural course of the self-originated essence, all objective appearances too are pure and naked in the

path. Insofar as the three dimensions of awakening are spontaneously present, these very [appearances] also stand as the fruit. Thus, the inseparability of path and fruit is said to be the base.

Moreover, the fundamental nature of things—the base—is the nature that is correlated in five ways, in the beginningless and endless three times, with appearances, emptiness, and pure awareness. Because this nature is spontaneously present from the beginning as the essence of the threefold fruit, the base and the fruit are said to be inseparable.

Once this nature is understood nakedly and without object through knowledge, familiarization with this [understanding] is the path. Therefore, the understanding that the base and the fruit are inseparable is said to be the path.

Just as pure awareness and emptiness inseparable are present in relation to appearances, wherever the dimension of emanation is present, the dimensions of enjoyment and reality are inseparably present. Just as appearance and emptiness inseparable are present in relation to pure awareness, wherever the dimension of enjoyment is present, the dimensions of emanation and reality are inseparably present. Just as appearance and pure awareness inseparable are present in relation to emptiness, wherever the reality dimension of awakening is present, the dimensions of emanation and enjoyment are also spontaneously present. The tantras say that this itself is the inseparability of cause and result, or the bodhicitta that has neither beginning nor end.

The fruit is asserted to be the exhaustion of the flaws of the base and path. Therefore, the base is the spontaneous presence of appearance, pure awareness, and emptiness as the essence of the three dimensions that are the fruit, and when these are realized to be not different, the flaws of the base are exhausted. Because it is the characteristic cause for the actualization of the three dimensions, when the natural course of the self-originated essence—which is the path—is perfected, the flaws of the path are exhausted. In relation to any appearance of the mind, any action that is performed, and any thought that occurs, the self-originated path is vividly present. This itself, without its edge being spoiled and without changing color, stands as the three dimensions that are the fruit. These two are inseparable, and when the impurity of the veil of obscuration is self-liberated, one reaches the perfect exhaustion. Therefore, it is asserted that the actualization of the inseparability of base and path is the fruit. (*SMC*, 5b1–6b3).

33. The five enlightened dimensions (*sku lnga*) consist of the three above-mentioned dimensions: dharmakāya, sambhogakāya, and nirmāṇakāya; the *abhisambodhikāya* (*mngon byang sku*), which is each of the three dimensions' distinct aspect of actual enlightenment; and the *vajrakāya* (*rdo rje sku*) or Vajra dimension that is of the "flavor" of dharmakāya, sambhogakāya, and nirmāṇakāya equally in the real condition (*dharmadhatu*). However, the five are listed differently in different sources.

34. *phar phyin theg pa*, Skt. *paramitayana:* the Mahayana, in which the six perfections (generosity, ethics, patience, effort, concentration, and discriminating intelligence) or the ten perfections (these six plus method, strength, aspiration, and wisdom) are applied as the means of attaining enlightenment.

35. *Samputa Tilaka Tantra (rgyud kyi rgyal po chen po dpal yang dag par sbyor ba'i thig le).* Derge Kangyur (henceforth Dg. K.). *rgyud'bum*, vol. Ga, 167b2–3 (Toh. 382). The *Samputa* is variously classified as an exegetical tantra. Some consider it an explanatory tantra of the *Hevajra Tantra.* According to Tāranātha, the *Samputa* is a general commentary to the *Hevajra, Cakrasamvara,* and *Catuhpītha Tantras.*

36. *chos kyi phung po brgyad khri bzhi stong.* In general, the "eighty-four thousand" refers to all the teachings included in the vehicles of the shravakas, pratyekas, bodhisattvas, and the Secret Mantra. The *All-Creating King (kun byed rgyal po)* states:

> The twenty-one thousand teachings of the division on Discipline were taught in order to overcome desire. The twenty-one thousand teachings of the division of the Discourses were taught to overcome aversion. The twenty-one thousand teachings of the division of Higher Knowledge were delivered in order to overcome ignorance. The twenty-one thousand teachings of the fourth division were taught in order to overcome all these [together]. In brief, although eighty-four thousand teachings were taught, all are intended to overcome emotions. Dg. K. *rgyud 'bum*, vol. Ka, 15b6–16a1 (Toh. 828).

37. *rdo rje.* "Here, it denotes inseparability." (*YC*).

38. This verse is not found in the *dpal nam mkha' dang mnyam pa'i rgyud kyi rgyal po (Khasama Tantraraja)* contained in Dg. K. *rgyud 'bum,* vol. Ga, 399–405 (Toh. 368).

39. Here, *heruka* means an enlightened being, a buddha.

40. *snying po'i kye rdo rje.* Here, this expression stands for the real condition of the individual.

41. *rdo rje rol pa zhes bya ba bar do rje phag mo'i rgyud.* This text has not been located.

42. The *Vajramāla* (*rdo rje 'phreng ba,* translated as *Indestructible Garland*) is a well known explanatory tantra of the *Guhyasamāja Tantra.* Although it has not been located in the *Vajramāla* contained in the Dg. K. (Toh. 445), the passage quoted is found in the *Nondual Victory Tantra (rnam rgyal gnyis med rgyud),* 111b1–2.

43. "The way in which [the body] is formed through five manifest awakenings." (*YC*).

44. The illnesses that can prevent conception are mentioned in an interlinear note, as follows:

    First, yellowish and thin kidney [menstrual] blood; second, dark spleen [menstrual] blood in which impure matter is present; third, dark liver [menstrual] blood; forth, vermillion lung [menstrual] blood; fifth, dark bluish heart [menstrual] blood. After this [faulty menstrual blood ceases], a child is conceived. On even [days], a male child; on odd [days], a female child is conceived. (*YC*).

45. For discussion of the energy-winds, see section "The Fundamental Nature of the Voice."

46. *'byung ba bzhi:* earth, water, fire, and air.

47. In the ancient Indo-Tibetan cosmology, at the formation of the universe, first the winds rose from the four directions. The powerful convergence and compression of these winds, represented by the fire element, brought clouds containing rain, the water element. Then gradually, through the churning of the masses of water by the wind, the earth element developed. See Kongtrul, *The Treasury of Knowledge, Book One: Myriad Worlds: Buddhist Cosmology in*

Abhidharma, Kalachakra, and Dzogchen, trans. Kalu Rinpoche Translation Group (Ithaca, NY: Snow Lion Publications, 1995).

48. Generally speaking, the bases of purification in the phase of creation of the Highest Tantras consist of death, the intermediate state, and rebirth. The meditations that are the agents of purification transform ordinary death, intermediate state, and rebirth, into the paths to attain the reality dimension, the dimension of enjoyment, and the dimension of emanation. In this process, the agents of purification are applied with forms according with that which is to be purified.

49. This is the stage in which the embryo is liquid with a thick surface.

50. "At the same time, the [fire-] accompanying [wind is formed]." (*YC*).

51. The text cited is the *phag mo mngon par byang chub pa'i rgyud* (Toh. 377), but this quotation is not found in it.

52. "This is explained in the *Vajramāla* and *Kālacakra* [tantras]." (*YC*). The *Kālacakra Tantra* presents the stages from conception to death as corresponding to the ten incarnations (Skt. *avātra*) of Viṣṇu. Only the first four stages occur in the womb, while the remaining stages occur during the lifetime. The *Vajramāla* only presents the pairings of the first five months of gestation with the first five incarnations. Alamkakalasha's *Commentary to the Vajramāla,* Derge Tengyur (henceforth Dg. T.) *rgyud,* vol. Gi, provides the pairings of the five later stages with the remaining five incarnations.

53. "Ramana, the son of Yene, and Ramana the magical king (*yan ne'i bu ra ma na dang 'phrul gyi rgyal po ra ma na*)." (*YC*).

54. In other lists, the tenth incarnation of Viṣṇu is Kirti, son of Kalki Brahmin (*rigs ldan bram ze'i bu kir ti*). For a description of the ten incarnations of Viṣṇu, see Khedrup Norzang Gyamtso, *phyi nang gzhan gsum gsal bar byed pa dri med 'od kyi rgyan,* 136–37. Translated by Gavin Kilty as *Ornament of Stainless Light: An Exposition of the Kālacakra Tantra* (Boston: Wisdom Publications, 2001).

55. "The hard and oval [stage] (*gor gor po*)." (*YC*).

56. "The stage of hardening (*khrang 'gyur kyi skabs*)." (*YC*).

57. "From this point on, the gender [of the fetus] will not change." (*YC*).

58. According to traditional Tibetan medicine, the seven organic components of the body (*lus zungs bdun*) are: the nutrient extracted from foods during digestion, blood, flesh, fat, marrow, bones, and vital essence or regenerative fluids.

59. Ten levels of realization (*sa bcu*) that mark the bodhisattva's path to awakening.

60. "[At this stage], the tongue turns inward, and the uvula projects the above it; instead of flowing outside, the upper winds flow inside, and therefore the body grows. This is also the essential point of the energy-wind related to the attainment of immortality." (*YC*).

61. "At the completion of the twelve months of interdependence." (*YC*).

62. "For this reason, the mother becomes emaciated." (*YC*).

63. "The [discomfort refers to the] fierce heat of the [stomach] swelling with food." (*YC*).

64. "This is the posture of the liberated lion that blocks the energy-wind [flowing through] the nine orifices of the body." (*YC*).

65. *'khrang gyur gyi skabs*: one of the five stages of embryonic development. Ratnakarashanti's *Commentary on the Saṃvarodaya Tantra (dpal sdom pa 'byung ba'i rgyud kyi rgyal po chen po'i bka' 'grel pad ma can)* explains the five stages as follows:

> The embryo of the first week is called "*nur nur po* (Skt. *kalaka*)," which means a slippery mixture of semen and ovum. The embryo of the second week is called "*mer mer po* (Skt. *arbuda*)," which means that its form resembles a bubble on water, empty inside. In the third week, it is called "*tar tar po* (Skt. *pesi*)," a form slightly more solid than that in the first week. In the fourth week, it is called "*gor gor po* (Skt. *ghana*)," which means that it is like flesh enveloped in a very soft membrane. Then, in the stage called "hardening" (Skt. *prasakha*), the fetus starts to show the five protuberances that are the beginnings of the four limbs and the head. Dg. T. *rgyud*, vol. Wa, 11a2 (Toh. 1420).

The *Saṃvarodaya* states that five stages of development represent the forms of the five buddhas: in the first week, the embryo is the form of Akṣobhya;

in the second week, that of Ratnasaṃbhava; in the third week, that of Amitābha; in the fourth week, that of Amoghasiddhi; and from the fifth week on, that of Vairocana. Dg. K. *rgyud 'bum,* vol. Kha, 266b2–3 (Toh. 373). It is to be noted that throughout the sutras and tantras there are inconsistencies in the naming of the initial stages of embryonic development.

66. *Hevajra Tantra,* Dg. K. *rgyud 'bum,* vol. Nga, 9a2–3 (Toh. 417).

67. A note in the text reads: "The *Mahāmudrātilaka* states: 'Listen, Lhamo of Great Fortune. The supreme origin of the wheels of channels consists of seventy-two thousand [channels]. These are said to be the family of all channels." (*YC*). *Mahāmudrātilaka Tantra,* Dg. K. *rgyud 'bum,* vol. Nga, 68a7 (Toh. 420). "In Jambudvīpa [likewise] there are seventy-two thousand rivers." (*YC*).

68. *yul.* On the sacred places, see note 6 above.

69. *bre gang dang phul gang. bre:* a measure of volume equaling approximately 0.94 liters; *phul gang:* a handful.

70. *zho gcig dang phul do.*

71. The quantities of organic components in the human body are also explained in the *Exegetical Tantra (bshad rgyud)* of Tibetan medicine, which states:

     The amount of the wind humor equals the volume of one's urinary bladder. The volume of bile equals the capacity of one's scrotum. The amount of phlegm is three cupped handfuls. The amount of blood and feces is seven cupped handfuls each. The amount of urine and lymph is four cupped handfuls each. The fat and adipose tissue each amount to two cupped handfuls. The vital fluids and semen each measure a single handful. The brain amounts to one cupped handful. As far as the quantity of flesh and muscle tissue is concerned, in the male body it amounts to five hundred close handfuls, while the female breasts and thighs additionally comprise ten closed handfuls each.... The major and minor bones are 360. (*sde dge rgyud bzhi.* TBRC W2DB4628, 32).

72. Dg. K. *rgyud 'bum,* vol. Nga, 2b1–2 (Toh. 417).

73. Kongtrul's *Phrase-by-Phrase Commentary to the Hevajra* explains:

There are indeed many types of channels, such as the seventy-two thousand, but there are thirty-two principal ones. In them flows thirty-two parts of the relative bodhicitta, the constituents [producing] teeth, nails, and so on. In particular, the main [constituent,] the lunar essence, flows to the place of great bliss, the navel, or the secret place (20b1–2).… Among the petals of the chakras and of the thirty-two channels just mentioned, the three channels that serve as the basis for all of them are thus known as the main channels. These are, to the left, the one called lalanā (*rkyang ma*); to the right, the one called rasanā (*ro ma*); to the center, the avadhūti, that is, *kun spang ma* or *kun 'dar ma* (20b5–6).

74. Dg. K. *rgyud 'bum,* vol. Nga, 2b7–3a1 (Toh. 417).

75. *YC* cites the following words of the *Hevajra Tantra:* "These symbolize, respectively, the sixty-four *daṇḍa* (*dbyu gu drug bcu rtsa bzhi*), the eight two-hour periods in a day (*thun chen po brgyad*), the sixteen transits (*'pho ba bcu drug*), and the thirty-two *ghaṭikā* (*chu tshod sum cu rtsa gnyis*)." Dg. K. *rgyud 'bum,* vol. Nga, 3a4 (Toh. 417). The two-hour periods (*thun*), transits (*'pho ba*), daṇḍa (*dbyu gu*), and ghaṭikā (*chu tshod*) refer to units of time, described variously in different tantras, through which the movements of the energy-winds are calculated.

76. According to the *Kālacakra Tantra,* the six chakras are as follows: the chakra of the secret region with its thirty-two channels, the navel chakra with sixty-four channels, the heart chakra with eight channels, the throat chakra with thirty-two channels, the forehead chakra (*dbral ba lhan cig skyes pa'i 'khor lo*) with sixteen channels, and the chakra of the crown of the head with four channels. See Kilty's translation of Khedrup Norzang's *Kālacakra,* 145.

77. The chakras of the forehead and of the secret region are the two immobile chakras (*mi g.yo ba'i 'khor lo*). The four mobile chakras (*g.yo ba'i 'khor lo*) are those of the head, throat, heart, and navel. The chakras of the twelve continents (*gling bcu gnyis kyi 'khor lo*) correspond to the major joints of the limbs. The chakras that perform actions (*las byed pa*) are those of the hands.

78. Dg. K. *rgyud 'bum,* vol. Nga, 2b7 (Toh. 417).

79. Kongtrul, explaining the literal meaning of these words, writes:

> The shape of E is the goddess that is the purity of earth: the earth element that, endowed with an unobstructed eye, is [called] Locanā (*spyan ma*). The shape of VAM is Māmakī—the purity of water—the *varuṇa* element, which in Tibetan is called *bdag gi ma* [Sovereign Lady]. The syllable MA is the goddess that is the purity of fire, the *maru* element that, holding a white cloth, is called Paṇḍāravāsinī (*gos dkar mo*). The shape of YA—the purity of air or *vayave* element—is Tārā (*sgrol ma*), who saves all beings from the suffering of samsara. (*PCH,* 27b6–28a2).

80. Four enlightened dimensions (*sku,* Skt. *kāya*): reality, enjoyment, emanation, and the dimension of great bliss (mahāsūkhakāya).

81. Dg. K. *rgyud 'bum,* vol. Nga, 21b1–2 (Toh. 418).

82. In the ancient meditative traditions of India and Tibet, the twenty-four hours of the day were subdivided into twelve periods of two hours each. Each of these periods is associated with one of the twelve animals that we find in the astrology of the elements (*nag rtsi*). The afternoon (associated with the sheep) and after midnight (associated with the ox) are the two periods in which the earth element exercises its strongest influence on the human organism.

83. The three lights (*snang ba gsum*)—white, red, and black—manifest at different moments in a lifetime and at the time of death. Those mentioned here are the three lights that manifest at the time of falling asleep. For an extensive discussion of the meaning of the three lights, see Kongtrul's *Systems of Buddhist Tantra,* 249–70.

84. "This is the talk of someone who does not have the slightest understanding of the Secret Mantra." (*YC*).

85. Yangönpa explains the four characteristics of the central channel above. Various characteristics are ascribed to the central channel. For example, in the *Stairway to Liberation,* Jigmed Lingpa states: "Straight like the stem of a plantain tree, slender as a lotus petal, luminous as a sesame oil lamp, and red like the lacquer tree's flower." (See Chögyal Namkhai Norbu, *The Precious Vase,* trans. Adriano Clemente). However, such characterizations do not seem to refer to inherent qualities of the central channel itself, but are descriptions intended to facilitate the practitioner's visualization. For

instance, in an oral communication, Rigzin Chanchub Dorje explained to Chögyal Namkhai Norbu that the central channel is a channel of wisdom, not materially present in the body as described.

86. *thabs lam.* Although it refers to the Mantrayana in general, in particular, this term is used in opposition to the "path of liberation" (*grol lam*), a path of pure contemplation. The "path of method" refers to the methods employed in the phase of completion of the Highest Tantras, in which one applies techniques involving the upper and lower doors of the central channels. For the upper door, one sequentially applies the inner heat in relation to the chakras of the upper part of the body to elicit the wisdom of bliss and emptiness. For the lower door, one relies on sexual practice with a consort, with the union of the two organs at the lower door of another's body (that is, the consort's) to instantly elicit the wisdom of bliss and emptiness. See Kongtrul, *Systems of Buddhist Tantra,* 324–26.

87. *Tantra of the Extraordinary Secret (thun mong ma yin pa'i gsang ba'i rgyud).* This work has not been located, and may no longer be extant. But this passage, with slightly different wording, is found in the *Mahāmudrātilaka,* Dg. K. *rgyud 'bum,* vol. Nga, 88b6 (Toh. 420). "This is also stated in the *Mahāmudrātilaka.*" (*YC*).

88. "The *Mahāmudrātilaka* explains that it is luminous like a lamp burning with sesame oil." (*YC*).

89. *Catuhpīṭha Tantra.* This passage has been found neither in the Dg. K. edition of this tantra (Toh. 428), nor in the *Catuhpīṭha Explanatory Tantra (dpal gdan bzhi pa'i rnam par bshad pa'i rgyud kyi rgyal po),* TBRC W26071.

90. "The essential points of [the practice related to] the six chakras are derived from these [six unions]." (*YC*). Here, "six unions" (*sbyor ba drug*) seems to be an explanation specific to the *Mahāmudrātilaka,* a tantra of the Hevajra class. In this tantra, it is stated that the root of all phenomena is the indestructible vital essence. When differentiated in accordance with its presence in the center of the six chakras of the body, it comprises six unions known as: potential for manifestation, vital essence, nature, mere nature, the supreme nature, and the other supreme alternative.

91. These are the six branches of yoga (*sbyor ba yan lag drug*) that, with different meanings and procedures, are applied in various tantras, such as the *Guhyasamāja, Kālacakra* and others. See Kongtrul, *Elements of Tantric Practice.*

92. "Because it is unrecognized by others, this central channel is very secret." (*YC*).

93. *Treasury of Doha,* Dg. T. *rgyud* (Toh. 2224). This passage is not found in the Dg. T. edition of this text.

94. *gnyer po che:* the crease that, in some people, is very evident in the lower abdominal region, above the pubic area.

95. Kotali or Kotalipa (*tog tse pa*). His hagiography is found among the life stories of the eighty-four mahasiddhas. This citation is not found in the two works contained in the Dg. T. that are attributed to him (Dg. T. *rgyud,* Toh. 2228–2339).

96. This may refer to the A of knowledge located at the juncture of the three channels below the navel.

97. *khams gsum:* the realms of desire, of form, and the formless realm. This statement may refer to the attainment of the clairvoyance of divine hearing (*lha'i rna ba'i mngon shes*) that enables one to hear all sounds, near and far.

98. The inverted syllable HAM at the crown of the head and the HAM at the area of the hair-tuft between the eyebrows represent the white vital essence.

99. "[This explains why] when male and female meet [in sexual intercourse], their nose [tip] splits; [why] the presence or absence of vital essence in the body is clearly indicated; and also why, when bloodletting is done at the tip of the nose in the case of fainting, it is also beneficial to massage [that point]." (*YC*).

100. This verse is not found in the Dg. K. edition of this tantra (Toh. 381).

101. "'Distinct' (*gsal ba*)] refers to the color and 'indistinct' (*mi gsal*) to the shape." (*YC*).

102. Center of the heart: "[Center] of the four chakras." (*YC*).

103. "The *dhuti.*" (*YC*).

104. *bdud bral ma:* "[The source of] the nonconceptual wisdom." (*YC*).

105   The fifth chapter of the *Kālacakra Condensed Tantra*, Dg. K. *rgyud 'bum*, (Toh. 362). These lines probably originate from the large root tantra of the *Kālacakra,* which is no longer extant.

106. The meaning of these lines are partially explained by the following interlinear notes:

> Line 1. "The sound, and a part of the vital essence."
>
> "At the throat [chakra], the vital essence of the Voice produces the dream state. At the heart [chakra], the vital essence of Mind produces the state of sleep."
>
> Line 2. "The places [to which] the nectar of wisdom has gone."
>
> "'Wisdom' [indicates that] at the forehead [chakra], the vital essence of Body produces the waking state. 'Nectar' [indicates that] the head [chakra] is the place where the vital essence dwells, and the genital [chakra], the place from which it seeps. 'Place' [indicates that], at the navel [chakra], during the day, the vital essence of wisdom produces the state of the avadhūti [that is, orgasm]. 'Has gone' [means that] feces, urine, and semen flow downward."
>
> Lines 3 and 4. "The channel bound with chains / The three paths of life and downward-voiding [winds]."
>
> "[In the channels] below, feces, urine, and semen flow; and [in the channels] above, the solar, lunar, and Rahu [energy-winds flow]. The central channel (dhuti) is bound by the knots of the rasanā and lalanā."
>
> Line 5. "The lotus with the vajra."
>
> "[This refers to] the crow-face (*kākamukha*) channel, the lower extremity of the central channel."
>
> Line 6. "And the vajra with the lotus."
>
> "[This means that, when] the extremity [of the crow-face channel] is good, the defects of the ten types of potent hermaphrodite are not present."
>
> Line 7. "When energy-winds meet at the center."

"[This refers to] the conceptual mind meeting with energy-wind, or alternatively, to the male and female life-sustaining and downward-clearing winds meeting at the secret place."

Line 8. "Through the objects and the senses."

"[This means that] the doors of the five sense objects, and the five senses, are closed."

Line 9. "There is arising and entering."

"'Arising' [refers to] the conceptual mind; 'entering' [means that] bliss enters the energy-winds." (*YC*).

107. "The names of the central channel include 'all shaking' (*kun 'dar ma*, Skt. *avadhūti*); 'seizer' (*sgra gcan*, Skt. *rahu*); 'crow-face' (*bya rog gdong ma*, Skt. *kākamukha*); 'conch woman' (*dung can ma*, Skt. *shankini*); 'good-minded female' (*yid bzang ma*, Skt. *susumna*); and 'dark one' (*mun pa 'bab*, Skt. *tamovaini*)." (*YC*).

108. Dg. K. *rgyud 'bum*, vol. Nga (Toh. 417), 2b2.

109. Explaining these words from the *Hevajra Tantra*, Kongtrul writes:

Having the nature of knowledge, lalanā (*rkyang ma*) creates the idea of the apprehended. Fifteen channels, such as the "undivided" (*mi phyed*), which are the purity of fifteen days of the waxing moon in the external [world], branch off from it. Its tip inserts in the left nostril. Rasanā (*ro ma*), which has the nature of method, creates the idea of the apprehender. Ten channels, such as "descending" (*gzhol ma*), which are the purity of the fifteen days of the waning moon in the external [world], branch off from it. Its tip inserts in the right nostril. The central channel (*kun 'dar ma*), which is of the nature of the inseparability of method and knowledge, stands straight in the body, its tip inserting into the Brahmā opening. In males, its lower extremity inserts in the door of the gem of the vajra; in females, it inserts in the clitoris. Since it is totally beyond apprehended and apprehender, it is called the "all-abandoner" (*kun spang ma*). Moreover, from the navel, having reached the Brahmā opening, the central channel turns toward the point between the eyebrows. It should be known that below the navel, where the three channels meet, the lalanā is at the back, the rasanā to the left, and the dhuti in front. (*PCH*, 21a1–b1).

110. "The energy-winds circulate by binding the two armpits and the breasts." (*YC*).

111. "[The rasanā and lalanā] enter [the central channel] by squeezing the hands in the meditation gesture." (*YC*).

112. *gla rtsi*: the abdominal gland of the musk deer, used as a sedative in traditional Tibetan and Ayurvedic medicine.

113. "As to their synonyms, lalanā is also called, 'the moon [channel] through which urine descends' (*zla ba dri chu 'bab*); rasanā, 'the sun [channel] through which blood descends' (*nyi ma khrag 'bab pa*)." (*YC*).

114. Dg. K. *rgyud 'bum*, vol. Nga, 2b, 2–3 (Toh. 417).

115. Kongtrul writes:

> As to the function of these three [channels], from the hollow cavity of the lower extremity of lalanā descends the urine that is called Akṣobhya. [In its] upper [part,] in the left nostril, the five winds of the lunar element that have the nature of Akṣobhya, flow in the order of [the elements'] arising. For *ro ma* (rasanā), likewise, its lower extremity expels or withholds the element of blood of the female. [In its] upper [part], in the right nostril, the five winds of the solar element flow in the order of [the elements'] dissolution. The lower extremity of the central channel, from the meeting point of the three channels [downward], causes the white portion of the lunar bodhicitta that has the nature of Nairātmyā—wisdom—to descend, and thus it is said to be filled with Vajradhāra (holder of the vajra). [The bliss] pervades all channels, and since bliss makes [the central channel] shake, [that channel] is called "all-shaking" (*kun 'dar ma*, Skt. *avadhūti*). (*PCH*, 21b2–6).

116. "As a result of strain and so forth, the channel opens, and there is loss of blood in the urine." (*YC*).

117. Such characteristics seem to parallel the shape of the female external genitals.

118. This citation is not found in the Dg. K. edition of this tantra (Toh. 381).

119. That is, from the navel down.

120. These words are from Virūpa's *Root Vajra Verses on the Path and Its Fruit* (*lam 'bras rdo rje tshig rkang ma*), 2b2–3.

> Regarding the "four channels of existence," above the navel the rasanā and lalanā exist depending on the right and left side of the body. Below the navel it is asserted that they split into four, to the right, left, front, and rear. The right channel expels and withholds frankincense [menstrual blood] (Skt. *sihalaka*) and energy-wind. The left extension expels and withholds camphor [semen] (Skt. *karpura*). The front extension expels and withholds musk [urine] (Skt. *kasturika*). The rear extension expels and withholds that which has four equal [tastes, that is, feces] (*bzhi mnyam*). These are known as "channels of existence" because they create the subject-object dichotomy that accompanies the body and mind produced by karma.

The "chakras" are the chakras of the forehead where the moon [lunar constituent] of the father dwells; and the secret region chakra where the blood [the solar constituent] of the mother dwells. These are the two immobile chakras (*mi g.yo ba'i 'khor lo*). Then there are four mobile chakras (*g.yo ba'i 'khor lo*) at the head, throat, heart, and navel, totaling six. These, plus the twelve chakras of the major joints (two wrists, two elbows, two shoulders, two ankles, two knees, and two hip joints), total eighteen chakras. Two action chakras are also mentioned: the six chakras of the lower wind, and the three chakras of the junction of the three channels (our paraphrase, from *gsung ngag rin po che lam 'bras bu dang bcas pa'i gzhung rdo rje'i tshig rkang gi 'grel pa*, TBRC W23605).

121. *bdud rtsi:* a reference to feces, urine, semen, and blood, which are considered to be the essences of the body.

122. Dg. K. *rgyud 'bum*, vol. Ka, 16a1–2 (Toh. 361).

123. "[These are] the four occasions on which, in an ordinary condition, the energy-winds enter the central channel." (*YC*).

124. *sgra can:* the ascending and descending nodes of the moon.

125. This passage is not found in the Dg. K. edition of this tantra (Toh. 381).

126. "All channels of the body branch off from the three [main] channels. Lalanā and rasanā also originate from the central channel. Since those who explain these channels have only the general meaning, they do not have the knowledge of how [the channels are arranged] in the body, of how to apply them in practice, and of which transformations occur. These essential points are very secret." (*YC*).

127. This passage is not found in the Dg. K. edition of this tantra (Toh. 381).

128. Kongtrul writes: "'Inseparable' (*mi phyed ma*)—the inseparability of the three vajras—abides at the head and produces nails and teeth." (*PCH*, 22a5).

129. *'tshogs ma*: the area located three fingers above the center of the hairline.

130. *bzang mo ma*. In some editions of our text (the *rdo rje lus kyi sbas bshad*) and in other sources as well, this channel is called "playful" (*rtse ba ma*). Kongtrul writes: "The [channel] 'playful' (*rtse ba ma*), [fond of] sensory enjoyments, resides at the right ear and produces skin and sweat." (*PCH*, 22a6).

131. Kongtrul writes: "The [channel called] 'that veers to the left' (*g.yon pa ma*) is at the nape of the neck. It produces the flesh of the back of the body." (*PCH*, 22a6–b1).

132. *'dul byed ma*. In the *Hevajra* and *Sampuṭa Tantras*, this channel is called *thung ngu ma*, meaning "short." Kongtrul writes: "The [channel called] 'round and short' is at the left ear. It produces tendons." (*PCH*, 22b1).

133. Kongtrul writes: "The [channel called] 'tortoise's generator' (*rus sbal skye ma*) resides at the point between the eyebrows, and produces bones."(*PCH*, 22b2).

134. *srid pa ma*. This channel seems to be the same as the one called "meditator" (*sgom pa ma*) in the *Hevajra Tantra*. Kongtrul writes: "The channel [is called] 'meditator' because it illuminates all phenomena of existence (*srid pa*), resides in the liver, and generates the two eyes." (*PCH*, 22b2).

135. Kongtrul writes: "The [channel is] called 'empowering' (*dbang skur ma*) because it cleanses all concepts, is connected to the base of the shoulders, and produces the heart and shoulders." (*PCH*, 22b2–3).

136. *sdang ma*. This channel, the first of the channels branching off from the throat chakra, seems to be same as that called *skyon bral ma* in the *Hevajra*

Tantra. Kongtrul writes: "The [channel called] 'faultless' (*skyon bral ma*), because it repudiates negative emotions, is connected to the two armpits and generates the flesh of the liver and the eyes." (*PCH*, 22b2–3).

137. *gshang ba ma.* This channel is the same as the one called "entering" (*'jug pa ma'*) in the *Hevajra Tantra*. Kongtrul writes: "The [channel] that causes the body to enter into the action of movement (*jug pa ma*) resides at the two breasts and produces the large intestine and bile." (*PCH*, 22b4).

138. *ma mo ma.* Kongtrul writes: "The [channel is called] 'mother deity' (*ma mo*) [because] it resembles a mother, resides in the lungs and is connected to the navel. It generates the lungs." (*PCH*, 22b4–5).

139. *mtshan mo ma.* Kongtrul writes: "The [channel called] 'night,' whose nature is the subsidence of appearances, extends from the intestine to the tip of the nose, and generates the abdomen." (*PCH*, 22b5).

140. *bsil sbyin ma.* Kongtrul writes: "The [channel called] 'soother' (*bsil sbyin ma*) reaches from the side of the mouth and resides at the jaw and ribs; it produces the entrails." (*PCH*, 22b6).

141. *'gro ba ma.* Spelling is doubtful. This channel seems to be the same as the one called "hot" (*tsha ba ma*) in the *Saṃpuṭa Tantra* (113a4). Kongtrul writes: "The [channel called] 'heating' (*tsha ba ster ba ma*) or 'warm' (*drod mo*) runs from the neck to the intestines, and produces the stomach and [long abdominal] creases. Lalanā that is never satiated with bliss is the basis for these channels." (*PCH*, 22b6–23a1).

142. This channel seems to be the same as the *gzhol ma* channel listed in the *Hevajra Tantra*. Kongtrul writes: "This [channel], which is descending (*gzhol ba*) to bliss from the heart, reaches the rectum and generates feces." (*PCH*, 23a4).

143. *mchu ma.* This channel seems to be the same as the one called "delighting" (*rangs par byed pa ma*). Kongtrul writes: "This [channel], which satisfies and delights with bliss, connects the anterior fontanel to the bladder. It generates the spinal fluid that fills the [spinal cord] in between the two." (*PCH*, 23a5).

144. *'thung gcod dang nye ba'i 'thung gcod.* In the *Saṃpuṭa* and in Kongtrul's *General Meaning of the Hevajra Tantra/Topical Commentary*, the first of these

places is called "enjoying drinking" (*'thung spyod*) and the second, "abstinence from drinking" (*'thung bcod*), (76a1–4).

145 *kun dha* (from the Sanskrit *kunda*), "jasmine flower": a metaphor for the white vital essence, which in its coarse form is the male semen.

146 *kun gzhi'i rnam shes*, Skt. *alayavijñana*. The "consciousness base of all" that, in the system of the Yogachara, proponent of the existence of eight consciousnesses, is considered to be the person itself and the repository of the traces of the person's actions.

147. *nyi ma*. The solar constituent stands for the red vital essence, which in its coarse form is the blood of the female.

148. *nyon mongs pa can gyi yid*. According to the Yogachara system, the emotional consciousness, focused on the consciousness base of all, grasps the existence of an "I."

149. *yid kyi rnam par shes pa*. One of the eight groups of consciousness asserted in the Yogachara system, the "mental consciousness" is a subjective consciousness that conceptually elaborates the information gathered by the sense consciousnesses.

150. Kongtrul writes: "The [channel called] 'three circles' (*sum skor ma*, Skt. *traivritta*) winds three times around the central and the cardinal petals of the heart and serves as the dominant condition for visual perception." *PCH*, 23b4.

151. *'dod pa ma*, Skt. *kamini*. Kongtrul writes: "The channel 'possessed of all desires' [serves as the dominant condition for] auditory perception." (*PCH*, 23b5).

152. Kongtrul writes: "The [channel] 'householder' (*khyim ma*, Skt. *geha*), which abides as the female householder of channels and winds, is known as [the dominant condition for] olfactory perception." (*PCH*, 23b5).

153. *sna'i 'dom sor*.

154. Kongtrul writes: "The [channel called] 'fierce' (*gtum mo*, Skt. *chandika*), which performs fierce action [serves as the dominant condition for] taste perception." (*PCH*, 23b6).

155. Kongtrul writes: "The [channel called] 'liberator from the demon' (*bdud bral ma*, Skt. *maradarika*), which frees one from the demon of death [serves as the dominant condition for] tactile perception. Another aspect of its function is to draw the white [vital essence] upward." (*PCH*, 23b6).

156. Here, the interlinear notes tell us:

> In these petal [-like] channels flows energy-wind mixed with nectar [that is, vital essence]; therefore, they are the [eight] guardians of the gates [of the mandala] (*sgo mtshams ma brgyad*) who have two forms [male and female]. They are also the eight bodhisattvas (*byang chub sems dpa' brgyad*): Maitreya, Kshitigarbha, Vajrapani, Khagarbha, Lokeshvara, Sarvanivarana Vishkambhin, Mañjuśrī, and Samantabhadra; the eight wrathful (*khro bo brgyad*) ones; and so on. (*YC*).

157. "The tips of these channels have the shape of the five syllables: DZAM at the eyes, DZIM at the ears, KSHIM at the nose, GHAM at the tongue, and KAM between the eyebrows. Their purity is the five bodhisattvas." (*YC*).

158. *mdog mdzes ma*. In the *Hevajra* and *Samputa* tantras, this channel is called "extremely beautiful" (*shin tu gzugs can ma*). Kongtrul writes: "The [channel called] 'beautiful,' which pertains to form (*bem pos bsdus pa*), is at the genitals and produces phlegm." (*PCH*, 23a6).

159. *thun mong ma*. This seems to be the same as the channel called "all-pervader" (*spyi khyab ma*) mentioned in the *Hevajra Tantra*. Kongtrul writes: "The [channel called] 'all-pervader' that is equal in all, resides at the anus, and produces mucus." (*PCH*, 23a6).

160. *rnag*. "The mucus always comes mixed with feces." (*YC*).

161. *rgyu ster ma*. In the *Hevajra* and *Samputa* tantras this channel is called "bestower of the cause" (*rgyu sbyin ma*). Kongtrul writes: "This [channel, called] 'bestower of all causes' (*rgyud thams cad sbyin par byed pa*), resides in the sides of the thighs and produces blood." (*PCH*, 23a6–b1).

162. *bral ba ma*. In the *Hevajra* and *Samputa* tantras, this channel is called "separator from acquisition" (*sbyor bral ma*). Kongtrul writes: "This [channel, called] 'separator from acquisition of suffering,' abides at the calves, and produces sweat." (*PCH*, 23b1).

163. "At the moment of fear comes sweat." (*YC*).

164. *mdza bo ma.* In the *Hevajra* and *Samputa* tantras, this channel is called "pleasant" (*sdu gu ma*). Kongtrul writes: "The [channel, called] 'pleasant' because it causes attachment, abides at the fingers and toes and produces fat." (*PCH,* 23b1–2).

165. "Whether the vital essence is present or not is evident from the nails." (*YC*).

166. *grub ma.* The *Hevajra* and *Samputa* tantras call this channel "extremely accomplished" (*shin tu grub ma*). Kongtrul writes: "The [channel called] 'accomplisher of powers' (*dngos grub grub par byed ma*) resides at the back or top of the foot, and produces tears." (*PCH,* 23b2).

167. "It produces suffering." (*YC*). "Existence" (*srid pa ma*) is one of the channels branching off from the head chakra mentioned above.

168. *me ma:* "The jewel channel (*rtsa nor bu*)." (*YC*). This channel in the *Hevajra* and *Samputa* tantras is called *tshed ba ma.* Kongtrul writes: "The [channel called] 'cooking' (*'tshed ma*) because it has the nature of fire, abides at the thumbs and big toes, and produces mucus and saliva." (*PCH,* 23b3).

169. "Below, this channel produces the hair of the big toes." (*YC*).

170. *yid 'ong ma.* This channel seems to be the same as the one called "good mind" (*yid bzang ma*) in the *Hevajra Tantra.* Kongtrul writes: "The [channel called] 'good mind,' and 'giver of bliss' has the nature of the water element and resides four fingers above the knees. It produces snivel." (*PCH,* 23b3).

171. In the Mahayana, the ten levels of realization (*sa,* Skt. *bhumi*) are named: joyful, stainless, luminous, flaming, realized, invincible, going far, unshakable, fine intelligence, and cloud of teachings.

    The *Samvarodaya Tantra,* Dg. K. *rgyud 'bum,* vol. Kha, 276a1–2 (Toh. 373), relates the ten levels to the sacred places, as follows: the "joyful" corresponds to the four main sacred places; the "stainless" corresponds to the four related sacred places; the "luminous," to the fields; the "flaming," to the related fields; the "realized," to the meeting places; the "invincible," to the related meeting places; the "going far," to the gathering places; the "unshakable," to the related gathering places; the "fine intelligence," to the charnel grounds; and the "cloud of teachings," to the related charnel grounds.

    Individual tantras and their commentaries contain different names and descriptions of the levels of realization. The number of levels range from ten to sixteen. The differentiation into twelve is found in the *Kālacakra*, the *Samputa*, the *Ocean of Ḍākinīs*, the *Guhyasamāja*, the *Ornament of the Vajra Essence,* and others. In this last tantra, for example, the first of the twelve, known as "aspirational conduct" (*mos spyod*), is a level at which the practitioner is still an ordinary being. The next ten levels correspond to the ten explained in Mahayana manner, from "joyful" to "cloud of teachings." The twelfth is the stage of Vajradhāra. In this case, the last two levels would be associated with the last two of the twelve places mentioned here: "abstinence from drinking," and "related abstinence from drinking." See Sertog Lozang Tsultrim's *Presentation of the Stages and the Paths of the Indestructible Way: The Jewel Staircase (gsang chen rdo rje theg pa'i sa dang lam gyi rnam par gzhag pa zung 'jug khang bzang du bgrod pa'i rin chen them skas). blo bzang dgongs rgyan mu tig phreng mdzas*, Book 21, 49–62. For a different interpretation of the twelve levels, see Lakshmi's *Elucidation of the Meaning of the Five Stages*, Dg. T., *rgyud 'grel*, vol. Chi, 188b4–189a3 (Toh. 1842).

172. The interlinear notes explain why the locations of channels are known by the names of various sacred places.

"The 'sacred places' (*gnas*, Skt. *pitha*) are so-called because in these areas, the vital essences dwell without increase or decrease.

"The 'related sacred places' (*nye ba'i gnas*, Skt. *upapitha*) are so-called because in these areas [the vital essences] are at times pure and at other times impure.

"The 'fields' (*zhing*, Skt. *kshetra*) are so-called because in these areas [the vital essence of] bodhicitta increases and spreads.

"The 'related fields' (*nye ba'i zhing*, Skt. *upakshetra*) are so-called because [the vital essence of] bodhicitta occasionally increases in these [areas].

"The 'meeting places' (Skt. *chandoha*) are so-called because the pure portion of the constituents [that is, the vital essence] is able to collect and flow in these [areas].

"The 'related meeting places' (Skt. *upachandoha*) are so-called because the pure portions of the constituents occasionally collect in these [areas].

"The 'gathering places' (*'du ba*, Skt. *melakapa*) are so-called because these are the areas where the red and white constituents gather.

"The 'related gathering places' (*nye ba'i 'du ba*, Skt. *upamelakapa*) are so-called because the red and white vital essences occasionally gather in these [areas].

"The 'charnel grounds' (*dur khrod*, Skt. *smasana*) are so-called because the flow of the constituents is halted in these [areas].

"The 'related charnel grounds' (*nye ba'i dur khrod*, Skt. *upasmasana*) are so-called because there, the flow of the constituents is at times halted and at other times not halted.

"The 'abstinence from drinking,' (*'thung gcod*) [areas] are so-called because] there, the pure portion of the constituent is differentiated [from the impure portion].

The 'related abstinence from drinking' (*nye ba'i 'thung gcod*) [areas] are so-called because] there, the pure portion of the constituent is sometimes differentiated [from the impure] and at other times, not differentiated." (*YC*).

The interlinear notes also state, "The head of the individual corresponds to the higher realms; the middle part, up to the arms, to the human realm; and the legs, to the lower realms." (*YC*).

173. This passage is not found in the Dg. K. edition of this tantra (Toh. 381).

174. "These [channels] are said to be present as two sets of the sixteen Sanskrit vowels, one [arranged] clockwise, and the other, counterclockwise." (*YC*).

175. "Like an open umbrella." (*YC*).

176. "This is the reason why there are many problems related to the channels." (*YC*).

177. *'phar rtsa*. Lit. "pulsating channels."

178. This refers to the two channels, lalanā and rasanā, at the neck.

179. "For this reason, binding these fingers and toes has the effect of withholding the vital essence." (*YC*).

180. "There is also the assertion that [these channels] are present as the sixteen Sanskrit vowels placed counterclockwise." (*YC*).

181. "This is the reason why, when shouting, one places the right hand in front of the ear; why, when one kneels or gets up, loud sounds are emitted; and why, when one eats coarse food, the senses close." (*YC*).

182. "[At the ears, the channels' tips] are like a coiled snake." (*YC*).

183. "This is the reason why the throat is narrow." (*YC*).

184. "This is the assertion of the *Two Examinations* [*of the Hevajra Tantra*]." (*YC*).

185. *dug lnga:* desire, anger, ignorance, pride, and envy.

186. Buddhas of the five families: Akṣobhya, Vairocana, Ratnasaṃbhava, Amitābha, and Amoghasiddhi, who are, respectively, the lords of the vajra, tathāgata, jewel, lotus, and action families. The five syllables just mentioned are also the seed-syllables of these five buddhas.

187. Dg. K. *rgyud 'bum,* vol. Ga, 112b6 (Toh. 381).

188. Dg. K. *rgyud 'bum,* vol. Ca, 223a6 (Toh. 445).

189. Dg. K. *rgyud 'bum,* vol. Ga, 104b7 (Toh. 381).

190. "[This channel] is a part of lalanā." (*YC*).

191. "The pure white vital essence the size of a subtle particle." (*YC*).

192. "In the medical treatises this is called 'physical radiance.'" (*YC*).

193. Dg. K. *rgyud 'bum,* vol. Ga, 112a8–9 (Toh. 381).

194. Dg. K. *rgyud 'bum,* vol. Ca, 220b7–221a1 (Toh. 445).

195. *spyod bsdus pa'i sgron ma.* Dg. T. *rgyud 'bum,* vol. Ngi, 86a3–4 (Toh. 1803).

196. "Light, spread of light, and culmination of light." (*YC*).

197. *ka ra na:* a yogic posture.

198. "The essential point of being in the state of instant presence by way of gazing is also related to this." (*YC*).

199. A, NU, TA, RA are the syllables visualized on four petals at the heart chakra, with OṂ or HŪṂ at the center, in most dream practices belonging to the completion phase of Anuttara tantra practice, in the context of dream yoga involving the recognition of the luminous clarity of sleep.

200. "Here one can make mistakes. If one meditates [on the syllables] on the outer channels [of the heart], the luminous clarity will not be recognized." (*YC*).

201. Dg. K. *rgyud 'bum*, vol. Ca, 96a6–97b2 (Toh. 442). Yangönpa's rendering of the last line, *rnal 'byor rig pas rtag tu bsgom*, differs slightly from the version found in the Dg. K., which reads: *rnal 'byor gyis ni rtag tu bsgom.*

202. In the completion phase of the Guhyasamāja practice, a sphere of substance, light, or mantra of five colors symbolizing the five wisdoms is visualized at the tip of the nose. Three such "nose tips" (*sna rtse, na sa gra*) are identified in the *Guhyasamāja Tantra*: one at the chakra of the secret place, one on the face, and one at the heart chakra within the central channel. See Wayman, *Yoga of the Guhyasamāja Tantra.*

203. Dg. K. *rgyud 'bum*, vol. Nga, 225a6–7 (Toh. 428).

204. *slob dpon nag po pa*, Skt. *krishna-acharya* or *kanhapa*. One of the eighty-four Buddhist mahasiddhas of ancient India, Krishna was the source of the three most important transmissions of the *Cakrasaṃvara* disseminated in Tibet. For his life, see Dowman, *Masters of Mahāmudrā,* 123–31.

205. Krishna deals with this topic in his *Vital Essence of Spring* (*dpyid kyi thig le*, Skt. *vasantatilaka*) Dg. T. *rgyud*, vol. Wa, 301a4–5 (Toh. 1448), and in the *Extensive Commentary on the Vital Essence of Spring* (*dpyid kyi thig le'i rgya cher 'grel pa*, Skt. *vasantatilakatika*) Dg. T. *rgyud*, vol. Tsu, 115a–120a (Toh. 3714).

206. *rdo rje dril bu pa*, Skt. *vajra ghanthapa:* another of the eighty-four Buddhist mahasiddhas of ancient India, and another source of one of the three most important systems of the *Cakrasaṃvara* disseminated in Tibet. For his life, see Dowman, *Masters of Mahāmudrā,* 267–75.

207. *thig le'i rnal 'byor.*

208. "The *Vajramāla* states:
'Sixty-four, eight, and four petals
'Face upward and downward
'And are present as if united.'" (*YC*).
Dg. K. *rgyud 'bum*, vol.Ca, 234a5–6 (Toh. 445).

209. "The red vital essence." (*YC*).

210. *rgod ma kha:* In ancient Indian cosmology, a name for the flaming mountains to the south of the outer ocean.

211. *rgod ma kha yi me'i gzugs//bdag med tig la ka zhes brjod.* The same passage in the Dg. K. edition of this tantra reads: *rgod ma'i me yi gzugs kyis ni//bdag med ma ni thig ler brjod.* Dg. K. *rgyud 'bum,* vol. Ga, 112a7 (Toh. 381).

212. "The crucial point of placing the two hands in the meditation gesture at two fingers below the navel, also relates to this." (*YC*).

213. *dus kyi me.* The raging fire that, at the end of the era of abiding, destroys a world system.

214. These lines are probably from the no longer extant larger root tantra of the *Kālacakra.*

215. "This means, 'separating the nutrients [in food] from the waste.'" (*YC*).

216. Dg. T. *rgyud,* vol. Wa, 301a3 (Toh. 1448).

217. *dus sbyor,* Skt. *lagna:* "The [solar] mansions [of the inner zodiac represented by these twelve channels] where the energy-winds move." (*YC*). In the external world, this refers to the duration of the arising of the twelve signs of the zodiac. Internally, it refers to the duration of the flow of the energy-winds in the twelve channels of the navel.

218. The solid organs (*don*) are the heart, liver, kidney, spleen, and lungs. The hollow organs (*snod*) are the stomach, intestine, colon, gall bladder, bladder, and seminal vesicles or ovaries.

219. *bha ga'i yig ge bcu bzhi.* Here, *bhāga,* as specified a few paragraphs below in the text, refers to the space in the secret place where there are channels whose knots have the shape of the syllables from which samsara and nirvana originate.

220. "This is the reason why the long crease forms." (*YC*).

221. The "base" (*rtsa ba*) should be understood as being located just above the sexual organ.

222. "Regarding the A taught in the *Path and Its Fruit:* the A of the outer form, the A of wisdom, the A of the essence, and the A of the syllable exist as the nature of all channels." (*YC*).

223. In our text, this syllable appears as *Sum.*

224. In our text, this syllable appears as *Dum.*

225. "The wandering in the six realms and the essential point of the closing of their doors should be understood [from the above]." (*YC*).

226. "First, they arise; second, they are purified; and third, they are destroyed." (*YC*).

227. Chen Ngawa writes:

    When mind enters the channels, meditative experiences related to the body arise; when it enters the seed-syllables, meditative experiences related to the voice arise; and when it reaches the vital essence within the seed-syllables, meditative experiences related to the mind arise. When the place left by the seed-syllables is filled with pure essence, the channels are purified. (*YC*).

228. "The OṂ [stands for] the form realm; the A, for the formless realm; and the HŪṂ, for the realm of desire." (*YC*).

229. *yum chen mo.* This refers to the condition of emptiness, the dharmadhatu from which all phenomena arise.

230. See note 208 in Part One.

231. *thab kyi dbyibs.* In some versions of our text, the word is *tha mig.*

232. *'bar ka.*

233. Although three openings are mentioned here, only two are listed. The third probably discharges feces.

234. The five elements (*byung ba lnga*) are earth, water, fire, air, and space. The five classes of beings (*'gro ba lnga*) are the gods, humans, animals, tormented spirits, and denizens of hell. The five emotions (*nyon mongs pa lnga*) are desire, anger, ignorance, pride, and envy.

235. This passage has not been located in the Derge Kangyur edition of this tantra (Toh. 381).

236. This may refer to the chakras at the crown of the head, the heart, and the navel.

237. "Eight" may refer to the eight inner channels of the navel chakra, "sixteen" may be the inner channels of the crown of the head chakra, and "four" may refer to the channels in the cardinal directions of the heart chakra.

238. "Sixty-four" are the channels of the navel; "thirty- two" are those at the crown of the head.

239. Tsami Sangye (*tsa mi sangs rgyas grags pa*), a twelfth- century Tangut translator and Sanskrit scholar, was the only person of the Tibetan region who ascended to the throne of abbot of Nalanda University in India.

240. *sbyor ba'i phreng ba*. bstan 'gyur, vol. 14, 253a3. TBRC W1GS66030.

241. Amended. For some reason, the text reads: "*gsum po 'dus dang phye ba yis drug dang lnga ni go rim bzhin zhes pas 'dus pa la 'khor lo drug 'ong la phye ba las lnga ru 'gro'o.*" (Regarding the three [channels and chakras, by sub-suming and dividing there are six and five [chakras], respectively. Thus, if summarized, the chakras are six; if divided, they become five)." Both the quotation and the text read: "if summarized, are six; if divided, are five."

242. *btsan:* lit. "chieftain." These are beings of a wrathful nature who, along with the Nyen (*gnyan*), dominate the space between earth and sky and can provoke serious illnesses such as cancer.

243. *rgyal po:* lit. "king." These are beings of a wrathful nature who can cause mental illness and epilepsy.

244. *ma mo:* lit. "mother." This is a class of wrathful female beings who can cause epidemics, famine, and war. They correspond to the *matraka* of the Indian tradition.

245. *the rang*. These beings, belonging to the Nyen (gnyan) class, dominate the space between earth and sky.

246. *klu*, Skt. *nāga:* serpent-like beings who dominate the waters and the world underground. They can cause infectious diseases and skin problems.

247. The words in square brackets are from *YC*.

248. "Thus, it is said to bind the ring fingers and the fourth toe of the feet." (*YC*).

249. "If one sleeps in a wrong position, [one can have the experience of] being pressed down." (*YC*). This temporary inability to move that occurs during sleep is accompanied by the impression of being held down by an invisible being.

250. "This is why, when one experiences fear, the backs of the knees become rigid." (*YC*).

251. *nags tshal ma:* one of the channels of the throat chakra, mentioned above.

252. *rlugs.* Some editions of Yangönpa's text have *lkugs pa,* "mutism."

253. *pho rtsa, mo rtsa, ma ning gi rtsa.* These channels reflect the characteristics of the veins and arteries of different people.

254. "[These channels produce] numerous qualities as well as numerous obstacles." (*YC*).

255. "[These channels produce] many qualities and few obstacles." (*YC*).

256. "[These channels produce] few obstacles and few qualities." (*YC*).

257. "Energy-winds depend on the channels, vital essences depend on energy-winds, and mind depends on vital essence. Each exists depending on the other as in a pole tent." (*YC*).

258. *kham sum cu so gnyis:* the thirty-two constituents that flow in the thirty-two channels branching off from the main chakras, producing teeth, nails, and so on.

259. "These [microorganisms (*srin bu*)] feed on the residues of the seven organic components, and on odors." (*YC*).

260. This passage is found, with slightly different wording, in Dg. K. *rgyud 'bum,* vol. Nga, 225a2–3 (Toh. 420).

261. "The four great elements are to be understood as the support of a life, or [the means] by which a life is revealed. Understand [this], Legge Wangmo (*legs dges dbang mo*)." (*YC*.) These words are drawn from the *Mahāmudrātilaka,* Dg. K. vol. Nga, 69b4 (Toh. 420).

262. Regarding this last line, some editions of our text have "*rnal 'byor pa yi gnas lta ba'o,*" while others have "*rnal 'byor pa yis gnas bta ba'o.*"

263. This passage has not been located in the Dg. K. (Toh. 445), but it exists in the *Nondual Victory Tantra (rnam rgyal gnyis med rgyud)* as found in the *Grand Dharma Treasury of the Glorious Drigung Kagyüd Tradition (dpal 'bri gung bka' brgyud kyi chos mdzod chen mo),* 111b2–3.

264. This passage has not been found in the Dg. K. edition of this text (Toh. 420).

265. *dgongs pa lung bstan pa zhes bya ba'i rgyud.* In the Dg. K. *rgyud 'bum,* vol. Ca, 168b5–6 (Toh. 444), this passage appears with a slightly different wording and line order.

266. "Energy-wind consciousness." (*YC*). In its specific usage in the father tantra, here bodhicitta denotes the energy-wind that is inseparable from consciousness.

267. "It is neither outside nor inside." (*YC*).

268. "[The five] elements." (*YC*).

269. "Root and branch [energy-winds] (*rtsa ba yan lag gi rlung*)." (*YC*).

270. "Exhalation, inhalation, and pause." (*YC*).

271. *rdo rje sgo zhes bya ba rgyud.* This scripture has not been identified.

272. The *Vajramāla* describes the corresponding energy-winds and buddhas in the following way: "The life [-holding wind] is Akṣobhya; the downward-clearing, at the pubis, is Ratnasaṃbhava; the upward-moving is Amitābha; the fire-accompanying is Amoghasiddhi; and the pervasive is Vairocana." (276b1–2).

273. The five bodhisattvas (*byang chub sems dpa' lnga*): possibly Vajrapani, Khagarbha, Kshitigarbha, Lokeshvara, and Sarvanivarana Vishkambhin.

274. Dg. K. *rgyud 'bum,* vol. Ca, 158b7–159a1 (Toh. 444). The last two lines of this passage as found in Yangönpa's text: "*de dag bdag gzugs bud med dang// slar yang sprul pa'i mdzad pa yin,*" differ from those found in the Derge Kangyur: "*'di dag tu ni nyid sku mdzad//bud med gzugs su slar sprul te.*"

275. "The five root energy-winds." (*YC*).

276. "The five branch energy-winds." (*YC*).

277. "[Enter] the dhuti [central channel]." (*YC*).

278. "The wisdom energy-wind." (*YC*).

279. "The male energy-wind." (*YC*).

280. "The female energy-wind."(*YC*).

281. "The neuter energy-wind." (*YC*).

282. "The five [branch] winds related related to these [root winds]." (*YC*).

283. Dg. K. *rgyud 'bum,* vol. Ca, 158b7–159a1 (Toh. 444).

284. This passage appears in the Dg. K. *rgyud 'bum,* vol. Ka, 44b1–3 (Toh. 362) with a slightly different wording.

285. *nor las rgyal:* another name for the victorious with the bow (*gzhu las rgyal*) wind.

286. This text has not been identified, but the quoted passage is found vol. 20, p. 41, of the *Sakya Lamdre.*

287. *sangs rgyas thams cad dang mnyam par sbyor ba mkha' 'gro ma sgyu ma bde ba'i mchog ces bya ba'i rgyud phyi ma.* Dg. K. *rgyud 'bum,* vol. Ka, 151b–193a (Toh. 366).

288. Dg. K. *rgyud 'bum,* vol. Ka, 186b5 (Toh. 366). In Aryadeva's *Lamp Summary of Tantric Practice (spyod pa'i bsdus pa'i sgron ma),* Dg. T. vol. Ngi, 68b2–3 (Toh. 1803), TBRC, W23703-1351-115-214, the ten names appear as follows:

    Kotakhya, kotabha, kota, kotabasha, kotiraga,
    kolakhya, kolabha, kola, kolabasha, kolatatha.

289. "These are the five root energy-winds." (*YC*).

290. "These are the five branch energy-winds." (*YC*).

291. The distinction between male, female, and neuter energy-winds is made with regard to the characteristics of the individual's breathing, which probably reflects the condition of the internal energy-wind.

292. These are the thirty-two channels that branch off from the navel chakra, described above.

293. "This is why one does not bind the lower wind at first. Instead, one balances them by warming the upper wind that is of a cold nature; then one mixes them." (*YC*). This may refer to the practice of vase-like breathing (*bum pa can,* Skt. *kumbhaka*).

294. This passage has not been found in the *Saṃpuṭa Tantra* contained in the Dg. K. (Toh. 381).

295. "[This is related] to the essential point of inhaling the air from above." (*YC*).

296. "Inhalation, exhalation, and pause are brought under one's power." (*YC*).

297. *thun bcu gnyis:* twelve periods of two hours each.

298. The Beijing edition of Yangönpa's text has *'pho ba phyed dang nyi shu rtsa bzhi* (23.5 transits).

299. *chu tshod,* Skt. *ghaṭikā.* In the Kālacakra system, six breaths including inhalation, exhalation, and pause, amount to one *panipala,* or *lipta;* 360 breaths amount to sixty *panipala,* equivalent to one ghaṭikā (*chu tshod*) (twenty-four minutes), or daṇḍa (*dbyu gu*); 7,776,000 breaths amount to 360 solar days, or one year; and 77,760,000 breaths make up a human life span of one hundred years. See also Vesna A. Wallace, *The Inner Kālacakratantra: A Buddhist Tantric View of the Individual* (New York: Oxford University Press, 2001), n. 108.

300. *dbyu gu.* Some editions of our text have "64 daṇḍa." The daṇḍa and ghaṭikā measures are usually considered equivalent in the *Kālacakra Tantra,* but in other tantras the daṇḍa is a smaller unit than the ghaṭikā. It is unclear why here, when referring to the *Kālacakra,* Yangönpa gives different measures for the two.

301. "It flows equally through the solar and lunar [channels]." (*YC*).

302. "At birth, at death, at the shifting of the houses [that is, the channels of the navel chakra] from right to left, from left to right, and during sexual intercourse." (*YC*).

303. Dg. K. *rgyud 'bum,* vol. Ca, 171a3 (Toh. 444).

304. The winds of the four goddesses—Pāṇḍaravāsinī, Tārā, Locanā, and Māmakī—are the winds of fire, air, earth, and water. See Wayman, *Yoga of the Guhyasamāja,* 219–20.

305. "The *Lamp Summary of Tantric Practice* states: 'The "pervasive" is the wind that flows in all the four [mandalas of the elements]. This pervading light, which does not exit [from the body], is the tathāgata Vairocana, the very essence, equal to space.'" (*YC*).

306. "It flows within the body 21,600 times in the mode of the [winds] of the five elements." (*YC*).

307. This passage is not found in the *Vajramāla* contained in the Dg. K. (Toh. 445). But a similar, though not identical, passage is found in Tāranātha's *rim lnga'i 'grel chen rdo rje 'chang chen po'i dgongs pa* (TBRC, W1PD45495:010:0001): "*lus kun la ni gnas pa'i rlung/bya ba kun la 'jug pa po/'di ni rnam snang ngo bo ste/'chi ba'i lus las 'byung bar 'gyur*," and in other works as well.

308. "[The support is] the body; [the supported] is the mind." (*YC*).

309. "It is said: 'This pervasive [wind] is of the essence of Vairocana, and at death it will leave [the body].'" (*YC*).

310. On the mundane paths, see note 65 in Part One.

311. The "half-moon" may refer to the lunar constituent, which, in the heart region within the central channel, is joined with the red constituent as the two halves of a sphere.

312. In the tantras mentioned, these measurements match the numbers of channels of the four main chakras: eight channels of the heart chakra, sixteen channels of the throat chakra, thirty-two channels of the crown of the head chakra, and sixty-four channels of the navel chakra.

313. In Dg. K. *rgyud 'bum*, vol. Ga, 111a5–6 (Toh. 381), this passage appears as follows: "*me nyid gang dang rlung dang ni/dbang chen dang ni de bzhin chu/l'khor lor sems kyi kun spyod pa/lsteng dang ngos dang brang 'og 'gro.*" In Yangönpa's text it reads: "*me dang de bzhin nyid gan rlung dang ni/dbang chen dang ni de bzhin chu/l'khor lo sems kyi 'tsho ba ste/lsteng 'og dang logs dang thad ka'o.*"

314. "In the upper part [of the nostrils] flows the wind of fire; in the lower part, that of water; on the [nostrils'] walls, that of air; and straight [through the center of the nostrils], that of earth." (*YC*).

315. *rtsom pa, longs spyod, thims pa.* These three phases represent the moments in which the energy-wind begins its function, performs its function, and ceases its function. These phases, as indicated by interlinear notes, are associated with the three phases of breathing: inhalation, pause, and exhalation, respectively.

316. *mi phyed ma.* One of the eight channels that branch off from the great bliss chakra at the crown of the head, described above.

317. "Exhalation." (*YC*).

318. *phra gzugs ma*. One of the eight channels that branch off from the great bliss chakra at the crown of the head, described above.

319. "Pause." (*YC*).

320. *bzang mo ma*. One of the eight channels that branch off from the great bliss chakra at the crown of the head, described above.

321. "Inhalation." (*YC*).

322. *g.yon ma*. One of the eight channels that branch off from the great bliss chakra at the crown of the head, described above.

323. *yid 'ong ma*. The last of the eight channels branching off from the navel chakra, described above.

324. *rim pa bzhi pa*. This probably refers to Krishna-Acharya's (Kanhapa's) *Analysis of the Four Stages (rim pa bzhi'i rnam par 'byed pa, kramachatustayavibhanga)* Dg. T. *rgyud*, vol. Wa, 338b–367a (Toh. 1452).

325. *ngag gi dbang phyug*. One of the six scholar-gatekeepers of Vikramashila monastery, the Indian master Vagishvarakirti was the teacher of Drogmi Lotsawa, founder of the Sakya school of Tibetan Buddhism.

326. *gling bzhi*. In ancient Indo-Tibetan cosmology, the world comprises four continents centered around Mount Meru, the axis mundi.

327. The navel chakra is composed of a total of sixty-four channels. Four root channels branch off from the central channel. Each of these splits into three, forming twelve channels. These twelve form the pathways for the energy-winds of the twelve time junctures (*dus sbyor*, Skt. *lagna*) or major transits (*'pho chen*). One major transit equals 1,800 breaths, 120 minutes, or one-twelfth of a solar day. Each of these twelve channels splits into five, forming sixty branches. These, plus the four root channels, constitute the sixty-four channels of the navel. The sixty branches form the pathways for the winds of the minor transits (*'pho chung*). One minor transit equals 360 breaths, twenty-four minutes, or one-sixtieth of a solar day. See Kongtrul's *Commentary on [Rangjung Dorje's] Profound Inner Reality (rnal 'byor bla na med pa'i rgyud sde rgya mtsho'i snying po bsdus pa zab mo nang gi don nyung ngu'i tshig gis rnam par 'grol ba zab don snang byed)*, 56a5–b5.

328. In Tibetan astrology, each year is associated with one of twelve animals.

329. The six periods include three of the day and three of the night.

330. The ancient system used in India and Tibet distinguishes six seasons, including the four usual seasons and then dividing winter and summer into two parts, thus totaling six.

331. "Thus, one should learn the great calculation of the energy-winds." (*YC*).

332. This passage is found, with slightly different wording, in Dg. K. *rgyud 'bum*, vol. Ga, 75a1–2 (Toh. 381).

333. "The pervasive wind." (*YC*).

334. "The upward-moving wind." (*YC*).

335. "The fire-accompanying wind." (*YC*).

336. "The downward-clearing wind." (*YC*).

337. "[On] the life-sustaining wind." (*YC*).

338. "The life-sustaining wind." (*YC*).

339. "The central [channel]." (*YC*).

340. This passage seems to emphasize the primary role that the life-sustaining wind has in yoga practice. The practices implied would include the so-called Tsalung (*rtsa rlung*) exercises, most of which are based on vase-like breathing (*bum pa can*, Skt. *kumbhaka*), yogic exercises, postures (*'phrul 'khor*, Skt. *yantra*), and others.

341. "These should be known from oral explanations." (*YC*).

342. *snying po nas:* lit. "from within the heart."

343. Dg. K. *rgyud 'bum*, vol.Ca, 154b2 (Toh. 443).

344. *brtan*, amended to *brtag* as in the Dg. K.

345. "The *vasanta* [channel] at the heart." (*YC*).

346. "The energy-wind at the door of the nose performs the functions of inhalation and exhalation." (*YC*).

347. This passage has not been located in the Dg. K. edition of the *Vajramāla* (Toh. 445).

348. "The five elements, the five solid organs such as the heart, and all fivefold [phenomena]." (*YC*).

349. "[The dream energy-wind] refers to the life-sustaining wind." (*YC*).

350. Although this passage is not found in the Dg. K. edition of the *Mahāmudrā-tilaka*, it is found, with slightly different wording, in the *Vajramāla*, Dg. K. *rgyud 'bum*, vol. Ca, 276b 2–3 (Toh. 445).

351. Dg. K. *rgyud 'bum*, Dg. T. *rgyud*, vol. Ngi, 49a5–6 (Toh. 1802).

352. Dg. K. *rgyud 'bum*, vol. Ca, 168b6–169a1 (Toh. 444). After the words *brten pa yin*, meaning "is dependent," the following lines of the original tantra for some reason have been omitted by Yangönpa: "*zhi ba dang ni rgyas pa dang//dbang dang de bzhin mngon spyod rnams//de nyid gsum gnas la rten nas//de kun byang chub sems kyis byed.*"

353. Regarding the integration as one of the outer and inner winds, in his *zhal dams* (5/1–5) Chen Ngawa writes:

> This integration as one (*rlung phyi nang bsre ba*) of the external and internal energy-winds is extremely profound. In this regard, the general place of [the energy-wind] is the lungs, the door [of the energy-wind] is the two nostrils, the essence of energy-wind is vitality and exertion, and the action of the energy-wind is to create all faults and qualities of samsara and nirvana. Applying the essential points through energy-winds and bliss, one passes beyond misery, and all good qualities are produced. In this context, if, having integrated mind and energy-wind as one, one practices the blazing and trickling that is the essential point through which all qualities are developed at the extremity of the central channel, all other energy-winds are inserted in the central channel, and the energy-winds do not flow outside: this is asserted to be a state of nonconceptual, crystal-clear luminosity. In this context, the energy-wind and mind flowing outside or remaining inside are considered to be equally positive. For when the energy-wind and mind flow outside, in a state of clear space of the inseparability of wind and mind, the visions of the eight consciousnesses are purified in the unsupported state. When wind and mind remain inside, their movement is purified, and one remains in a state of inseparable bliss-emptiness beyond [the grasping to] subject

and object. In this way, the energy-winds are integrated without and within. When energy-wind and mind are inserted in the ultimate central channel, they become pure like space, and one is free from internal and external subject and object [grasping], and they become one; this is the integration of external and internal energy-winds and mind.

354. "In the embryonic phase called 'watery' (*mer mer po*), OM is formed; in the phase called lump (*ltar ltar po*), A is formed; and in the phase called 'hard and oval' (*gor gor po*), the syllable HŪM is formed. At birth, one is born reciting these three syllables." (*YC*).

355. *rdo rje'i bzlas pa.* See note 135 in Part Two.

356. *a thung.* The short A represents the solar energy and refers to the final single stroke of the Tibetan letter A (ཨ). In the inner heat (*gtum mo*) practices, it is visualized upside down, as a slender triangle, four fingers below the navel. At this time of day, the red vital essence is said to be at the chakra of the secret place.

357. Dg. K. *rgyud 'bum,* vol. Ka, 3a3 (Toh. 360).

358. With regard to A, this "sacred syllable of the great meaning" (*don chen yig ge dam pa yin*), Garab Dorje's *Commentary to the Mañjuśrīnāmasaṅgīti* states:

> "A is the supreme of all syllables," means that, just as the syllable A is the essence of all syllables, pure awareness is superior to the five wisdoms and the [five] elements. "It is the sublime syllable of total reality," means that, unlike the syllable A or the words and names that depend on it, pure awareness is the meaning of the inseparable, self-originated dimension of reality that is naturally pure. For example, the syllable A comes from within, and is like the abode of other syllables; thus, it is a self-originated sound. Being self-originated, it is unborn. Dg. T. *rgyud,* vol. Tshi, 42b2–4 (Toh. 2093).

Commenting on the same lines of the *Mañjuśrīnāmasaṅgīti* (Dg. K. *rgyud 'bum,* vol. Kha, 3a2–3, Toh. 360), Vimalamitra writes:

> A is the supreme of all syllables. Why is it supreme? Since it is the syllable that reveals the total reality of phenomena, "it is the sublime syllable of total reality." Why is that? Since it reveals the meaning of

the unborn, which is the total reality, "it comes from within and is unborn." All other syllables depend on the teeth, tongue, lips, upper palate, and so on, but the syllable A does not depend on them. It arises naturally from within, and is therefore the supreme of all syllables. (Dg. T. *rgyud,* vol. Tshi, 10a6–b1; Toh. 2092).

359. *rgyal ba'i yum:* the *Prajñāpāramitā Sutra.*

360. That is, the vowels and consonants of the Sanskrit alphabet.

361. "This is the reason why, in a particular country, its particular language is understood." (*YC*).

362. "This is why each country has its own particular language." (*YC*).

363. "[Your] language changes." (*YC*).

364. Dg. K. *rgyud 'bum,* vol. Ca, 167a5 (Toh. 444).

365. *dbyangs:* lit. "melody" or "vowel." However, here Yangönpa seems to be using this word to indicate the sound of the voice, or resonation.

366. *mi'am ci'i rgyal pos zhus pa'i mdo.* This may be a reference to the *mi'am ci'i rgyal po sdong pos zhus pa'i mdo* (Toh. 157), but the passage quoted is not found in this sutra.

367. *gsung yan lag drug cu.* Sixty qualities are ascribed to the Buddha's voice. According to the tantras, it is like the voice of Brahmā, like cymbals, like a song, like the singing of the Kalapinga bird, like thunder, and like the music of a sitar. Each of these aspects is multiplied by the following ten for a total of sixty: it generates understanding, is comprehensible, worthy of respect, without discord, extremely profound, acceptable, indomitable, pleasing to hear, unconfused, and exceedingly distinct.

368. This passage has not been located in the *Vajramāla* contained in Dg. K. (Toh. 445), but is found in the *Nondual Victory Tantra (rnam rgyal gnyis med rgyud)* as contained in the *Grand Dharma Treasury of the Glorious Drigung Kagyüd Tradition,* 111b4–5. However, the *Nondual Victory Tantra* has *snang ba gsum* (the three lights) instead of *ting nge 'dzin* (contemplation).

369. *khams dgu:* the pure essences of the four elements (*'byung ba bzhi*) and of the five nectars (*bdud rtsi lnga*), explained below.

370. *khams bcu drug.* This may refer to the sixteen parts of the vital essence descending from the chakra of great bliss during sexual intercourse and at other occasions in tantric practice.

371. *khams sum cu rtsa bdun.* These are included in the thirty-two bodily constituents that originate from the vital essence present in the channels branching off from the four main chakras.

372. The tantras contain various listings of the five nectars (*bdud rtsi lnga*). One common list gives the five as follows: feces (*dri chen,* Skt. *purisha*), urine (*gla rsti,* Skt. *kasturika*), menstrual blood (*khrag,* Skt. *sihlaka*), semen (*ga bur,* Skt. *karpura*), and brain (*klad pa*). Occasionally, in place of brain, there is human flesh (*sha chen,* Skt. *mahamamsa*). The "great pure essence" (*mdangs chen*) that Yangönpa lists here as one of the five nectars probably refers to the brain.

The *Mahāmudrātilaka* (74b6) states that menstrual blood is Ratnasaṃbhava; semen is Amitābha; human flesh, Amoghasiddhi; urine, Akṣobhya; and feces, Vairocana.

373. Dg. K. *rgyud 'bum,* vol. Ga, 110b4–5 (Toh. 381).

374. *bad kan.* "Phlegm" in this passage stands out as an odd term. It probably refers to the "great pure essence" (*mdangs chen*) in Yangönpa's list of the five nectars in the preceding paragraph.

375. As we have seen, here the five nectars are equated with the pure essence of the chakras, which, along with the channels branching off from them, are responsible for the production of the different aspects of body and mind.

376. *khams sum cu so gnyis.* The thirty-two bodily constituents are those mentioned in the explanation of the thirty-two channels that branch off from the four main chakras: teeth, nails, and so on.

377. "When the wastes are balanced, they also contribute to the development of the organic components [of the body]. If they are destroyed by the decomposing phlegm, they cause illness." (*YC*).

378. In the interlinear notes, we have:

> With the addition of wind. Phlegm (*bad kan*) has five aspects: the supporting phlegm that is located at the heart, the decomposing

phlegm located in the stomach, tasting phlegm located in the tongue, acting phlegm located in the head, and connecting phlegm located in the joints. (*YC*).

In traditional Tibetan medicine, the acting phlegm is known as satisfying (*tshim byed*).

379. Bile (*mkhris pa*) has five aspects: digestive bile, bile that clarifies the complexion, bile of endeavor, bile that acts on the sight, and bile that lightens the complexion." (*YC*). The bile humor is found mainly in the digestive tract, liver, gall bladder, and blood. The digestive bile is found mainly in the areas between the stomach, where the food has not yet been assimilated, and the large intestine, where the food has already been assimilated. Color-transforming bile is found mainly in the liver. Bile of endeavor is found mainly in the heart. Bile that acts on the sight is found mainly in the eyes. Bile that lightens the complexion is found mainly in the skin.

380. *khrag gnas skam po.*

381. "If [lymph is] excessive or is lacking at the joints, illness will occur." (*YC*).

382. On the seven organic components; see note 58 above.

383. Here, "phlegm" seems to refer to one of the stages of extraction of the nutrients from food during the digestive process.

384. In Tibetan medicine, this is the pure essence of food (*dwangs ma*) that is ready to turn into blood.

385. *thig le.* Some editions of our text instead have *khu ba* (Skt. *shukra*), which usually refers to semen. However, here *thig le* or *khu ba* stands for the potency from which the source of the generative fluids for both genders is produced. In Tibetan medicine, this potency has both a subtle and a coarse manifestation. The subtle aspect spreads from the heart to all regions of the body, infusing it with strength and radiance. In men, the coarse aspect becomes semen, and in women, menstrual blood that was believed to contain the element of fertility.

386. *dwangs chen.* The "great essence" mentioned here must be the same as the "great pure essence" (*mdangs chen*) in the list of five nectars given above, referring to the brain.

387. This manner of listing these factors, with one characterized as lesser than another, may refer to the process of bodily regeneration that starts with the intake of food and ends with the formation of the vital essence, the final product. In this chain, the great essence—that is, brain, belonging to the category of marrow—is the organic component just before the vital essence. And before that comes blood, which is the basis for the nourishment contained in the organic components. Urine and feces, which are residues, come at the end of the scale.

388. "These syllables generate all [the syllables that are] the vital essence present within the central channel in the form of syllables. The syllables at the knots of the channels outside [the central channel] are generated in the womb [during gestation]." (*YC*).

389. *dus bzhi*. See above section on the reasons for the names of the chakras.

390. *kundha:* the vital essence that is the basis of the body's vitality and of the white and red constituents.

391. The white constituent that resides in the chakra of the head in the form of the syllable HAM.

392. "The wind of fire having moved upward and the vital essence downward, the constituents become weak; thus, fever arises." (*YC*).

393. "Turns the fire wind downward, and reverses the vital essence upward." (YC).

394. This refers to the path of skillful means that employs sexual relations with a qualified tantric consort, here called the "messenger" (*pho nya*).

395. See note 356 above.

396. "This is why the ascetics of the past, knowing this, prevented themselves from sleeping [at midday]." (*YC*).

397. "Most quarrels occur at midday." (*YC*).

398. *dpa' bo; mkha' 'gro*. This refers to the tantric practitioners who gather at the sacred places.

399. This passage has not been found in the Dg. K. edition of this text (Toh. 381).

400. "[That is,] because the energy-wind of fire blazes upward." (*YC*).

401. "[This means that] the [white] constituent develops." (*YC*).

402. "[This means that] the vital essence inside the channels is purified." (*YC*).

403. "This [is true] for men. For women, [it occurs] during the waning moon." (*YC*).

404. "In those places, the vital essence gradually develops more and more. [Externally,] the moon also becomes fuller and goes farther and farther away from the sun." (*YC*).

405. This is true for men. For women, it is the opposite.

406. "When the red vital essence has reached [the crown of the head], the lunar [essence] is present only as a seed." (*YC*).

407. The *Kālacakra Tantra*.

408. *ri bong can:* a poetic synonym for the moon, since Tibetans traditionally see a rabbit in the shadow appearing in the full moon. Here, it refers to the white vital essence of the head chakra.

409. This sentence may refer to the practice of inner heat in which the white vital essence is melted by the energy-winds, thus giving rise to the experience of the four joys as the vital essences descend from the head to the other chakras.

410. The waning phase of the moon.

411. "If the neck is blocked, [the vital essence is] increased." (*YC*).

412. Our text has this verse as: "*sa yi dkyil 'khor bzhi* [amended to *gzhi*] *yi khyon//rkang pa ya gcig mthil kyis mnon//rkang mthil sen mo'i khyon gyis kyang//mtshang pa'i yu las rtse nas gnon.*" In the Dg. K. the words read as follows: "*rkang pa gcig gis mthil gnon pa//sa yi snying po'i mthil la gnas//tshangs pa'i sgo nga'i rtse mo gnan//rkang mtheb sen mo la gnas pa.*" (*rgyud 'bum,* vol. Ka, 6b7–7a1; Toh. 360).

413. "[This refers to] the waning moon." (*YC*).

414. "[This refers to] the waxing moon." (*YC*). Here, "the mandala of the earth" seems to refer to the feet, where, at the new moon, the vital essence is found.

The "tip of Brahmā's shaft," probably refers to the tip of the central channel where the vital essence dwells during the full moon.

415. "That is, [the solar and lunar essence] enter the opening of the central channel." (*YC*).

416. "Because of this essential point, in the external environment, the sun is one league larger [than the moon]." (*YC*). *dpag tshad*, Skt. *joyana*, translated here as "league," is an Indian measure of distance equal to sixteen thousand cubits or about 4.5 miles.

417. "This is why each year the sun moves northwest, and each month the moon moves northwest." (*YC*).

418. *bsnyen gnas*. See note 53 in Part Two. Here, the precept directly related to the above discussion is to refrain from engaging in sex, as this would lead to the loss of vital essence.

419. "Since [the vital essence] holds two places [possibly, those of the red and of the white vital essence]." (*YC*).

420. *dwags po bka' brgyud*: the Tagpo Kagyüd lineage as transmitted through Gampopa.

421. *myur ba dang yul myur ba 'jug pa*: moves swiftly and quickly enters the areas [of the body], amended to *myur ba dang yul nyung bar 'jug pa* (as translated).

422. "[This means that] by controlling the [white] vital essence, wealth is gathered." (*YC*).

423. This passage has not been found in the *Saṃpuṭa* in Dg. K. (Toh. 381).

424. Water represents the lunar vital essence that has a cold nature.

425. Fire represents the solar vital essence that has a hot nature.

426. This passage appears in a slightly different wording in the Dg. K. *rgyud 'bum*, vol. Ga, 114a2 (Toh. 381).

427. "The nectars of the day and night" refers to the red and white vital essences. "The fire brings joy" stresses Yangönpa's point, above, that the increasing phase of both the lunar and solar essences depends on the power of the fire-accompanying wind located below the navel. "[The 'names' refers to the phases of] increase and decrease of the vital essence." (*YC*).

428. "[At the time of realization,] the five nectars [become] the forms of the tathāgatas, and so on." (*YC*).

429. *kun rdzob byang chub sems; don dam pa'i byang chub sems.* Here, these two terms are used in the Mahayana sense. Relative bodhicitta is the wish to attain enlightenment for the benefit of others. Ultimate bodhicitta is the realization of emptiness, permeated by the essence of compassion, which is attained by a bodhisattva on the path of seeing. The former serves as a cause or support for the latter.

430. Dg. K. *rgyud 'bum,* vol. Nga, 15b3–4 (Toh. 418).

431. Dg. K. *rgyud 'bum,* vol. Nga, 11b7–12a1 (Toh. 417).

432. Dg. K. *rgyud 'bum,* vol. Nga, 15b4–5 (Toh. 418).

433. The bhāga, or vagina of the vajra queen, refers to emptiness, the real nature of body, mind, and of all phenomena.

434. Dg. K. *rgyud 'bum,* vol. Nga, 20b3 (Toh. 418).

435. This refers to the vital essence, particularly the white vital essence, as semen.

436. *snang ba rdo rje 'char ba'i rgyud.* Not identified.

437. The five classes of beings (*'gro ba lnga*) are the gods (*lha*), humans (*mi*), animals (*dud 'gro*), tormented spirits (*yid dwags*), and denizens of hell (*myal ba*). Here, the demigods (*la ma yin*) are included among the gods.

438. *tin nge 'dzin lnga.* These five contemplations may be: the contemplation of consciousness (*shes pa'i ting nge 'dzin*), the contemplation of peace (*zhi ba'i ting nge 'dzin*), the contemplation that touches the extreme joy of body and mind (*lus dang sems rab tu dga' ba la reg pa'i ting nge 'dzin*), the contemplation of the absence of joy (*dga' ba med pa'i ting nge 'dzin*), and the contemplation that leads to bravery (*dpa' bar 'gro ba'i ting nge 'dzin*) taught in the bodhisattva path. However, the sutras and tantras contain various listings of the five contemplations.

439. *yon tan brgya phrag bcu gnyis:* the qualities attained by bodhisattvas on the first level of realization. In an instant they can see one hundred buddhas; receive one hundred blessing from them; live for one hundred eons; see the past and future for one hundred eons; enter and arise from one hundred contemplations; shake up one hundred world systems; illuminate one hundred

world systems with their radiance; ripen one hundred sentient beings; travel to one hundred pure lands; open one hundred spiritual gateways through teaching; emanate in one hundred bodies; and have each body surrounded by one hundred bodhisattvas.

440. Although the passage quoted here is not found in this tantra as contained in Dg. K. (Toh. 441)—as has been pointed out by Willa Blythe Miller in her exhaustive study, *Secrets of the Vajra Body: Dngos po'i gnas lugs and the Apotheosis of the Body in the work of Rgyal ba Yang dgon pa* (doctoral dissertation, Cambridge, MA: Harvard University, 2013), 61, n. 733—it does appear in Aryadeva's *spyod pa bsdus pa'i sgron ma* as found in the *bstan 'gyur dpe bsdur ma*, where it is also attributed to the *Equal to the Sky Tantra;* and in Padma Karpo's *'byung ba ro snyoms kyi rnam bshad ku mu ta, The Collected Works (gsung 'bum) of Kun khyen Padma dkar po,* 110/6–111/2.

441. "In regard to this, some people think it is incorrect to count the five wisdoms as part of the mind of ordinary beings, because even though [the ordinary mind] is asserted to be wisdom, it is [actually] consciousnesses. If one understands them as [being] of one flavor, then that fault does not exist, as is clear from passages of the *Catuḥpīṭha* and other [tantras], and from the characteristics of wisdom explained below." (*YC*).

442. These words are found in *mkhas grub mnyam med dpal na ro pa'i rnam par thar pa dri med legs bshad bde chen 'brug sgra* of *lha'i btsun pa rin chen rnam rgyal.* See Günther, *Life and Teaching of Nāropā.*

443. *kun gzhi rgyu'i rgyud. kun gzhi* (*alaya*) or "base of all" is a term that Tantra has borrowed from the Cittamātra philosophy in which, in association with consciousness (*kun gzhi rnam shes*), it indicates the consciousness that is the repository of karmic imprints. In Tantra, *kun gzhi* came to be used alone to refer to the very reality that is the source of everything, equivalent to the mind essence.

The term *rgyu'i rgyud* or "causal continuum" is a tantric term used in threefold scheme in which all the content of the Highest (Anuttara) Tantras is included: causal continuum, method continuum, and resultant continuum. These correspond to the base, path, and fruit. For an exhaustive explanation, see Kongtrul's *Systems of Buddhist Tantra,* 14–15, 295–96.

444. Here, Bhagavān is a general name for the figures that appear as teachers in the various Anuttara tantras.

445. This citation has not been found in the Dg. K. version of this text (Toh. 443).

446. "The [central channel is the] primordially present organ (*gnyug ma'i dbang po*)." (*YC*).

447. Dg. K. *rgyud 'bum*, vol. Ca, 149b3–4 (Toh. 443).

448. "The base of purification, the agent of purification, the phase of creation and the phase of completion, and their union." (*YC*).

449. Some editions of Yangönpa's text have the additional sentence "*las kyi rlung 'du 'phros ni shes rab*": "The activity of the karmic wind is knowledge."

450. *mer mer po*. See notes 65 and 354 above.

451. *nur nur po*. See note 65 above.

452. On how the five manifest awakenings are applied in the context of the phase of creation of various tantras, see Kongtrul's *Elements of Tantric Practice*, 149–52.

453. *skye gnas bzhi:* birth from womb, egg, moisture, and miraculous birth.

454. *dur khrod.* The celestial palace, residence of the deity, is encircled by eight cemeteries. See Kongtrul, *Elements of Tantric Practice*, 92–93.

455. *srung 'khor.* The circle of protection usually consists of the visualization of an impenetrable tent made of vajras. See Kongtrul, *Elements of Tantric Practice*, 90–91.

456. Dg. K. *rgyud 'bum*, vol. Nga, 16a1 (Toh. 418).

457. *rdo rje'i bzlas pa*. See note 135 in Part Two.

458. *snang ba gsum:* the white, red, and black lights from which the eighty innate thoughts or natural concepts (*rang bzhin brgyad cu'i rtog pa*) originate. For an exhaustive discussion of the three lights, see Kongtrul, *Systems of Buddhist Tantra*, 35–36, 251–60.

459. *rims pa lnga*. These five stages comprise key elements applied in all the Anuttara tantra praxis. As a presentation style, and as a way of delimiting

the progressive steps of the completion phases, they are specific to the Arya tradition of the *Guhyasamāja Tantra*. They comprise the practices called vajra recitation (*rdo rjei bzlas pa*), focusing on the mind (*sems la dmigs pa*), illusory body (*sgyu lus*), luminous clarity (*od gsal*), and union (*zung jug*). The first two are also called voice isolation (*ngag dben*) and mind isolation (*sems dben*), respectively. See Kongtrul, *Elements of Tantric Practice*, 138–45.

460. *phyag rgya bzhi.* The "four symbols" originally stem from the Yoga tantra tradition, where they are inclusive of all aspects of that tantric system's practice. In the Anuttara tantras, these four have rather different meanings, and belong mainly to the completion phase. But they can also be related to the phase of creation as well as to the resultant phase. The four are defined in different ways in the various Anuttara tantras. See Kongtrul, *Systems of Buddhist Tantra*, 245–47.

461. *byin sreg*, Skt. *homa.* A rite associated with the four activities called appeasing, increasing, dominating, and wrathful. A mandala base is prepared on the ground in a shape that accords with the chosen action. The wood for the fire is arranged on this base. And after the officiant has visualized the fire deity, the fire is lit and several substances are offered, including melted butter poured on the fire with two long spoon-like instruments. This rite is also customarily performed at the end of a tantric retreat, to effect the attainment of powers.

462. *gzhung rdo rje'i tshig rkang.* TBRC, W23891, 1b3–2a1.

463. The body is the "tantra of method" because, when the auspicious coincidence is formed in the body, the root tantra of samsara and nirvana—the base of all—is understood and perfectly realized. To apply the path, one must first be initiated, and the words "seats, and so on," refer to all four mandalas of initiation, including the one made of colored sand, and so on. The seats are three: those of the of buddhas and bodhisattvas, of the consort and goddesses (such as Vajrarupini), and of the wrathful deities. This refers to the arrangement of the deities in the mandala of colored sand used for the initiation. The "third and fourth" refers to the third or secret initiation, and the fourth, the initiation of the word. The "causal initiation" is the initiation that is first received from the master. This is a paraphrase of Sachen Kunga Nyingpo, *gzhung bshad gnyags ma*, 6a5–7a2.

464. *gzhung rdo rje'i tshig rkang.* TBRC, W23891, 2a3.

465. *gyad kyi nor.* This metaphor for the Buddha-nature present in all beings was taken from the twelfth chapter of the *Mahaparinirvanasutra,* called "On the Nature of Tathāgata." The "wrestler's jewel" refers to a diamond bead on a wrestler's brow that enters his skin when impacted by another wrestler's head, at which point it becomes invisible and is thus deemed lost.

466. Dg. K. *rgyud 'bum,* vol. Nga, 27b5–6 (Toh. 418).

467. Here, the characteristics of solidity, wetness, heat, movement of the vital essence, and bliss generated by the action of the sexual intercourse stand for the five elements: earth, water, fire, air, and space.

468. This passage is found with a slightly different wording in Dg. K. *rgyud 'bum,* vol. Nga, 165–66 (Toh. 418).

469. *Bola* is the vajra, or penis; *kakkola* is the lotus, or vagina.

470. This may mean that by the fifth month it is difficult to kill the fetus by means of medicines or mantras.

471. Dg. K. *rgyud 'bum,* vol. Nga, 21b6–7 (Toh. 418).

472. On the thirty-two major marks, see note 20 in Part Two.

473. *rang bzhin brgyad cu'i rtog pa.* See Kongtrul, *Systems of Buddhist Tantra,* 264.

474. See note 20 in Part Two.

475. On the ten powers, see note 86 in Part One.

476. *khams gsum:* see note 98 above.

477. *sa gsum:* the planes of celestial beings above the earth, of human beings upon the earth, and of nāgas beneath the earth.

478. *ji snyed pa mkhyen pa:* the knowledge, possessed by a realized being, of all possible existing things.

479. *ji lta ba mkhyen pa:* the knowledge, possessed by a realized being, of the real nature of things.

480. "Perfect freedom" (*spangs ba phun sum tshogs pa*) and "perfect realization" (*rtogs pa phun sum tshogs pa*) are qualities of enlightened beings. These include freedom from emotions, and so on; and realization of reality, and so on.

481. *mchog gi sprul pa:* emanations that appear as a fully enlightened beings who enact the twelve deeds.

482. *ston pa drug:* the six buddhas who manifest in the six realms in order to spiritually uplift beings.

483. *skye ba'i sprul sku:* emanations of enlightened beings that do not display the signs and deeds of a supreme emanation.

484. This passage is found in the *dpal he ru ka nges par brjod pa,* 245b5, where it contains the extra line: *"dpal ldan khrag 'thung rgyal po che/'dod pa kun gyi dbang phyug gtso/kun tu phyag dang zhabs ldan zhing/thams cad du ni spyan zhal dbu/kun tu thos ldan 'jig rten na/thams cad gyogs te rnam par zhugs."*

485. The essential meaning of this verse is that the state of enlightenment is the heruka who has overcome the four demons. Since it accomplishes the desires of yogins through their practice of the stages of creation and completion, it is the sovereign of all desires. Externally, it is present in the form of deities possessing arms, legs, and so forth, and is renowned for great learning. Possessed of these qualities, it is present, pervading everything as the mandala of the Body, as channels, and as vital essences. See *sa skya bka' 'bum,* TBRC W3JT13366:003:0008.

486. See his *yan lag bdun pa,* W23703, 190a4–5.

487. This passage is not found in the version of the *Saṃpuṭa Tantra* contained in the Dg. K. (Toh. 381).

488. Dg. K. *rgyud 'bum,* vol. Nga, 22a5 (Toh. 418).

489. These words are actually found in the *Hevajra Tantra,* 22a3 (Toh. 418).

490. *sems kyi rdo rje:* one of the names of Yangönpa, occasionally appearing in the honorific as *thugs kyi rdo rje.*

491. *'bri gung chung rin chen:* one of the five main teachers of Yangönpa. See Yangönpa's biography, above.

492. Sakya Paṇḍita.

493. *rgod tshang pa mgon po rdo rje.*

494. On the four demons, see note 15 above.

495. *rgyal mtshan dpal bzang.*

496. The last paragraph and the line of good wishes translated here, which appear in some editions of Yangönpa's text, were probably added by others.

Appendix One

1. *thon chos* amended to *thun chos.*
2. It is unclear why these Discourses of the Buddha figure in Yangönpa's Collected Works.

Appendix Two

1. *chos ma.* Elsewhere, it appears as *bcos ma.*
2. *rje mi bskyod rdo rje.* The eighth Karmapa.
3. *rje tsong kha pa.* The eminent scholar and saint (1357–1419) who founded the Gelug school.
4. *grub dbang a phu rin po che.* The grandson of Shakya Shri.

Bibliography
Works Cited by the Authors

SCRIPTURES

All-Creating King
sarvadharmamahāsantibodhicittakulayarāja
kun byed rgyal po/chos thams cad rdzogs pa chen po byang chub kyi sems kun byed rgyal po

Several editions are extant:
mtshams brag edition, vol. Ka, 1–251 (Thimphu: 1982);
Dilgo Khyentse (*dil mgo mkhyen brtse*) edition, vol. Ka, 1–220 (Thimphu, 1973);
snga 'gyur bka' ma, vol. Tsa, 5–285, *si khron bod kyi rig gnas zhib 'jug khang* edition;
bKa' 'gyur, 1–126, The Tibetan Tripitaka, Beijing Edition (Tokyo-Kyoto, 1957);
snga 'gyur bka' ma, vol. Ka, 383–435 (Leh, 1971) (contains only the *phyi ma'i rgyud and the phyi ma'i phyi ma'i rgyud*)

Includes *The Unwaning Standard of Victory: Total Space of Vajrasattva*, listed below.

Amoghapāśa Scripture
amoghapāśahṛdayasūtra
don yod zhags pa snying po'i mdo
Dg. K. *rgyud 'bum*, vol. Ba, 278b–284a (Toh. 682)

Buddhasamāyoga Tantra
sarvabuddhasamāyogaḍākinījālasambaranāmottaratantra
sangs rgyas thams cad dang mnyam par sbyor ba mkha' 'gro ma sgyu ma bde ba'i mc- hog ces bya ba'i rgyud phyi ma
Dg. K. *rgyud 'bum*, vol. Ka, 151b–193a (Toh. 366)

Cakrasaṃvara Tantra
saṃvarakhasamātantra

bde mchog nam mkha' dang mnyam pa'i rgyud
Dg. K., vol. Ca, 174–180 (Toh. 441)

Chanting the Names of Mañjuśrī/Mañjuśrīnamasamgiti
mañjuśrījñānasattvasyaparamārthanāmasaṃgīti
'jam dpal ye shes sems pa'i don dam pa'i mtshan yang dag par brjod pa
Dg. K. *rgyud 'bum*, vol. Kha, 1b–13b (Toh. 360);
rnying ma rgyud 'bum, vol. 21
mtshams brag edition (*mtshams brag dgon pa'i bris ma* TBRC W21521);
bka' ma shin tu rgyas pa, vol. Nga (*'jam dpal mtshan brjod*), 449–73
Kathog (*Kaḥ thog*) edition, edited by Kathog Khenpo Jamyang (*kaḥ thog mkhan po 'jam dbyangs*)
Translation: Alex Wayman, *Chanting the Names of Mañjuśrī*

Catuḥpīṭha Tantra
catuḥpīṭhamahāyoginītantrarāja
rnal 'byor ma'i rgyud kyi rgyal po chen po dpal gdan bzhi pa
Dg. K. *rgyud 'bum*, vol. Nga, 363–464 (Toh. 428)

Dialogue with the Four Goddesses Tantra
caturdevīpariprcchātantra
lha mo bzhis yongs su zhus pa
Dg. K. *rgyud 'bum*, vol. Ca, 277b–281b (Toh. 446)

Equal to the Sky Tantra/Glorious Equal to the Sky Tantra
khasamātantrarāja
dpal nam mkha' dang mnyam pa'i rgyud kyi rgyal po
Dg. K. *rgyud 'bum*, vol. Ga, 399–405 (Toh. 368)

Guhyasamāja Tantra
Sarvatathāgatakāyavākcittarahasyaguhyasamājanāmamahākalparāja
de bzhin gshegs pa thams cad kyi sku gsung thugs kyi gsang chen gsang ba 'dus pa zhes bya ba brtag pa'i rgyal po chen po
Dg. K. *rgyud 'bum*, vol. Ca, 90a–148a (Toh. 442)
Translation: Alex Wayman, *The Yoga of the Guhyasamāja Tantra*

Continuation of the Guhyasamāja Tantra
gsang ba 'dus pa'i rgyud phyi ma
Dg. K. *rgyud 'bum,* vol. Ca, 297–316 (Toh. 443)

Hevajra Tantra
hevajratantrarāja
kye'i rdo rje zhe bya ba rgyud kyi rgyal po
Dg. K. *rgyud 'bum,* vol. Nga, 3–61 (Toh. 417–18)
Translation: David L. Snellgrove, *Hevajra Tantra*

Indestructible Garland
see *Vajramāla Tantra*

Kālacakra Tantra/Glorious Kālacakra Tantra/Tantra of the Primordial Buddha
paramādibuddhoddhṛtaśrīkālacakranāmatantrarāja
mchog gi dang po'i sangs rgyas las phyung ba rgyud kyi rgyal po dpal dus kyi 'khor lo
Dg. K. *rgyud 'bum,* vol. Ka, 22b–128b (Toh. 362)

Kālacakra Condensed Tantra
laghutantra/paramādibuddhoddhṛtaśrīkālacakranāmatantrarāja
*bsdus pa'i rgyud/ mchog gi dang po'i sangs rgyas las phyung ba rgyud kyi rgyal po
    dpal dus kyi 'khor lo*
Dg. K. *rgyud 'bum,* 22b–128b (Toh. 362)

Mahāmudrātilaka Tantra
mahāmudrātilakatantra
phyag rgya chen po'i thig le'i rgyud
Dg. K. *rgyud 'bum,* vol. Nga (Toh. 420)

Narrative of Former Lives (of the Buddha)
jātakanidāna
skyes rabs kyi gleng gzhi
Dg. K. *shes phyin,* vol. Ka, 183a–250a (Toh. 32)

Net of Magical Manifestations of Mañjuśrī, see Chanting the Names of Mañjuśrī
Nondual Victory Tantra
rnam rgyal gnyis med rgyud

Grand Dharma Treasury of the Glorious Drigung Kagyüd Tradition (*dpal 'bri gung bka' brgyud kyi chos mdzod chen mo*)
TBRC W000J501203, Lhasa, 2004

Perfection of Wisdom in 8,000 Lines
āryāṣṭasāhasrikāprajñāpāramitā
'*phags pa shes rab kyi pha rol tu phyin pa brgyad stong pa*
Dg. K. *shes phyin,* vol. Ka, 1b–286a (Toh. 12)
TBRC, W22084, vol. 918

Perfection of Wisdom in 100,000 Lines
śatasāhasrikāprajñāpāramitāsūtra/mahāprajñāpāramitāsūtra
phar phyin chen po/ rgyal ba'i yum
Dg. K. *shes phyin,* vol. Ka, 1–394 (Toh. 8)

Heart Sutra of the Perfection of Wisdom
prajñāpāramitā hṛdaya
shes rab snying po/shes rab kyi pha rol du phyin pa'i snying po
Dg. K., *shes phyin,* vol. Ka, 144a–146b (Toh. 21)

Prophetic Declaration of Intention Tantra
sandhivyākaraṇatantra
dgongs pa lung bstan pa zhes bya ba'i rgyud
Dg. K. *rgyud 'bum,* vol. Ca, 158a–207b (Toh. 444)

Saṃpuṭa Tantra
sampuṭanāmamahātantra
yang dag par sbyor ba zhes bya ba'i rgyud
Dg. K., *rgyud 'bum,* vol. Ga, 73b–158b (Toh. 381)

Saṃpuṭa Tilaka Tantra
rgyud kyi rgyal po chen po dpal yang dag par sbyor ba'i thig le
Dg. K. *rgyud 'bum,* vol. Ga, 158b–184a (Toh. 382)

Saṃvarodaya Tantra
mahāsamvarodayatantra
bde mchog 'byung ba'i rgyud

Dg. K. *rgyud 'bum,* vol. Kha, 265a–311a (Toh. 373)

Summary of the (Kālacakra) Initiation
sekoddeśa
dbang mdor bstan pa
Dg. K. *rgyud 'bum,* vol. Ka, 14a–21a (Toh. 361)

Tantra of the Extraordinary Secret
thun mong ma yin pa'i gsang ba'i rgyud
(Not located)

Tantra of the Manifest Enlightenment of Vārāhī
phag mo mngon par byang chub pa'i rgyud
Dg. K. *rgyud 'bum,* vol. Ga 52–60 (Toh. 377)

Tantra of Vajravārāhī Called Vajra Manifestation
rdo rje rol pa zhes bya bar rdo rje phag mo' i rgyud
(Not located)

The Unwaning Standard of Victory/Total Space of Vajrasattva
mi nu pa'i rgyal mtshan/rdo rje sems dpa' nam mkha' che
Chapter 30 of the All-Creating King
Dg. K. *rnying rgyud,* vol. Ka, 1b–86a (Toh. 828)
Translation: Adriano Clemente, *Total Space of Vajrasattva*

Two Examinations
see *Hevajra Tantra*

Vajraḍāka Tantra
vajraḍākatantra
rgyud kyi rgyal po chen po dpal rdo rje mkha' 'gro zhes bya ba
Dg. K. *rGyud 'bum,* vol. Kha, 1b–125a (Toh. 370)

Vajramāla Tantra/Indestructible Garland
vajramālatantra
rdo rje phreng ba'i rgyud
Dg. K. *rgyud 'bum,* vol. Ca, 208a–277b (Toh. 445)

Vajramukha Tantra
rdo rje sgo zhes bya ba brgyud
(Not located)

Vajra Peak Tantra
vajraśekharamahāguhyayogatantra
rdo rje tse-mo'i rgyud
Dg. K. *rgyud*, vol. 142b–274a (Toh. 480)

Treatises

Treatises of Indian Origin

Alamkakalasha (Alaṃkakalaśa)

Commentary on the Vajramāla (Indestructible Garland) Tantra
vajramālātantraṭīkāgaṃbhīrārthadīpikā
rnal 'byor chen po'i rgyud dpal rdo rje phreng ba'i rgya cher 'grel pa zab mo'i don gyi 'grel pa.
Dg. T. *rgyud*, vol. Gi, 1–220a7 (Toh. 1795)

Aryadeva (Āryadeva)

Lamp Summary of Tantric Practice
caryāmelāpakapradīpa
spyod bsdus pa'i sgron ma
Dg. T. *rgyud*, vol. Ngi, 57a–106b (Toh. 1803)
TBRC, W23703-1351-115-214 *bstan 'gyur dpe bsdur ma*
Beijing: *krung go'i bod rig pa'i dpe skrun khang,* 2006–09

Atiśa (Atīśa)

Vajra Song of the Vajra Seat
Vajarasanāvajragiti
rDo rje gdan gyi rdo rje'i glu
Dg. T., *rgyud 'grel,* vol. Zha, 208a–209b (Toh. 1494)

Garab Dorje (dga' rab rdo rje)

Commentary to the Mañjuśrīnamasamgiti
Āryamañjuśrīnāmasaṁgītiārthalokaranāma
'phags pa 'jam dpal mtshan gyi mtshan yang dag par brjod pa'i grel pa don gsal bar byed pa
Dg. T. *rgyud,* vol. Tshi, 38b–84b (Toh. 2093)

Krishna Acharya (Kṛṣṇācarya); Kanhapa

Vital Essence of Spring
vasantatilaka
dpyid kyi thig le
Dg. T. *rgyud,* vol. Wa, 298b–306b (Toh. 1448)

Extensive Commentary on the Vital Essence of Spring
vasantatilakaṭikā
dpyid kyi thig le'i rgya cher 'grel pa
Dg. T. *rgyud,* vol. Wa. 306b–349a (Toh. 1449)

Analysis of the Four Stages
kramacatuṣṭayavibhaṃga
rim pa bzhi'i rnam par 'byed pa
Dg. T. *rgyud,* vol. Wa, 338b–367a (Toh. 1452)

Lakshmi (Lakṣmī)

Elucidation of the Meaning of the Five Stages
pañcakramavrttārthavirocana
rim pa lnga'i don gsal bar byed pa
Dg. T., *rgyud 'grel,* vol. Chi, 187b–277b (Toh. 1842)

Nagārjuna (Nāgārjuna)

Five Stages
pañcakrama
rim pa lnga pa
Dg. T. *rGyud,* vol. Ngi, 45a–57a (Toh. 1802)

Nāropā

Five Points that Dispel Obstacles
gegs sel ser lnga'i man ngag
In Kongtrul, ed., *Treasury of Precious Key Instructions*
gdams ngag rin po che'i mdzod
Paro, Bhutan: Lama Ngodrup and Sherab Drimey, 1979–1981, 259–80
Delhi: N. Lungtok and N.Gyaltsen, 1971

Ratnakarashanti (Ratnakaraśanti)

Commentary on the Saṃvarodaya Tantra
Śrīsaṃvarodayamahātantrarājapadminīnāmapañjikā
dpal sdom pa 'byung ba'i rgyud kyi rgyal po chen po'i 'dka' grel ba pad ma can zhes bya ba
Dg. T. *rgyud,* vol.Wa, 1b–101b (Toh. 1420)

Saraha

Treasury of Doha
dohakośagīti
do ha mdzod kyi glu
Dg. T. *rgyud,* vol. Wi, 70b–77a (Toh. 2224)
Translation: H. V. Günther, *Ecstatic Spontaneity*

Tilopa

Perfect Words: Esoteric Instructions of the Ḍākinīs
bka' yang dag pa'i tshad ma zhes bya ba mkha' 'gro ma'i man ngag
TBRC W20877, vol. Ja
Nāropā's account is preserved in Jamgön Kongtrul Lodrö Thaye (*'jam mgon kong sprul blo gros mtha' yas*), *Treasury of Precious Key Instructions* (*gdams ngag rin po che'i mdzod*) vol. 7. Delhi: N. Lungtok and N.Gyaltsen, 1971; Paro, Bhutan: Lama Ngodrup and Sherab Drimey, 1979.

Vimalamitra

Commentary on the Mañjuśrīnamasamgiti

nāmasaṃgītivṛttītnāmārthaprakāśakaraṇadīpanāma
mtshan yang dag par brjod pa'i 'grel pa mtshan don gsal byed pa'i sgron ma zhes bya ba
Dg. T. *rgyud,* vol. Tshi, 1b–38b (Toh. 2092)

Virūpa

Root Vajra Verses on the Path and Its Fruit
lam 'bras rdo rje tshig rkang ma
Digital format: *gzhung rdo rje'i tshig rkang ma,* TBRC, W23891

Vitapada (Vitapāda)

Commentary on the Liberating Essence
muktitilakanāmavyākhyāna
grol ba'i thig le zhes bya ba'i rnam par shad pa
Dg. T. *rGyud,* vol. Ni, 45b–59a (Toh. 1870)

Treatises of Tibetan Origin

Anthologies

Little Pithy Volume of Many Oral Instructions on Vajrayoginī of the Sakya
sa skya'i mkha spyod be'u bum
3 vols., TBRC W1PD5284

The Collected Works of the Founding Masters of the Sakya
dpal ldan sa skya bka' 'bum
TBRC W22271; 20751

Sakya Lamdre
dpal sa skya pa'i lam 'bras
39 vols. *Sde dge rdzong sar lnga rig slob gling: sde dge rdzong sar,* 2007

The Collected Works of Kun khyen Padma dkar po (Padma Karpo)
Darjeeling: Kargyud Sungrab Nyamso Khang, 1973–1974.

Collected Works of Gyalwa Yangönpa
rgyal ba yan dgon pa rgyal mtshan dpal gyi gsung 'bum
rta mgo chos dbyings pho brang, 3 vols.

Thimphu, Bhutan: Kunsang Tobgey, 1976
See Appendix One

Unpublished Works and Spoken Teachings of Gyalwa Yangönpa
See Appendix Two

Individual Treatises

Exegetical Tantra (of Tibetan medicine)
bshad rgyud kyi rgyud
sde dge rgyud bzhi, TBRC W2DB4628
Beijing: mi rigs dpe skrun khang, 2007

Yangönpa (*rgyal ba yan dgon pa rgyal mtshan dpal*)

Hidden Description of the Vajra Body
rdo rje lus kyi sbas bshad
Collected Works, vol. 2, 399–466
Thimphu, Bhutan: Kunsang Tobgey, 1976.

Praise Called the Precious Thunder Sound
bstod pa rin po che 'brug sgra
(Not located)

Praise Called the Thunder Sound of the State of Union
bstod pa zung 'jug 'brug sgra
(Not located)

Ritual for Auspiciousness Called One Sufficient for All
rten 'brel chig chog ma
(Not located)

Teaching on the Profound HŪṂ
zab mo'i hUM chos
Possibly the same as *HŪṂ Teaching of the Ḍākinīs of the Four Families and the
    Manner of Conferral*
rigs bzhi da ki'i hUM chos gnang tshul dang bcas pa
Collected Works, vol. 2, 275–82
Thimphu, Bhutan: Kunsang Tobgey, 1976

Reference Bibliography

Tibetan Works

Chen Ngawa Rinchen Den (*spyan snga ba rin chen ldan*). The following works by Chen Ngawa are found in the three volumes of the *Collected Works* (*gsung 'bum*) of Gyalwa Yangönpa. Thimphu, Bhutan: Kunsang Tobgey, 1976.

rdo rje lus kyi sbas bshad gyi bsdus don. Collected Works (*gsung 'bum*), 397–403.

rdo rje lus kyi sbas bshad kyi zhal gdams sbas pa gnad kyi gter mdzod. Collected Works, 499–511.

rgyal ba yang dgon pa'i rnam thar bstod pa ma'am me long chen mo. Swayambhu, Kathmandu: Gam-po-pa Library, 2002.

ri chos brgyud tshul gyi lo rgyus. Collected Works, 1–10.

ri chos (b)skor gsum du grags pa zab chos (b)rgyan bzhi'i dkar chag, Collected Works, 155–66.

rin po che lha gdong pa'i rnam thar me long chen mo bstod pa ma. Collected Works, 21–104.

sbas bshad kyi dka' 'grel. Collected Works, 405–20.

Drigung Konchog Gyamtso (*'bri gung dkon mchog rgya mtsho*).*'bri gung chos 'byung.* Beijing: *Mi rigs dpe skrun khang,* 2004, 351–58. TBRC W27020.

Drigung Tendzin Padme Gyaltsen (*'bri gung bstan 'dzin pad ma'i rgyal mtshan*),*'bri gung gdan rabs gser phreng.* Lhasa: *Bod ljongs bod yig dpe rnying dpe skrun khang,* 1989.

Drogön Tsangpa Gyare (*'gro mgon gtsang pa rgya ras*). *Seven Successive Points of Interdependence: Collection of Treasured Instructions on the Practice of the rten 'brel rab bdun ma* (*rten 'brel rab bdun ma'i zhal gdams phyogs bsgrigs*).Thimphu: National Library of Bhutan, 1985.

Gö Lotsawa (*'gos lo tsa ba gshon nu dpal*). *deb ther sngon po.* Varanasi: Vajra Vidya, 2002. Trans. Gendun Chöpel and G. N. Roerich, *The Blue Annals,* 2nd ed. Delhi: Motilal Banarsidass, 1976.

Khedrup Norzang Gyamtso (*nor bzang rgya mtsho*). *Detailed Elucidation of the Outer, Inner, and Alternative Levels of the Kālacakra Tantra: Ornament of the Stainless Light* (*phyi nang gzhan gsum gsal bar byed pa dri med 'od kyi rgyan*), reproduced from an ancient print from Gemur Monastery in Lahaul by Topden Tshering. Published by Thopden Tshering. Distributed by the Tibetan Bönpo Monastic Centre, Dolanji (H.P.), 1975. Courtesy of the Library of Tibetan Works and Archives, Dharamsala. Trans. by Gavin Kilty as *Orna-*

ment of Stainless Light: An Exposition of the Kālacakra Tantra. Boston: Wisdom Publications, 2001.

Konchog Gyamtso (*dkon mchog rgya mtsho*). *gdan rabs grags pa 'byung gnas.* In *'bri gung chos 'byung.* Beijing: *Mi rigs dpe skrun khang,* 2004, 351–57. TBRC W27020.

Kongtrul Lodrö Thaye, Jamgön (*'jam mgon kong sprul blo gros mtha' yas*). *Commentary on [Rangjung Dorje's] Profound Inner Reality (rnal 'byor bla na med pa'i rgyud sde rgya mtsho'i snying po bsdus pa zab mo nang gi don nyung ngu'i tshig gis rnam par 'grol ba zab don snang byed),* Rumtek, Sikkim: Dharma Chakra Centre, 1981.

——. *Disclosing the Secret of the Invincible Vajra: Phrase-by-Phrase Commentary on the Hevajra Tantra—Two Examinations (dpal kye'i rdo rje'i rgyud kyi rgyal po brtag pa gnyis pa'i tshig don rnam par 'grol ba bzhom med rdo rje'i gsang ba 'byed pa).* Rumtek, Sikkim: Dharma Chakra Centre, 1981.

——. *General Meaning of the Hevajra Tantra/Topical Commentary (spyi don legs par bshad pa gsang ba bla na med pa rdo rje drva ba'i rgyan).* Palpung Monastery: *dPal spungs thub bstan chos 'khor gling* (woodblock print).

——. *Treasury of Precious Key Instructions (gdams ngag rin po che'i mdzod).* Delhi: N. Lungtok and N. Gyaltsen, 1971; Paro, Bhutan: Lama Ngodrup and Sherab Drimey, 1979.

Kunga Rinchen (*kun dga' rin chen*). *spyan snga grags pa 'byung gnas kyi rnam thar 'khor ba'i g.yul las rnam par rgyal byed.* In *gsung 'bum kun dga' rin chen,* vol. 1. Delhi: Drigung Kargyu Publications, 2003, 177–82. TBRC W23892.

Longchenpa (*klong chen rab 'byams pa*). *snyan brgyud 'bring bo bar do'od gsal rang snang.* In *bla ma yang thig yid bzhin nor bu,* Collection: 82. A Dzam edition. Also in *snying thig ya bzhi:* TBRC W12827.2:369-387. Delhi: *sherab gyaltsen lama,* 1975.

——. *phyogs bcu mun sel.* Commentary to the *Guhyagarbha Tantra.* Shechen Monastery: Shechen Publications, 1998.

Minyag Gönpo (*mi nyag mgon po*) et al. *spyan snga pa grags pa 'byung gnas kyi rnam thar mdor bsdus.* In *gangs can mkhas dbang rim byon gyi rnam thar mdor bsdus,* vol. 2. Beijing: *Krung go'i bod kyi shes rig dpe skrun khang,* 1996–2000. TBRC W25268.

Ngagwang Kalden Gyamtso (*ngag dbang skal ldan rgya mtsho*). *History of the White Crystal (shel dkar chos 'byung): Religion and Politics of Southern La stod,* vol. 252, Veröffentlichungen zur Sozialanthropologie; Bd. 1 Vienna: Verlag der Österreichischen Akademie der Wissenschaften, 1966; TBRC W1KG13996, Dharamsala (H.P.): Library of Tibetan Works and Archives, 2012.

Old Lady Yulo (*ma rgan g.yu lo*) and Chen Ngawa Rinchen Den (*spyan snga ba rin chen ldan*). *Secret Accounts of the Life of the Unequaled Gyalwa Yangönpa* (*mnyam med rgyal ba yang dgon pa'i gsang ba'i rnam thar*). In Yangönpa's Collected Works, Tango, Thimphu, Bhutan: Tango Monastic Community, 1984, TBRC W23654, vol. 1, Ka, 113–33.

Padma Karpo (*padma dkar po*). *The Sun That Blooms the Lotus of the Doctrine: A Religious History* (*chos 'byung bstan pa'i padma rgyas pa'i nyin byed*). Lhasa: Bod ljongs bod yig dpe rnying dpe skun khang, 1992, 444; *Collected Works (gsung 'bum)*. Kargyu Sunrab, TBRC 10736, 2: 1–619.

———. *'byung ba ro snyoms kyi rnam bshad ku mu ta*. In his *Collected Works (gsung 'bum)*. Kargyu Sunrab, TBRC 10736, 24: 53–287.

Pawo Tsulag Trengwa (*dpa' bo gtsug lag phreng ba*). *A Feast for the Learned Ones: A Religious History* (*chos 'byung mkhas pa'i dga' ston*), vol. 1. Varanasi: Vajra Vidya Library, 2003.

Sachen Kunga Nyingpo (*sa chen kun dga' snying po*). *gzhung bshad gnyags ma*. In *dpal sa skya pa'i lam 'bras kyi chos skor gces btus*. TBRC W1KG13617.

Sengdrag Rinpoche (*seng 'brag rin po che*) and Khenpo Sherab Chöphel (*mkhan po shes rab chos 'phel*). *stod 'brug bstan pa'i mnga' dpal rgyal ba yang dgon pa'i rnam thar gsol 'debs 'gyur med rdo rje'i sgra dbyangs kyi 'grel ba skal bzang rna ba'i bdud rtsi*. Kathmandu: *Nub lung bkra shis phun tshogs*, 2001.

Sertog Lozang Tsultrim (*gser tog blo bzang tshul khrims rgya mtsho*). *Presentation of the Stages and the Paths of the Indestructible Way: The Jewel Staircase* (*gsang chen rdo rje theg pa'i sa dang lam gyi rnam par gzhag pa zung 'jug khang bzang du bgrod pa'i rin chen them skas*). In *blo bzang dgongs rgyan mu tig phreng mdzas*, Book 21. Karnataka, India: Drepung Loseling Educational Society, 1977. TBRC W29702.

Sogdogpa Lodrö Gyaltsen (*so bzlog pa blo gros rgyal mthsan*). *Instructions on Dzogchen Semde* (*rdzogs chen sems sde'i khri yig*). Found in *snga 'gyur bka' ma*, trans. Adriano Clemente in *Ati Samten Gondzöd*, the *Ati Treasure of Contemplation*. Arcidosso, Italy: Shang Shung Edizioni, 2008.

Tāranātha (*tā ra nā tha*). *rim lnga'i grel chen rdo rje chang chen po'i dgons pa*. TBRC W1PD45495.

Tse Wangyal (*tshe dbang rgyal*). *lho rong chos 'byung*. Lhasa: *Bod ljongs bod yig dpe rnying dpe skrun khang*, 1994.

Yangönpa (*rgyal ba yan dgon pa rgyal mtshan dpal*). *Inner Autobiographical Accounts of the Glorious Yangönpa* (*dpal yang dgon pa chen po'i nang gi rnam thar gyi dbu lags*). In Yangönpa's *Collected Works*, Tango, Thimphu, Bhutan: Tango Monastic Community, 1984, TBRC W23654, vol. 1, Ka, 97–104.

———. *Secret Autobiographical Accounts of the Unequaled Gyalwa Yangönpa (mnyam med rgyal ba yang dgon pa'i rnam par thar pa gsang ba ma)*. In Yangönpa's *Collected Works,* Tango, Thimphu, Bhutan: Tango Monastic Community, 1984, TBRC W23654, vol. 1, Ka, 135–46.

Yönten Gyamtso (*yon tan rgya mtsho*). *Refulgence of the Sun (yon tan rin po che'i mdzod kyi 'grel pa zab don snang byed nyi ma'i 'od zer)*. In Dudjom Rinpoche (*bdud 'joms 'jigs bral ye shes rdo rje*), ed., *rnying ma bka' ma rgyas pa* (expanded edition of the *Nyingma Kahma* in 58 volumes). Kalimpong: Dupjung Lama, 1982–1987, vol. 40 (Thi).

Other Works and Translations

Aris, Michael. *Bhutan: the Early History of a Himalayan Kingdom,* vol. 1. Warminster, UK: Aris & Phillips, 1979.

Bhikkhu Ñāṇamoli, trans. *Buddhaghoṣa's Visuddhimagga: The Path of Purification.* Berkeley, CA: Shambhala, 1976.

Chögyal Namkhai Norbu. *The Precious Vase (Santi mahā sangha'i rmang gzhi'i khrid rin chen bum bzang)*. Trans. Adriano Clemente. Arcidosso, Italy: Shang Shung Edizioni, 2001.

———. *The Ati Treasure of Contemplation, First Level of the Santi Maha Sangha Training (Santi mahā sangha'i bslab rim dang po a ti bsam gtam dgongs mdzod ces bya ba)*. Trans. Adriano Clemente. Arcidosso, Italy: Shang Shung Edizioni, 2008.

Adriano Clemente, trans. *Total Space of Vajrasattva.* Arcidosso, Italy: Shang Shung Edizioni, 1999.

Davidson, Ronald M., *Tibetan Renaissance: Tantric Buddhism in the Rebirth of Tibetan Culture.* New York: Columbia University Press, 2005.

Deshung Rinpoche. *The Three Levels of Spiritual Perception: An Oral Commentary on the Three Visions of Ngorchen Konchog Lhundrub.* Trans. Jared Rhoton. Boston: Wisdom Publications, 2003.

Dowman, Keith, trans. *Masters of Mahāmudrā: Songs and Histories of the Eighty-Four Buddhist Siddhas.* Albany, NY: SUNY Press, 1985.

Günther, H. V. *Ecstatic Spontaneity: Saraha's Three Cycles of Doha.* Fremont, CA: Asian Humanities Press, 1993.

———, trans. *The Royal Song of Saraha: A Study in the History of Buddhist Thought.* Seattle: University of Washington Press, 1970; paperback ed. Boston: Shambhala Publications, 1973.

————, trans. *The Life and Teaching of Nāropā*. UNESCO Collection of Representative Works: Tibetan Series. Oxford, UK: Clarendon Press, 1963; repr. Oxford, UK: Oxford University Press, 1971.

Kapstein, Matthew. *The Tibetan Assimilation of Buddhism: Conversion, Contestation, and Memory*. New York: Oxford University Press, 2000.

Kongtrul Lodrö Thaye, Jamgön (*'jam mgon kong sprul blo gros mtha' yas*). *The Treasury of Knowledge, Book One: Myriad Worlds: Buddhist Cosmology in Abhidharma, Kalachakra, and Dzogchen*. Trans. Kalu Rinpoche Translation Group. Ithaca, NY: Snow Lion Publications, 1995.

————. *The Treasury of Knowledge, Book Six, Part Four: Systems of Buddhist Tantra: The Indestructible Way of Secret Mantra*. Trans. Elio Guarisco and Ingrid McLeod, Kalu Rinpoche Translation Group. Ithaca, NY: Snow Lion Publications, 2005.

————. *The Treasury of Knowledge, Book Eight, Part Three: The Elements of Tantric Practice*. Trans. Elio Guarisco and Ingrid McLeod, Kalu Rinpoche Translation Group. Ithaca, NY: Snow Lion Publications, 2008.

————. *The Treasury of Knowledge, Books Nine and Ten: Journey and Goal*. Trans. Richard Barron (Chokyi Nyima), Kalu Rinpoche Translation Group. Ithaca, NY: Snow Lion Publications, 2011.

Longchen Yeshe Dorje and Kangyur Rinpoche. *Treasury of Precious Qualities, Book 2: Vajrayana and the Great Perfection*. Trans. Padmakara Translation Group. Boston: Shambhala, 2013.

Miller, Willa Blythe. *Secrets of the Vajra Body: Dngos po'i gnas lugs and the Apotheosis of the Body in the work of Rgyal ba Yang dgon pa*. Doctoral dissertation, Cambridge, MA: Harvard University, 2013.

Smith, E. Gene. *Among Tibetan Texts: History and Literature of the Himalayan Plateau*. Boston: Wisdom Publications, 2001.

Snellgrove, David L., ed. and trans. *Hevajra Tantra*. Parts I and II. London: Oxford University Press, 1959.

Stearns, Cyrus. *Taking the Fruit as the Path: Core Teachings of the Sakya Lamdre Tradition*. 1st ed., vol. 4, Library of Tibetan Classics. Boston: Wisdom Publications, 2006.

————. *Hermit of Go Cliff: Timeless Instructions from a Tibetan Mystic*. Boston: Wisdom Publications, 2000.

Wallace, Vesna A. *The Inner Kālacakratantra: A Buddhist Tantric View of the Individual*. New York: Oxford University Press, 2001.

Wayman, Alex. *Chanting the Names of Mañjuśrī: The Mañjuśrī-Nāma-Saṃgīti*. Boston: Shambhala, 1985; repr. Delhi: Motilal Banarsidass, 2006.

————, trans. *The Yoga of the Guhyasamāja Tantra: The Arcane Lore of Forty Verses, a Buddhist Tantra Commentary.* Repr. in Buddhist Tradition Series, vol. 17. Delhi: Motilal Banarsidass, 1991.

Index

Bhagavān (*bcom ldan 'das*) 231, 305, 431
Bhagavati (*bcom ldan 'das ma*) 156
Bhrikuti Devi (*lha mo khro gnyer can*) 184
Bhuta hermitage (*bhu ta'i ri khrod*) 150
Bhutan (*mon*) 10, 28, 169, 327, 347, 350, 353, 443, 445-449
bile (*mkhris pa*) 44, 60, 141, 242, 288-289, 393, 403, 425
bliss (*bde ba*) vi, viii, ix, 23, 31, 33, 36-38, 41, 48, 50, 55, 57, 74-75, 78, 80-81,
    86-87, 92, 95-97, 100, 104-105, 110, 114, 119, 123-124, 139, 157, 193, 203,
    207, 219-220, 226, 229, 231-234, 241, 248, 255, 258, 260, 277, 287, 290, 298,
    301-304, 307-308, 311, 314, 316, 320-321, 325, 353-354, 357, 370, 378, 381,
    385, 394-396, 399-400, 403, 418-419, 421, 424, 433
    autonomous (*rang dbang can gyi* —) 302
    devoid of self-nature (*rang bzhin med pa'i* —) 302
    great (— *chen po*) 33, 36-37, 87, 95-97, 104-105, 114, 123-124, 219, 226, 231,
        233-234, 241, 248, 255, 258, 277, 301-304, 308, 314, 316, 320-321, 325, 357,
        378, 381, 394-395, 418-419, 424
    great bliss endowed with seven facets (*yan lag bdun dang ldan gyi bde ba chen po*):
    inconceivable (*bsam gyis mi khyab pa'i* —) 302
    natural (*ngo bo nyid kyi* —) 302
    nondual (*gnyis su med pa'i* —) 302
    uncompounded (*'dus ma byas kyi* —) 302
    uncontaminated (*zag pa med pa'i* —) 301
blood, menstrual blood, *rakta* (*khrag*) 38, 44, 51-52, 56, 60, 64, 88-89, 101, 178,
    220, 224-225, 229-231, 239, 245, 257, 267, 287-291, 320, 351, 357, 390, 392-
    393, 400-401, 404-405, 424-426
bodhicitta, vital essence (*byang chub sems*, Skt. *bodhicitta*) v, vi, viii, ix, 24, 31, 53,
    57-60, 70, 81, 84, 86-87, 91-96, 99-100, 105, 110, 189, 223, 228, 233, 236-
    237, 239-240, 246-254, 256, 258, 260-262, 280, 284, 287, 289-301, 307, 309-
    311, 319, 333, 353-354, 392, 396-398, 404-410, 412, 414, 422, 424, 426-429,
    433, 442
    relative (*kun rdzob* —) 113
    ultimate (*don dam* —) 113
body (*lus*) 1, 3-4, 12, 15, 17-20, 23-24, 26, 28-32, 34-54, 57-72, 82, 84-96, 99-107,
    110-111, 116, 119, 121, 124, 126, 130-131, 138, 141-142, 145, 147, 150, 153-
    158, 160, 163, 168, 175, 179-180, 182, 186-187, 194-195, 199, 205, 207-212,
    214-215, 219-231, 233-235, 237-241, 247, 250, 253-254, 256-258, 260-264,
    267-272, 274, 276, 279-281, 283-294, 296-301, 305-325, 329-330, 349-350,
    355-357, 359, 363-364, 372-377, 379-382, 384-386, 390, 392-393, 396-399,
    401-403, 412, 417-418, 424-425, 428-430, 432, 434, 445, 450

eight that branch off from the chakra of enjoyment (*long spyod kyi 'khor lo las gyes pa'i rtsa brgyad*) 242-243

eight that branch off from the chakra of great bliss (*bde chen gyi 'khor lo nas gyes pa'i rtsa brgyad*) 241-242

eight that branch off from the chakra of phenomena (*chos kyi 'khor lo las gyes pa'i rtsa brgyad*) 243-245

extension (*rtsa ba'i rgyud*) 240

female (*mo —*) 261

fire lady (*me ma*) 239, 246, 255, 257

fire of the eon (*dus kyi me zhes bya ba'i —*) 238

five hidden (*sbas pa'i rtsa lnga*) 248

good-minded female (*yid bzang ma*) 399

immobile, unmoving, veins (*sdod —*) 41, 44-45, 414

kākamukha (*bya rog gdong ma —*) 398-399

knot (*— mdud*) 54, 226, 241-243, 245, 248, 252-253, 255-256, 290, 361

lalana (*rkyang ma*) viii, 45, 51-54, 56, 84, 90, 231, 233, 237-239, 241-244, 251, 255-256, 290, 295, 313, 394, 398-403, 408-409

lesser bell-possessing (*dril can mchog ma yin pa'i —*) 236

liberator from the demon, māradārikā (*bdud bral ma*) 57, 237, 244, 249, 251-252, 254

life (*srog pa'i/srog —*) 46, 49-51, 64, 234, 236, 242, 351

male (*pho —*) 261

mare's face (*rgo ma kha*) 57-58, 253-254

minor (*— phran*) 284

neuter (*ma ning gi —*) 261

of qualities (*yon tan gyi —*) 249, 252

of sorrow (*myan ngan kyi —*) 259-260

of the four chakras (*'khor lo bzhi'i —*) 247-259, 317, 341

of the provocations (*'dre'i —*) 259

ox eye (*glang mig*) 226, 253

pulsating, arterial system (*phar —*) 45, 247, 408

radial (*— 'dab*) 231, 247

rasanā (*ro ma*) 45, 51-54, 56, 84, 90, 231, 233, 237-239, 241, 243-245, 251, 255-256, 290, 313, 394, 398-402, 408

seizer (*sgra gcan gyi —*) 399

sleepy (*gnyid ma*) 239, 255

stable (*gnas pa'i —*) 28, 158

supreme bell-possessing (*dril can mchog —*) 236

thirty-two in which vital essences descends (*byang chub kyi sems 'bab pa'i rtsa sum*

K

Kadampa (*bka' gdams pa*) 8, 17, 19
Kailash (*gangs ti se*) 151
kakkola 316, 433
Kal (*skal*) 176
Kala (*ka la*) 174
Kālacakra 9, 17, 44, 77, 159, 228, 231-232, 237, 253, 269, 272, 277, 364, 391,
    394, 397-398, 407, 411, 417, 427, 438, 440, 446-447
Kālacakra Tantra 9, 44, 228, 231-232, 237, 253, 272, 364, 391, 394, 417, 427, 438,
    446-447
Kaliṅga 243, 342, 379
Kāmarūpa 242, 379
Kāñcī 342
Kang Pule (*gangs bu le*) 20
Karmapa Mikyöd Dorje (*karma pa mi bskyod rdo rje*) 25, 333
Karmapa Rangjung Dorje (*karma pa rang 'byung rdo rje*) 25
Khenchen Tsultrim Nyingpo (*mkhan chen tshul khrims snying po*) 18, 365
Khog (*khog*) 176, 328
Khyungkar (*khyung dkar*) 11, 20
Khyungkar cave (*khyung dkar phug*) 11
King of the West (*nub kyi rgyal po*, Skt. *virūpākṣa*) 152
knowledge (*shes rab* or *mkhyen pa*) ix, x, xvi, xvii, 6, 8-9, 14, 20-21, 30, 34-36, 39,
    43, 45, 47, 52-53, 56, 62, 64, 71, 73, 75, 77-78, 87, 95, 97, 101-102, 108, 122,
    137, 139, 174, 178, 208, 221, 234, 236, 238, 255, 273, 294, 309-311, 319,
    349-350, 354, 357-358, 363-364, 376, 378, 386, 388-390, 397, 399, 402, 431,
    433, 450
    knowledge of the real nature of things (*ji lta ba mkhyen pa*) 319
    knowledge of the variety of things (*ji snyed pa mkhyen pa*) 319
Kog (*kog*) 176
Kolung (*go lung*) 174
Kośala 342
Könchog Pal (*dkon mchog dpal*) 26
Kong (*skong*) 176, 443, 447, 450
Kongched (*kong chad*) 177
Kotali, aka Kotalipa (*tog tse pa*) 236, 397
Kotrag (*ko brag*) 364
Kotragpa Sönam Gyaltsen (*ko brag pa bsod nams rgyal mtshan*) 9, 356
Kulutā 343, 379
kumbhaka (*see* vase-like breathing)

phase (*rim pa*) x, 94, 103, 157, 224, 275, 296-297, 311-313, 367, 391, 396, 409-410, 422, 427-428, 431-432
    phase of completion (*rdzogs* —) 103, 312, 396, 431
    phase of creation (*bskyed* —) 103, 224, 311-312, 391, 431-432
phlegm (*bad kan*) 60, 245, 288-289, 393, 405, 424-425
Pong river (*bong chu*) 178, 212
Pongshöd (*bong shod*) 175-176, 180
prāṇāyāma (*srog rtsol*) 68, 73, 235
preceptor (*slob dpon*) 104, 144, 204, 318, 372
Pretāpurī 245, 343, 379
Prophetic Declaration of Intention 82, 264, 266, 268, 272-273, 282, 284, 439
Pule (*bu le*) 20, 151, 165, 168, 194
Pullīramalaya 241, 379
Pulmar (*bul dmar/pul dmar*) 7-8, 18, 108, 127-129, 132, 135-137
pure awareness (*rig pa*) 114, 123, 136, 151, 214, 305, 319, 354, 387-388, 422
pure essence, essence (*dwangs ma*) 66, 88-89, 229, 237, 244, 249, 258, 268, 287-291, 293-294, 301, 307, 310, 412, 424-425
    acquired from the father (*pha las thob pa'i* —) 55
    acquired from the mother (*ma las thob pa'i* —) 55
    great, great pure (— *chen*) 89, 237, 288, 424-425
    of the five chakras (*'khor lo lnga'i* —) 89, 288
    of the five nectars (*bdud rtsi lnga'i* —) 287, 310
    of the four elements (*'byung ba bzhi'i* —) 310
    white (— *dkar po*) 94
purification (*byang ba*) 39, 59, 224, 256, 314, 367, 374, 391, 431, 449
    basis of purification (*sbyang gzhi*) 314
    purifying agent (*sbyang byed*) 314

R
Raga Asya (*ra ga a sya*) 25
Ralung (*ra lung*) 11
Ramoche temple (*ra mo che gtsug lag khang*) 161, 372
Rāmeśvara 242, 341
Rangön, *see* Shri Rangön
Ratnasaṃbhava (*rin chen 'byung ldan*) 65, 316, 393, 409, 415, 424
Ravisher (*'phrog byed*) 219, 383
real condition (*chos dbyings*) 105, 109, 230, 378, 389-390
realization, perfect (*rtogs pa phun sum tshogs pa*) 319, 322, 433
realization, siddhi (*dngos grub*) xiii, 8, 11-12, 19-20, 26, 32-33, 46, 59, 70, 91, 100,

480 ✹ Secret Map of the Body

Yönten Gyamtso, *see* Tsibri Yönten Gyamtso
Yönten Zangpo (*yon tan bzang po*) 27

Z
Zhonseng, *see* Lobpön Zhongseng

CPSIA information can be obtained
at www.ICGtesting.com
Printed in the USA
FSOW01n1137291217
42880FS